Praise for

Drawn to Change

"With vivid, compelling, and often amusing graphics, *Drawn to Change* makes working people's diverse history of struggle leap off the page. Full of inspiring yet honest portrayals, this book should be required reading for anyone who wants to understand what it takes—personally and collectively—to transform our world for the better."
– **Stephanie Ross**, Work & Labour Studies Program, York University

"A brilliantly creative, richly researched, and determinedly accessible history of working-class organizations, personalities, and struggles. Bravo!"
– **Leo Panitch**, Distinguished Research Professor, York University and co-editor of *The Socialist Register*

"*Drawn to Change* is a visually rich collection of stories that cleverly captures the spirit and struggles of the ordinary working people. Keep *Drawn to Change* on your shelf for inspiration."
– **David H. T. Wong**, author of *Escape to Gold Mountain: A Graphic History of the Chinese in North America*

"This book is a brilliant example of what exciting things can happen when artists and writers collaborate. The fascinating visual storytelling in these pages combines wonderfully imaginative artwork and lively text. What better way to bring to life many dramatic moments in Canadian workers' history—from the battles of industrial workers in the 1880s to the struggles of Filipina women in the 21st century. This is 'active history' at its best."
– **Craig Heron**, Department of History, York University

"The future of the labour movement will be shaped by three things: 1) Remembering the history of workers' struggles and honouring their victories; 2) Learning from lessons past to help inform the future; 3) Broadening the tent so the movement grows. *Drawn to Change* will serve as a vital resource on all three fronts."
– **Trish Hennessy**, director, Canadian Centre for Policy Alternatives, Ontario

"These engaging comics bring vividly to life important moments in working-class history, focusing on the historical achievements and travails of ordinary working people as they struggled to pose real alternatives to unchecked capitalist development."
– **Steve Brier**, founding director, American Social History Project, CUNY, and co-developer of *Who Built America?*

"*Drawn to Change* is a potent collection of little-known histories of Canadian workers. Its use of engaging images makes the stories of struggle accessible for activists of any age, and any experience with the labour movement. This kind of storytelling is invaluable."
– **Nora Loreto**, labour activist and author of *From Demonized to Organized: Building the New Labour Movement*

"A feisty, entertaining, contentious, and informative introduction to dramatic stories in Canadian labour history."
– **Ian McKay**, Wilson Chair in Canadian History, McMaster University

"*Drawn to Change* is a vibrant and invaluable collection of important stories from Canada's working-class history. These stories of struggle and organizing are as beautifully presented as they are insightful. This collection will be a source of knowledge and inspiration for all those fighting to build a militant working-class movement."
– **David Bush**, Editor, *RankandFile.ca*

"The Graphic History Collective has created another engaging and multi-faceted portrait of how—and why—women and men have not only shaped but made history. The result is both informative and inspiring."
– **Kendra Coulter**, Centre for Labour Studies, Brock University

"As Albert Camus once said, 'Beauty, no doubt, does not make revolutions. But a day will come when revolutions will have need of beauty.' The beautiful comics of *Drawn to Change* inspire us to take revolutionary action and create social change."
– **Elettra Stamboulis** and Gianluca Costantini, non-fiction comic writers and artists, founders of the Komikazen International Festival of Reality Comics

"There are so many exciting and vitally important stories from the history of social movements, and the most engaging way to tell those stories is through art, in its various forms. The Graphic History Collective is brilliantly doing just that."
– **David Rovics**, singer, songwriter, activist

"Canadian workers have never lacked intelligence, integrity, or organizational talent. National histories, however, rarely tell that story. *Drawn to Change* is the entertaining antidote. You can enjoy learning about what reactionaries would have us forget."
– **Veronica Strong-Boag**, activist and women's historian

Drawn to Change
Graphic Histories of
Working-Class Struggle

**Edited by the Graphic History Collective
with Paul Buhle**

Between the Lines
Toronto

Drawn to Change

First published in 2016 by
Between the Lines
401 Richmond Street West
Studio 277
Toronto, Ontario M5V 3A8
Canada
1-800-718-7201
www.btlbooks.com

Library and Archives Canada Cataloguing in Publication
Drawn to change : graphic histories of working-class struggle / edited by The Graphic History Collective ; with Paul Buhle.
Includes bibliographical references.
Issued in print and electronic formats.
ISBN 978-1-77113-257-2 (paperback).--ISBN 978-1-77113-258-9 (epub).--ISBN 978-1-77113-259-6 (pdf)
1. Labor movement--Canada--History--Comic books, strips, etc. 2. Working class--Canada--Social conditions--Comic books, strips, etc. 3. Graphic novels. I. Buhle, Paul, 1944-, editor II. Graphic History Collective, editor
HV6524.D67 2016 331.880971 C2015-907932-2
C2015-907933-0

Cover art by Kara Sievewright
Printed in Canada

GCC/IBT

MIX
Paper from responsible sources
FSC® C103567

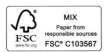

As winner of the 2012 Wilson Prize for Publishing in Canadian History, Between the Lines thanks the Wilson Institute for Canadian History for its recognition of our contribution to Canadian history and its generous support of this book.

We acknowledge for their financial support of our publishing activities the Government of Canada through the Canada Book Fund, the Canada Council for the Arts, which last year invested $153 million to bring the arts to Canadians throughout the country, and the Government of Ontario through the Ontario Arts Council, the Ontario Book Publishers Tax Credit program, and the Ontario Media Development Corporation.
Fourth Printing October 2021

Canada Council for the Arts
Conseil des Arts du Canada
Canada
ONTARIO ARTS COUNCIL
CONSEIL DES ARTS DE L'ONTARIO
an Ontario government agency
un organisme du gouvernement de l'Ontario

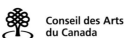

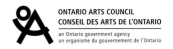

Contents

Preface: Changing the World with Comics
Paul Buhle

The Graphic History Collective's marvellous new anthology, *Drawn to Change: Graphic Histories of Working-Class Struggle*, sets its own standard artistically, historically, and politically. With this preface, I wish only to contextualize the collection's significance and to help the reader understand the impressive contribution that it makes.

Comics, of course, have been beloved by popular audiences for well over a century. Yet despite a long and vibrant tradition of activist comics reaching back to the 1910s, only in the past decade or so has the so-called graphic novel, fiction or non-fiction, with a focus on progressive politics, truly arrived on the public scene. This trend has dovetailed with the general resurgence of comics. Now, museum exhibits of current comics art have made a splash in various cities across the United States, Canada, Europe, Japan, and elsewhere. Comics festivals, with old-time artists from the 1960s or even the 1940s on hand, have sprung up in the wake of Comic-Con events with tens of thousands of visitors (a certain portion of them dressed in amusing costumes). The business pages of major newspapers carry comics information mainly due to the popularity of superhero films and television productions, and the arts pages cover a small field of newly appearing printed works by iconic comics figures like Art Spiegelman. In the academic world, where enrolment matters, courses on comics are in high demand, and comics are even being embraced by school teachers and librarians. In short, comics are back in vogue.

While the GHC is on the cutting edge of this new comics movement, its work differs decidedly from that of much of the industry. The comics medium, for the most part, continues to be controlled by large corporations like DC and Marvel; it is male dominated and saturated with safe storylines that protect the status quo. The GHC shows that this need not be the case. *Drawn to Change* embodies the best of proletarian art by showcasing a kind of do-it-yourself representation—comics about workers by workers—that is essential to revolutionary empowerment. In a highly commercialized world, it is commendable that the GHC is a volunteer-run, not-for-profit arts collective focused on making social change. Moreover, the majority of the contributors are women, and the collection features comics by Indigenous and female artists of colour as well as comics that highlight the strength and agency of working women and women of colour. This is both unique and encouraging. New voices and fresh perspectives that reflect the complexity and diversity of working-class life are sorely needed in comics. The contributors to this collection use a variety of different styles and themes, emphasizing that workers of all shapes, sizes, colours, genders, and abilities are capable of changing the world. This collection is the start of something special for the GHC and is exciting for fans of history and of comics.

Overall, *Drawn to Change* presents a much-needed popular account of working-class struggle in North America. The work of the GHC generally, and this collection in particular, blends the traditions of people's history or "history from below" and activist comics and repackages the lessons of working-class history for a wider and younger audience. This is not only an admirable pursuit but also a desperately needed project for our present age, in which workers are too often told that there are no alternatives to the capitalist status quo. This important collection shows us that alternatives are always possible but that they are not simply given by the powers that be; they must be fought for and won by working people. In illustrating how radical history in comics form can be used as a resource to restore hope for social change, *Drawn to Change* will undoubtedly inspire new generations of informed activists.

Comics art, so often during the last century being the art closest to the blue-collar reader, returns to its origins but with fresh vigour. Onward!

Acknowledgements

Sam Bradd, Sean Carleton, Robin Folvik, Julia Smith

Comics are collaborative projects, and the Graphic History Collective (GHC) would like to thank the many special people who helped make this anthology possible. It is difficult to thank everyone and to adequately express how grateful we are for all the support we have received, but we are going to try.

The GHC is a not-for-profit arts collective. As GHC members, we volunteer and share our artistic, writing, and administrative skills. Nevertheless, comics take time and energy to produce, and though most of the contributors to this collection created their comics on a volunteer basis, a number of organizations provided funding to support the project and to ensure that contributors received some compensation for their labour. The History Education Network (THEN/HiER), the Canadian Committee on Labour History, Canadian Union of Public Employees Local 3908, and the Simon Fraser University Labour Studies Program and Morgan Centre for Labour Research donated funds to help us recognize peoples' work with honorariums. The Sâkêwêwak Artists' Collective provided support for artist Tania Willard. THEN/HiER also provided a timely grant to pay Kara Sievewright to redesign the GHC's website to better feature the finished comics. Thank you to all of these organizations.

As well, a number of people enthusiastically encouraged our efforts. Paul Buhle has been a wonderful mentor, passing along his expertise and advice whenever it seemed like we needed direction. We thank comics producers Alex Alkana, Linda Alkana, Lorna Alkana, Steph Hill, Sarah Mirk, Josiah Neufeld, Khris Soden, and Cynthia Williams for their willingness to share their work as part of the Graphic History Project, and we are grateful to Noam Chomsky for his kind comments and support of the GHC generally. We also thank Sarah Beuhler, Ken Boesem, Valentina Brooks, Caelie Frampton, David Frank, Natasha Henry, Jaimie Kendall-Ward, Sarah Leavitt, Mark Leier, Jay MacPherson, Todd McCallum, Trevor McKilligan, Anna Rambow, Jason C. Ross, Maleah Schmitke, and Daniel Tseghay for their feedback, assistance, and guidance at varying stages.

We have also benefited from many opportunities to share our work. Nancy Janovicek invited GHC members to discuss comics and history with her class at the University of Calgary. Jarrett Henderson arranged for GHC members to travel to Calgary to give a keynote presentation at the Foothills Colloquium at Mount Royal University. In addition, we had the good fortune to be interviewed by many folks interested in the GHC, including Wojtek Gwiazda (CBC), Scott Neigh (Talking Radical Radio), Open Door Toronto, CJSF Radio, and Simon Fraser University's Department of History. We thank the beloved Rhizome Café in Vancouver for hosting some of our first talks and the Cumberland Museum and Archives for co-ordinating our installation *Illustrate! Educate! Organize!* for the annual Miners' Memorial Weekend. We are also grateful for the crucial support we have received from *ActiveHistory.ca*, *Canada's History*, *Canadian Dimension*, the Canadian Historical Association, the Canadian Union of Public Employees, the Employee Action and Rights Network, the Labor and Working-Class History Association, LeftWords Festival of Books and Ideas, Murray Bush at Flux Design, Marine Printers Inc., Mayworks Festival of Working People and the Arts, *Our Times Magazine*, the Pacific Northwest Labor History Association, *rabble.ca*, *RankandFile.ca*, Vancouver Co-op Radio, the Canadian Freelance Union (Unifor), and the Word on the Street National Book and Magazine Festival. These groups and organizations helped profile our work and get the word out about the GHC.

Most importantly, this collection would never have come together without its generous contributors. Collective work can be frustrating, confusing, and time-consuming, but in the end the ability to produce something bigger than yourself is both rewarding and powerful. We are thankful to the activists and academics who wrote original and insightful introductions to the comics that accompany the different projects in the collection: David Camfield, Conely de Leon, Gregory S. Kealey, Mark Leier, Andrée Lévesque, Zenee May Maceda, Dale McCartney, Bryan D. Palmer, Andrew Parnaby, Joan Sangster, and Ron Verzuh. Most of all, we are extremely grateful to our fellow artists and writers whose works are showcased in this collection: Jo SiMalaya Alcampo, Althea Balmes, Christine Balmes, Nicole Marie Burton, Ethan Heitner, Orion Keresztesi, David Lester, Doug Nesbitt, Kara Sievewright, and Tania Willard. It has been a tremendous pleasure working with and learning from you all. Special thanks to Kara Sievewright for designing the collection's beautiful original cover.

Lastly, we thank Between the Lines Press, and specifically Amanda Crocker, for taking a chance on us several years ago and for sticking with us and supporting our vision of changing the world with comics.

Our hearts are full. Thank you to everyone!

In love and solidarity,
The Graphic History Collective

Introduction: Hope, History, and Comics
The Graphic History Collective

Hope is crucial to struggles for social change. At times, however, it can be difficult to feel hopeful. Currently, income inequality and attacks on working people are increasing, prejudice and corporate greed run rampant, and climate change threatens our collective existence. But in such moments of difficulty and despair, we can look to the past to create hope for social change. Indeed, historian and activist Howard Zinn explains, "To be hopeful in bad times is not just foolishly romantic. It is based on the fact that human history is a history not only of cruelty, but also of compassion, sacrifice, courage, kindness."[1]

To help inspire hope, we present *Drawn to Change: Graphic Histories of Working-Class Struggle*, a collection of comics—or graphic histories—that highlights a variety of important people, events, and struggles from Canada's working-class history.[2] Working people are too often ignored or pushed to the margins of official history. As a result, we don't see ourselves in the stories that surround us, at least not in positive ways. Indeed, much of what we learn about history in school, at the movies, or on the History channel revolves around the lives of individuals with the most money and power in society, such as monarchs, capitalists, and politicians. But workers' lives matter too; without our labour, society would cease to function. We are important agents of social transformation, and our power is magnified when we work together.

The graphic histories that make up this collection do not always depict successful working-class struggles, but they highlight the strength of working people when they band together to try to improve their lives.[3] Like those workers before us, we must continue to fight for a better world, even in the face of uncertainty. No One Is Illegal activist Ruby Smith Días argues that "dreaming in a time where we are told that it is foolish, futile, or not useful is one of the most revolutionary things we can do."[4] So, drawing on the lessons of the Knights of Labor, a 19th-century labour organization featured in the pages that follow, this collection asks people to "dream of what might be" and to work collectively with others to bring about positive social change.[5]

By blending lessons from Canada's working-class history with the popular medium of comics, this collection offers short, easily readable, and inspiring histories.[6] Working people have always included art—songs, banners, poems, and performances—in their social movements, and comics are increasingly becoming a part of this tradition. Comics can make complex ideas interesting and accessible, and they can be read anywhere, from the classroom to the bus, and by people with varying levels of literacy. As well, comics offer readers the opportunity to piece together the incomplete information in each panel/sequence to make meaning, and thus comics can be an active and empowering form of education.[7] As a result of the medium's renewed popularity in the last twenty years, comics producers have more opportunities to publish radical comics and graphic histories with politically progressive content. In producing this collection, we offer historical comics that we hope spark conversations about the tactics and strategies necessary for new struggles for social transformation today.

In this introduction, we provide a brief history of the tradition of activist comics, with an eye to its Canadian dimensions, and we explain how the Graphic History Collective was formed. We then outline how the comics of this collection were created and show how, together, they remind us that radical social change is always possible.

A Brief History of Activist Comics

While the origins of the "comic book" are debatable, it is generally agreed that the mixture of words and sequential art—often taking the form of different panels on a page—emerged as a distinct artistic medium in the late 19th century. Inspired by the political cartoons of 19th-century European newspapers, Richard Felton Outcault's 1895 strip *Hogan's Alley* in *New York World* is often credited with popularizing the comics medium in North America. Due to increased public demand, illustrated strips like *Hogan's Alley* started appearing in the Sunday editions of newspapers in greater frequency in the early 20th century. By the 1930s, these strips, referred to as "comics" because they were often humorous, were bound together and sold separately in a distinct magazine format.[8] For the most part, people considered early comics to be light comical diversions from the serious issues of the day.

Yet comics also had dissident dimensions, as some comic strips and graphic books combined the new medium of sequential illustrated art with radical politics. One of the first labour comics, Ernest Riebe's *Mr. Block*, published by the Industrial Workers of the World in the 1910s, poked fun at the proverbial patriotic, law-abiding, anti-union "block-head."[9] The proliferation of socialist politics in the 1920s and 1930s spawned a loosely defined leftist/communist comics scene in the United States, fostered by such publications as *Daily Worker, Picture Magazine, The Masses, New Masses*, and *Art Front*.[10] There were also many stand-alone graphic books—many of them wordless, with openly left politics—published in the 1930s and 1940s, including *One of Us: The Story of John Reed, The Ruling Clawss, Aesop Said So*, and *White Collar: A Novel in Linocuts*.[11]

By the late 1930s, comics had become an established medium, primarily for children and adolescents but with some popular and political appeal for adults as well. It was the invention of the superhero, however, that launched the comic book into the mainstream. In June 1938, Jerry Siegel and Joe Shuster introduced readers to Superman in an issue of *Action Comics*. Siegel and Shuster quickly started a self-titled series the following year to capitalize on the popularity of superhero characters. During World War II, new comic book superheroes and superheroines, such as Captain America and Wonder Woman, played a key role in American military propaganda and, consequently, comic books reached new heights of popularity.[12] Canadian contributions included the superheroine Nelvana of the Northern Lights.[13]

Anxious adults, however, began to see comics as potentially dangerous and subversive, and in the postwar period they challenged the medium's legitimacy.[14] Comic books became prime targets during the Cold War battle against a perceived crisis in youth delinquency. American psychiatrist Fredric Wertham led the moral panic around comics. In his book *Seduction of the Innocent*, Wertham attacked comics for their so-called controversial content. He singled out "crime comics" as part of a "youthful rebellion" that glorified violence and opposition to authority. In Canada, in 1949 the Canadian government passed Bill 10 as an amendment of Section 207 of the Criminal Code to designate crime comics as "obscene literature."[15]

In the face of Cold War pressures and tighter regulations on the production and distribution of comics, many producers refused to sacrifice the social relevance of their work, and so they chose to create and distribute their art independently. Such writers and illustrators as Sharon Rudahl and Spain Rodriguez kept alive a dissident spirit in comics as they forged an underground "comix" movement, which overlapped with broader countercultural scenes in North America and the United Kingdom in the 1960s and 1970s. Publications with socially conscious content, such as *Zap Comix* and *Anarchy Comics*, became popular sources of information as well as political analysis. Comics like *Wimmen's Comix* and *It Ain't Me Babe* and, in Canada, the Corrective Collective's *She Named It Canada*

Because That's What It Was Called, made important feminist contributions to the comix movement.[16] By the early 1980s, underground comix was replaced by the alternative comics movement, which saw the rise of magazines such as *Raw* and *World War III Illustrated*.

As the intensity of the Cold War faded and the youth of the postwar period reached adulthood, it became clear that they had not abandoned their love for comics. The modern "graphic novel" was born in this context. Drawing on the themes and styles of the comix and alternative comics movements, such new projects as Will Eisner's *A Contract with God and Other Tenement Stories* (1978), Frank Miller's *Batman: The Dark Knight* (1986), and Alan Moore's *Watchmen* (1986–87) and *V for Vendetta* (1989) were published to rave reviews.[17] It was Art Spiegelman's *Maus: A Survivor's Tale*, however, that permanently altered the literary landscape and secured comics a place of prominence.[18] Published in two parts, Spiegelman's historical account of Nazism and the horrors of the Holocaust became a bestseller, won a Pulitzer Prize, and firmly established the graphic novel as being capable of capturing the attention of traditional comic book fans as well as those seeking more critical and serious engagements with history and politics.

Since then, comics have experienced an incredible mainstream resurgence. Superhero films are making millions at the box office and comics are becoming bestsellers. As a result of this popularity, more progressive comics are being published, carrying the tradition of activist comics to new heights. Indeed, since 2000 a variety of new comics have highlighted the lives of radicals such as Nat Turner, Emma Goldman, Rosa Luxemburg, and Che Guevara, examined events like the Spanish Civil War, the Israeli-Palestinian conflict, and Ireland's War of Independence, and covered the history of such groups as Students for a Democratic Society and the Industrial Workers of the World. In Canada, comics have told the stories of Louis Riel and Nellie McClung and illustrated the struggles of Indigenous peoples, the 1970s October Crisis, and the Winnipeg General Strike.[19]

The Graphic History Collective

The activist comics of the early 2000s greatly inspired the formation of the Graphic History Collective. The origins of the GHC trace back to the mid-2000s, when a group of labour historians associated with the Canadian Committee on Labour History and led by professors Joan Sangster and Bryan Palmer at Trent University answered a call from the Social Sciences and Humanities Research Council (SSHRC) for innovative research projects that would bring together nationwide clusters of research expertise. The group submitted a proposal entitled "Work and Society in Historical Perspective" to create awareness about Canadian working-class history through the publication of popular and accessible materials, including a comic book.[20]

After SSHRC agreed to fund the project, Mark Leier, a history professor at Simon Fraser University (SFU), took on the task of assembling a research, writing, and illustrating team, which eventually became the GHC. The team worked collectively to produce a comic book about the history of May Day—May 1 or International Workers' Day—as it was celebrated in Canada. After selling over two thousand copies of the finished project, *May Day: A Graphic History of Protest*, the GHC partnered with Between the Lines Press to release a revised edition of the comic book in 2012.[21] To date, close to five thousand copies of *May Day* have been sold to unions, social groups, and teachers, and the project has received praise from a variety of scholars and activists, including Noam Chomsky.

Though the GHC initially formed only to create the *May Day* comic book, members soon began to dream of new projects. In the fall of 2012, the GHC made a call for proposals to start a new endeavour called the Graphic History Project. We wanted to share our skills and knowledge of how to make activist comics with others. We hoped to encourage new comics writers and illustrators to come together to produce, on a volunteer basis, a number of short graphic histories that illustrated the various ways in which people from a diversity of backgrounds historically struggled for social change. Cognisant of the traditionally exploitative nature of the comics industry, the GHC promised to apply for all available grants and funds to provide teams, at the very least, with an honorarium for their work. Once completed, the finished comics would be made available on our website and then potentially collected, edited, and published with a progressive press.

Proposals quickly flooded our inbox, as people from around the world responded to the call. In early 2013, we began working with American historian and graphic history editor Paul Buhle (*Wobblies, A People's History of American Empire*, etc.) and a number of artists, activists, and academics. As each project was completed, it was posted on the GHC website. In total, twelve comics were completed. Projects examined disparate subjects, ranging from the 19th-century French feminist Susan Voilquin (by Linda Kelly Alkana, Lorna Alkana, and Alex Alkana) and Portland's Black Panthers (by Sarah Mirk and Khris Soden), to the environmental movement (by Steph Hill) and the 1936 sit-down strike in Flint, Michigan (by Ethan Heitner and edited by Paul Buhle). The vast majority of projects, however, focused on various aspects of Canadian labour and working-class history, from the oppositional efforts of the Knights of Labor in the 19th century, to the experiences of migrant care workers in the 21st century. As the Graphic History Project wound down, we realized that a collection of the graphic histories focused on working-class struggles in Canada would be an important contribution to Canadian history and to the tradition of activist comics. The result is the collection you hold in your hands.

Drawn to Change: An Outline

The current collection features nine comics completed as part of the Graphic History Project that highlight different aspects of Canadian labour and working-class history. The comics showcase the inspiring efforts of working people who united to fight for a better world. As you will see, the history of working-class struggle is a fascinating story of conflict and coercion and of resistance and triumph. It has the drama of defeat mixed with the thrill of victory, though not always in equal measure. At the same time, working-class history is not just interesting and exciting; it also contains important lessons that we can learn from and use to change the world today. As a whole, the comics in this collection illustrate the courage and determination of workers who struggled to bring about social change.

Dreaming of What Might Be: The Knights of Labor in Canada, 1880–1900, is illustrated by Sam Bradd and co-authored by Sean Carleton, Julia Smith, and Robin Folvik. It examines the Knights of Labor, a powerful labour organization in the late 19th century. To construct Canada as a capitalist settler society, the state dispossessed Indigenous peoples from their lands and pushed many people into cities to find work in factories. Working conditions in cities such as Toronto and Hamilton were often poor, and by mid-century workers started to organize to fight back. By the 1880s, the Holy Order of the Knights of Labor, which was founded in Philadelphia in 1869 as one of the first labour organizations in North America, had come to Canada. As Bryan D. Palmer and Gregory S. Kealey explain in their introduction to the comic book, the Knights of Labor appealed to workers because it asked them to "dream of what might be" rather than accept the poor conditions that were said to be unchangeable at the time.

Working on the Water, Fighting for the Land: Indigenous Labour on Burrard Inlet by Tania Willard (Secwepemc Nation), Robin Folvik, and Sean Carleton looks at Indigenous peoples' long history of work. Indigenous peoples have inhabited the diverse and overlapping territories of what is now known as "Canada" since time immemorial and have shaped the natural environment of Turtle Island, or North America, in innumerable ways. With an introduction by Andrew Parnaby, the project shows how X̱ʷməθkʷəy̓əm (Musqueam), Sḵwx̱wú7mesh (Squamish), and Səl̓ílwətaʔ (Tsleil-waututh) Coast Salish First Nations peoples, in what is now known as British Columbia, responded to the coming of colonialism and capitalism in the late 19th and early 20th centuries. *Working on the Water, Fighting for the Land* relies on transcripts of oral interviews with Indigenous labourers to demonstrate how Indigenous peoples worked on the waterfront and used the benefits of unionization to help fund their efforts to protect their lands and how they continue to do so today. Overall, the project highlights the strength, creativity, and resilience of Coast Salish peoples, both past and present.

David Lester's *The Battle of Ballantyne Pier: An Injury to One Is an Injury to All* also focuses on west coast labour history. Introduced by Dale McCartney, Lester's project recounts the story of his grandfather, Frederick Bruno Lester, who joined the Industrial Workers of the World (IWW) in Spokane, Washington before moving to Vancouver to become a longshore worker. In Vancouver, he participated in the dramatic Battle of Ballantyne Pier in June 1935. Earlier that year, the Shipping Federation locked out nearly one thousand waterfront workers and decided to hire non-union labourers to continue the work of unloading ships. In response, five thousand waterfront workers and supporters marched through the streets of Vancouver to Ballantyne Pier to protest. Armed city police intercepted them. Aided by the Royal Canadian Mounted Police, the city police attacked the marchers with clubs and tear gas and shot one worker in the back of his legs. The Battle of Ballantyne Pier lasted for more than three hours and resulted in many worker injuries. Though the workers were defeated that day in June, their struggle for justice on the waterfront continued, as they fought to form a stronger union, the International Longshore and Warehouse Union (ILWU), which they used to secure a number of longer-term victories.

Also set in the 1930s, Kara Sievewright's *Bill Williamson* recounts Williamson's fascinating life on the left as a hobo, Wobbly (or member of the IWW), communist, On-to-Ottawa Trekker, Spanish Civil War veteran, and photographer. As Mark Leier explains in his introduction, Williamson participated in many important moments in left and labour history during the first half of the 20th century in Canada and internationally. He joined the IWW in British Columbia and then, later, the mass of organized relief workers during the Great Depression that travelled across the country by rail as part of the On-to-Ottawa Trek to protest conditions in government relief camps. After leaving Canada and sailing around the world, Williamson sailed to Spain to fight fascism in the Spanish Civil War. In Spain, he joined Spanish forces as well as International Brigades, including the Mackenzie-Papineau Battalion (or "Mac-Paps") from Canada. Throughout his life, Williamson maintained his commitment to social justice and demonstrated that the fight for a better world is not relegated to one country or one event; it is a lifelong passion.

Nicole Marie Burton's *Coal Mountain: The 1935 Corbin Miners' Strike* returns to British Columbia. As Ron Verzuh explains in his introduction, though many are familiar with the mining struggles in places like West Virginia and Nova Scotia, the small town of Corbin, British Columbia, located near the Alberta border, witnessed a bitter strike in 1935 launched by the Corbin Miners' Association, a local of the militant Mine Workers' Union of Canada. In January, three hundred workers walked off the job to protest the firing of one of their fellow workers and sparked a protracted battle that came to a head in mid-April when the bosses of Corbin Collieries hired scab labour and employed a special police force to protect them. Miners and their families confronted the cops, with women taking the front lines. Similar to the events of 1935 on the Vancouver waterfront, the police attacked the Corbin miners to protect corporate interests. Though the workers did not win the day, their courageous struggle was part of a larger fight to pressure bosses and the state to recognize workers' rights, a fight which laid a foundation for future victories.

While the comics on the Knights of Labor and the Corbin strike discuss the roles of women in working-class struggles, *Madeleine Parent: A Life of Struggle and Solidarity*, illustrated by Sam Bradd and co-authored by Sean Carleton, Julia Smith, and Robin Folvik, is entirely dedicated to the inspiring life of Québécoise labour organizer and feminist Madeleine Parent. In her introduction, Andrée Lévesque notes that after being introduced to student politics at McGill University in Montréal, Parent came of age as a labour militant during her efforts to organize female textile workers in Québec in the 1940s and 1950s. The working conditions in the textile mills were atrocious and Parent, along with her husband Kent Rowley, fought long and hard to help workers organize and strike to win better wages and working conditions. Parent also played an integral role in the Canadian women's movement, constantly advocating for working women's rights. Parent believed in the importance of solidarity within the labour and women's movements. She was an advocate for the rights of Indigenous women in Canada and supported their campaign to implement Bill C-31 and amend the Indian Act to establish greater gender equity. Parent led an inspiring life of activism in which she showed a fearless sprit of struggle and solidarity.

In the 1970s and 1980s, a new movement of organized working women emerged in Canada, determined to push the connections between women and unions further. *An "Entirely Different" Kind of Labour Union: The Service, Office, and Retail Workers' Union of Canada*, illustrated by Ethan Heitner and co-authored by Julia Smith, Robin Folvik, and Sean Carleton, recounts the history of one group from this period, SORWUC. As Joan Sangster explains in her introduction, SORWUC differed from the established mainstream business unions of the time. SORWUC was a small, independent, and grassroots union committed to improving the lives of working women through a diversity of tactics, including direct action. SORWUC was also an explicitly feminist union, having grown out of the student and women's movements in Vancouver. As a smaller union, the success of SORWUC depended to a great extent on its engaged members and community solidarity initiatives, as the union sought to organize white-collar and low-paid service workers. SORWUC shows us the importance of democratic and feminist labour organizing, as well as the need to challenge the legitimacy of the state, business unionism, and the law in working-class struggle.

Though SORWUC disbanded in the 1980s, the struggle for workers' rights in Canada continued. *The Days of Action: The Character of Class Struggle in 1990s Ontario*, illustrated by Orion Keresztesi and co-authored by Doug Nesbitt and Sean Carleton, depicts the dramatic events of the Days of Action in Ontario during the 1990s. After the election of the Ontario New Democratic Party (ONDP) in the 1990 Ontario provincial election, Premier Bob Rae (who later became a Liberal Member of Parliament) watered down his election promises and resorted to implementing unpopular austerity policies that attacked workers' rights. Rae's tenure as premier split the labour movement on the issue of supporting the ONDP, with more progressive unions refusing to back the party in the 1995 election. Unfortunately, a divided labour movement created a perfect storm for the election of Progressive Conservative candidate Mike Harris, a right-wing politician determined to break public sector unions and drastically slash social spending. In an unprecedented wave of coalition-building, a committed social movement emerged that saw thousands protest the Harris regime in eleven different one-day strikes collectively known as the Days of Action. As David Camfield reminds readers in his introduction, the Days of Action hold important lessons for today's working-class activists about the strengths and weaknesses of party politics and protest.

The final project, *Kwentong Bayan: Labour of Love*, illustrated by Althea Balmes, written by Jo SiMalaya Alcampo, and edited by Christine Balmes, examines the real-life stories of Filipina migrant workers in the Canadian Live-in Caregiver Program. With introductions by Conely de Leon and Zenee May Maceda and produced in close collaboration with caregivers and supporters, the project highlights the work experiences of caregivers and showcases their stories of community and friendship, love and struggle, and empowerment. Balmes and Alcampo demonstrate how government policy intersects with workers' daily lives and how even the most vulnerable and precarious workers can struggle to find meaning and dignity in their paid work. In the Filipino language, "Kwentong Bayan" is the literal translation of "community stories," and "Labour of Love" reflects Balmes and Alcampo's understanding that community-based artwork and caregiving work are rooted in love, are valuable, and deserve respect.

Overall, a clear picture emerges from this collection of the strength and perseverance of working-class people in the face of adversity. These individual stories, though, only offer readers snapshots of a more fluid and complicated history of working-class struggle in Canada. The histories of this collection span more than 150 years, cover many geographic areas, and discuss a variety of people, events, and struggles, but they are in no way meant to be representative of Canadian labour and working-class history as a whole. Much is missing, and many more comics need to be created. Thus, we encourage readers to create their own comics to help fill in the gaps. For now, we hope these comics generate new interest in labour and working-class history and demonstrate the importance of learning from the past, as a resource, to help guide present and future struggles for social change.

Illustrate! Educate! Organize!

In his autobiography *You Can't Be Neutral on a Moving Train*, Zinn insists that if we are to remain hopeful about the future, we must learn to think both historically and optimistically. He explains, "What we choose to emphasize in this complex history will determine our lives. If we see only the worst, it destroys our capacity to do something. If we remember those times and places—and there are so many—where people have behaved magnificently, this gives us the energy to act, and at least the possibility of sending this spinning top of a world in a different direction."[22]

Historical storytelling, then, is not a neutral endeavour. It is a profoundly political act. In *Drawn to Change*, we recount the vibrant history of working-class struggle to foster hope for social justice. In doing so, we aim to reassert labour organizer and feminist Madeleine Parent's belief that if working-class victory does not come today, "it will be tomorrow, provided that we remain mobilized, all of us together."[23] We hope that the following historical comics will inspire you to work with others to organize and change the world.

Notes

1 Howard Zinn, *You Can't Be Neutral on a Moving Train* (Boston: Beacon Press, 2003), 208.

2 We use the terms "comics" and "graphic histories" interchangeably. For more background on terminology and comics theory, see Scott McCloud, *Understanding Comics: The Invisible Art* (New York: William Morrow Paperbacks, 1993); Robert C. Harvey, *The Art of the Comic Book: An Aesthetic History* (Jackson: University of Mississippi Press, 1996); Stephen Weiner, *Faster Than a Speeding Bullet: The Rise of the Graphic Novel* (New York: NBM Publishing, 2003); Douglas Wolk, *Reading Comics: How Graphic Novels Work and What They Mean* (New York: De Capo Press, 2007); Jeet Heer and Kent Worcester, eds., *A Comics Studies Reader* (Jackson: University of Mississippi Press, 2009); Bart Beaty, *Comics versus Art* (Toronto: University of Toronto Press, 2012).

3 Although many people think of "class" in terms of income, status, or lifestyle, we see class differently. Building on the work of historians like E.P. Thompson and economists like Michael Zweig, we view class as a social relationship that emerges from our interactions with one another when "producing goods and services." Class, then, is about the power you have at work and, related to that, the power you have in society. In a capitalist society, working-class people, or those who must work to produce goods and services in exchange for wages, make up the vast majority of the world's population; a handful of employers—the "capitalist class"—own factories and corporations and control most of the world's wealth. The struggle that goes on between these two classes for power at work and in society profoundly shapes human history, as this collection shows. See E.P. Thompson, *The Making of the English Working Class* (London: Penguin Books, 1991); Michael Zweig, *The Working Class Majority: America's Best Kept Secret* (Ithaca: Cornell University Press, 2000), 8–11. For the Canadian context, see Jim Stanford, *Economics for Everyone: A Short Guide to the Economics of Capitalism*, 2nd ed. (Halifax: Fernwood Publishing, 2015).

4 Ruby Smith Días as quoted in Harsha Walia, *Undoing Border Imperialism* (Oakland: AK Press, 2013), 236.

5 Gregory S. Kealey and Bryan D. Palmer, *Dreaming of What Might Be: The Knights of Labor in Ontario, 1880–1900* (New York: Cambridge Press, 1982), front page.

6 Many researchers have documented the important struggles and contributions of working people to Canadian history. See, for example, the select bibliography at the end of the collection.

7 Sean Carleton, "Drawn to Change: Comics and Critical Consciousness," *Labour/Le Travail* 73 (Spring 2014), 151–177.

8 Shirrel Rhoades, *A Complete History of American Comic Books* (New York: Peter Lang Publishing, 2008).

9 Ernest Riebe, *Mr. Block: Twenty-Four IWW Cartoons* (Chicago: Charles H. Kerr Publishing Company, 1984).

10 For more information on communist artists in the United States, see Andrew Hemingway, *Artists on the Left: American Artists and the Communist Movement, 1926–1956* (New Haven: Yale University Press, 2002).

11 Hugo Gellert, *Karl Marx: "Capital" in Lithographs* (New York: Ray Long & Richard R. Smith, 1934); Lynd Ward and Granville Hicks, *One of Us: The Story of John Reed* (New York: Equinox Cooperative Press, 1935); A. Redfield, *The Ruling Clawss* (New York: Daily Worker, 1935); Hugo Gellert, *Comrade Gulliver: An Illustrated Account of Travel into That Strange Country The United States of America* (New York: G.P. Putnam's Sons, 1935); Hugo Gellert, *Aesop Said So* (New York: Covici Friede, 1936); Giacomo G. Patri, *White Collar: A Novel in Linocuts* (San Francisco: Pisani Printing and Publishing Company, 1940). For more examples, see "Paul Buhle "The Left in American Comics: Rethinking the Visual Vernacular," *Science and Society* 71 (July 2007), 348–356.

12 For more on women and comics, see Jill Lepore, *The Secret History of Wonder Woman* (New York: Alfred A. Knopf, 2014); Mike Madrid, *Divas, Dames, and Daredevils: Lost Heroines of Golden Age Comics* (Minneapolis: Exterminating Angel Press, 2013).

13 Michael Hirsh and Patrick Loubert, *The Great Canadian Comic Books* (Toronto: Peter Martin Associates, 1971). See also John Bell, *Guardians of the North: The National Superhero in Canadian Comic-Book Art* (Ottawa: National Archives of Canada, 1992) and *Invaders of the North: How Canada Conquered the Comic Book Universe* (Toronto: Dundurn Press, 2006).

14 Robert Genter, "With Great Power Comes Great Responsibility: Cold War Culture and the Birth of Marvel Comics," *The Journal of Popular Culture* 40 (December 2007), 953–78.

15 See Mary Louise Adams, *The Trouble with Normal: Postwar Youth and the Making of Heterosexuality* (Toronto: University of Toronto Press, 1997), 142–150; Augustine Brannigan, "Mystification of the Innocents: Crime Comics and Delinquency in Canada, 1931–49," *Canadian Justice History* 7 (1986), 111–144. Joan Sangster argues that in Canada, communists even condemned the perceived "American cultural imperialism" of comics. Joan Sangster, *Girl Trouble: Female Delinquency in English Canada* (Toronto: Between the Lines Press, 2002), 58–59, 190.

16 See Mark James Estren, *A History of Underground Comics* (San Francisco: Straight Arrow Books, 1974); Patrick Rosenkranz, *Rebel Visions: The Underground Comix Revolution, 1963–1975* (Seattle: Fantagraphics Books, 2002); *Wimmen's Comics* (San Francisco: Last Gasp, 1972–1985); *It Ain't Me Babe* (San Francisco: Last Gasp, 1970); *She Called It Canada Because That's What It Was Called* (Vancouver: Corrective Collective, 1971).

17 Will Eisner, *A Contract with God and Other Tenement Stories* (New York: Baronet Books, 1978); Frank Miller, *Batman: The Dark Knight* (New York: DC Comics, 1986); Alan Moore, *Watchmen* (New York: DC Comics, 1986–1987) and *V for Vendetta* (London: Vertigo, 1982–1989).

18 Art Spiegelman, *Maus: A Survivor's Tale* (New York: Pantheon Books, 1986 and 1991).

19 See, for example, Joe Sacco, *Safe Area Gorazde* (Seattle: Fantagraphics Books, 2000); Marjane Satrapi, *Persepolis: The Story of Childhood* (New York: Pantheon Books, 2003) and *Persepolis: The Story of a Return* (New York: Pantheon Books, 2003); Chester Brown, *Louis Riel: A Comic Strip Biography* (Montréal: Drawn and Quarterly, 2003); Paul Buhle and Nicole Schulman, eds., *Wobblies! A Graphic History of the Industrial Workers of the World* (New York: Verso, 2005); Sharon Rudahl, *A Dangerous Women: A Graphic Biography of Emma Goldman* (New York: The New Press, 2007); Spain Rodriguez, *Che: A Graphic Biography* (New York: Verso, 2008); Howard Zinn, Mike Konopacki, and Paul Buhle, *A People's History of American Empire: A Graphic Adaptation* (New York: Metropolitan Books, 2008); Kyle Baker, *Nat Turner* (New York: Henry N. Abrams, 2008); Harvey Pekar, Paul Buhle, and Gary Dumm, *Students for a Democratic Society: A Graphic History* (New York: Hill & Wang, 2009); Rick Geary, Sylvain Lemay, and André St-Georges, *Pour en finir avec novembre* (Montréal: Les 400 coups, 2011); Brian Wright-McLeod, *Red Power: A Graphic Novel* (Markham: Fifth House, 2011); Gord Hill, *The 500 Years of Resistance Comic Book* (Vancouver: Arsenal Pulp Press, 2010) and *The Anti-Capitalist Resistance Comic Book* (Vancouver: Arsenal Pulp Press, 2012); Kate Evans and Paul Buhle, *Red Rosa: A Graphic Biography of Rosa Luxemburg* (London: Verso, 2015).

20 For more on the goals of this initiative, see Joan Sangster, "Work and Society in Historical Perspective: Creating a New Labour History Research Network," *Labor: Studies in Working Class History of the Americas* 3 (Spring 2006), 41–47.

21 Robin Folvik, Sean Carleton, Mark Leier, Sam Bradd, and Trevor McKilligan, *May Day: A Graphic History of Protest* (Toronto: Between the Lines Press, 2012).

22 Zinn, *You Can't Be Neutral on a Moving Train*, 208.

23 Madeleine Parent as quoted on "Madeleine Parent," The Confederation of Canadian Unions, www.ccu-csc.ca/about/madeleine-parent.

Dreaming of What Might Be

The Knights of Labor in Canada, 1880–1900

"Spreading the Light" in the 21st Century

Bryan D. Palmer, Gregory S. Kealey

The 19th-century labour organization known as the Noble and Holy Order of the Knights of Labor marked a turning point in Canadian working-class history: it proclaimed new ways of organizing all workers into "one big union," and in its refusal to limit class struggle to the "pure and (seemingly) simple" matter of higher wages, it proclaimed the necessity of a far broader-ranging labour reform.

The Knights of Labor perceived their project to be one of "spreading the light." In 1880s Canada, a young labour movement, in which the Knights represented the most advanced elements, first grappled with organizing skilled and unskilled workers in the same working-class association; first struggled with the complex issues of mobilizing women in the same unions as men, demanding variants of the modern, yet-to-be realized aim of equal pay; and seriously expanded understandings of "the labour question" beyond the issue of wages and job conditions, important as they were, and into realms of politics, culture, and everyday life. "Spreading the light," then as now, entailed a wide-ranging struggle to transcend inequality, in the workplace as well as the political arena. Once this complex initiative of popular, working-class struggle was extended, it could never be definitively turned back again, containing labouring people in the confinements of convention.

The Noble and Holy Order was indeed unconventional in what it did. Not just a trade union, it was also a secular brotherhood and sisterhood, in which solidarity reached beyond the wage relation into areas of ideas, values, and deep longings for alternative ways of reconfiguring society, in which impulses of co-operation and collectivity trumped the acquisitive individualism of the age. The Knights of Labor organized public lectures and Sunday "labour sermons." They established courts to ascertain the guilt or innocence of members with respect to a wide range of behaviours that violated the working-class community's sense of right and wrong, reaching from the abuse of wives, children, and workmates, to defrauding or stealing from fellow Knights of Labor, to exposing the secret, ritualized, inner workings of the Noble and Holy Order to non-members. These courts relied on understandings of what constituted working-class justice rather than turning questions of social transgression over to regulatory and disciplinary bodies presided over by those of a different, ostensibly superior, class. In an era that pre-dated the mass culture and mass communications of our own times, the Knights, not commercial interests, led the way in organizing dances and balls, picnics and parades. They set up newspapers to promote the cause of workers, and Knights of Labor intellectuals published books and pamphlets. Tracts of political economy and a poetry of the people emerged out of this "movement culture."

Of course the Knights also pressured employers for better conditions in factories, mills, and public works projects, just as they campaigned to elect working-class candidates to municipal, provincial, and federal office. In their lobbying efforts in the political arena, the Knights championed and secured important factory acts that bettered the lives of working men, women, and children. The consolidating apparatus of the state was forced to acknowledge the Order and its message of labour reform in all kinds of ways, including the establishment of a Royal Commission on the Relations of Labor and Capital that heard testimony across the length and breadth of industrial-capitalist Canada in the late 1880s. All of this made the labour movement of the time an educational, spiritual, cultural, and political happening of significance.

As the GHC's comic book suggests, this history of the Knights of Labor is often complicated.

Race, for instance, both divided workers in 19th-century North America and revealed how some workers were indeed struggling to rid the labour movement of the debilitating influence of racism. Racist jokes circulated within the correspondence of Knights of Labor leaders like Grand Master Workman Terence V. Powderly, and rank-and-file Knights could, sadly, demand segregation in their locals. The record of Chinese exclusion and scapegoating in the Knights of Labor is one of the saddest chapters of retreat into racist stereotyping in the late 19th century, with Victoria, British Columbia, and its labour newspaper, the *Industrial News*, a centrepiece of Pacific coast anti-Orientalism. And yet, on balance, the record of the workers' movement in this era improved in terms of confronting racism, especially with respect to the relations of black and white workers. An alternative to past decades of Jim Crow racial separation was emerging within the labour movement. As much as the Canadian history of this period is one of stark divides, in which white workers and Indigenous peoples seldom came together, there were hints in bodies like the Noble and Holy Order of the Knights of Labor that some working-class militants could indeed extend the hand of solidarity to Métis warriors like Louis Riel or Indigenous peoples working in northern woodlots or coastal fisheries.

The question of race in Canada was, moreover, complicated immensely by the racialization of francophone workers. The Knights of Labor galvanized French and English labour, bringing these components of the workforce together in dramatic ways. The Order came as close as any 20th-century labour movement to cultivating common struggles and organization among French and English workers in Québec, but it did not quite manage to override the linguistic, cultural, and religious divides that have kept central components of the Canadian working class apart.[1]

Finally, in their unique grappling with "the woman question," the Order embraced a medieval-like sense of protective chivalry that elevated "honest working-class womanhood" to a kind of isolating pedestal at the same time as it provided an environment of demand and militancy that was distinctly new. This brought women into strikes, promoted a sense of equal rights, and championed those Knights, male and female, who organized and agitated for the betterment of all workers. As this happened, labouring people started, albeit slowly and incompletely, to understand that the workplace and the family home were both sites where relationships needed to change and where equality needed to supplant hierarchy and privilege.

If the Noble and Holy Order of the Knights of Labor did not succeed in transforming 19th-century relations of inequality then, this pioneer labour organization played an important role in fighting for the kinds of social change that are still needed today. How and why the Knights failed is something that the workers' movement of today and all manner of social activists need to ponder. But what the Order struggled, against considerable odds, to create, and how it did this, is also worthy of note. Visualizing and reading this Knights of Labor history is, we hope, a way in which this project of understanding can be extended, "spreading the light" in our own times.

Notes

1 For arguably the most important scholarly study of the Knights of Labor in Canada to appear since the publication of *Dreaming of What Might Be*, see Peter C. Bischoff, "'Un chaînon incontournable': les Chevaliers du travail, 1882–1902," *Labour/Le Travail* 70 (Fall 2012), 13–59.

Dreaming of What Might Be

THE KNIGHTS OF LABOR IN CANADA 1880–1900

WRITERS: Sean Carleton, Julia Smith, Robin Folvik
ILLUSTRATOR: Sam Bradd

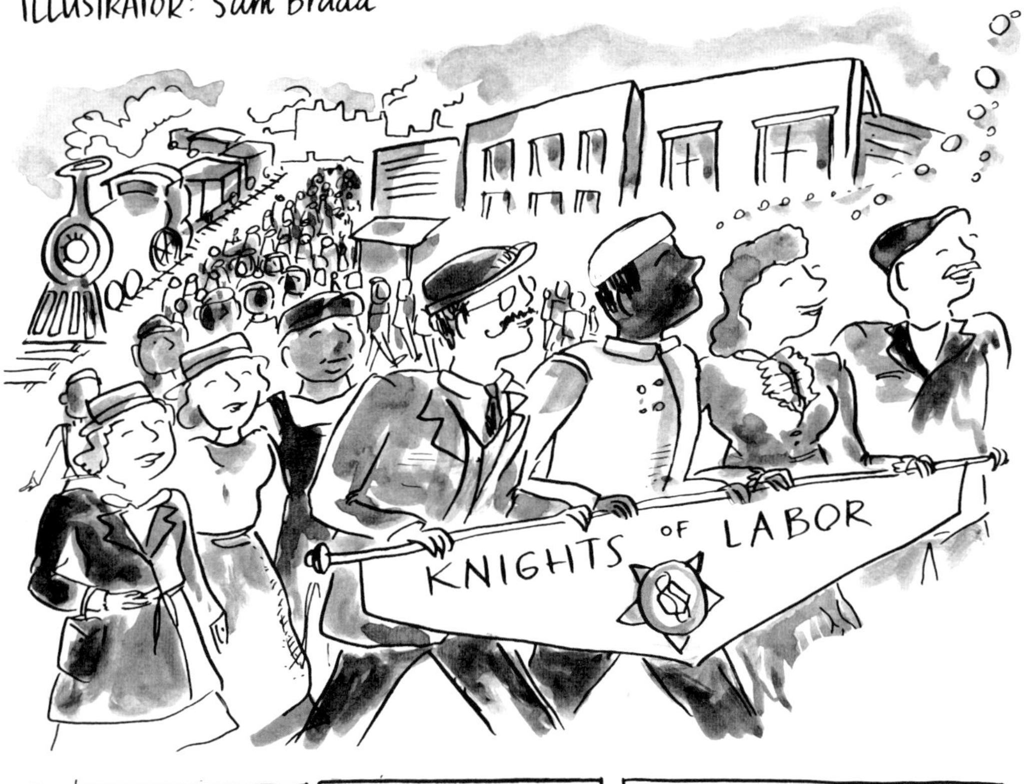
KNIGHTS OF LABOR

Workers in Canada have always had to fight to gain control at work and for power in society. This is the story of how one group,

the NOBLE AND HOLY ORDER of THE **KNIGHTS** of **LABOR**, quickly gained momentum in Canada…

…during the 1880s and 1890s by uplifting **working people** and inspiring them to struggle to improve their lives.

By forging their own distinct culture and by organizing large numbers of workers across divisions of skill, sex, and race, the Knights differed from many of the conservative labour organizations of the 1800s.

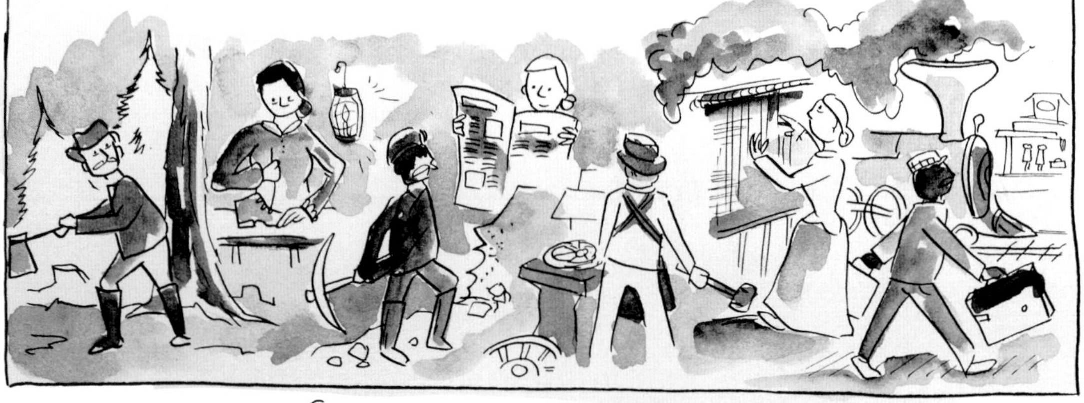

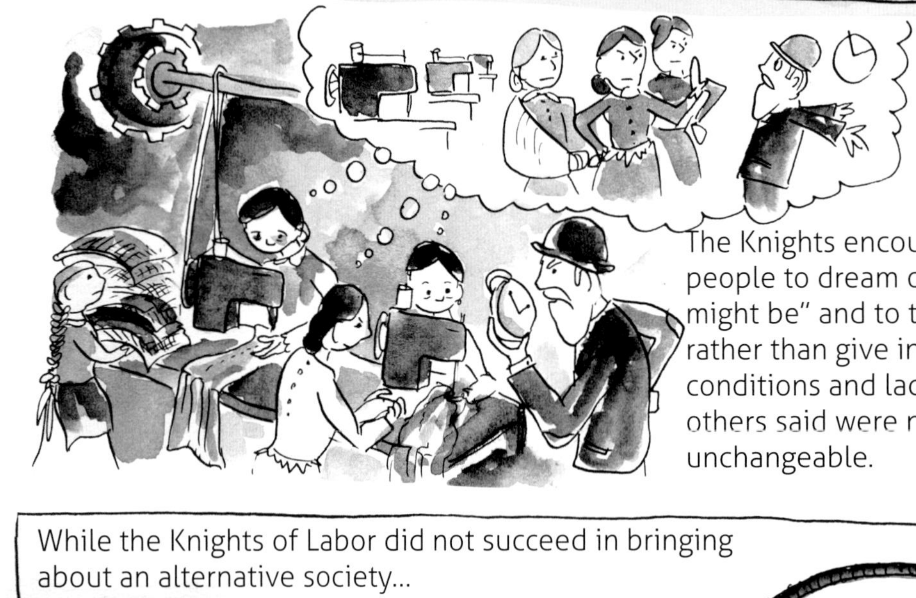

The Knights encouraged people to dream of "what might be" and to take action rather than give in to the poor conditions and lack of control others said were natural and unchangeable.

While the Knights of Labor did not succeed in bringing about an alternative society...

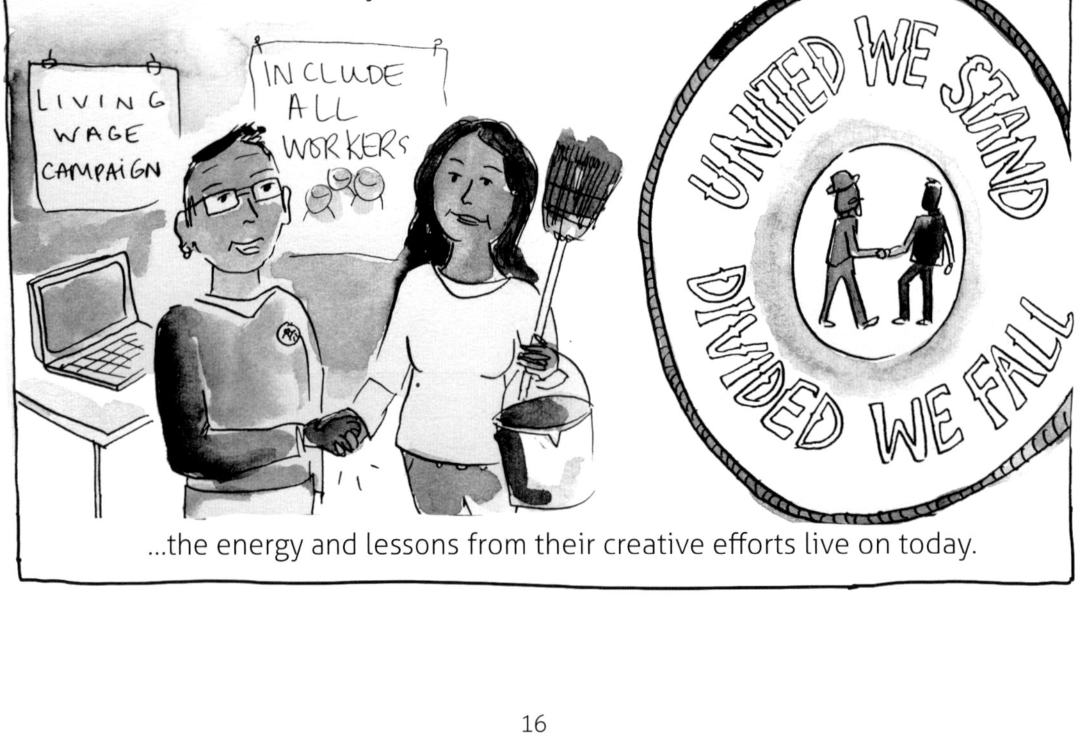
LIVING WAGE CAMPAIGN
INCLUDE ALL WORKERS
UNITED WE STAND
DIVIDED WE FALL

...the energy and lessons from their creative efforts live on today.

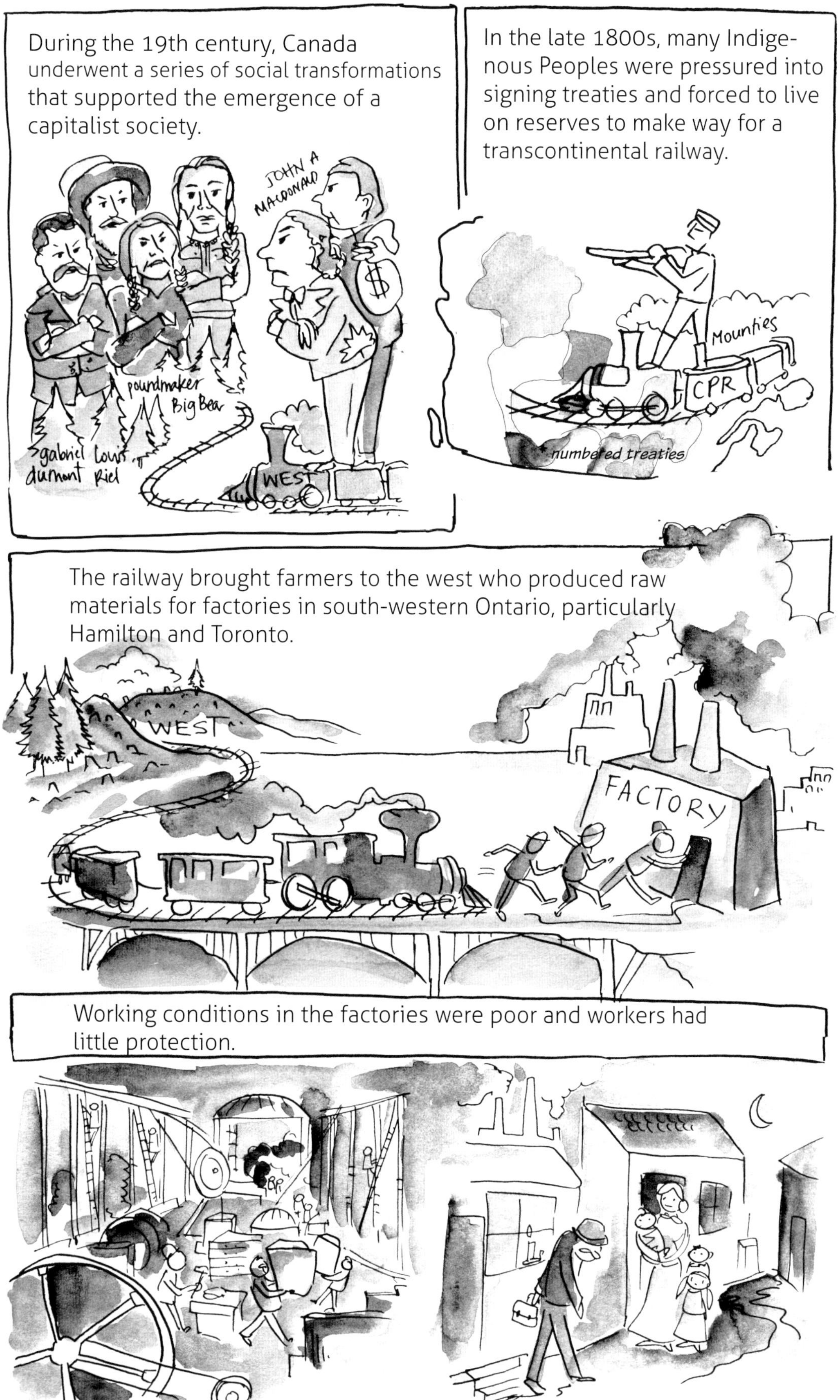
During the 19th century, Canada underwent a series of social transformations that supported the emergence of a capitalist society.
JOHN A MACDONALD
poundmaker
Big Bear
gabriel dumont
Louis Riel
WEST
In the late 1800s, many Indigenous Peoples were pressured into signing treaties and forced to live on reserves to make way for a transcontinental railway.
Mounties
CPR
numbered treaties
The railway brought farmers to the west who produced raw materials for factories in south-western Ontario, particularly Hamilton and Toronto.
WEST
FACTORY
Working conditions in the factories were poor and workers had little protection.

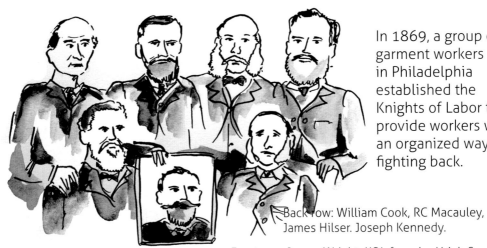

In 1869, a group of garment workers in Philadelphia established the Knights of Labor to provide workers with an organized way of fighting back.

Back row: William Cook, RC Macauley, James Hilser. Joseph Kennedy.

Front row: James Wright, KOL founder Uriah S. Stephens in the picture, Robert W Keen.

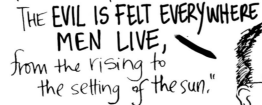

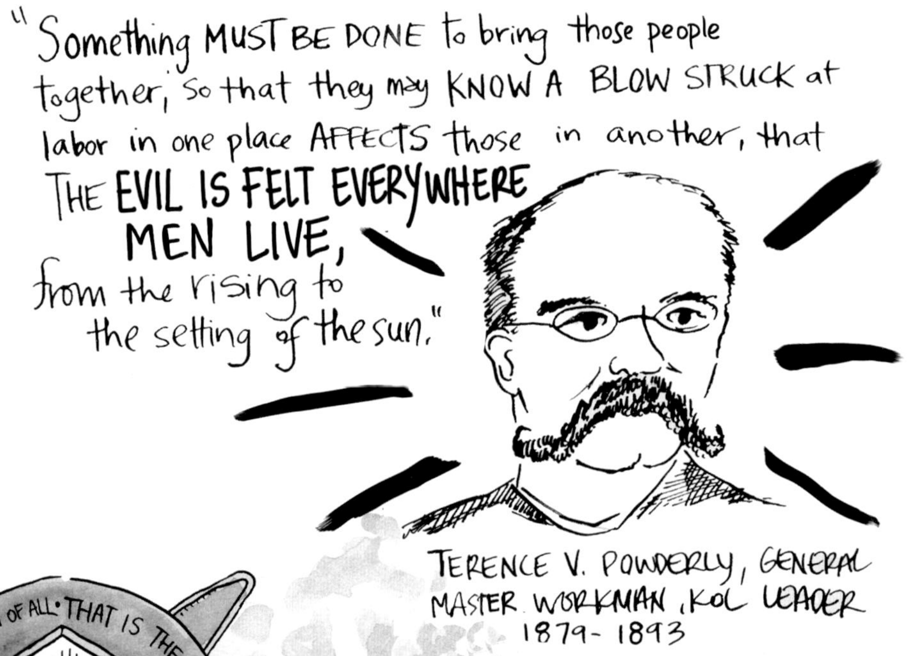

"Something MUST BE DONE to bring those people together, so that they may KNOW A BLOW STRUCK at labor in one place AFFECTS those in another, that THE EVIL IS FELT EVERYWHERE MEN LIVE, from the rising to the setting of the sun."
TERENCE V. POWDERLY, GENERAL MASTER WORKMAN, KOL LEADER 1879- 1893

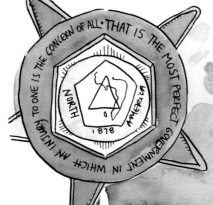

The Knights spread rapidly, arriving in Canada in the mid-1870s. Strongest in Ontario, Quebec, and British Columbia, the KOL also enjoyed success in Nova Scotia and Manitoba and established locals in New Brunswick and present-day Alberta.

THAT IS THE MOST PERFECT GOVERNMENT IN WHICH AN INJURY TO ONE IS THE CONCERN OF ALL
NORTH AMERICA
1878
Cities and towns with 3+ assemblies: 1881-1902

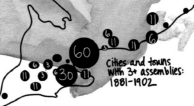

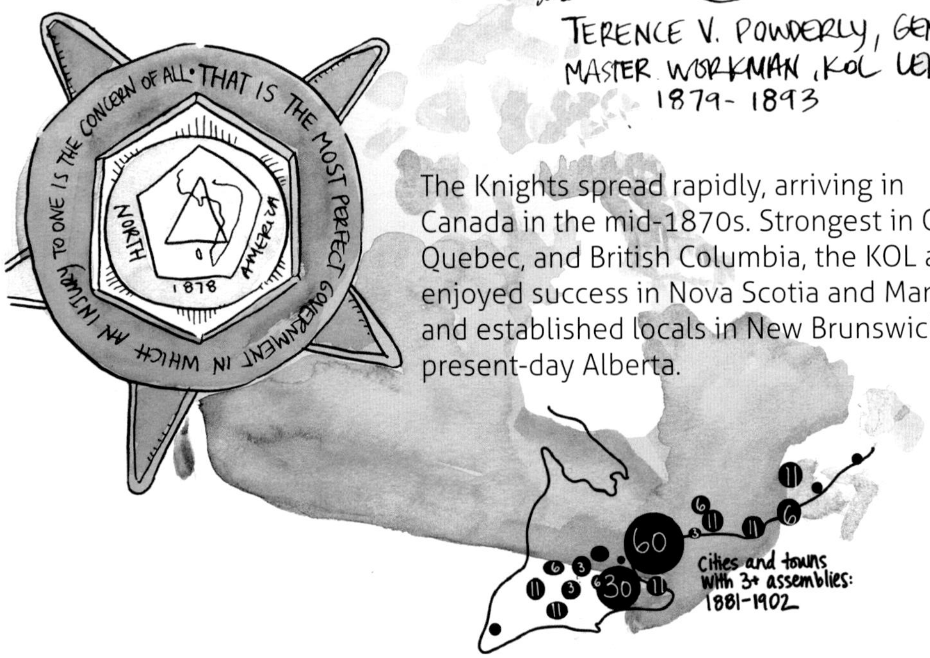

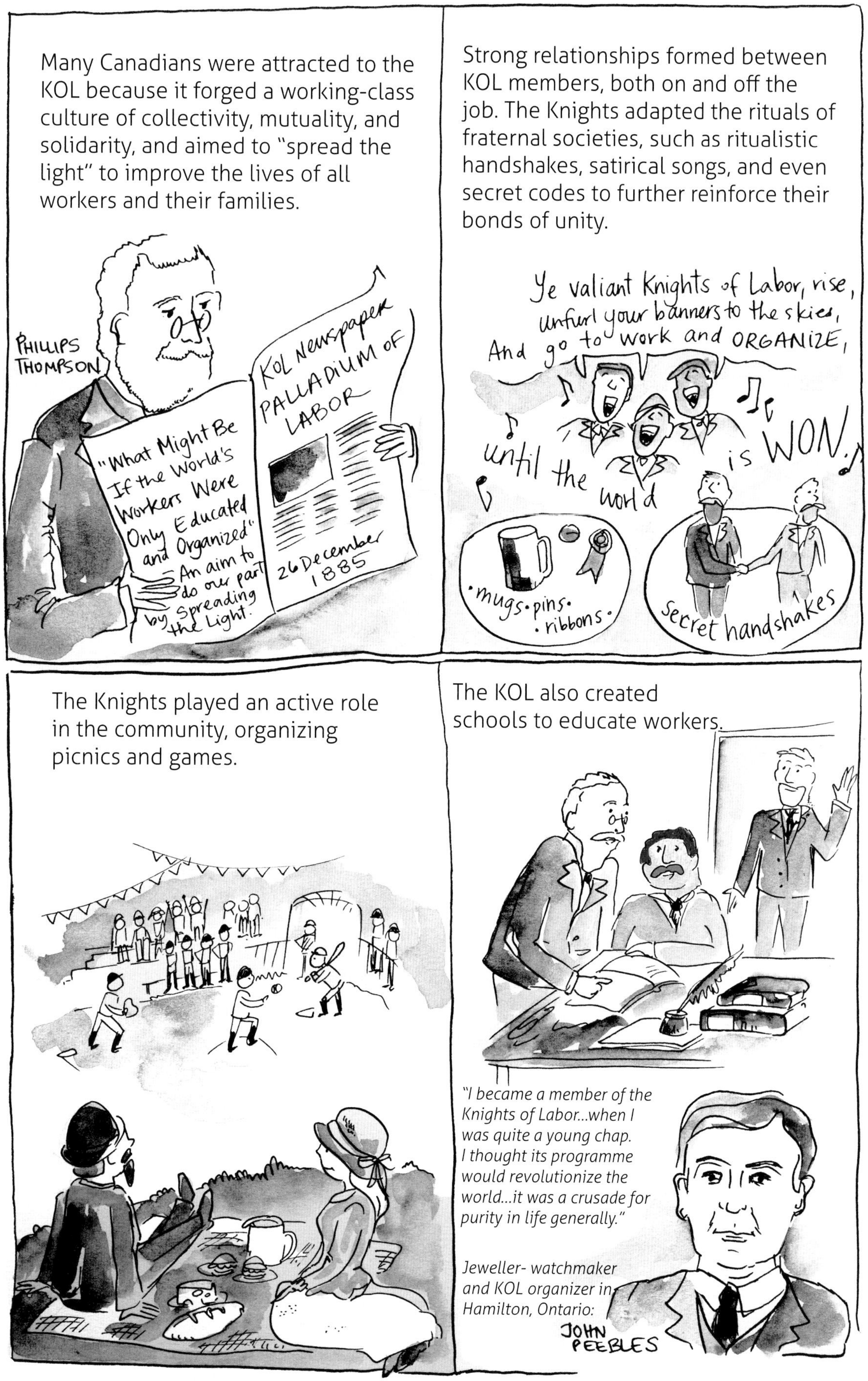
Many Canadians were attracted to the KOL because it forged a working-class culture of collectivity, mutuality, and solidarity, and aimed to "spread the light" to improve the lives of all workers and their families.
PHILLIPS THOMPSON
KOL Newspaper
PALLADIUM OF LABOR
"What Might Be If the World's Workers Were Only Educated and Organized" An aim to do our part by Spreading the Light.
26 December 1885
Strong relationships formed between KOL members, both on and off the job. The Knights adapted the rituals of fraternal societies, such as ritualistic handshakes, satirical songs, and even secret codes to further reinforce their bonds of unity.
Ye valiant Knights of Labor, rise, unfurl your banners to the skies, And go to work and ORGANIZE, until the world is WON.
•mugs•pins• •ribbons•
secret handshakes
The Knights played an active role in the community, organizing picnics and games.
The KOL also created schools to educate workers.
"I became a member of the Knights of Labor...when I was quite a young chap. I thought its programme would revolutionize the world...it was a crusade for purity in life generally."
Jeweller- watchmaker and KOL organizer in Hamilton, Ontario:
JOHN PEEBLES

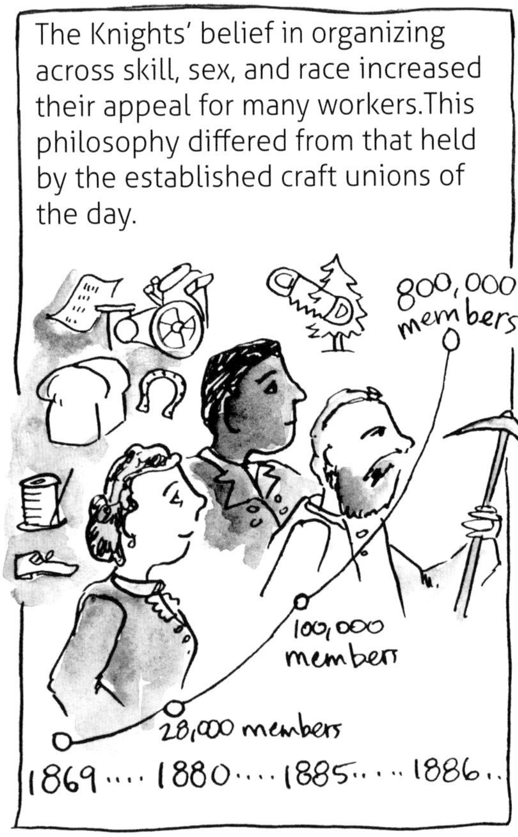
The Knights' belief in organizing across skill, sex, and race increased their appeal for many workers.This philosophy differed from that held by the established craft unions of the day.
800,000 members
100,000 members
28,000 members
1869.... 1880.... 1885..... 1886..

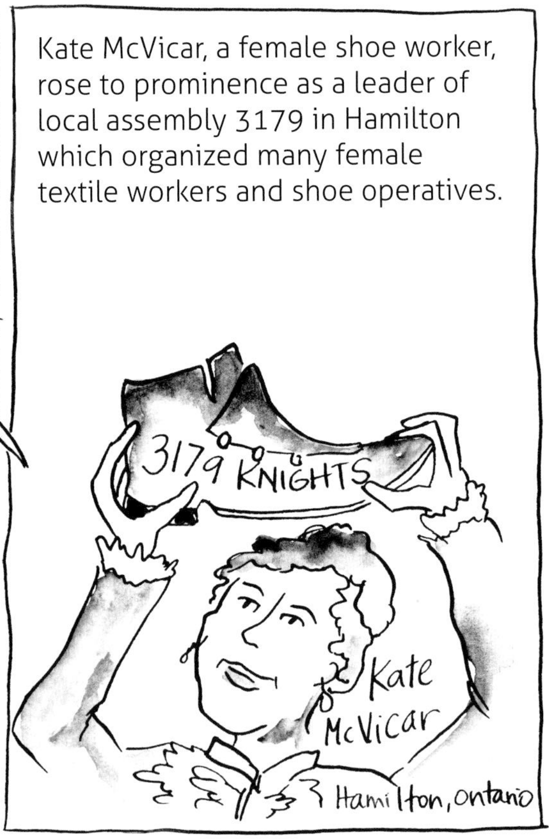
Kate McVicar, a female shoe worker, rose to prominence as a leader of local assembly 3179 in Hamilton which organized many female textile workers and shoe operatives.
3179 KNIGHTS
Kate McVicar
Hamilton, Ontario

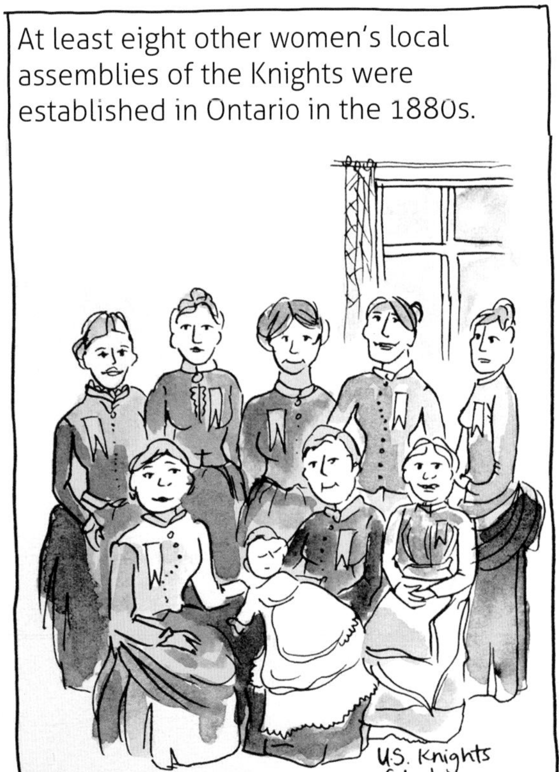
At least eight other women's local assemblies of the Knights were established in Ontario in the 1880s.
U.S. Knights of Labor

Black workers joined the Knights in Canada and the US.

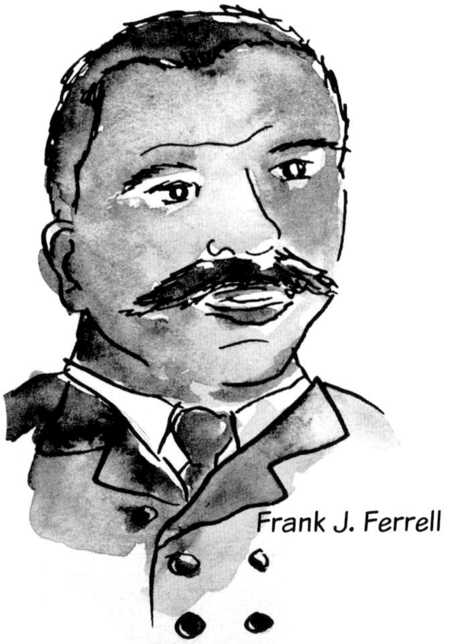
Frank J. Ferrell

Some members of the Knights even supported the 1885 Métis resistance.

While the Knights were progressive on many issues, their anti-Asian stance, particularly on the west coast, shows how deeply entrenched racist ideas were in the 1880s.

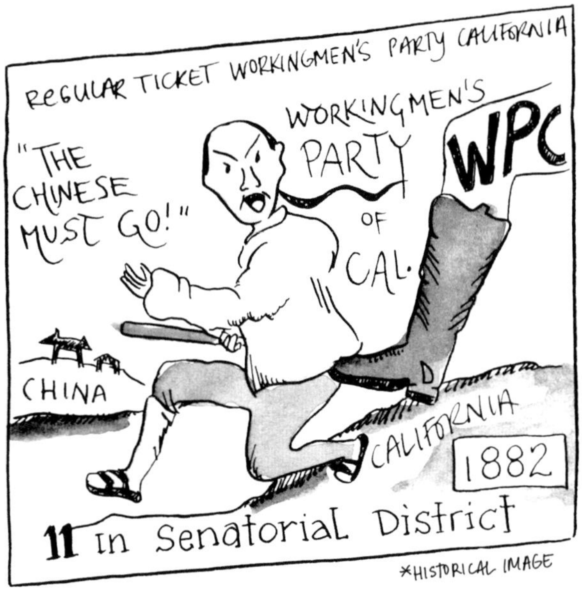
REGULAR TICKET WORKINGMEN'S PARTY CALIFORNIA
"THE CHINESE MUST GO!"
WORKINGMEN'S PARTY OF CAL.
WPC
CHINA
CALIFORNIA
1882
11 in Senatorial District
*HISTORICAL IMAGE

Whites saw Asian workers as a threat to job security. Many Asian workers felt compelled by their dire economic circumstances to accept lower wages and sometimes replace striking workers as "scabs."

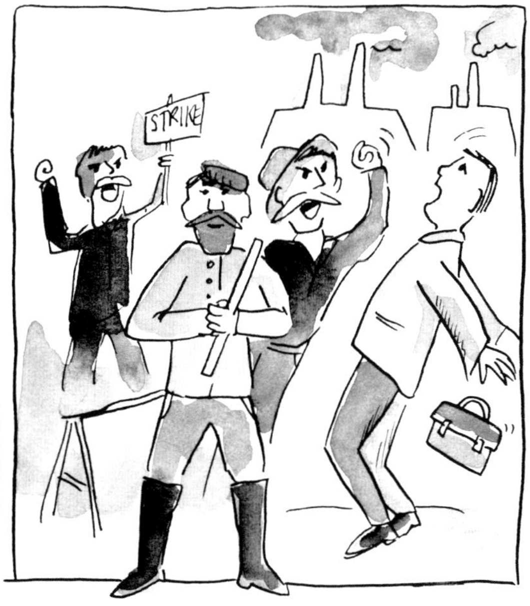
STRIKE

In British Columbia, the KOL excluded these Asian workers rather than including and working with them in their attempts to improve the lives of workers. Employers exploited this racial conflict to further divide workers and increase their profits.

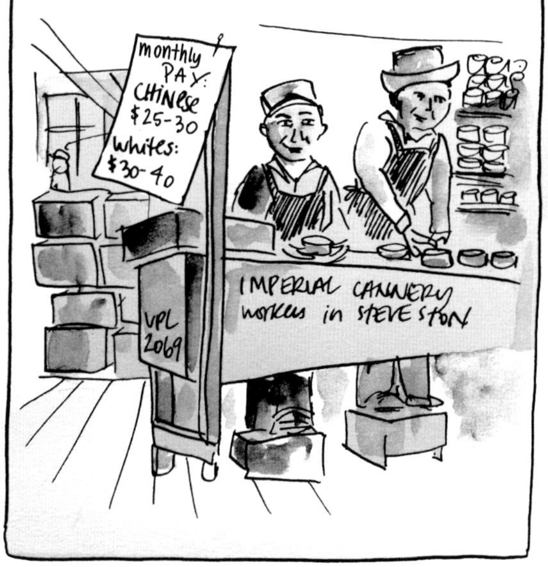
monthly PAY: CHINESE $25-30 Whites: $30-40
IMPERIAL CANNERY workers in STEVESTON
VPL 2069

More than 100 years later, racism continues to shape people's lives and divide working people.

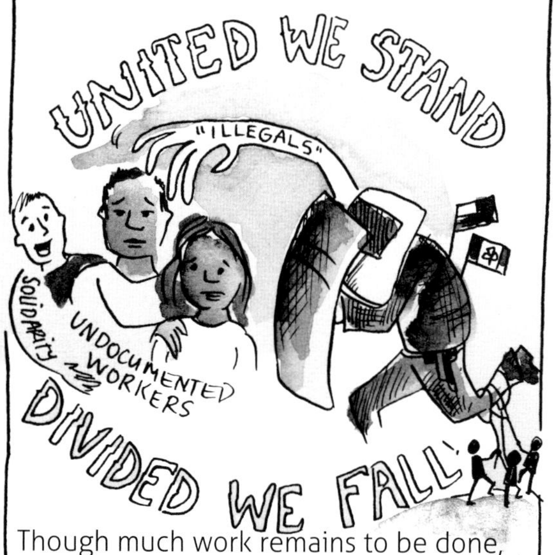
UNITED WE STAND
"ILLEGALS"
SOLIDARITY
UNDOCUMENTED WORKERS
DIVIDED WE FALL

Though much work remains to be done, today many unions are committed to challenging racism (or racist ideas, behaviours, and structures) in the labour movement, workplace, and society.

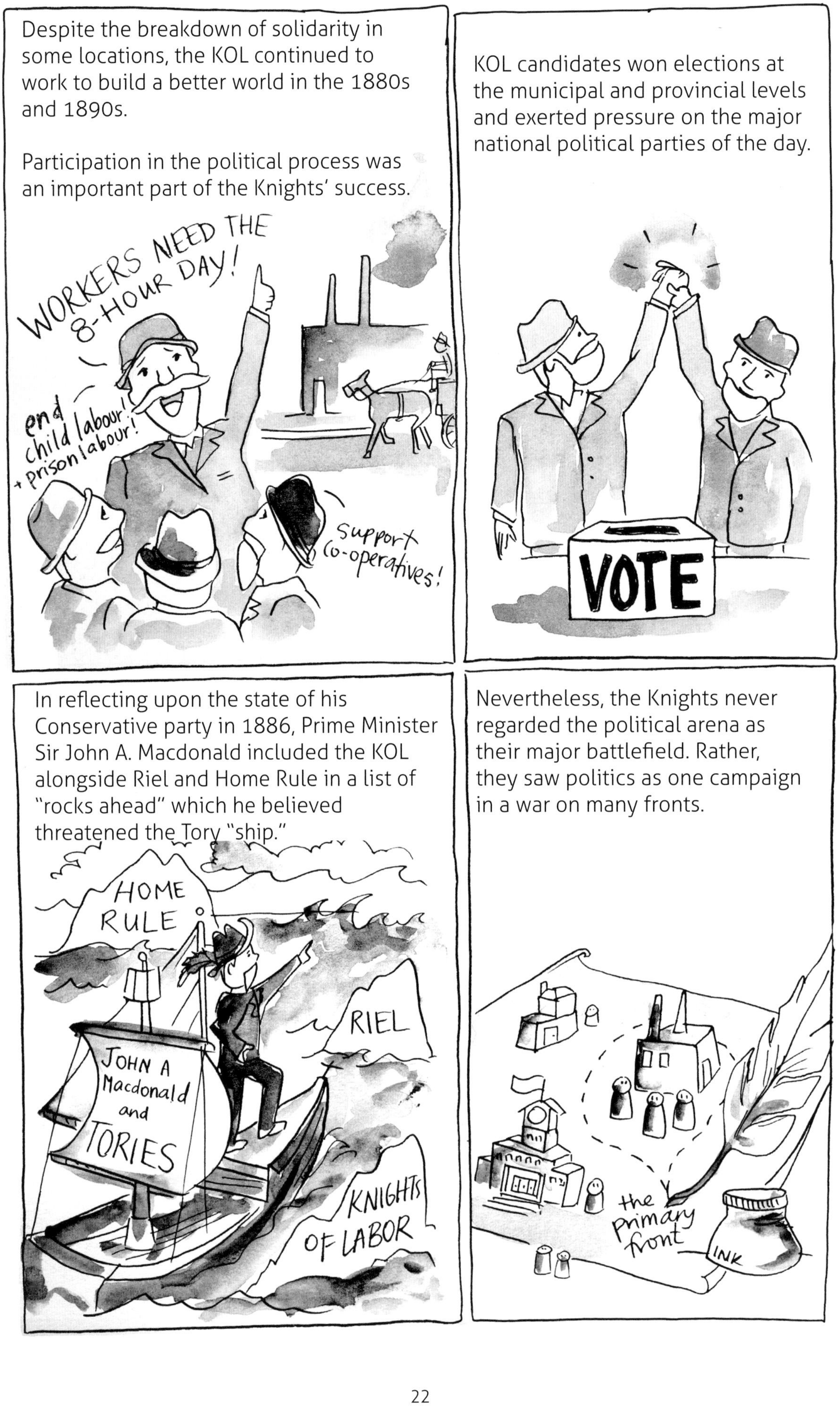
Despite the breakdown of solidarity in some locations, the KOL continued to work to build a better world in the 1880s and 1890s.
Participation in the political process was an important part of the Knights' success.
WORKERS NEED THE 8-HOUR DAY!
end child labour! + prison labour!
support co-operatives!
KOL candidates won elections at the municipal and provincial levels and exerted pressure on the major national political parties of the day.
VOTE
In reflecting upon the state of his Conservative party in 1886, Prime Minister Sir John A. Macdonald included the KOL alongside Riel and Home Rule in a list of "rocks ahead" which he believed threatened the Tory "ship."
HOME RULE
RIEL
JOHN A Macdonald and TORIES
KNIGHTS OF LABOR
Nevertheless, the Knights never regarded the political arena as their major battlefield. Rather, they saw politics as one campaign in a war on many fronts.
the primary front
INK

In the beginning the Knights used the withdrawal of labour power as an effective tactic.

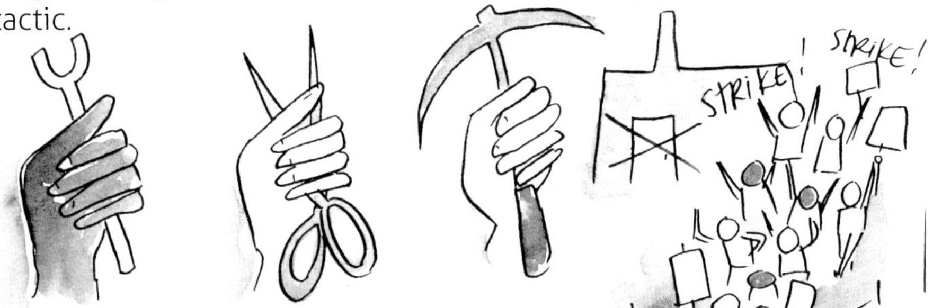
STRIKE!
STRIKE!

In Ontario, in 1886, the Knights played key roles in strikes in Chatham, Merritton, and Gravenhurst.

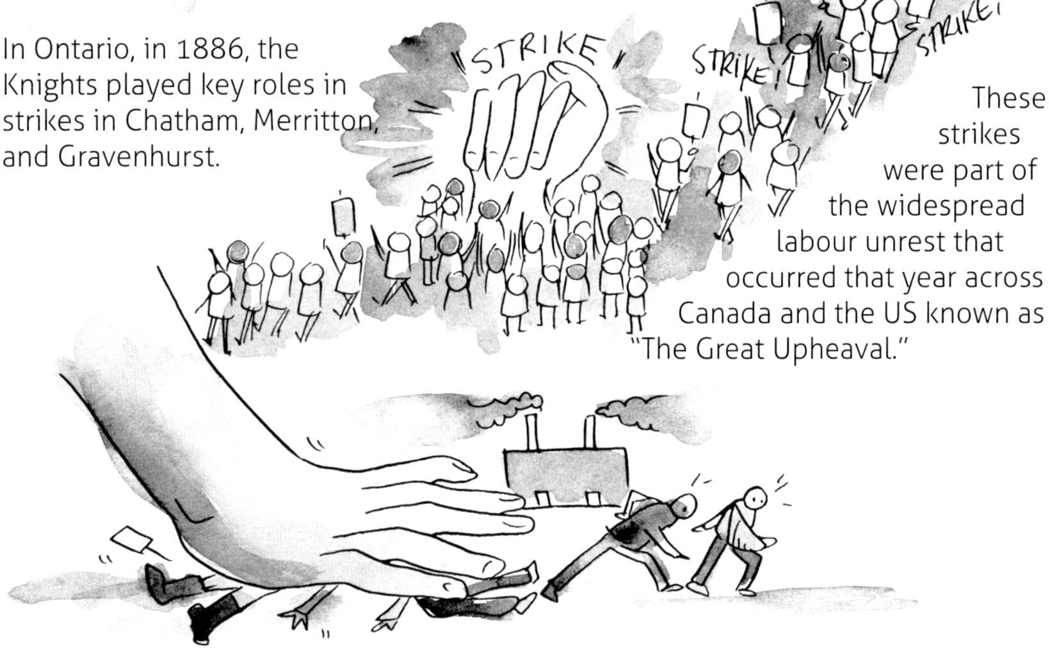
"STRIKE"
STRIKE!
STRIKE!

These strikes were part of the widespread labour unrest that occurred that year across Canada and the US known as "The Great Upheaval."

Although some strikes resulted in victory, others ended in bitter defeat. After losing a number of prominent strikes, the KOL began to view strikes as a last resort in industrial conflict.

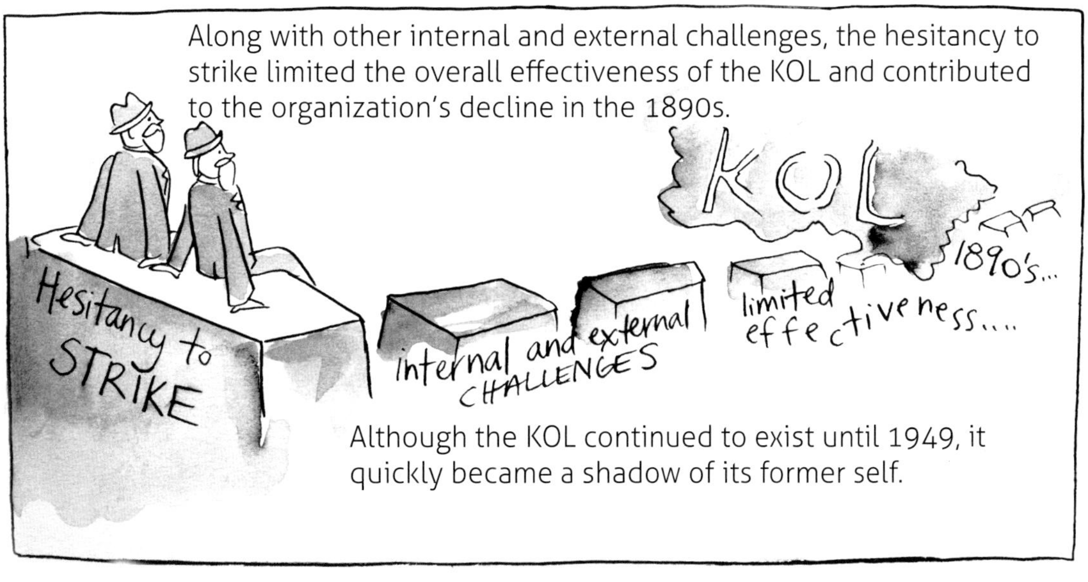
KOL
1890's...
Hesitancy to STRIKE
internal and external CHALLENGES
limited effectiveness....

Along with other internal and external challenges, the hesitancy to strike limited the overall effectiveness of the KOL and contributed to the organization's decline in the 1890s.

Although the KOL continued to exist until 1949, it quickly became a shadow of its former self.

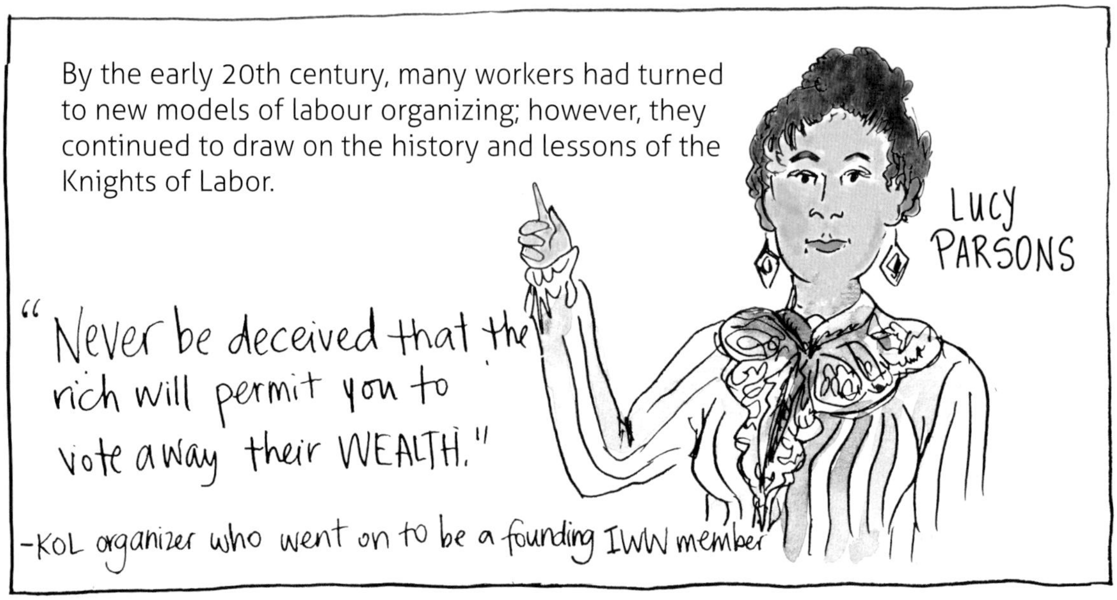
By the early 20th century, many workers had turned to new models of labour organizing; however, they continued to draw on the history and lessons of the Knights of Labor.
LUCY PARSONS
"Never be deceived that the rich will permit you to vote away their WEALTH."
-KOL organizer who went on to be a founding IWW member

Though not without its faults, the Knights of Labor can still be drawn upon for inspiration.

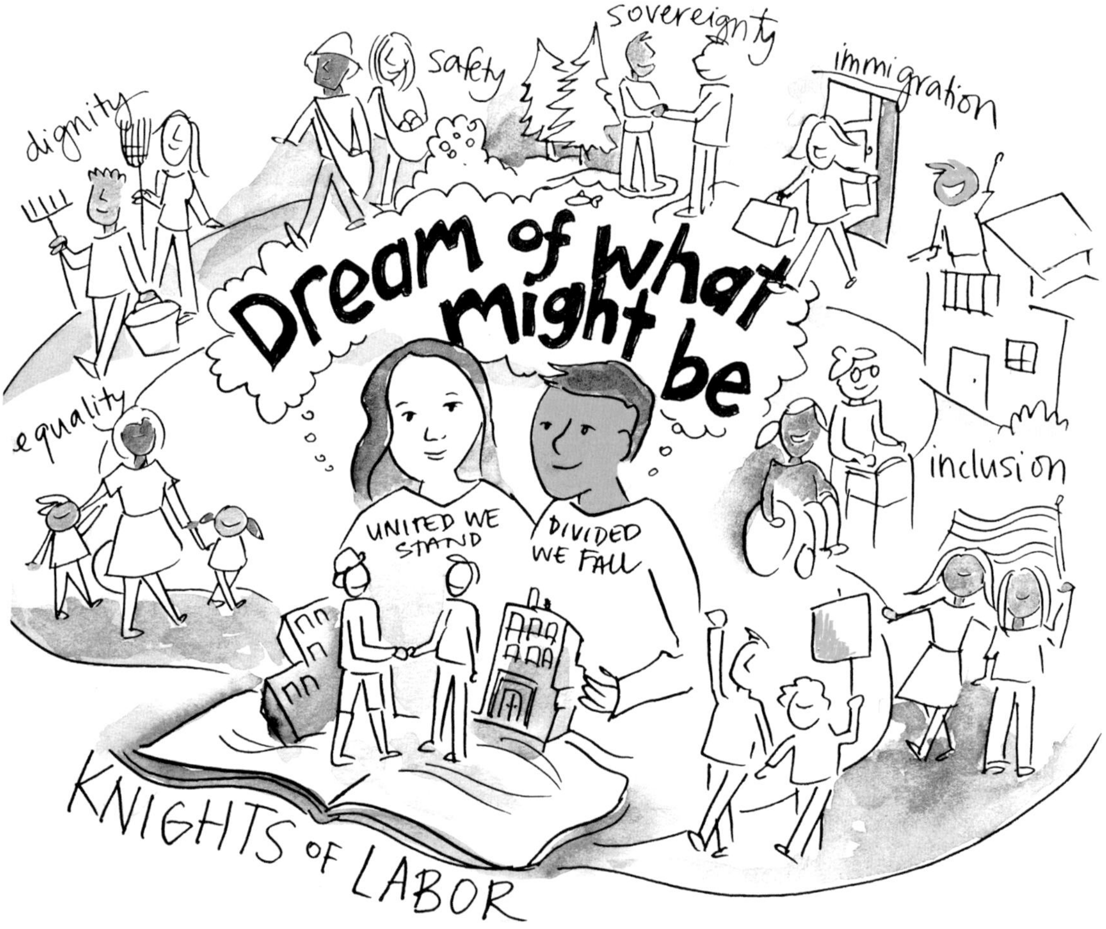
dignity
safety
sovereignty
immigration
Dream of what might be
equality
inclusion
UNITED WE STAND
DIVIDED WE FALL
KNIGHTS OF LABOR

Today, as we work to develop new cultures and movements of opposition, the Knights' call to "dream of what might be" reminds us that an alternative society is always possible.

Acknowledgements

The Graphic History Collective is grateful for the financial support we received from the Canadian Committee on Labour History (www.cclh.ca). We also acknowledge the activists and academics who have previously studied the Knights of Labor and whose works assisted us in producing our comic book, in particular Bryan D. Palmer and Gregory S. Kealey.

Notes

Page 15: The opening image for the comic book was inspired by a photograph of the Knights of Labor (KL) in Hamilton parading down King Street during the 1880s. Library and Archives Canada, PA-103086.

Page 16, Panel 3: The image of two figures shaking hands with the slogan "United We Stand, Divided We Fall" was inspired by a series of KL plates from the 1880s depicting a similar image. Minnesota Historical Society Collections, 70.39.23.

Page 18, Panel 1: This is a reproduction of a sketch of the founders of the KL. The original sketch appears to have been drawn by H.J. Skeffington in 1886. Everett Collection, 4048-7533.

Page 18, Panel 2: This is a quote from Terence V. Powderly, General Master Workman for the KL from 1879 to 1893. Terence V. Powderly, *Address Delivered in Music Hall, Providence Rhode Island* (Boston: 1886), 19–20.

Page 19, Panel 1: The image of Phillips Thompson reading a newspaper combines two primary sources: a reproduction of a photograph of Thompson (Library and Archives Canada, C-38581) and headlines from the December 26, 1885, issue of the KL newspaper, *Palladium of Labor*.

Page 19, Panel 2: The song lyrics and images of KL cultural material, such as ribbons and mugs, are taken from Robert E. Weir's book *Beyond Labor's Veil: The Culture of the Knights of Labor* (University Park: Pennsylvania State University Press, 1996), 111.

Page 19, Panel 4: This is a quote from John Peebles, "Recollections of John Peebles, Mayor of Hamilton, 1930–1933," February 7, 1946, Hamilton Collection, Hamilton Public Library.

Page 20, Panel 3: This is a reproduction of a photograph of KL women delegates attending the 1886 United States national convention. American Catholic History Research Center and University Archives, Box 2, Item 63.

Page 21, Panel 1: This image is based on Carl Albert Browne, "Regular Ticket Workingmen's Party California. The Chinese Must Go! 11th Senatorial District," 1878, lithograph. California Historical Society, Fine Arts collection, FN-30623.

Page 22, Panel 3: This image is based on a quote from John A. Macdonald. Sir John A. Macdonald to Sir Charles Tupper, June 21, 1886, in Sir Joseph Pope, ed., *The Correspondence of Sir John A. Macdonald* (Toronto: Oxford University Press, 1921), 382.

Page 24, Panel 1: Picture of Lucy Parsons and quote attributed to her. Labadie Photograph Collection, University of Michigan, LPF.0862.

Working on the Water, Fighting for the Land
Indigenous Labour on Burrard Inlet

On the Indigenous Waterfront
Andrew Parnaby

This comic book tells the dramatic story of a group of Coast Salish peoples who were deeply involved in the political upheaval that characterized Indigenous and working-class lives in 19th and early 20th century British Columbia.

As Indigenous peoples, they felt the heavy pressures of white settlement. The appearance of sawmills along Burrard Inlet—part of their ancestral territories—beginning in 1863 heralded a new era of intensified settler colonialism. Yet, as workers, they took advantage of the employment opportunities that emerged as the port of Vancouver industrialized: they became longshorers. Never fully shedding their attachments to older, customary ways of Indigenous life and labour, they developed a sharp, well-defined consciousness of the issues that confronted them, both as "Indians" and workers: title to land and rights to resources; low wages, dangerous working conditions, and oppressive bosses. Consistently, this consciousness spurred political action, both on their reserves and on the job. Their solidarities extended to other Indigenous groups in the province and to non-Indigenous waterfront workers, who also faced hard times in the rough world of dockside employment. These are extraordinary lives worth knowing about—and learning from.

For an awfully long time, the writing of history ignored both Indigenous and working people. But beginning in the 1960s, the definition of who mattered historically began to expand and change shape; it became more open, more democratic. This shift in perspective was partly due to the activism of the era, as the Indigenous, women's, labour, and civil rights movements gained momentum, forcing formerly hidden histories out into the open for broader consideration. That post-secondary education came within reach of people from diverse backgrounds was also important, for these new students wanted to learn more about people in the past whose lives more resembled their own. This comic book, as Paul Buhle explains in the preface, is indebted to this tradition. And in this spirit, it embodies two of the tradition's most basic, yet enduringly powerful ideas: all peoples have a history and what they did, felt, and thought mattered.

This comic book also pushes that tradition in new directions. Until quite recently, Indigenous history and labour history were thought of as two distinct stories—researched and taught separately. Yet as *Working on the Water, Fighting for the Land* illustrates, the links between the two are too tight and too numerous to divide the historical narrative up so neatly. Lessons learned by the likes of Squamish leader Andrew Paull in the search for Indigenous solidarity and collective rights were also applied to the politics of waged work—and vice versa. It's not stretching the point too far to say that generations of Squamish men were—and continue to be—integral to the labour history of the Pacific province: their experiences propelled economic change, produced a range of influential unions, and shaded the electrifying political debates that raged on the docks and in the union movement down to the 1940s. Inseparable and no less significant are the contributions of Squamish women, whose own history of domestic, community, and industrial work is hinted at in the comic book and exemplified by the figure of Valentina Brooks in the conclusion. Like the making of a traditional woven basket depicted on the book's cover, each narrative—Indigenous and labour, male and female—is drawn together through the placement of text and image to make something new and original: history from below.

Visually this comic book is powerful. Yet perhaps more compelling are the stylistic elements that the artist—Tania Willard of the Secwepemc Nation—has brought to bear on this project. Non-Indigenous people have been representing "Indians" visually since the first illustrated edition of Columbus's letters was published in the late 15th century. Prints, paintings, photographs, sculptures, and movies all followed—collectively entrenching the stereotypes of the "bloodthirsty savage," noble savage, and dying Indian in Western visual culture. Utilizing the lino-cut style of print making, Willard offers readers an alternative to these malignant colonialist projections in her images of Indigenous peoples that capture their complicated histories, motivations, and actions.

The arrangement of the images on each page in collage-like patterns extends this sentiment further. The layout weaves Indigenous people into the complicated patterns of historical change that transformed B.C.'s Lower Mainland during this era; it makes clear that they did not sit outside it all, unchanging, helpless, and thus in need of the white man's pity or salvation. Graphic elements borrowed from the visual traditions of the union movement—especially the Industrial Workers of the World—lend the comic book an additional, radical edge. That Willard has based some of her prints on photographic images originally taken by non-Indigenous photographers for other purposes illustrates in a few frames what the book, overall, is designed to do: change our perspective.

Reading a comic book is not like reading a traditional text. Its form forces the reader to move constantly from text to image, flit from panel to panel across the spaces in between, and thus to actively engage in the process of storytelling. In this heightened mode, readers might find themselves questioning commonly held beliefs about the past. Or perhaps they might be more open to the idea that history does not happen *to* people, but is made *by* them. Readers might also stop seeing the present as the only or best way to organize a society, and start working to change it, as the "best men that ever worked the lumber" did in British Columbia not so long ago.

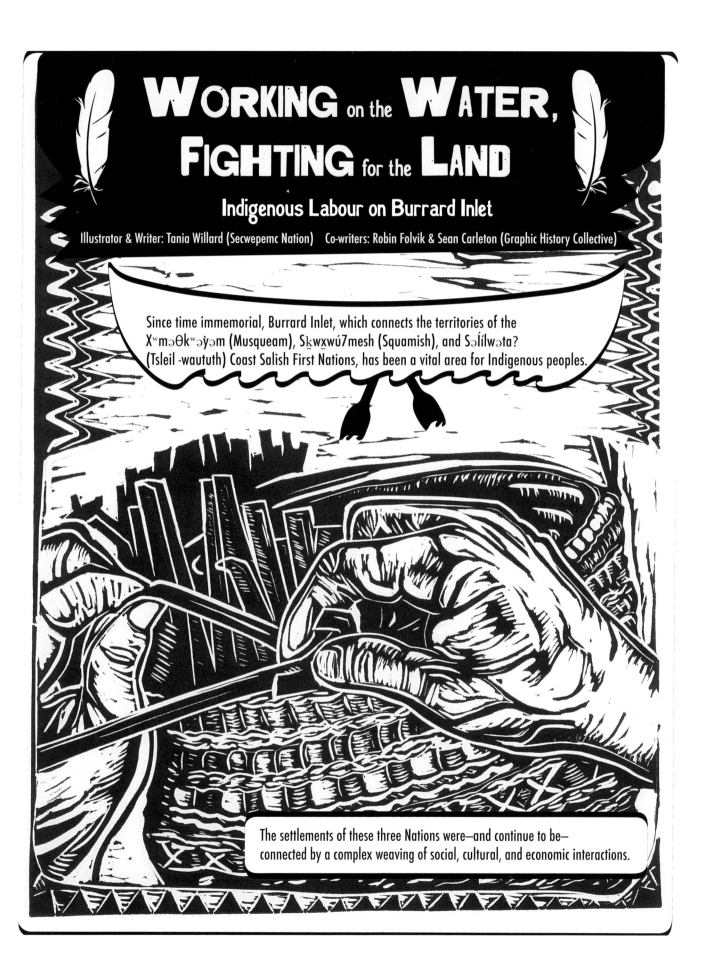

WORKING on the WATER, FIGHTING for the LAND

Indigenous Labour on Burrard Inlet

Illustrator & Writer: Tania Willard (Secwepemc Nation)   Co-writers: Robin Folvik & Sean Carleton (Graphic History Collective)

Since time immemorial, Burrard Inlet, which connects the territories of the Xʷməθkʷəy̓əm (Musqueam), Sḵwx̱wú7mesh (Squamish), and Səl̓ílwəta? (Tsleil-waututh) Coast Salish First Nations, has been a vital area for Indigenous peoples.

The settlements of these three Nations were—and continue to be—connected by a complex weaving of social, cultural, and economic interactions.

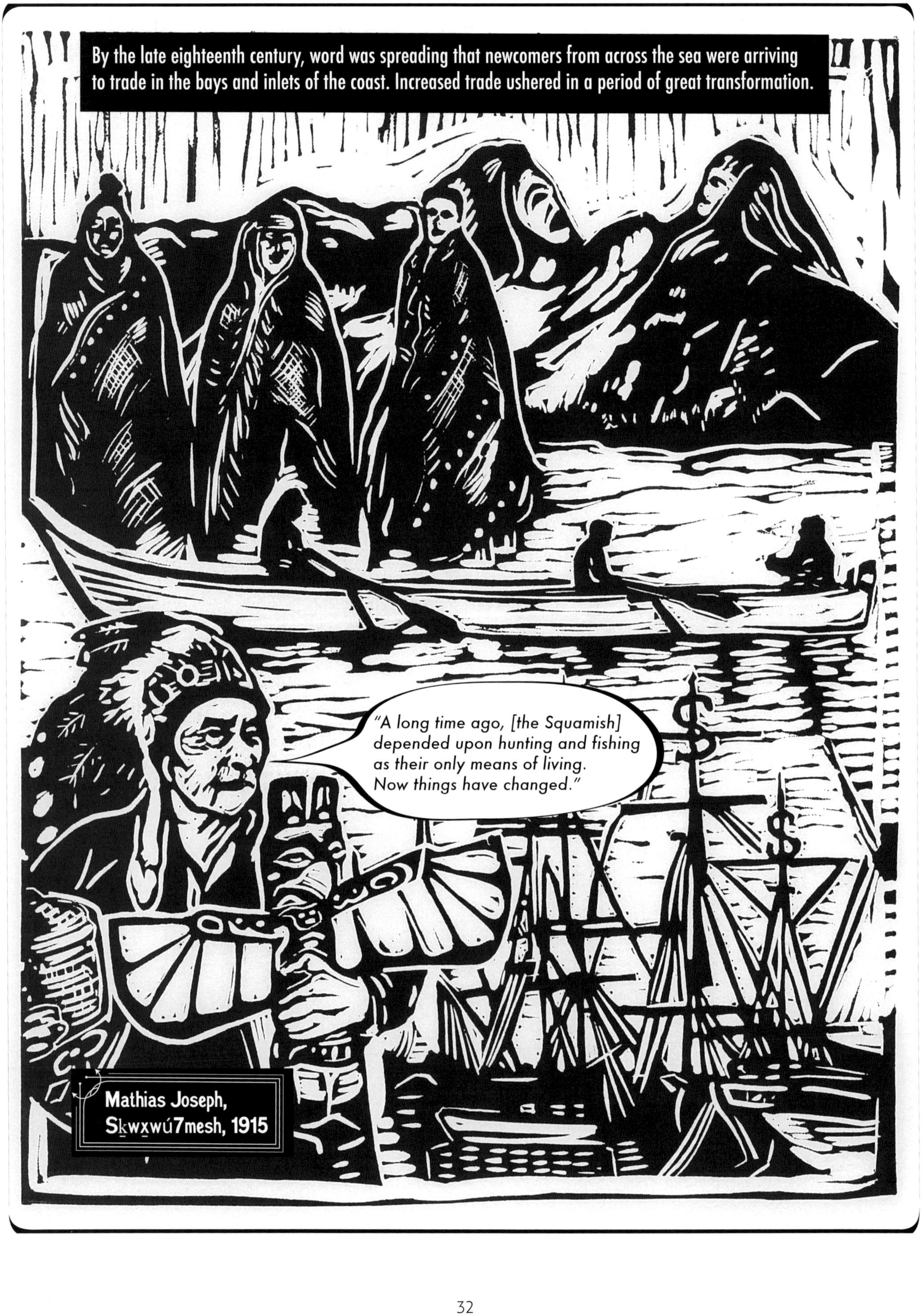
By the late eighteenth century, word was spreading that newcomers from across the sea were arriving to trade in the bays and inlets of the coast. Increased trade ushered in a period of great transformation.
"A long time ago, [the Squamish] depended upon hunting and fishing as their only means of living. Now things have changed."
Mathias Joseph, Sk̲wx̱wú7mesh, 1915

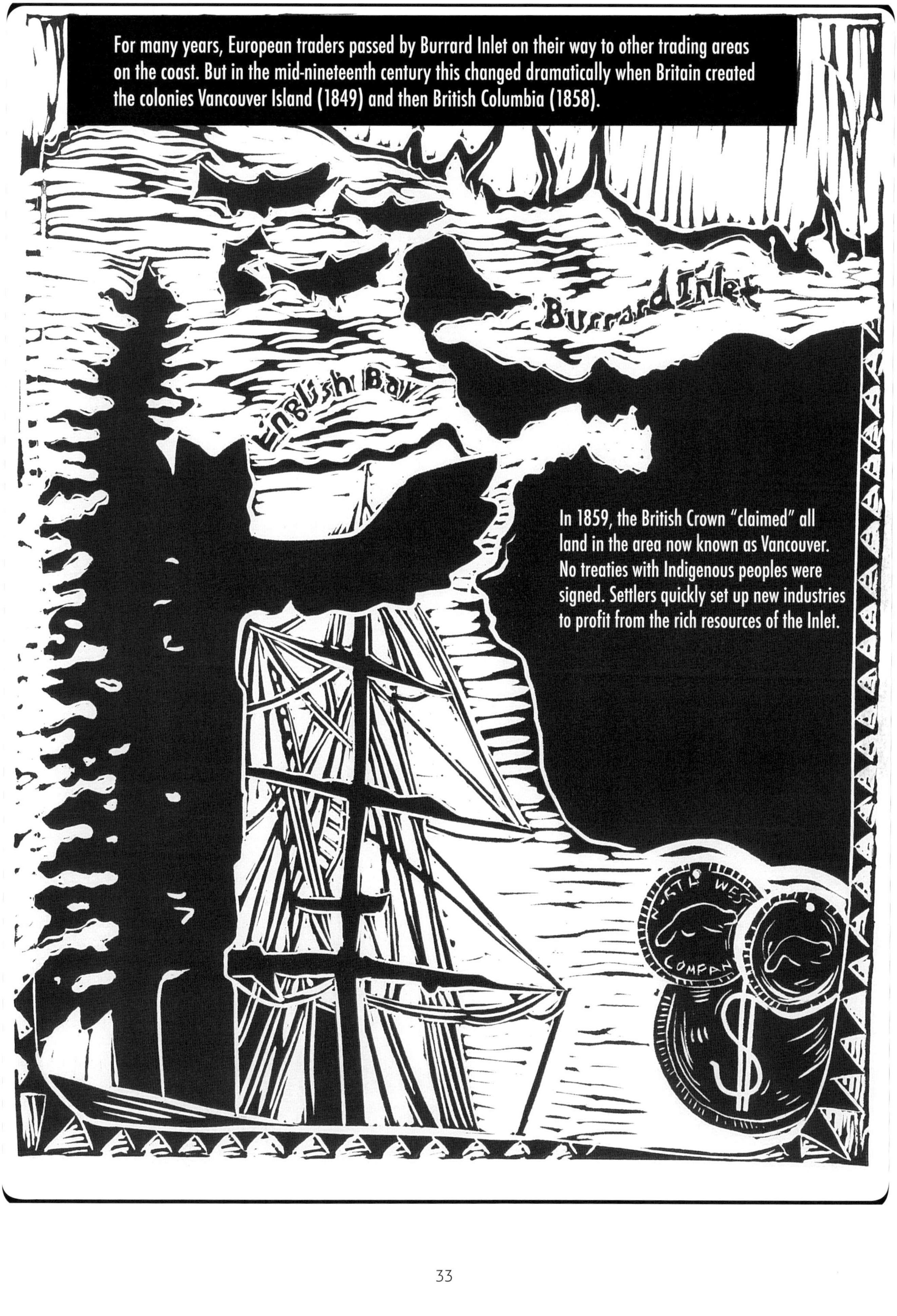
For many years, European traders passed by Burrard Inlet on their way to other trading areas on the coast. But in the mid-nineteenth century this changed dramatically when Britain created the colonies Vancouver Island (1849) and then British Columbia (1858).
Burrard Inlet
English Bay
In 1859, the British Crown "claimed" all land in the area now known as Vancouver. No treaties with Indigenous peoples were signed. Settlers quickly set up new industries to profit from the rich resources of the Inlet.

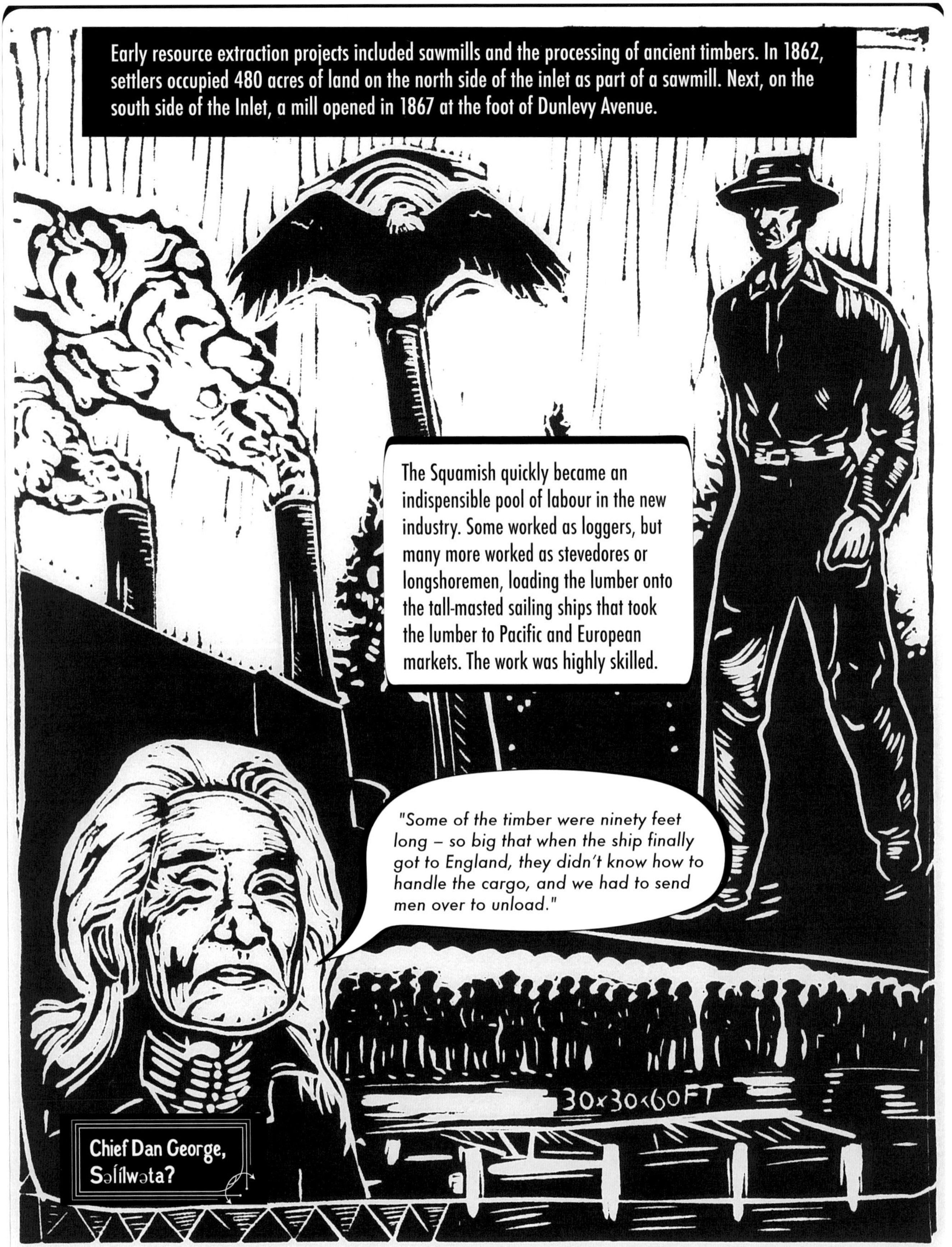
Early resource extraction projects included sawmills and the processing of ancient timbers. In 1862, settlers occupied 480 acres of land on the north side of the inlet as part of a sawmill. Next, on the south side of the Inlet, a mill opened in 1867 at the foot of Dunlevy Avenue.
The Squamish quickly became an indispensible pool of labour in the new industry. Some worked as loggers, but many more worked as stevedores or longshoremen, loading the lumber onto the tall-masted sailing ships that took the lumber to Pacific and European markets. The work was highly skilled.
"Some of the timber were ninety feet long – so big that when the ship finally got to England, they didn't know how to handle the cargo, and we had to send men over to unload."
30x30x60FT
Chief Dan George, Səlílwəta?

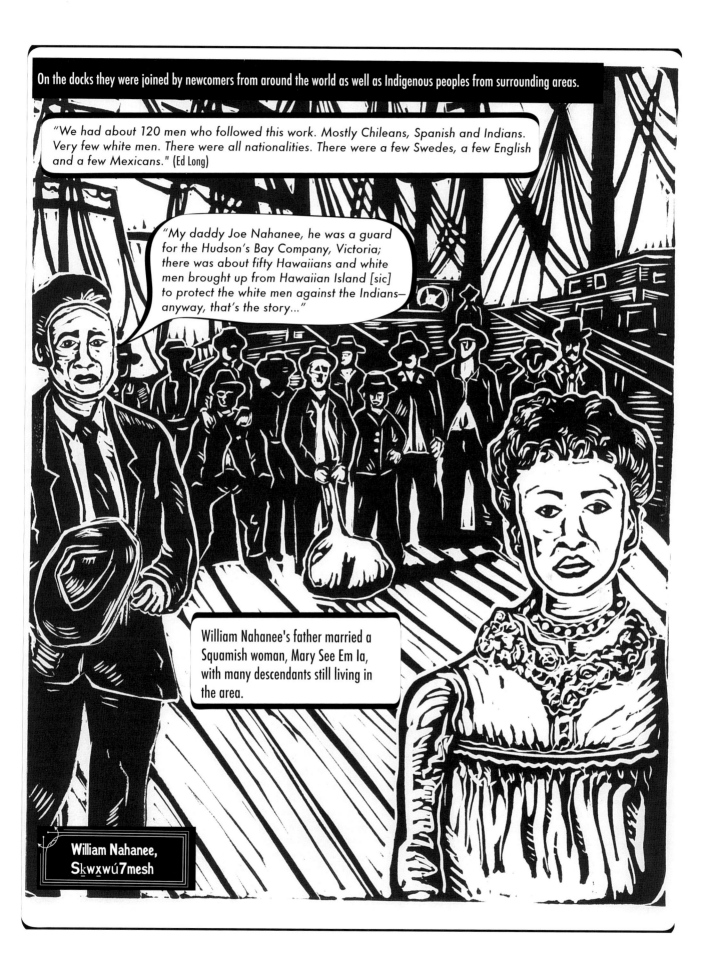

On the docks they were joined by newcomers from around the world as well as Indigenous peoples from surrounding areas.

"We had about 120 men who followed this work. Mostly Chileans, Spanish and Indians. Very few white men. There were all nationalities. There were a few Swedes, a few English and a few Mexicans." (Ed Long)

"My daddy Joe Nahanee, he was a guard for the Hudson's Bay Company, Victoria; there was about fifty Hawaiians and white men brought up from Hawaiian Island [sic] to protect the white men against the Indians— anyway, that's the story..."

William Nahanee's father married a Squamish woman, Mary See Em Ia, with many descendants still living in the area.

William Nahanee, Sḵwx̱wú7mesh

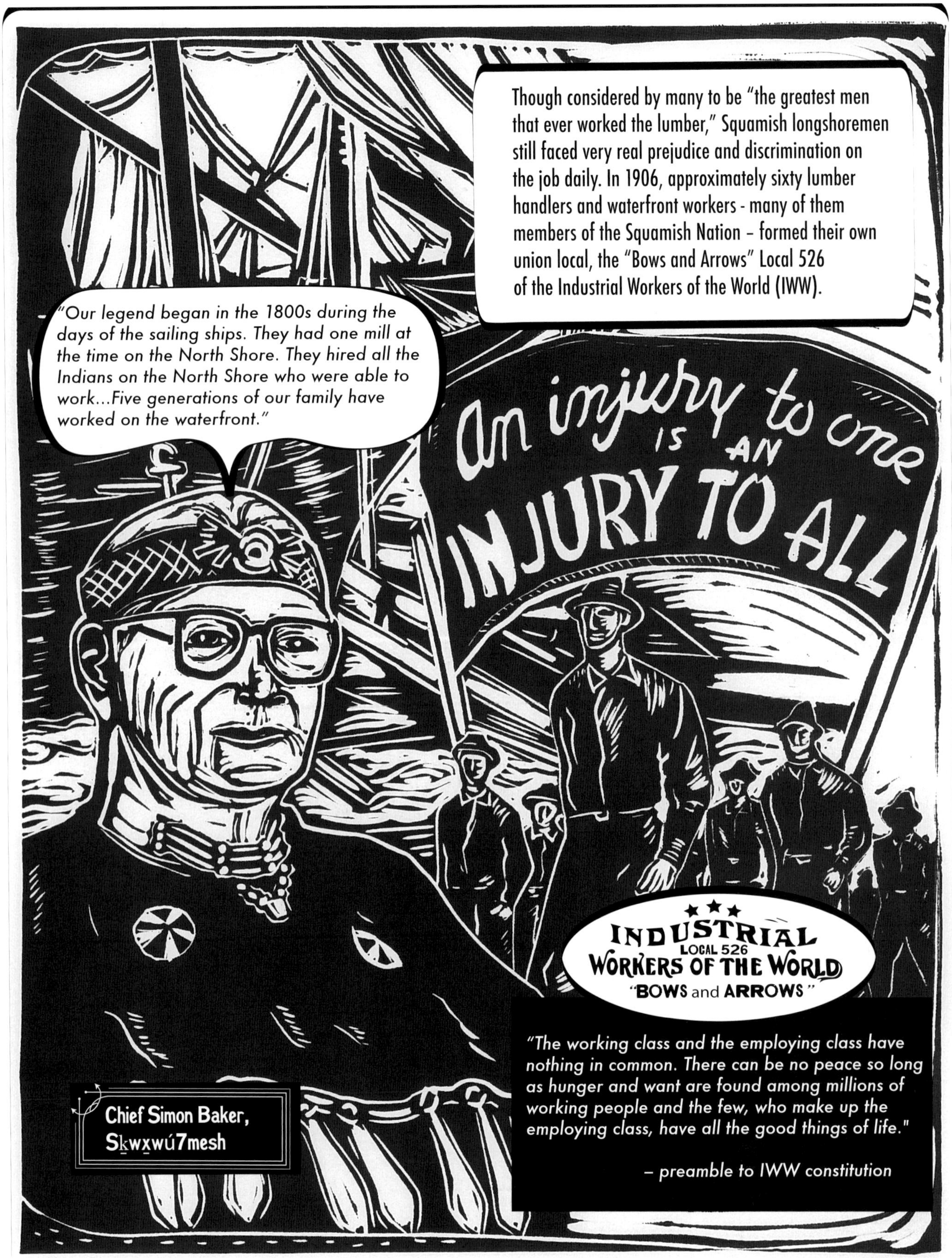
Though considered by many to be "the greatest men that ever worked the lumber," Squamish longshoremen still faced very real prejudice and discrimination on the job daily. In 1906, approximately sixty lumber handlers and waterfront workers - many of them members of the Squamish Nation – formed their own union local, the "Bows and Arrows" Local 526 of the Industrial Workers of the World (IWW).
"Our legend began in the 1800s during the days of the sailing ships. They had one mill at the time on the North Shore. They hired all the Indians on the North Shore who were able to work...Five generations of our family have worked on the waterfront."
An injury to one IS AN INJURY TO ALL
INDUSTRIAL LOCAL 526 WORKERS OF THE WORLD "BOWS and ARROWS"
Chief Simon Baker, Sḵwx̱wú7mesh
"The working class and the employing class have nothing in common. There can be no peace so long as hunger and want are found among millions of working people and the few, who make up the employing class, have all the good things of life."
– preamble to IWW constitution

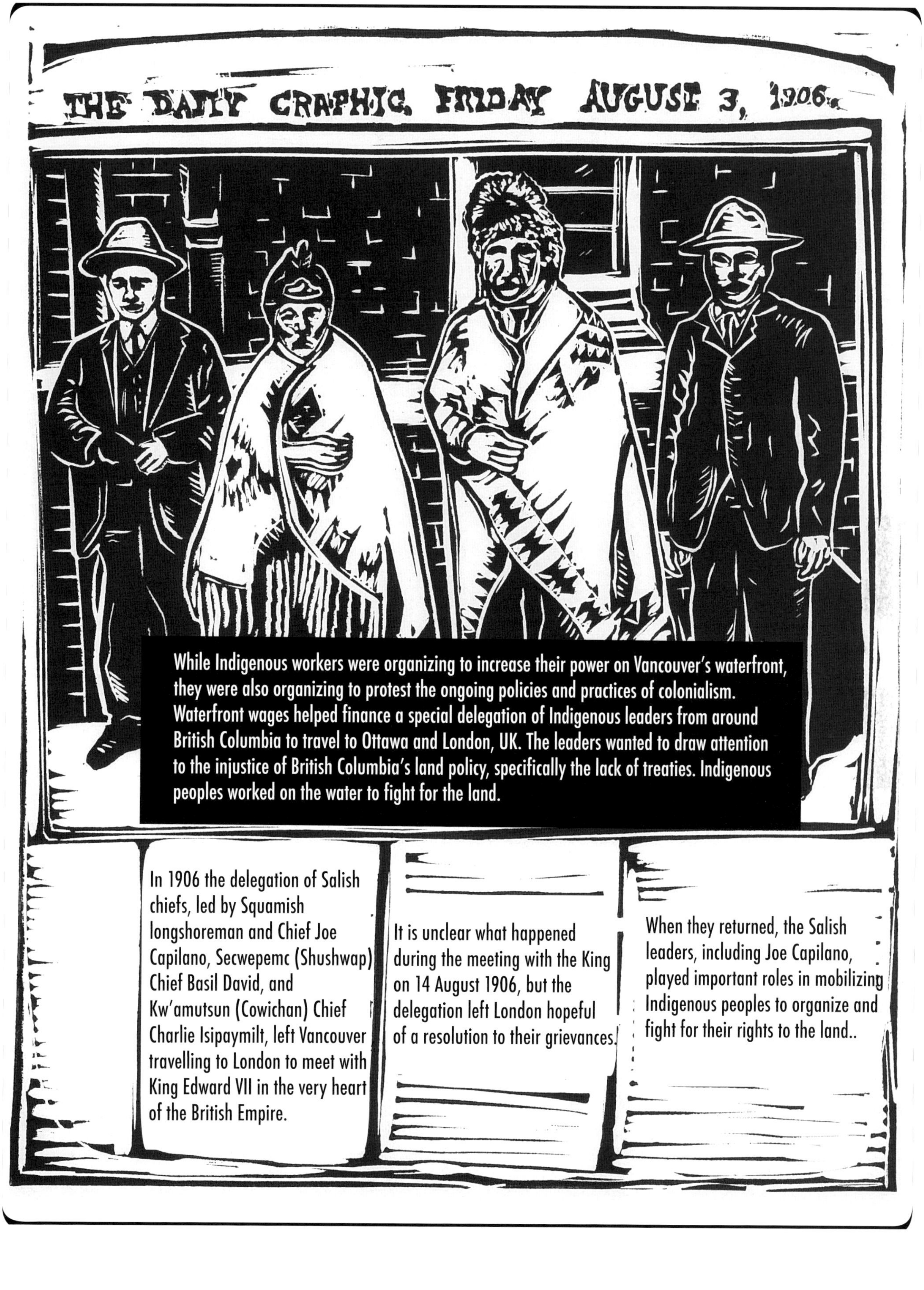
THE DAILY GRAPHIC, FRIDAY AUGUST 3, 1906.
While Indigenous workers were organizing to increase their power on Vancouver's waterfront, they were also organizing to protest the ongoing policies and practices of colonialism. Waterfront wages helped finance a special delegation of Indigenous leaders from around British Columbia to travel to Ottawa and London, UK. The leaders wanted to draw attention to the injustice of British Columbia's land policy, specifically the lack of treaties. Indigenous peoples worked on the water to fight for the land.
In 1906 the delegation of Salish chiefs, led by Squamish longshoreman and Chief Joe Capilano, Secwepemc (Shushwap) Chief Basil David, and Kw'amutsun (Cowichan) Chief Charlie Isipaymilt, left Vancouver travelling to London to meet with King Edward VII in the very heart of the British Empire.
It is unclear what happened during the meeting with the King on 14 August 1906, but the delegation left London hopeful of a resolution to their grievances.
When they returned, the Salish leaders, including Joe Capilano, played important roles in mobilizing Indigenous peoples to organize and fight for their rights to the land..

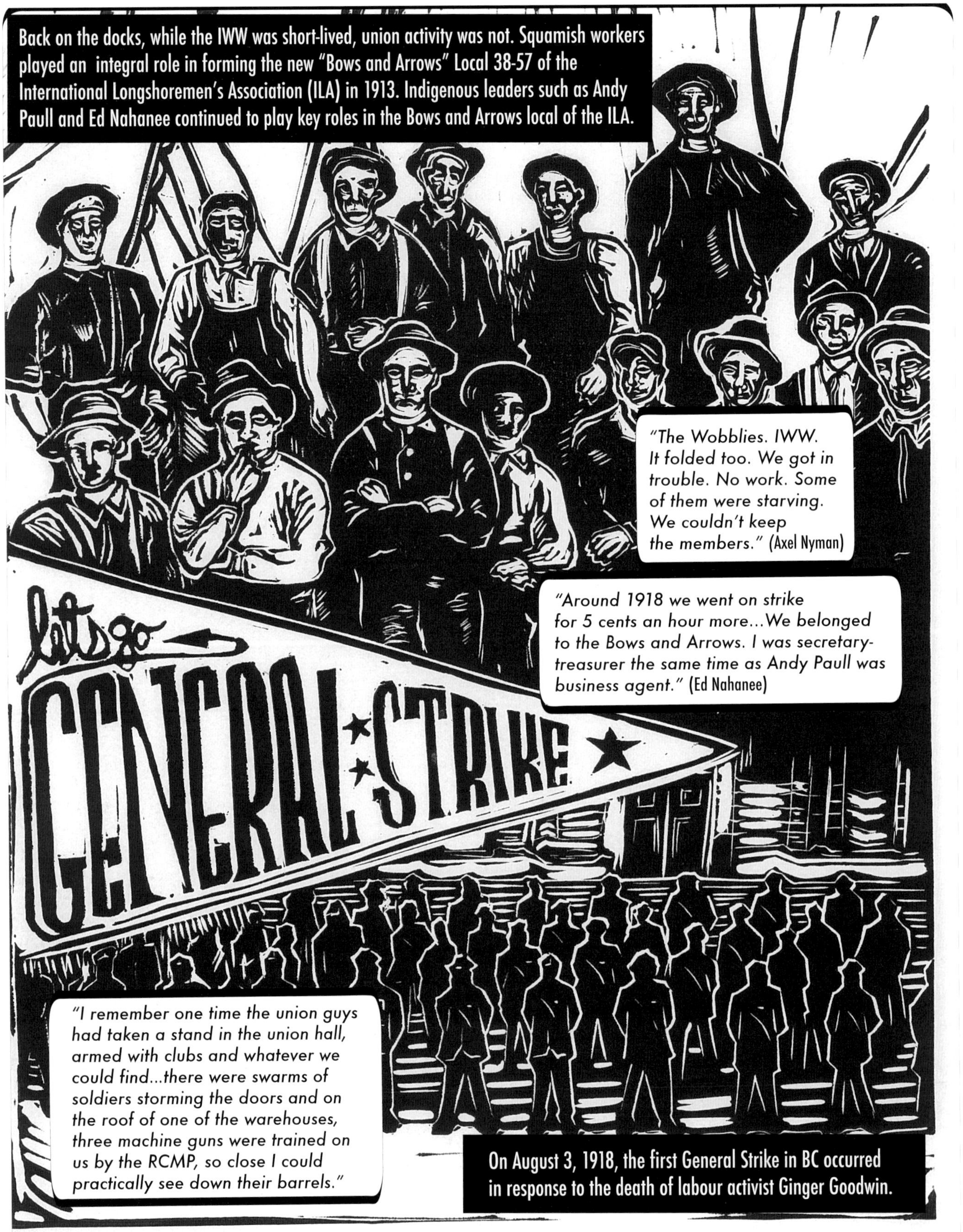

Back on the docks, while the IWW was short-lived, union activity was not. Squamish workers played an integral role in forming the new "Bows and Arrows" Local 38-57 of the International Longshoremen's Association (ILA) in 1913. Indigenous leaders such as Andy Paull and Ed Nahanee continued to play key roles in the Bows and Arrows local of the ILA.
"The Wobblies. IWW. It folded too. We got in trouble. No work. Some of them were starving. We couldn't keep the members." (Axel Nyman)
"Around 1918 we went on strike for 5 cents an hour more...We belonged to the Bows and Arrows. I was secretary-treasurer the same time as Andy Paull was business agent." (Ed Nahanee)
let's go
GENERAL STRIKE
"I remember one time the union guys had taken a stand in the union hall, armed with clubs and whatever we could find...there were swarms of soldiers storming the doors and on the roof of one of the warehouses, three machine guns were trained on us by the RCMP, so close I could practically see down their barrels."
On August 3, 1918, the first General Strike in BC occurred in response to the death of labour activist Ginger Goodwin.

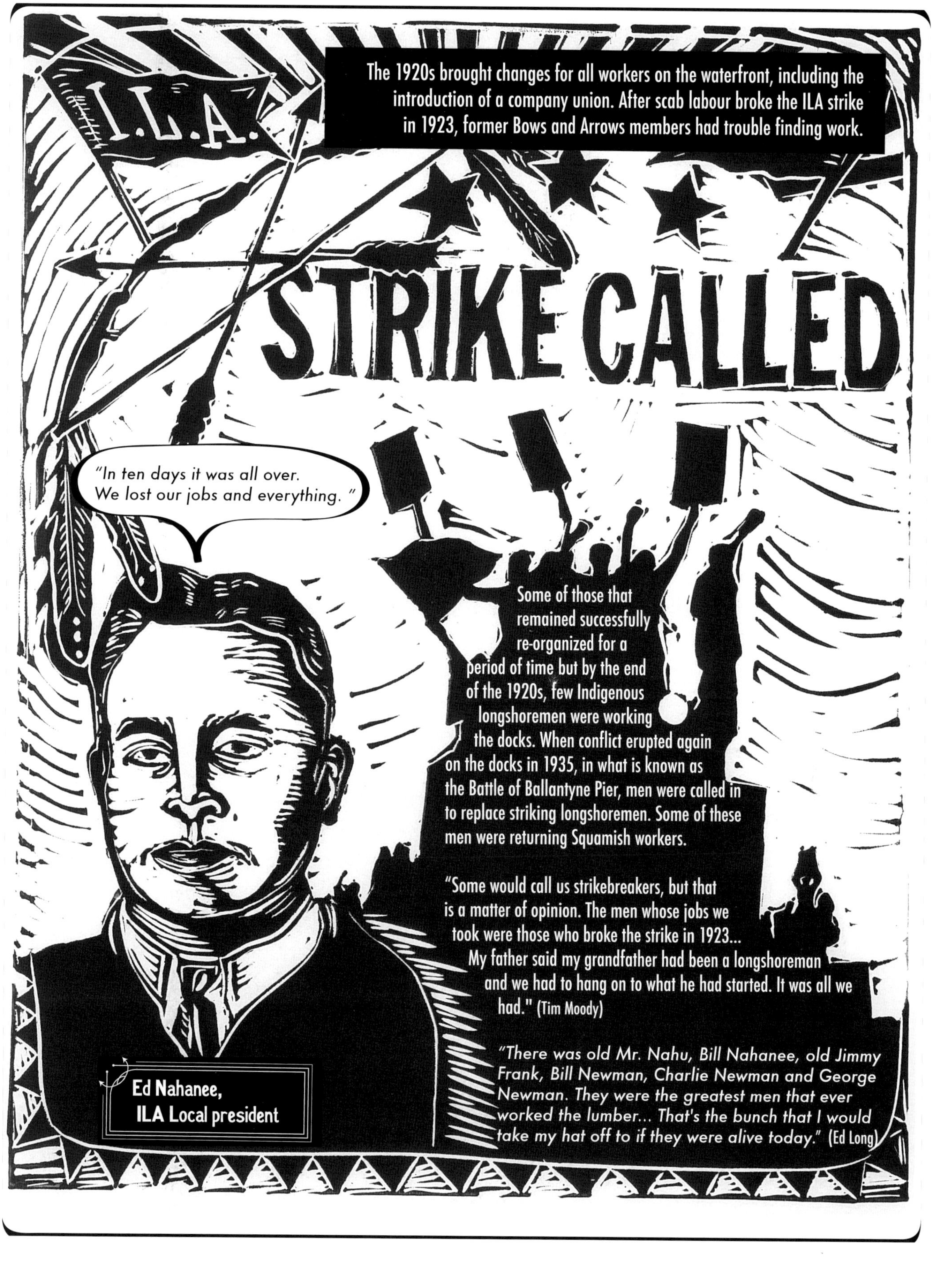
I.L.A.
The 1920s brought changes for all workers on the waterfront, including the introduction of a company union. After scab labour broke the ILA strike in 1923, former Bows and Arrows members had trouble finding work.
STRIKE CALLED
"In ten days it was all over. We lost our jobs and everything."
Some of those that remained successfully re-organized for a period of time but by the end of the 1920s, few Indigenous longshoremen were working the docks. When conflict erupted again on the docks in 1935, in what is known as the Battle of Ballantyne Pier, men were called in to replace striking longshoremen. Some of these men were returning Squamish workers.
"Some would call us strikebreakers, but that is a matter of opinion. The men whose jobs we took were those who broke the strike in 1923... My father said my grandfather had been a longshoreman and we had to hang on to what he had started. It was all we had." (Tim Moody)
"There was old Mr. Nahu, Bill Nahanee, old Jimmy Frank, Bill Newman, Charlie Newman and George Newman. They were the greatest men that ever worked the lumber... That's the bunch that I would take my hat off to if they were alive today." (Ed Long)
Ed Nahanee, ILA Local president

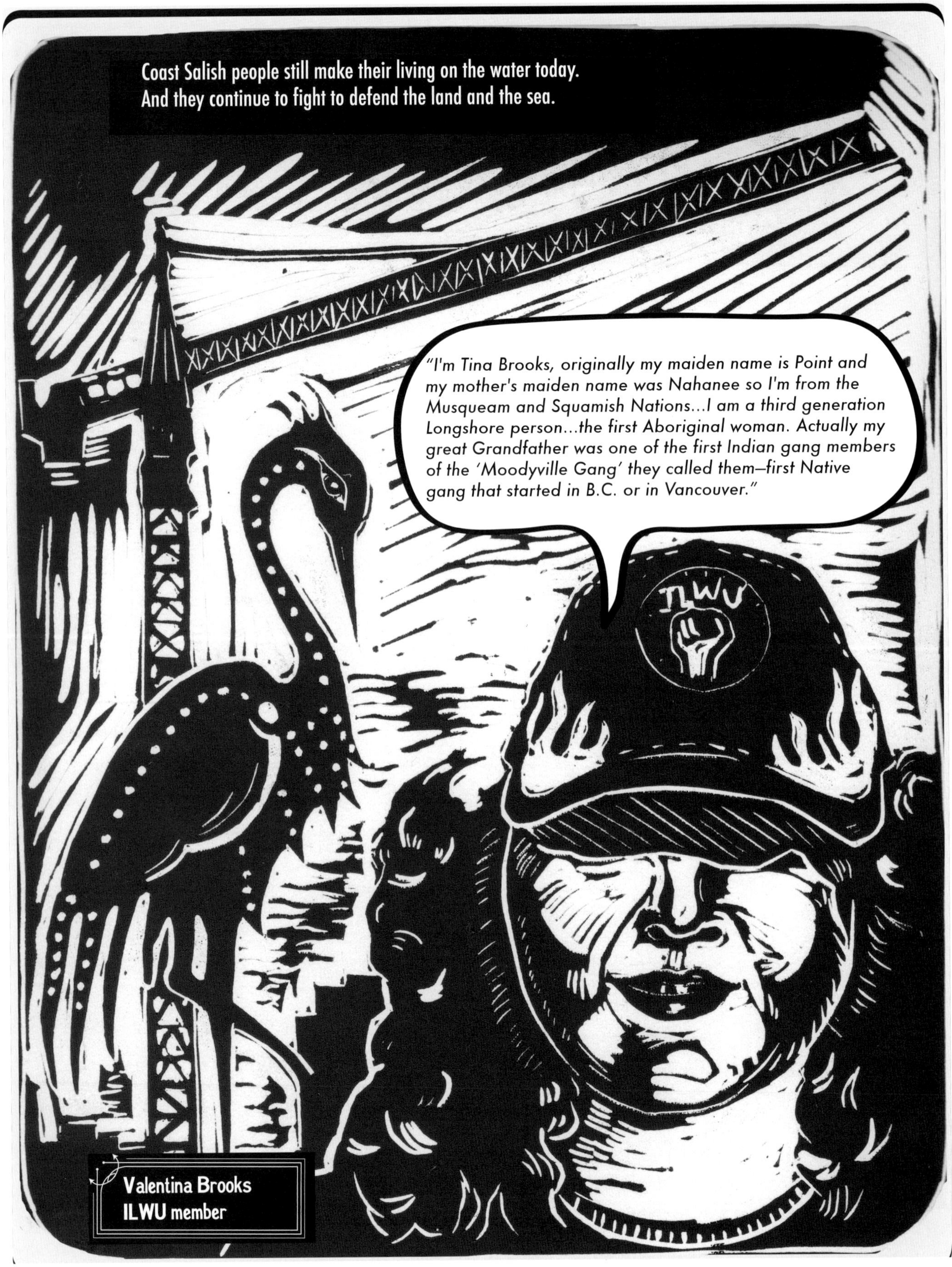
Coast Salish people still make their living on the water today.
And they continue to fight to defend the land and the sea.
"I'm Tina Brooks, originally my maiden name is Point and my mother's maiden name was Nahanee so I'm from the Musqueam and Squamish Nations...I am a third generation Longshore person...the first Aboriginal woman. Actually my great Grandfather was one of the first Indian gang members of the 'Moodyville Gang' they called them—first Native gang that started in B.C. or in Vancouver."
ILWU
Valentina Brooks
ILWU member

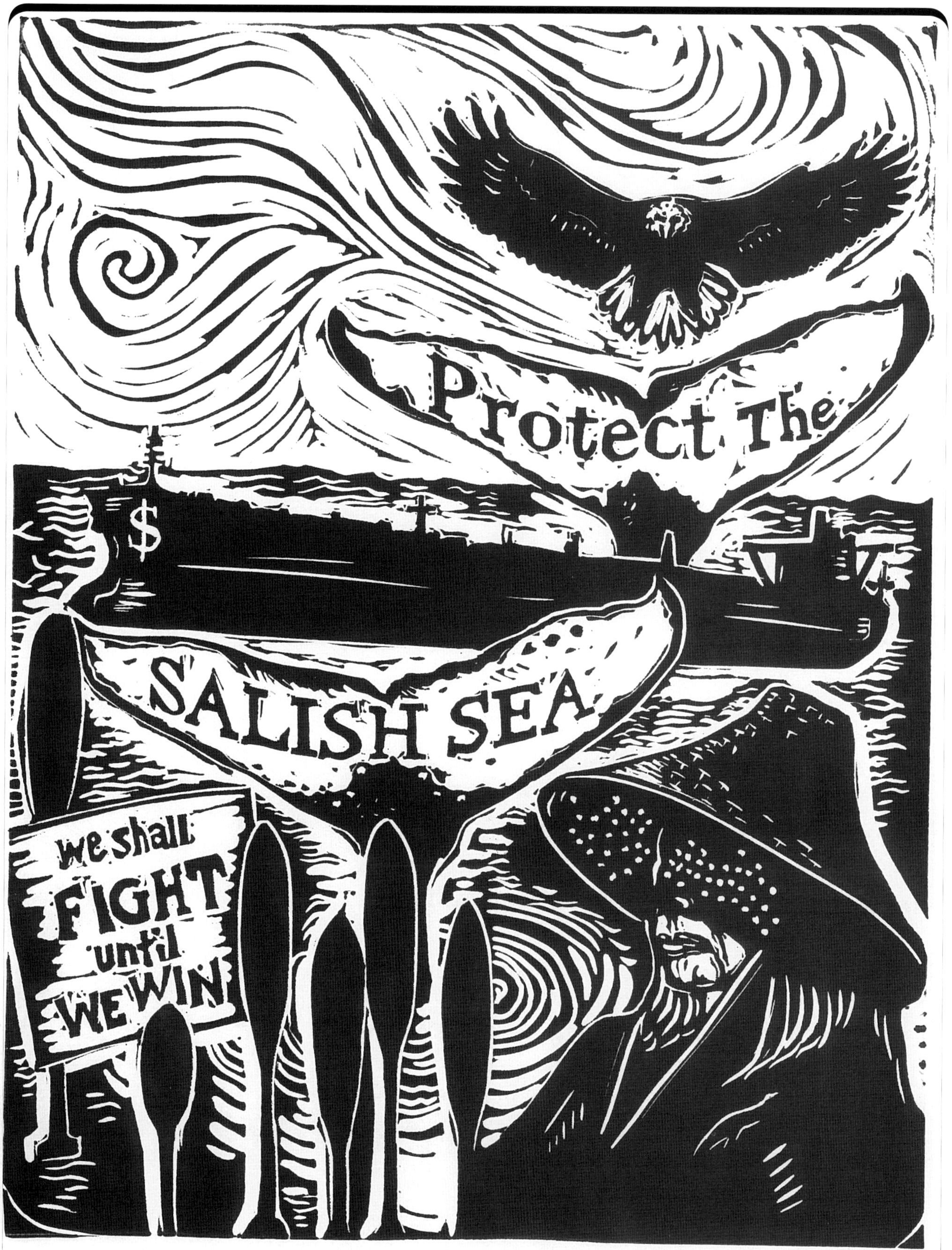
Protect the
SALISH SEA
$
we shall
FIGHT
until
WE WIN

Acknowledgements

Thanks to the Sâkêwêwak Artists' Collective and Articulate Ink in Regina for their assistance with parts of the project, as well as Kamala Todd and her work with Storyscapes Vancouver. Thanks are also due to Valentina Brooks for sharing her experiences as a Squamish woman working on the water.

This graphic history is produced in memory and solidarity with all Coast Salish peoples, working, dancing, and fighting for culture and land.

Notes

Page 32: Dugout canoe on Burrard Inlet, see City of Vancouver Archives, CVA-99-2122. Mathias Joe, see City of Vancouver Archives, CVA 6-108 and CVA-99-2507. Ships in Burrard Inlet, see Glenbow Museum, NA-47-45.

Page 34: Row of workers standing on scaffolding at Hastings Sawmill, see City of Vancouver Archives, CVA-SGN 40. Chief Dan George, see Aboriginal Multi-Media Society, www.ammsa.com/content/chief-dan-george-footprints.

Page 35: Longshore Workers, Members of the Bows and Arrows, see City of Vancouver Archives, CVA Mi P2. William Nahanee, see City of Vancouver Archives, Port P569.3

Page 36: Chief Simon Baker, see Simon Baker, *Khot-La-Cha: The Autobiography of Chief Simon Baker*, ed. Verna J. Kirkness (Vancouver: Douglas & McIntyre, 1994).

Page 37: Salish Delegation in England, see British Library, 081745.

Page 38: Inspired by a photo of the longshore workers that appears in Vancouver Longshoremen/ ILWU Local 500 Pensioners, *"Man along the Shore!" The Story of the Vancouver Waterfront as Told By Longshoremen Themselves* (Vancouver: ILWU Local 500 Pensioners, 1985).

Page 39: Edward Nahanee, see Ancestry.ca, www.ancestry.ca.

The Battle of Ballantyne Pier

An Injury to One Is an Injury to All!

Organizing in the Hardest of Times
Dale McCartney

David Lester's project highlights an exceptionally important moment in the history of Canadian workers. Long overshadowed by the On-to-Ottawa Trek, which happened at roughly the same time, the Battle of Ballantyne Pier was the culmination of more than a decade of union organizing on the Vancouver waterfront. It stands out as a singular event, but also one example of a broader worker-led fight back in the 1930s. For unionists today, it is a reminder that there have been periods in the past in which employers have been intractable, the state has been an enemy, and organizing has seemed impossible, and yet, as Lester shows us, progress is possible.

Longshore workers had been militant pretty much since the docks opened in Vancouver. And so in 1923 the employers on the shore turned to a new method of pacifying their employees, the company union. Company unions offered the façade of union membership to workers, but the actual control of the union rested in the hands of the employer. They were first a public relations initiative, started after the Ludlow Massacre of 1912 by a Rockefeller family concerned about its public image. Like contemporary human resource approaches, they used the power of names to disguise a system that remained largely unchanged. Similar to modern companies who call their workers "team members," "associates," or "partners"—yet still treat them as expendable employees—company unions were set up to allow employers to insist they respected their employees, even as the unions worked to placate workers rather than represent them.

As Lester shows us, longshore workers (including his grandfather Frederick Lester) overcame this tactic, again and again electing leaders like Ivan Emery, who forced the company unions to become actual unions, representing the interests of their members instead of the interests of the employers. These campaigns bear some resemblance to contemporary campaigns for better conditions in the retail and fast food sector, as the organizing was happening outside of the broader union movement at first, and was driven by the workers themselves. Despite enormous obstacles, workers still organized and fought for their rights.

Another important lesson that Lester's graphic history teaches us is that the state is often an opponent of progressive change for workers. The On-to-Ottawa Trek is an example, as it resulted in an RCMP attack on the protestors in Regina, similar to the Vancouver Police Department attack that Lester draws so movingly. The era was characterized by state neglect of workers interests, and open hostility from the government toward unions. Much like today, the government consciously positioned the interests of workers as different than the interests of the public.

Lester's account of the battle is also important because he humanizes the activists involved, and reminds us that people just like us overcame these challenges in the past. By telling the story through the eyes of his grandfather, Lester shows how everyday people can contribute to moments of great historical importance. Similarly, the gritty realism of the images captures recognizable sites in Vancouver, allowing us to see ourselves in the efforts of the longshore workers, and prompting us to recognize modern-day efforts to make Canada more just as part of a long history of working class struggle.

Workers today find themselves facing challenges that their parents had thought permanently overcome. Declining wages, lengthening workdays, and the loss of opportunities for advancement or meaningful work are only the start. As unions decline and governments beholden to free trade agreements continue to break down labour laws, workers confront an unregulated and unprotected future. But Lester has shown us with this comic book that there are victories to be won even when workers are organizing in difficult conditions.

For these reasons, Lester's graphic history is both wonderful and timely. As the contemporary labour movement confronts declining density, anti-union employers who use everything from propaganda videos to targeted firings to prevent unionization, and a state that is neglectful at best and openly hostile at worse, it is important for contemporary activists to look back at periods with similar challenges.

It is easy to forget that some of the basic rights modern workers take for granted today were won through confrontations like the Battle of Ballantyne Pier, and won by people like Lester's grandfather. This beautiful graphic history reminds us of the importance of past battles, and inspires us to believe we can win them again.

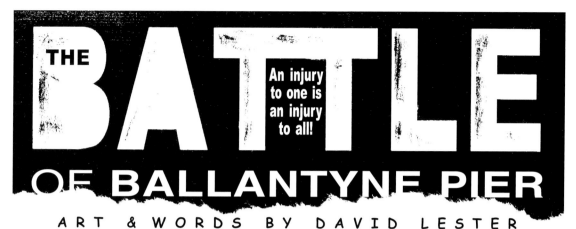

THE BATTLE

An injury to one is an injury to all!

OF BALLANTYNE PIER

ART & WORDS BY DAVID LESTER

Vancouver, British Columbia, Canada

My grandpa worked most of his life on the Vancouver waterfront unloading the holds of ships like this. He even escaped death when the SS Greenhill Park blew sky high in 1945. Grandpa was the winch driver. Blown right off. He was 54, same age as I am now.

Grandpa was born in Berlin as Frederick Bruno Lester. He emigrated to North America in the early part of the twentieth century. After reaching Spokane, Washington he took a job paving sidewalks and joined the Industrial Workers of the World (IWW). Moving on to Vancouver he joined the 1912 free speech battles and in 1918, he defended the IWW hall against an attack by hundreds of right-wing soldiers who had just returned from World War One and wanted to "sort those Reds out."

Grandpa even played trombone in the IWW marching band, until he was booted out for being late to a practice because he'd been carousing with a woman. When I told grandpa I was learning to play guitar, he told me it was a good way to meet girls.

By 1924, he was a longshoreman in Vancouver. By 1935, he was 44 years old, married to a Scottish immigrant, with a son named Freddy, and... out on the strike that leads us to the battle of Ballantyne Pier.

AUTHOR's NOTE: All text in quotation marks are the actual words spoken by the historical characters.

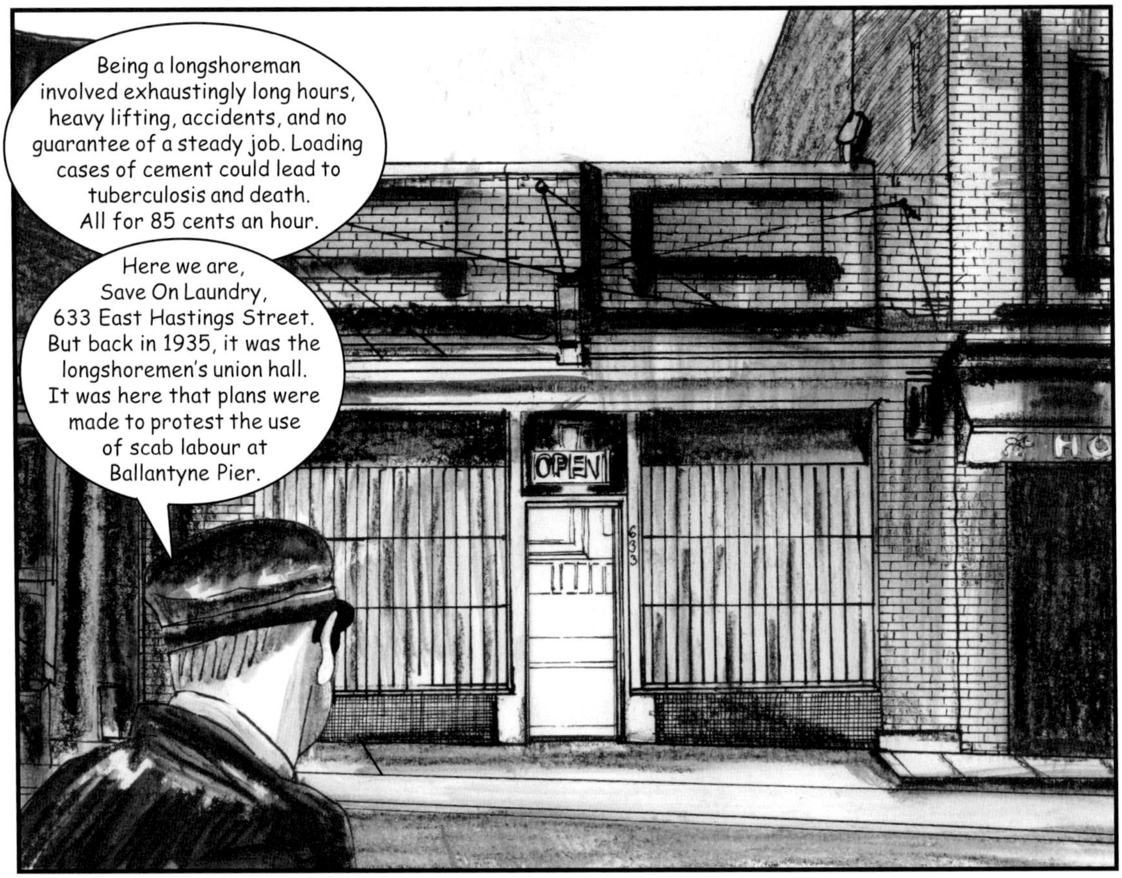
Being a longshoreman involved exhaustingly long hours, heavy lifting, accidents, and no guarantee of a steady job. Loading cases of cement could lead to tuberculosis and death. All for 85 cents an hour.
Here we are, Save On Laundry, 633 East Hastings Street. But back in 1935, it was the longshoremen's union hall. It was here that plans were made to protest the use of scab labour at Ballantyne Pier.
OPEN
633

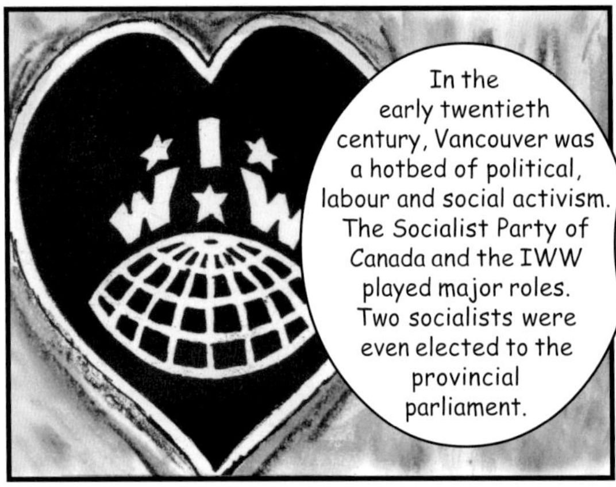
I
W W
In the early twentieth century, Vancouver was a hotbed of political, labour and social activism. The Socialist Party of Canada and the IWW played major roles. Two socialists were even elected to the provincial parliament.

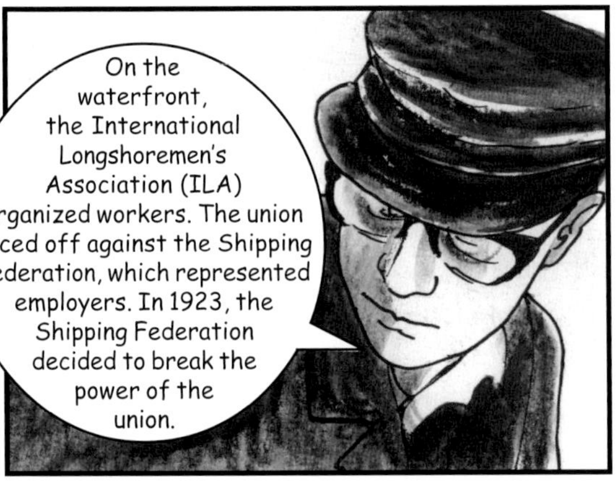
On the waterfront, the International Longshoremen's Association (ILA) organized workers. The union faced off against the Shipping Federation, which represented employers. In 1923, the Shipping Federation decided to break the power of the union.

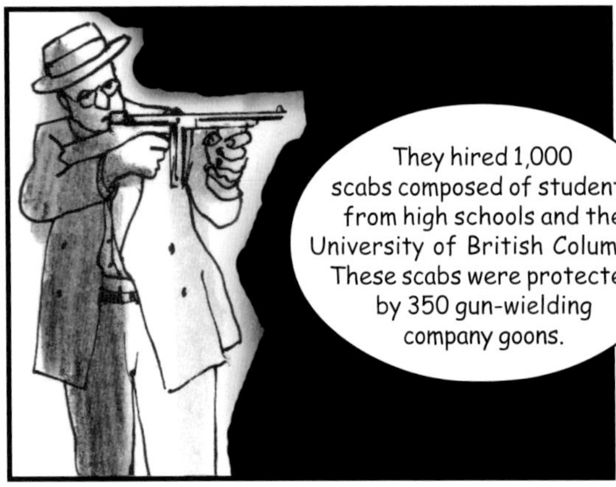
They hired 1,000 scabs composed of students from high schools and the University of British Columbia. These scabs were protected by 350 gun-wielding company goons.

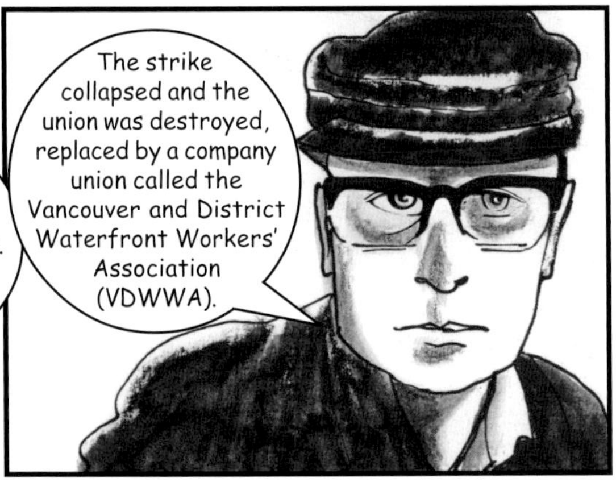
The strike collapsed and the union was destroyed, replaced by a company union called the Vancouver and District Waterfront Workers' Association (VDWWA).

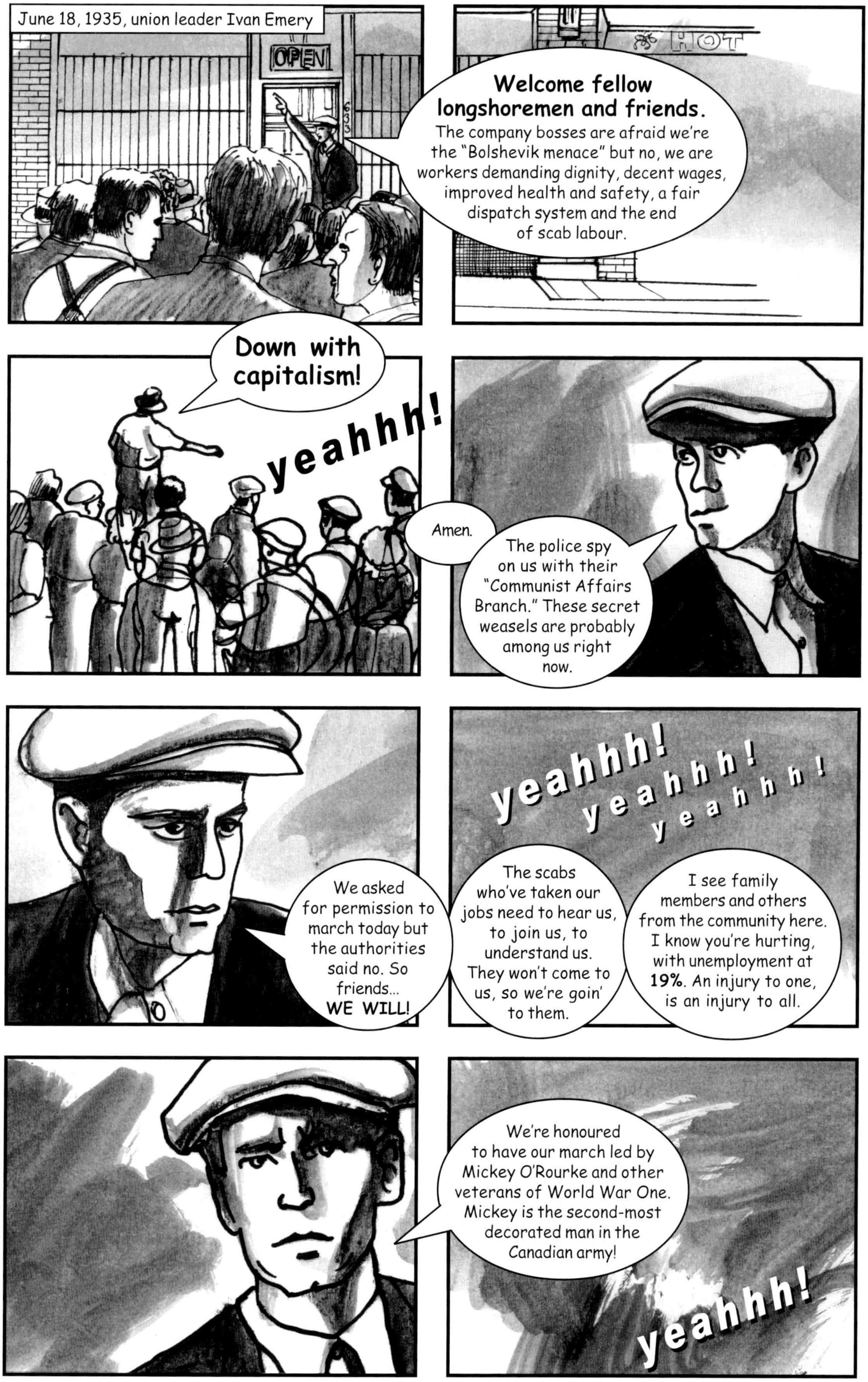
June 18, 1935, union leader Ivan Emery
OPEN
633
HOT
Welcome fellow longshoremen and friends. The company bosses are afraid we're the "Bolshevik menace" but no, we are workers demanding dignity, decent wages, improved health and safety, a fair dispatch system and the end of scab labour.
Down with capitalism!
yeahhh!
Amen.
The police spy on us with their "Communist Affairs Branch." These secret weasels are probably among us right now.
We asked for permission to march today but the authorities said no. So friends... WE WILL!
yeahhh! yeahhh! yeahhh!
The scabs who've taken our jobs need to hear us, to join us, to understand us. They won't come to us, so we're goin' to them.
I see family members and others from the community here. I know you're hurting, with unemployment at 19%. An injury to one, is an injury to all.
We're honoured to have our march led by Mickey O'Rourke and other veterans of World War One. Mickey is the second-most decorated man in the Canadian army!
yeahhh!

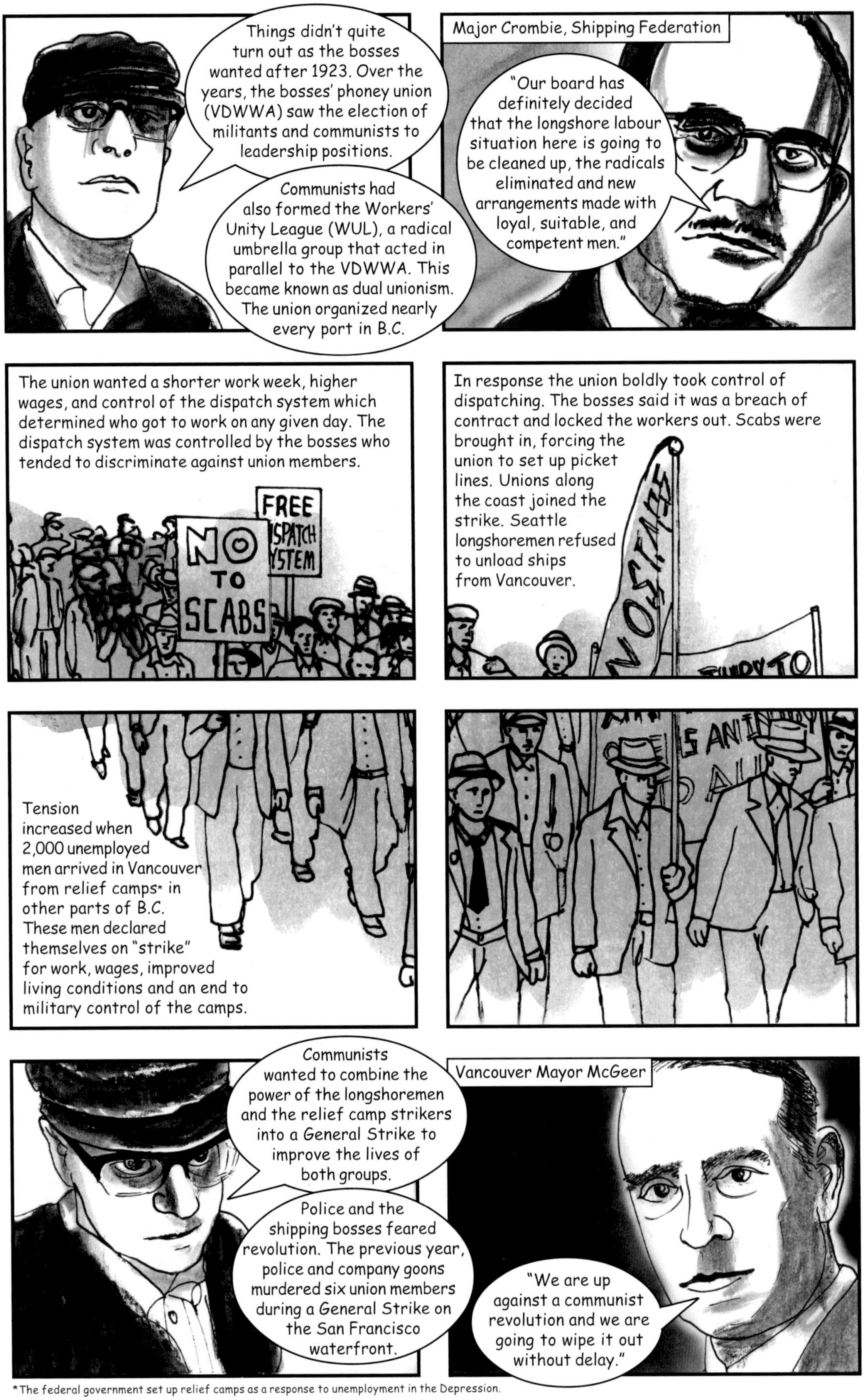
Things didn't quite turn out as the bosses wanted after 1923. Over the years, the bosses' phoney union (VDWWA) saw the election of militants and communists to leadership positions.
Communists had also formed the Workers' Unity League (WUL), a radical umbrella group that acted in parallel to the VDWWA. This became known as dual unionism. The union organized nearly every port in B.C.
Major Crombie, Shipping Federation
"Our board has definitely decided that the longshore labour situation here is going to be cleaned up, the radicals eliminated and new arrangements made with loyal, suitable, and competent men."
The union wanted a shorter work week, higher wages, and control of the dispatch system which determined who got to work on any given day. The dispatch system was controlled by the bosses who tended to discriminate against union members.
FREE
NO TO SCABS
In response the union boldly took control of dispatching. The bosses said it was a breach of contract and locked the workers out. Scabs were brought in, forcing the union to set up picket lines. Unions along the coast joined the strike. Seattle longshoremen refused to unload ships from Vancouver.
Tension increased when 2,000 unemployed men arrived in Vancouver from relief camps* in other parts of B.C. These men declared themselves on "strike" for work, wages, improved living conditions and an end to military control of the camps.
Communists wanted to combine the power of the longshoremen and the relief camp strikers into a General Strike to improve the lives of both groups.
Police and the shipping bosses feared revolution. The previous year, police and company goons murdered six union members during a General Strike on the San Francisco waterfront.
Vancouver Mayor McGeer
"We are up against a communist revolution and we are going to wipe it out without delay."

*The federal government set up relief camps as a response to unemployment in the Depression.

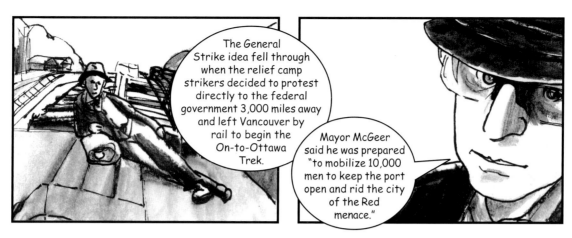

The General Strike idea fell through when the relief camp strikers decided to protest directly to the federal government 3,000 miles away and left Vancouver by rail to begin the On-to-Ottawa Trek.

Mayor McGeer said he was prepared "to mobilize 10,000 men to keep the port open and rid the city of the Red menace."

Next into the drama came the The Citizens' League of British Columbia, a right-wing vigilante group funded by the shipping bosses. The League's spokesman, Colonel Charles Edgar Edgett viewed communism as an international Jewish conspiracy.

PLANNED DESTRUCTIVENESS OF COMMUNISTS TO BE EXPOSED

Citizens Unite to Defend Law and Order

BRITISH COLUMBIA in recent months has seen her decent and orderly institutions imperilled by the deliberate cunning of a small group of Communists pledged only to destroy all that now exists and to offer no adequate substitute. The immediate past has brought the movement dangerously near culmination. In Vancouver the spearhead of this subversive action has operated to foment strikes, to intimidate business, to discredit constitutional authority and to jeopardize the safe and proper operation of commercial and industrial enterprise.

The CITIZENS LEAGUE of B.C.
an ANTI-LABOR LEAGUE of BRITISH

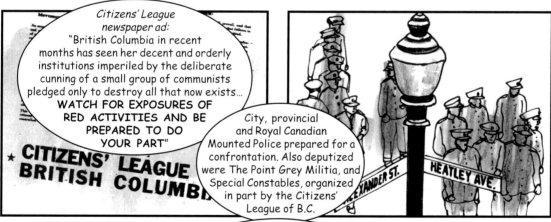

Citizens' League newspaper ad: "British Columbia in recent months has seen her decent and orderly institutions imperiled by the deliberate cunning of a small group of communists pledged only to destroy all that now exists... **WATCH FOR EXPOSURES OF RED ACTIVITIES AND BE PREPARED TO DO YOUR PART"**

City, provincial and Royal Canadian Mounted Police prepared for a confrontation. Also deputized were The Point Grey Militia, and Special Constables, organized in part by the Citizens' League of B.C.

★ CITIZENS' LEAGUE BRITISH COLUMB

ALEXANDER ST.   HEATLEY AVE.

Police were equipped with machine guns and tear gas (the first city in Canada to use chemical weapons). After World War One, weapons manufacturers had aggressively promoted their products to police departments in North America.

Mayor McGeer said that the people of Vancouver had to decide between "constituted authority or Communism."

But... public sympathy with the strikers was strong.

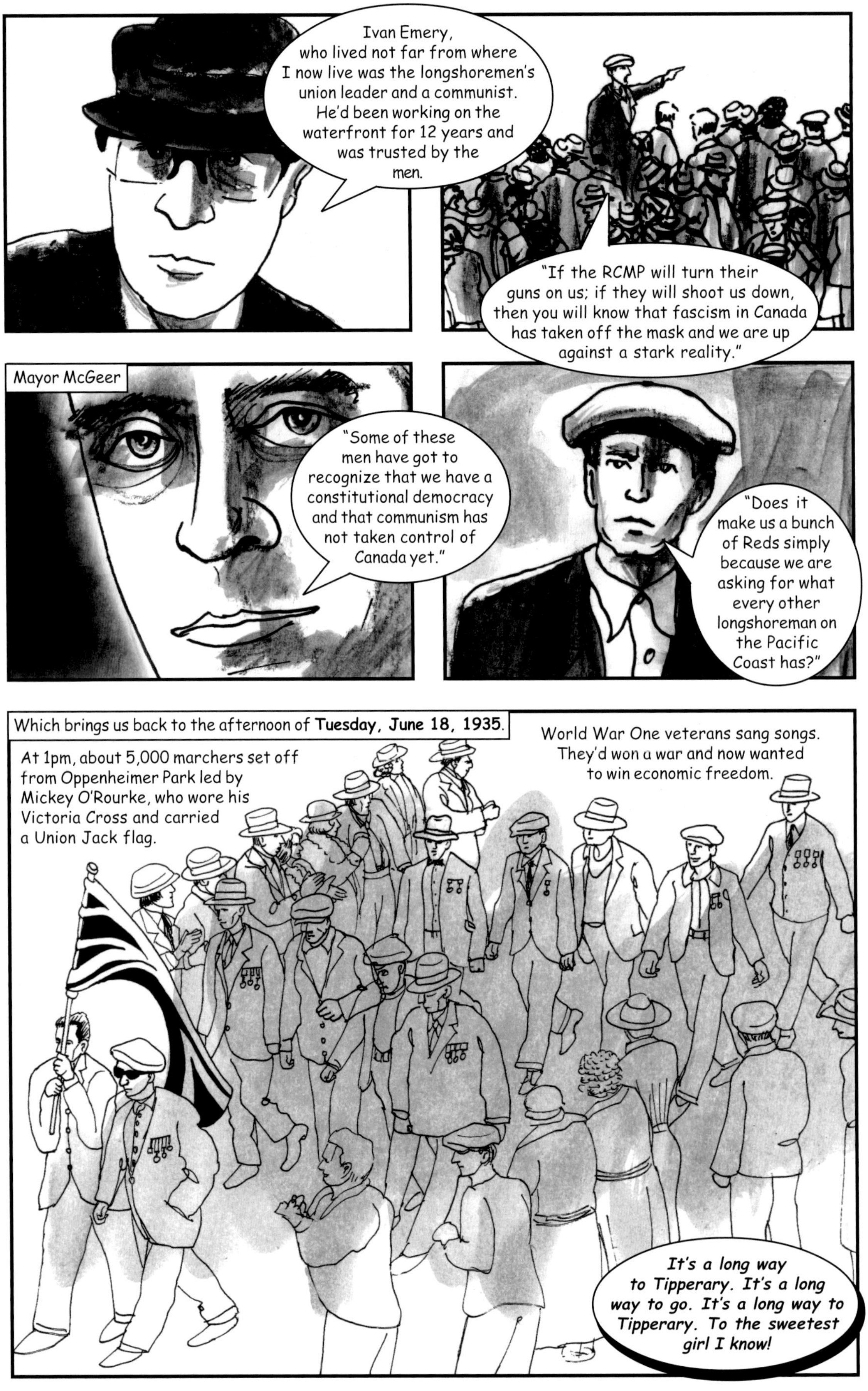

Ivan Emery, who lived not far from where I now live was the longshoremen's union leader and a communist. He'd been working on the waterfront for 12 years and was trusted by the men.
"If the RCMP will turn their guns on us; if they will shoot us down, then you will know that fascism in Canada has taken off the mask and we are up against a stark reality."
Mayor McGeer
"Some of these men have got to recognize that we have a constitutional democracy and that communism has not taken control of Canada yet."
"Does it make us a bunch of Reds simply because we are asking for what every other longshoreman on the Pacific Coast has?"
Which brings us back to the afternoon of **Tuesday, June 18, 1935**.
At 1pm, about 5,000 marchers set off from Oppenheimer Park led by Mickey O'Rourke, who wore his Victoria Cross and carried a Union Jack flag.
World War One veterans sang songs. They'd won a war and now wanted to win economic freedom.
It's a long way to Tipperary. It's a long way to go. It's a long way to Tipperary. To the sweetest girl I know!

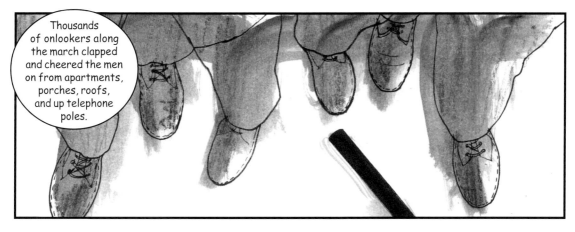

Thousands of onlookers along the march clapped and cheered the men on from apartments, porches, roofs, and up telephone poles.

Provincial police hid behind boxcars with Thompson machine guns as other officers stood by with clubs.

As the marchers neared the railway tracks at Ballantyne Pier, Police Chief W. W. Foster met them.

"Just a minute, boys."

Chief Foster was the one who organized the Shipping Federation's goons during the 1923 strike.

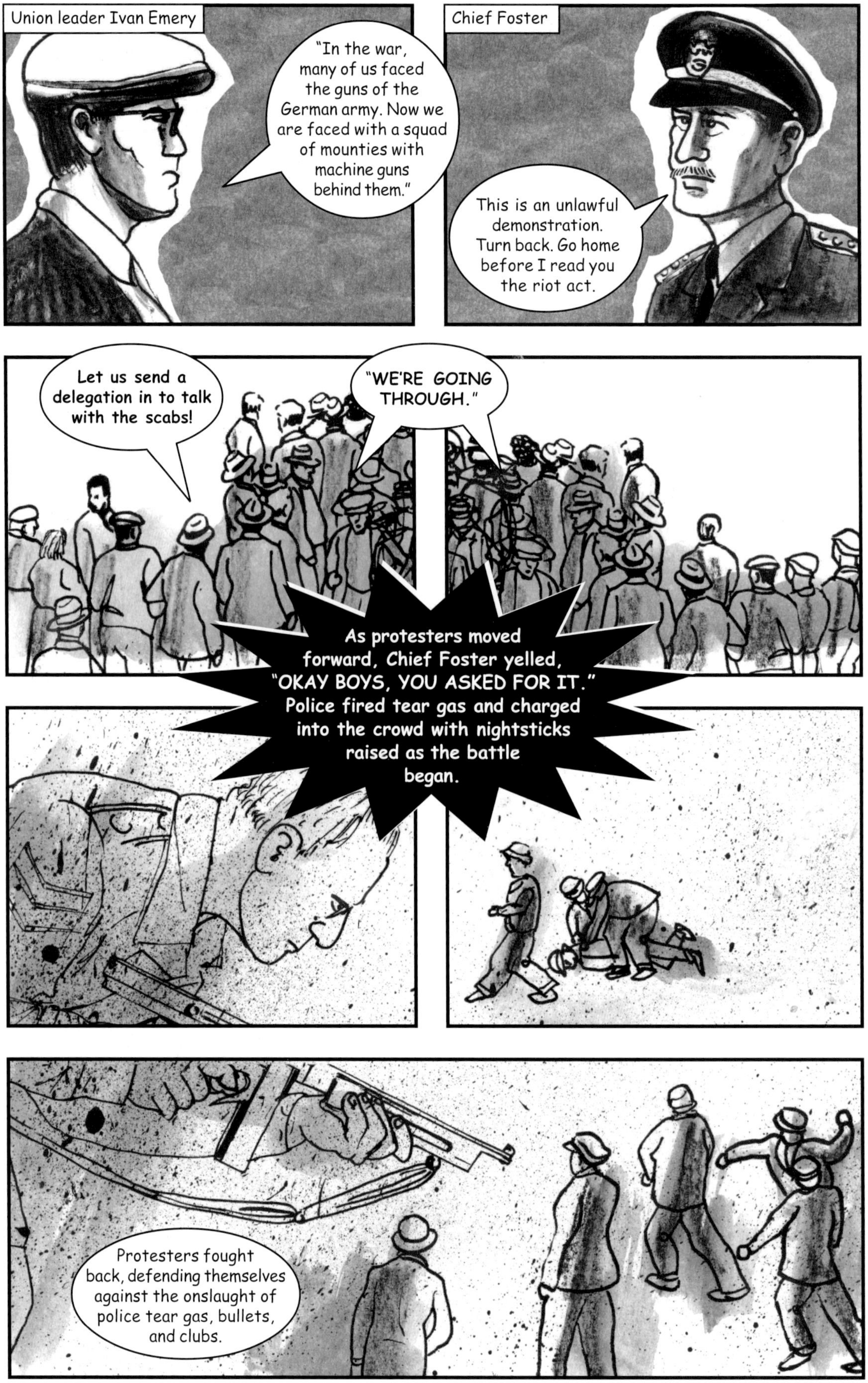

Union leader Ivan Emery
"In the war, many of us faced the guns of the German army. Now we are faced with a squad of mounties with machine guns behind them."
Chief Foster
This is an unlawful demonstration. Turn back. Go home before I read you the riot act.
Let us send a delegation in to talk with the scabs!
"WE'RE GOING THROUGH."
As protesters moved forward, Chief Foster yelled, "OKAY BOYS, YOU ASKED FOR IT." Police fired tear gas and charged into the crowd with nightsticks raised as the battle began.
Protesters fought back, defending themselves against the onslaught of police tear gas, bullets, and clubs.

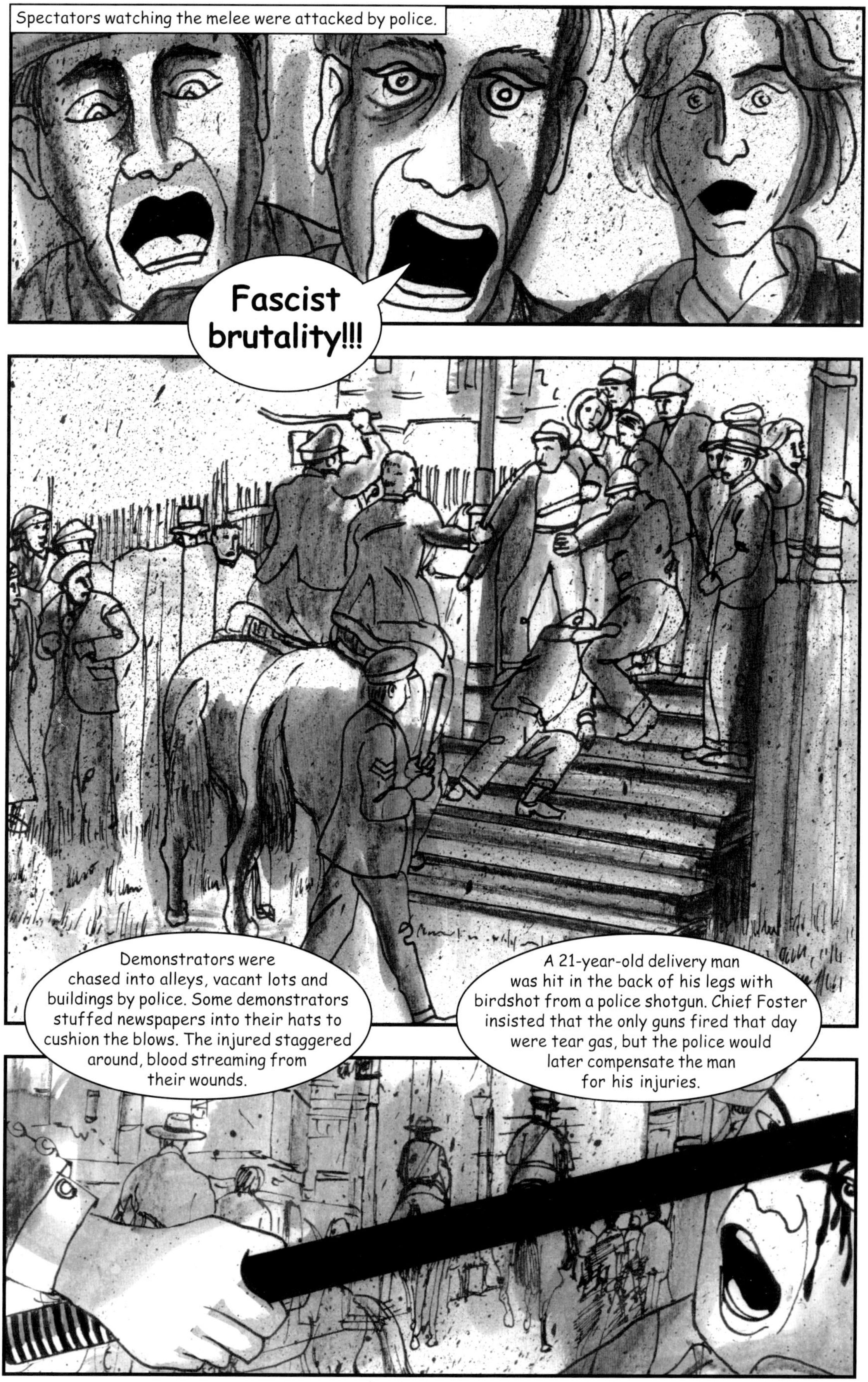
Spectators watching the melee were attacked by police.
Fascist brutality!!!
Demonstrators were chased into alleys, vacant lots and buildings by police. Some demonstrators stuffed newspapers into their hats to cushion the blows. The injured staggered around, blood streaming from their wounds.
A 21-year-old delivery man was hit in the back of his legs with birdshot from a police shotgun. Chief Foster insisted that the only guns fired that day were tear gas, but the police would later compensate the man for his injuries.

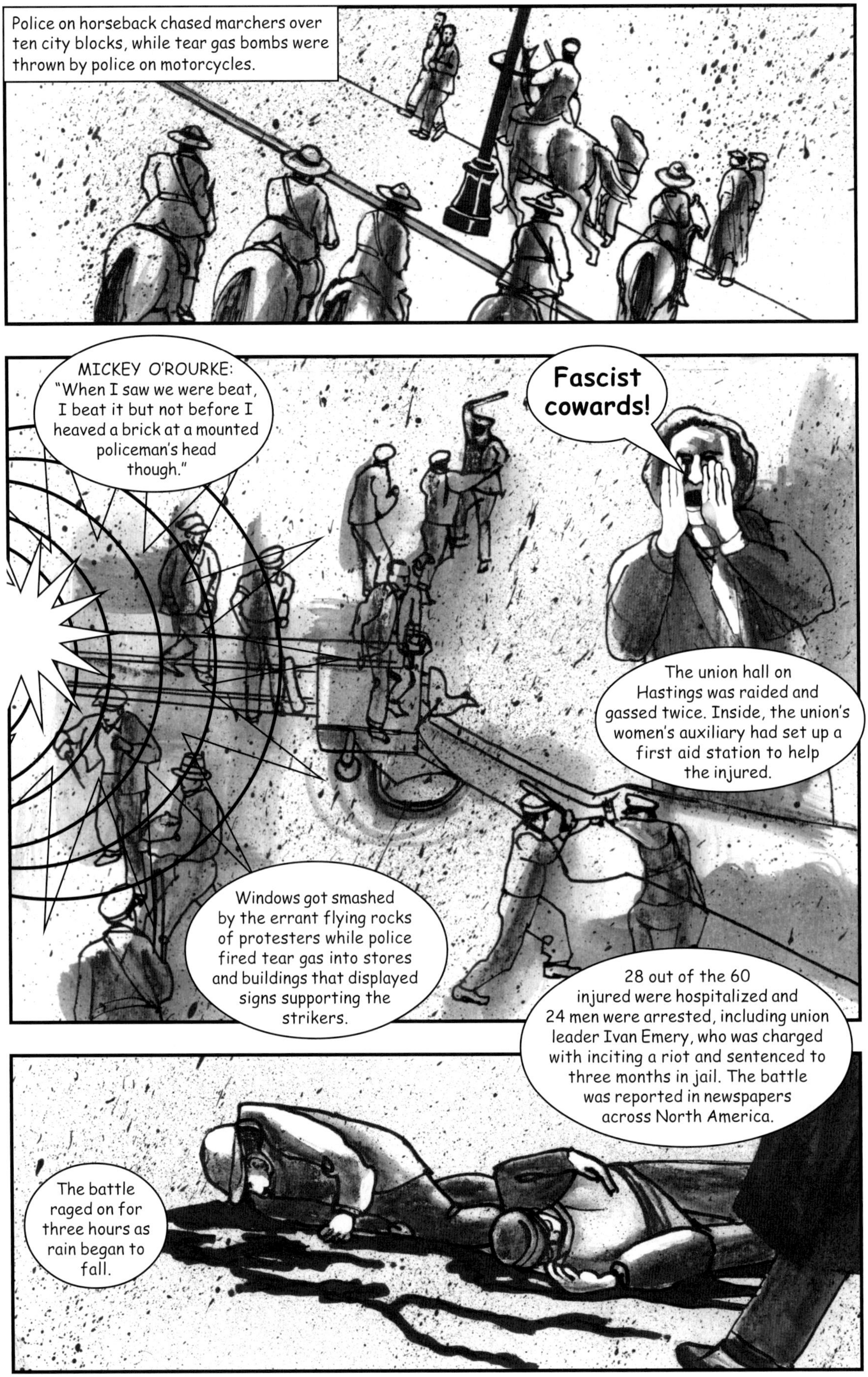
Police on horseback chased marchers over ten city blocks, while tear gas bombs were thrown by police on motorcycles.
MICKEY O'ROURKE: "When I saw we were beat, I beat it but not before I heaved a brick at a mounted policeman's head though."
Fascist cowards!
The union hall on Hastings was raided and gassed twice. Inside, the union's women's auxiliary had set up a first aid station to help the injured.
Windows got smashed by the errant flying rocks of protesters while police fired tear gas into stores and buildings that displayed signs supporting the strikers.
28 out of the 60 injured were hospitalized and 24 men were arrested, including union leader Ivan Emery, who was charged with inciting a riot and sentenced to three months in jail. The battle was reported in newspapers across North America.
The battle raged on for three hours as rain began to fall.

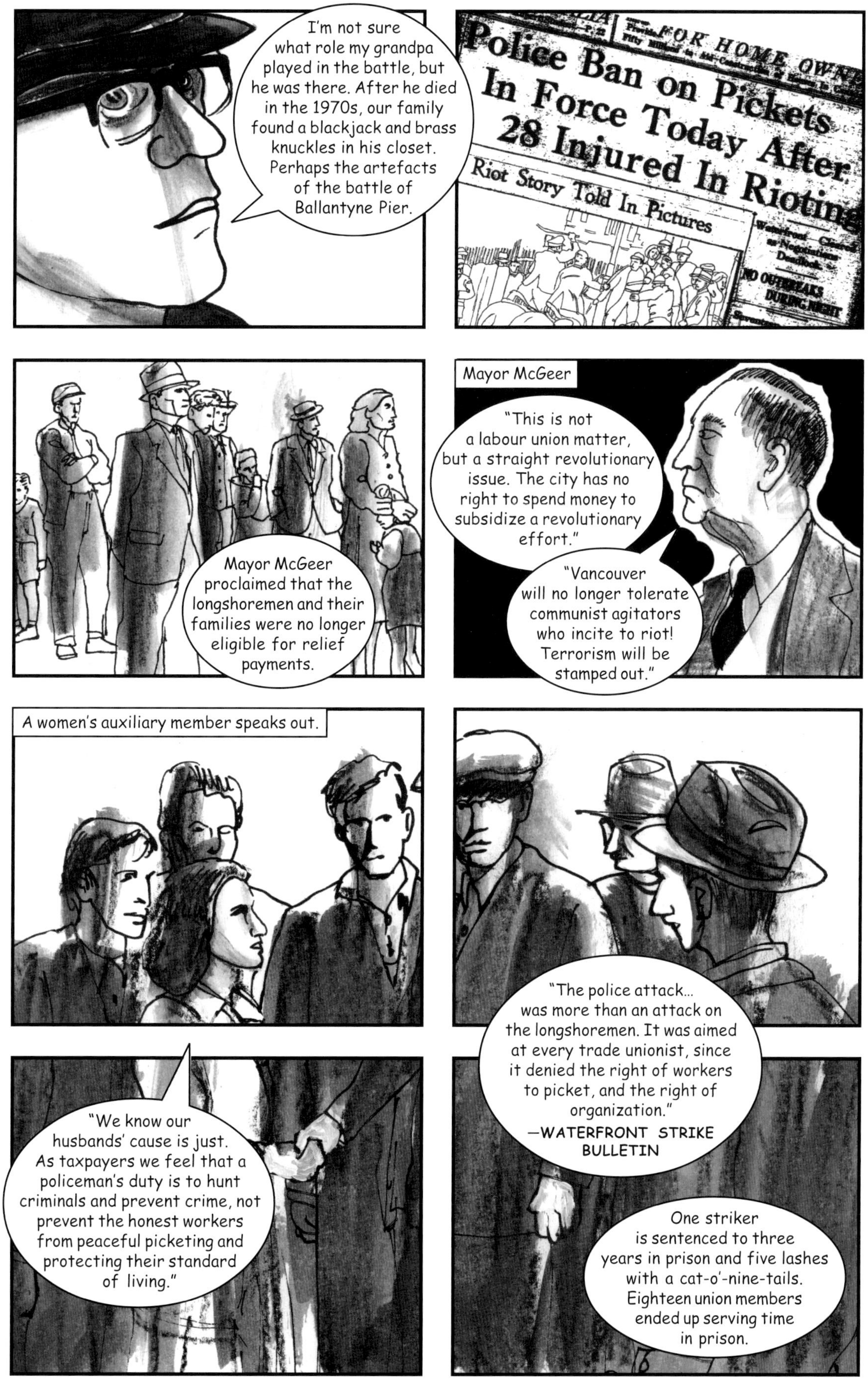
I'm not sure what role my grandpa played in the battle, but he was there. After he died in the 1970s, our family found a blackjack and brass knuckles in his closet. Perhaps the artefacts of the battle of Ballantyne Pier.
Police Ban on Pickets In Force Today After 28 Injured In Rioting
Riot Story Told In Pictures
NO OUTBREAKS DURING NIGHT
Mayor McGeer proclaimed that the longshoremen and their families were no longer eligible for relief payments.
Mayor McGeer
"This is not a labour union matter, but a straight revolutionary issue. The city has no right to spend money to subsidize a revolutionary effort."
"Vancouver will no longer tolerate communist agitators who incite to riot! Terrorism will be stamped out."
A women's auxiliary member speaks out.
"We know our husbands' cause is just. As taxpayers we feel that a policeman's duty is to hunt criminals and prevent crime, not prevent the honest workers from peaceful picketing and protecting their standard of living."
"The police attack... was more than an attack on the longshoremen. It was aimed at every trade unionist, since it denied the right of workers to picket, and the right of organization."
—WATERFRONT STRIKE BULLETIN
One striker is sentenced to three years in prison and five lashes with a cat-o'-nine-tails. Eighteen union members ended up serving time in prison.

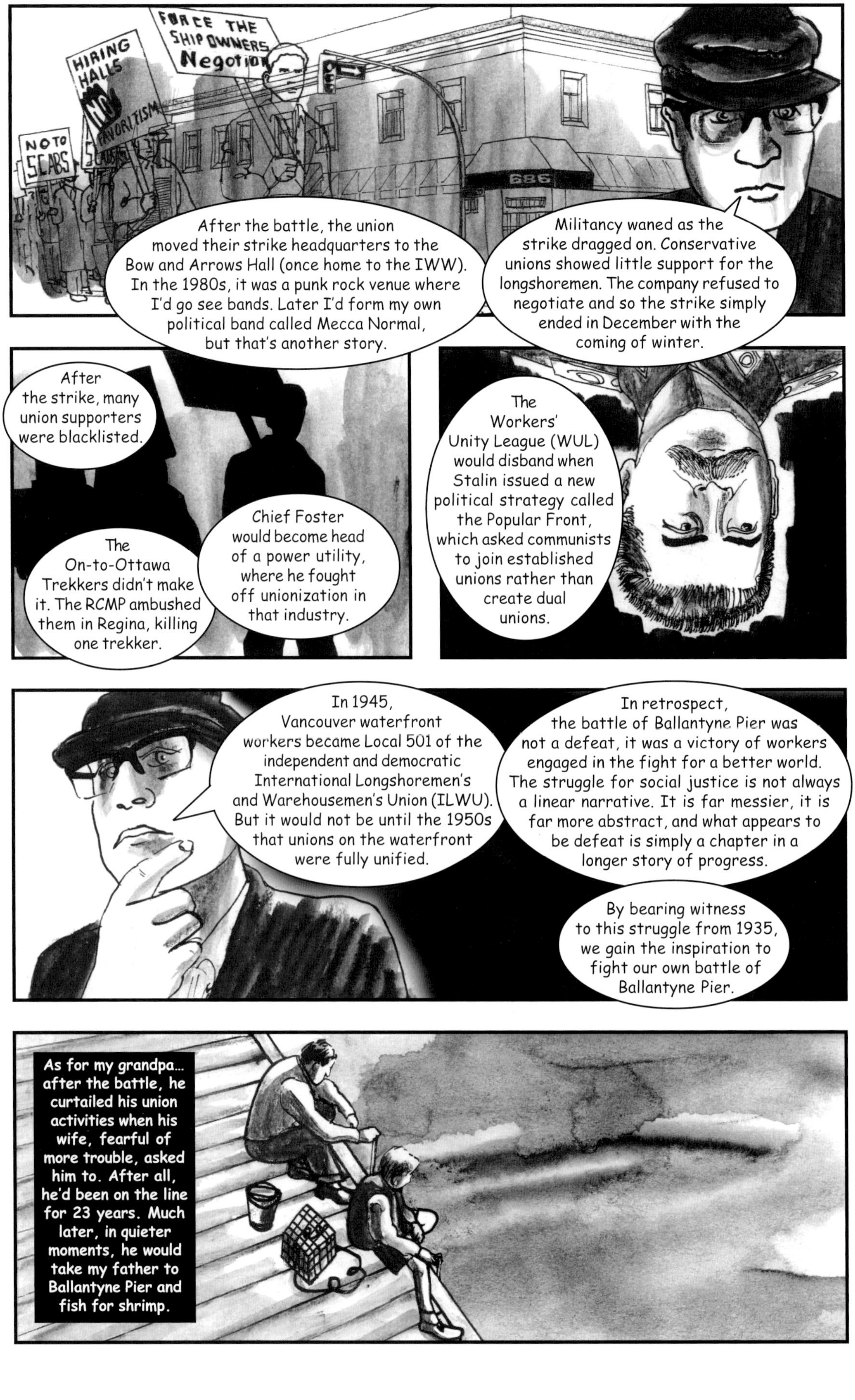
HIRING HALLS
NO FAVORITISM
NO TO SCABS
After the battle, the union moved their strike headquarters to the Bow and Arrows Hall (once home to the IWW). In the 1980s, it was a punk rock venue where I'd go see bands. Later I'd form my own political band called Mecca Normal, but that's another story.
Militancy waned as the strike dragged on. Conservative unions showed little support for the longshoremen. The company refused to negotiate and so the strike simply ended in December with the coming of winter.
After the strike, many union supporters were blacklisted.
The On-to-Ottawa Trekkers didn't make it. The RCMP ambushed them in Regina, killing one trekker.
Chief Foster would become head of a power utility, where he fought off unionization in that industry.
The Workers' Unity League (WUL) would disband when Stalin issued a new political strategy called the Popular Front, which asked communists to join established unions rather than create dual unions.
In 1945, Vancouver waterfront workers became Local 501 of the independent and democratic International Longshoremen's and Warehousemen's Union (ILWU). But it would not be until the 1950s that unions on the waterfront were fully unified.
In retrospect, the battle of Ballantyne Pier was not a defeat, it was a victory of workers engaged in the fight for a better world. The struggle for social justice is not always a linear narrative. It is far messier, it is far more abstract, and what appears to be defeat is simply a chapter in a longer story of progress.
By bearing witness to this struggle from 1935, we gain the inspiration to fight our own battle of Ballantyne Pier.
As for my grandpa... after the battle, he curtailed his union activities when his wife, fearful of more trouble, asked him to. After all, he'd been on the line for 23 years. Much later, in quieter moments, he would take my father to Ballantyne Pier and fish for shrimp.

Acknowledgements

Thanks for editorial input and inspiration from Wendy Atkinson, Jean Smith, and Norman Nawrocki; Ken Lester for information on our grandfather, Frederick Bruno Lester; Lani Russwurm, for his research tips and excellent website, Past Tense Vancouver; Jill Teasley, Digital Archivist at the City of Vancouver Archives; the Vancouver Public Library for their newspaper microfilm collection; and the enthusiasm of Robin Folvik.

I also want to note that my brother Ken Lester was the National Vice-President of the Service and Office Workers Union of Canada (SORWUC), which will be discussed later in this collection.

Notes

Reference images came from printouts the artist made from microfilm copies of *The Daily Province* and *The Vancouver Sun* (June 1935) held by the Vancouver Public Library. *The Vancouver Sun* photos were credited to Sydney Williamson, Sun staff photographer.

Bill Williamson

Hobo, Wobbly, Communist, On-to-Ottawa Trekker, Spanish Civil War Veteran, Photographer

A Life on the Left

Mark Leier

Through a combination of luck, temperament, conviction, and choice, Bill Williamson was a participant in some of the most significant movements and events in working-class history, in Canada and globally.

As a teenager in British Columbia, he met members of the Industrial Workers of the World (IWW), also known as the Wobblies. Their message of radicalism, militancy, and rank and file democracy appealed to the independent young man, as did the union's relaxed yet lively culture. One IWW song, by Matti Valentine Huhta, better known as T-Bone Slim, summed up Williamson's life to that point:

> *I grabbed a hold of an old freight train*
> *And around the country traveled,*
> *The mysteries of a hobo's life*
> *To me were soon unraveled.*
> *I ran across a bunch of "stiffs"*
> *Who were known as Industrial Workers,*
> *They taught me how to be a man—*
> *And how to fight the shirkers.*
> *I kicked right in and joined the bunch*
> *And now in the ranks you'll find me.*
> *Hurrah for the cause—To Hell with the boss!*
> *And the job I left behind me.*

In B.C., the IWW led strikes of railway navvies, rallied civic workers, loggers, and miners, and fought for the right of organizers to speak on city street corners despite being banned by local ordinances. The preamble to the union's constitution made its politics clear: "The working class and the employing class have nothing in common.… Between these two classes a struggle must go on until the workers of the world organize as a class, take possession of the earth and the machinery of production, and abolish the wage system."

State repression during and after World War I, factional fights within the organization and the labour movement more broadly, corporate welfarism, and the depression of the 1920s meant the IWW's formal strength had waned by the time Williamson met individual Wobblies in the camps and bunkhouses of the province. Its politicized working-class culture, however, infused and influenced the politics of generations of radicals, from those in the Communist Party and intellectuals such as C. Wright Mills to the Yippies of the New Left and activists today. That cultural legacy is as important as any of the bread and butter gains the union fought for.

By the 1930s, the Communist Party (CP) replaced the IWW as a centre of activism and radicalism. The Communist Party of Canada was formed in 1921 as radicals and workers from left-wing parties and unions hoped to replicate the success of the Bolsheviks in Russia by utilizing similar strategies and tactics. Historians still debate the role of the CP. Some see it as an authoritarian, sectarian party that was little more than a tool of Soviet foreign policy. Others point to rank and file organizers who were not much interested in the grand policy and political machinations of leaders at home or abroad. Instead, they were inspired by a broader vision and saw their organizing work sustained and supported by the institutions, such as newspapers, halls, legal aid, and training the party provided. What cannot be denied is that Communist Party organizers were crucial during the Great Depression of the 1930s.

Williamson was one of many radicals who combined the earlier message of the IWW with the pragmatism of the CP to organize workers during the Great Depression of the 1930s. Unemployment soared to over 30 per cent of the workforce in some years while most unions did little more than retrench to protect the dwindling membership. While a new political party, the Co-operative Commonwealth Federation, now the New Democratic Party, was created in 1932, organizing the resistance by the unemployed was largely left to the Communist Party.

The success of CP organizers pushed the federal government to create relief camps to siphon off resistance and put unemployed men to work far from urban centres. Housed in crude barracks, clothed in army surplus, and forced to labour on make-work projects for 20 cents a day—the price of two packs of cigarettes—men found the conditions of the camps themselves reason to organize and protest, and the CP created the Relief Camp Workers Union (RCWU) to take up their cause. Demands for better conditions were backed up with protests and ultimately a strike of relief camp workers, who walked out of the camps and headed to Vancouver, where they won considerable support among the general public.

The most dramatic action of the RCWU was the On-to-Ottawa Trek. At one mass meeting of the unemployed, someone suggested that they take the fight right to the federal government. Why not jump on a freight train and head en masse to Ottawa? Party organizers were cautious, even timid. Riding the rails was illegal; individuals might escape the police, but how could hundreds avoid being spotted and arrested? More daunting, how could so many people be fed and sheltered and protected on a cross-country trip that would take several days? How could unity and discipline be maintained? But the idea caught the imagination of the rank and file, and organizers scrambled to gather supplies and tools for the Trek.

One of those tools was taken from the IWW: a song to carry the message of the Trek and to build solidarity. Legend has it that a "Comrade Marsh" had an accordion, but he only knew one tune, that of an American hymn, long since transformed by the English Transport Workers Union, the Knights of Labor, and the IWW into a labour song: "Hold the Fort." Trekkers combined the traditional lyrics with a version written by Wobbly Ralph Chaplin in 1919 called "All Hell Can't Stop Us." The chorus became the rallying cry of the Trek:

> *Scorn to take the crumbs they drop us,*
> *All is ours by right!*
> *Onward, men! All Hell can't stop us,*
> *Crush the parasite!*

While Williamson correctly observes that the demands of the Trekkers were not met, it would be a mistake to conclude the Trek was a failure. The dramatic tactic, its repression by the government, and the harsh reality of the depression moved Canadians to throw out the federal Conservative government of R.B. Bennett in 1935. Furthermore, the lessons learned by organizers were applied effectively as Communists and others created industrial unions such as the International Woodworkers of America and the United Autoworkers. Even Jack Munro, long-time Canadian president of the International Woodworkers of America and fervent anti-Communist, later reflected that whatever one might think of their politics, "the Communists were goddammed good trade unionists." Those unions led the upsurge in union organizing during World War II and a wave of strikes across Canada during and after the war. That militancy warned successive governments and businesses that measures such as unemployment insurance, welfare, postsecondary education, medicare, and fiscal policy to maintain full employment had to be at the top of their agenda. As we have seen over the last thirty years, without that sustained pressure, the state and capital will only squeeze us harder.

Thus Williamson's story, told so evocatively in his own words and Kara Sievewright's art, holds lessons for activists today. We need the spirit of internationalism that underlay the IWW and the International Brigade that Williamson joined during the Spanish Civil War. We need the inspiration that comes from a coherent radical vision and the creative, militant tactics that bring people together and empower them. We need organization—democratic, grassroots organization—to build mass movements and institutions to sustain it. And we need the glue of culture, a culture of opposition and resistance and humour. Part of that culture is the history of struggle and resistance. This graphic history beautifully recaptures some of our past and so helps us build the future.

65

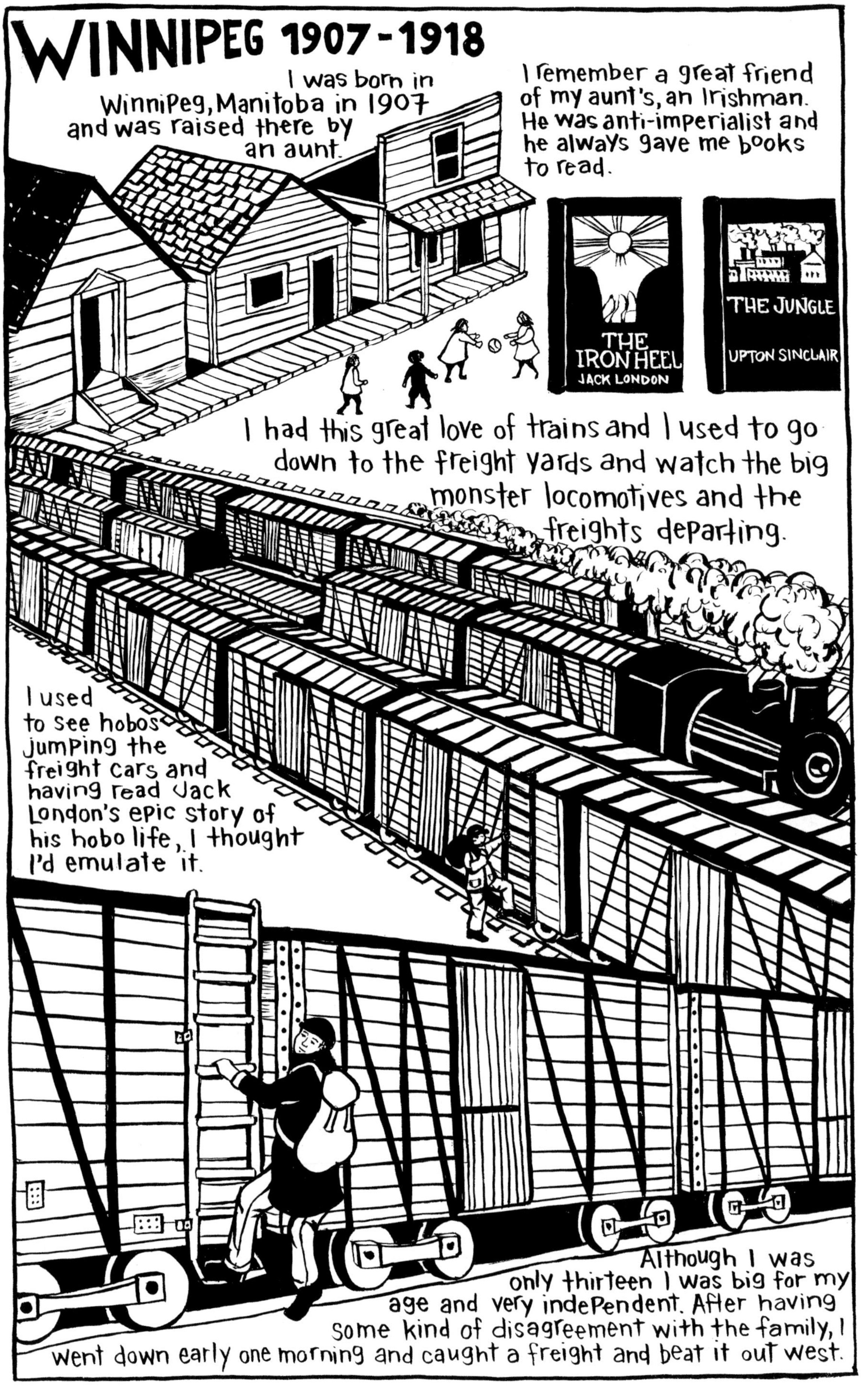

WINNIPEG 1907-1918
I was born in Winnipeg, Manitoba in 1907 and was raised there by an aunt.
I remember a great friend of my aunt's, an Irishman. He was anti-imperialist and he always gave me books to read.
THE IRON HEEL
JACK LONDON
THE JUNGLE
UPTON SINCLAIR
I had this great love of trains and I used to go down to the freight yards and watch the big monster locomotives and the freights departing.
I used to see hobos jumping the freight cars and having read Jack London's epic story of his hobo life, I thought I'd emulate it.
Although I was only thirteen I was big for my age and very independent. After having some kind of disagreement with the family, I went down early one morning and caught a freight and beat it out west.

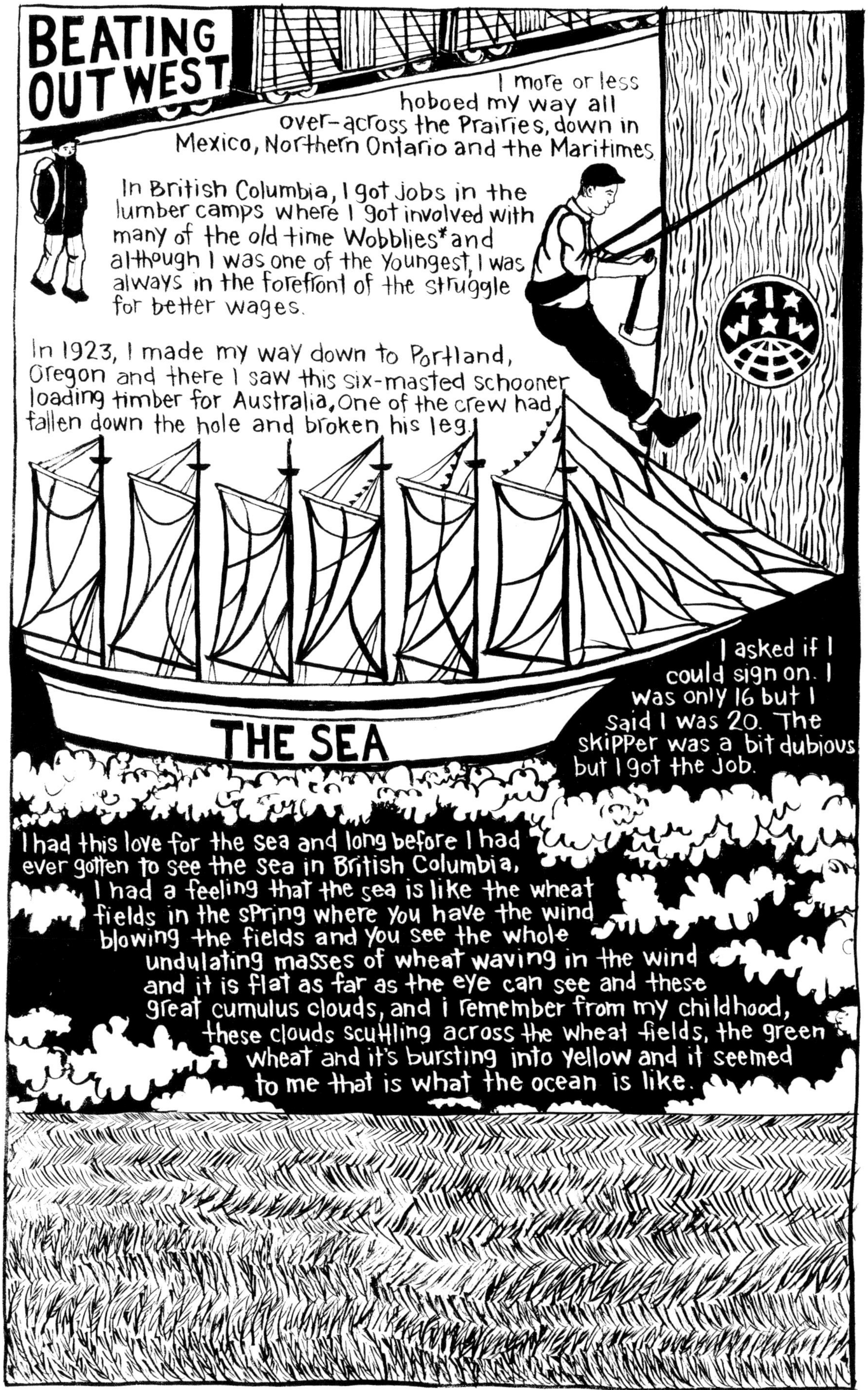
BEATING OUT WEST
I more or less hoboed my way all over–across the Prairies, down in Mexico, Northern Ontario and the Maritimes.
In British Columbia, I got jobs in the lumber camps where I got involved with many of the old time Wobblies* and although I was one of the youngest, I was always in the forefront of the struggle for better wages.
I W W
In 1923, I made my way down to Portland, Oregon and there I saw this six-masted schooner loading timber for Australia. One of the crew had fallen down the hole and broken his leg.
THE SEA
I asked if I could sign on. I was only 16 but I said I was 20. The skipper was a bit dubious but I got the job.
I had this love for the sea and long before I had ever gotten to see the sea in British Columbia, I had a feeling that the sea is like the wheat fields in the spring where you have the wind blowing the fields and you see the whole undulating masses of wheat waving in the wind and it is flat as far as the eye can see and these great cumulus clouds, and i remember from my childhood, these clouds scuttling across the wheat fields, the green wheat and it's bursting into yellow and it seemed to me that is what the ocean is like.

*The Industrial Workers of the World (IWW)

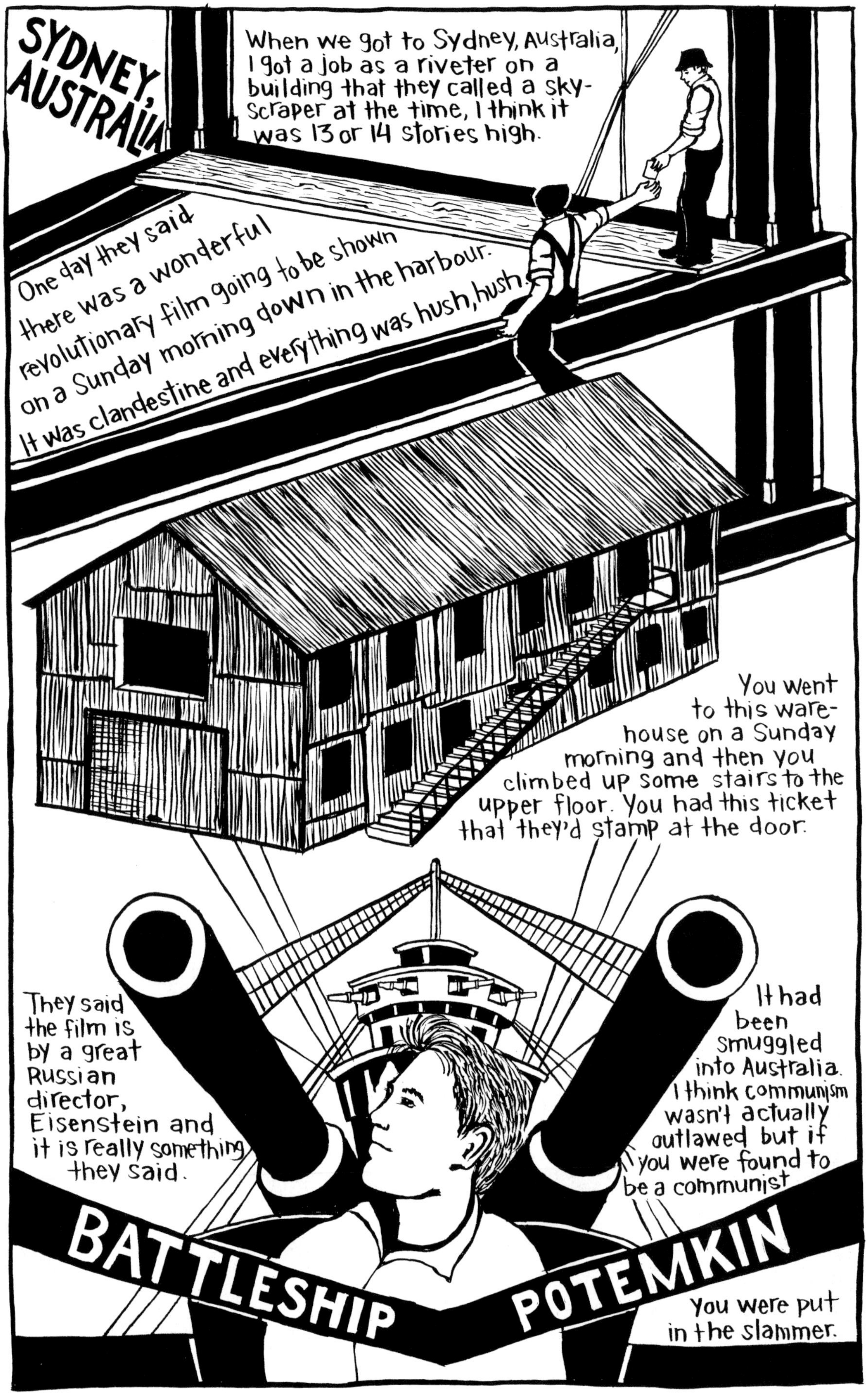
SYDNEY, AUSTRALIA
When we got to Sydney, Australia, I got a job as a riveter on a building that they called a sky-scraper at the time, I think it was 13 or 14 stories high.
One day they said there was a wonderful revolutionary film going to be shown on a Sunday morning down in the harbour. It was clandestine and everything was hush, hush.
You went to this ware-house on a Sunday morning and then you climbed up some stairs to the upper floor. You had this ticket that they'd stamp at the door.
They said the film is by a great Russian director, Eisenstein and it is really something they said.
It had been smuggled into Australia. I think communism wasn't actually outlawed but if you were found to be a communist
BATTLESHIP POTEMKIN
You were put in the slammer.

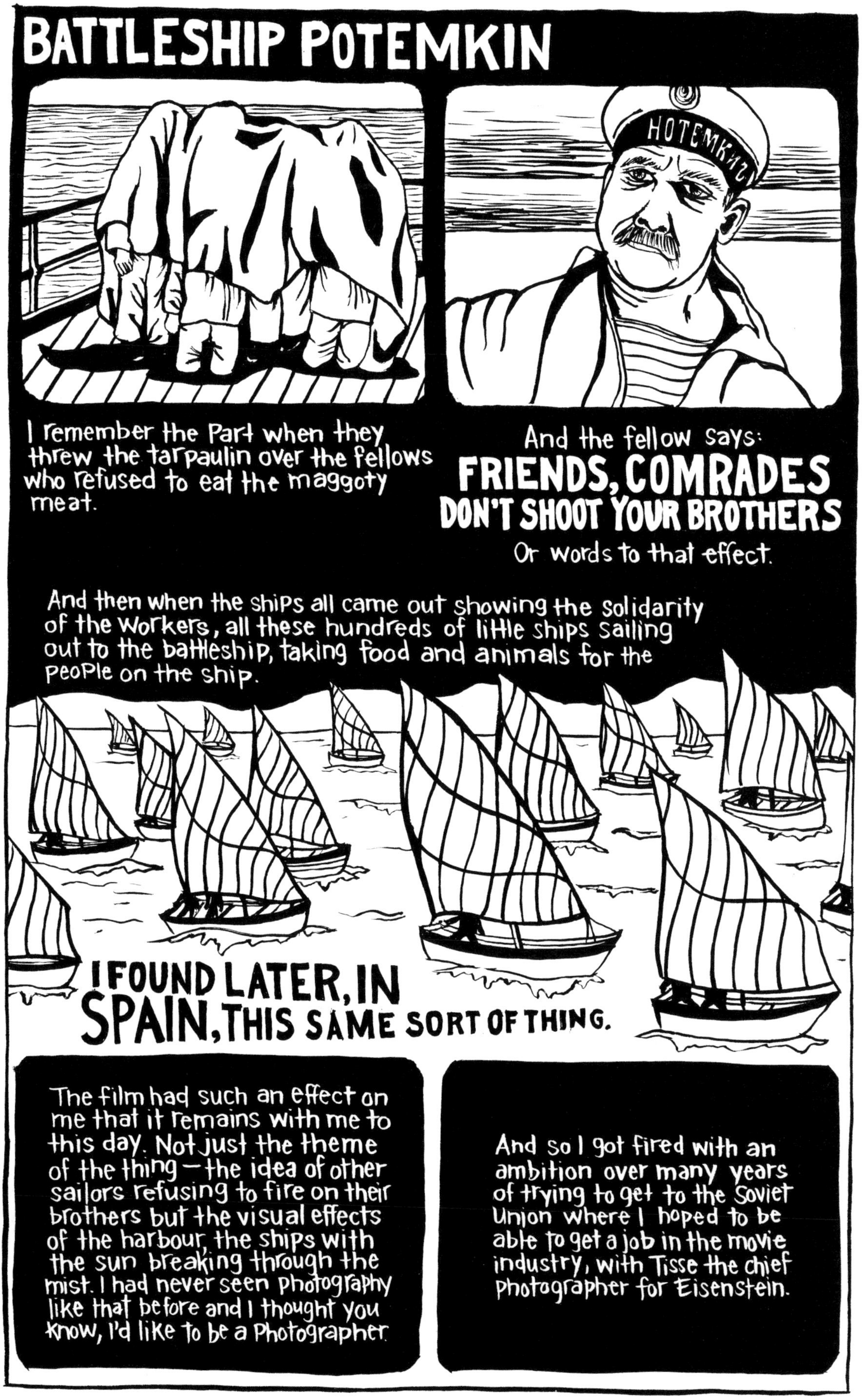
BATTLESHIP POTEMKIN
I remember the Part when they threw the tarpaulin over the fellows who refused to eat the maggoty meat.
And the fellow says: FRIENDS, COMRADES DON'T SHOOT YOUR BROTHERS Or words to that effect.
And then when the ships all came out showing the solidarity of the Workers, all these hundreds of little ships sailing out to the battleship, taking food and animals for the People on the ship.
I FOUND LATER, IN SPAIN, THIS SAME SORT OF THING.
The film had such an effect on me that it remains with me to this day. Not just the theme of the thing — the idea of other sailors refusing to fire on their brothers but the visual effects of the harbour, the ships with the sun breaking through the mist. I had never seen photography like that before and I thought you know, I'd like to be a Photographer.
And so I got fired with an ambition over many years of trying to get to the Soviet Union where I hoped to be able to get a job in the movie industry, with Tisse the chief photographer for Eisenstein.

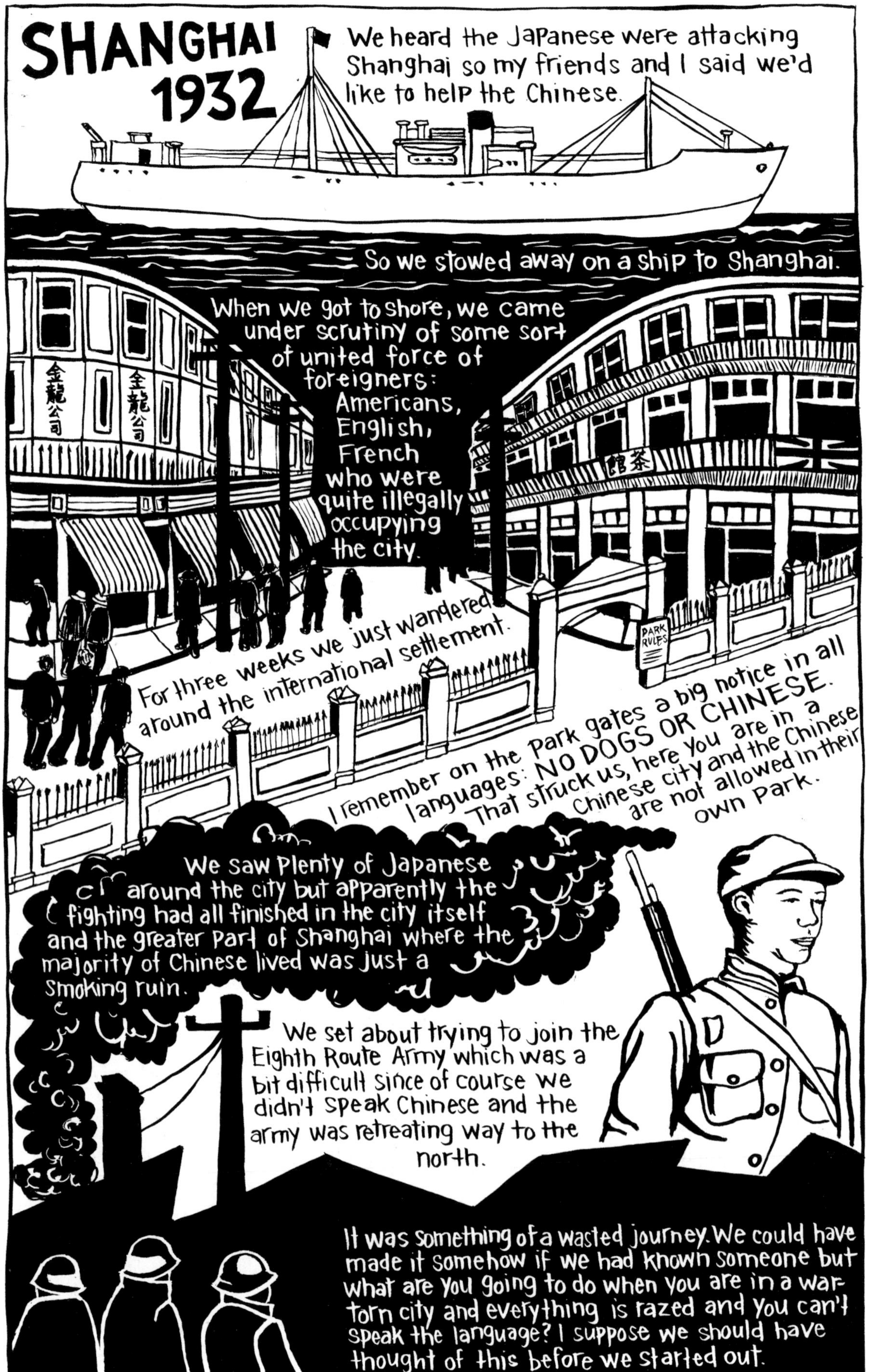
SHANGHAI 1932
We heard the Japanese were attacking Shanghai so my friends and I said we'd like to help the Chinese.
So we stowed away on a ship to Shanghai.
When we got to shore, we came under scrutiny of some sort of united force of foreigners: Americans, English, French who were quite illegally occupying the city.
金龍公司
金龍公司
茶館
For three weeks we just wandered around the international settlement.
PARK RULES
I remember on the park gates a big notice in all languages: NO DOGS OR CHINESE. That struck us, here you are in a Chinese city and the Chinese are not allowed in their own park.
We saw plenty of Japanese around the city but apparently the fighting had all finished in the city itself and the greater part of Shanghai where the majority of Chinese lived was just a smoking ruin.
We set about trying to join the Eighth Route Army which was a bit difficult since of course we didn't speak Chinese and the army was retreating way to the north.
It was something of a wasted journey. We could have made it somehow if we had known someone but what are you going to do when you are in a war-torn city and everything is razed and you can't speak the language? I suppose we should have thought of this before we started out.

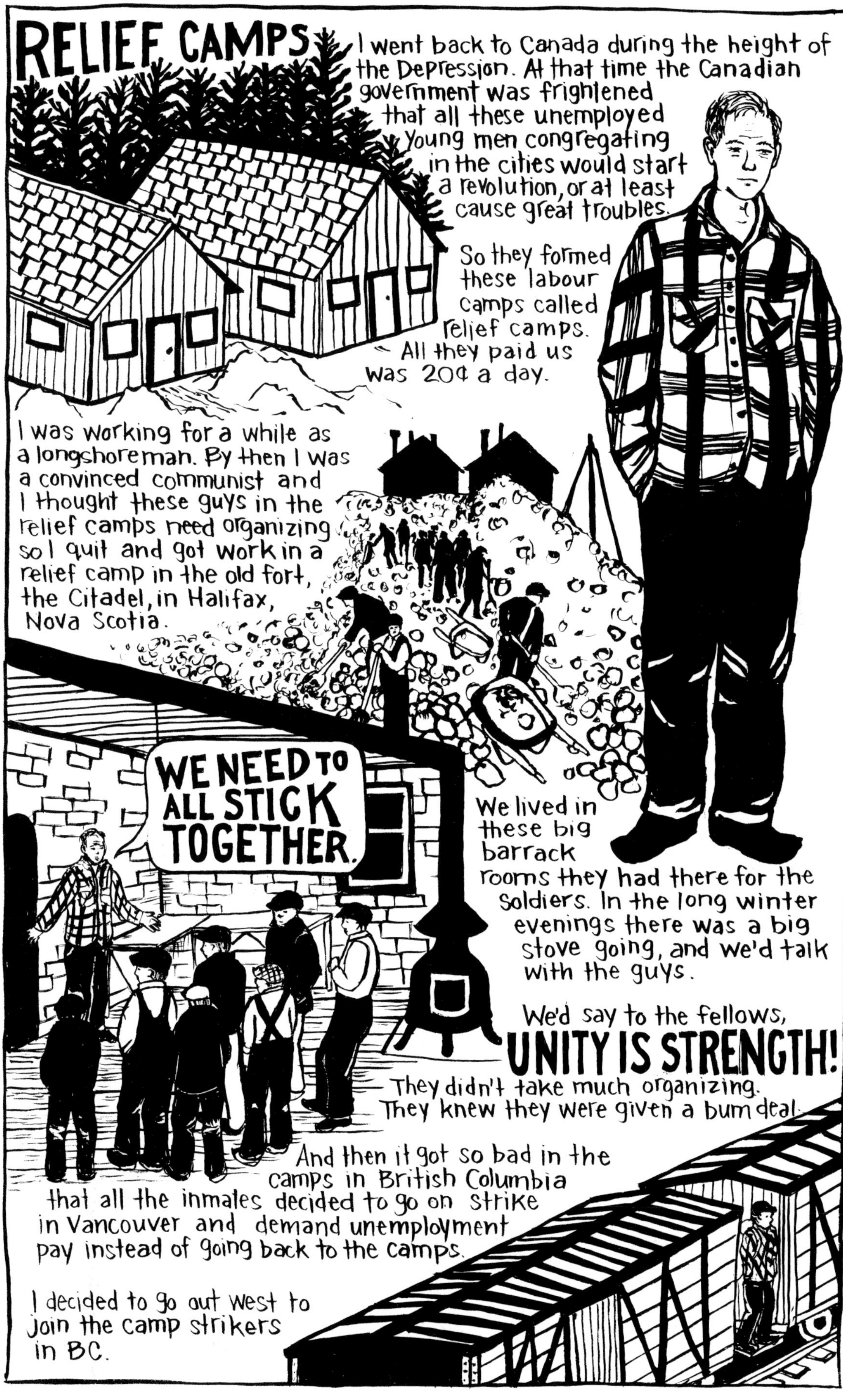

RELIEF CAMPS
I went back to Canada during the height of the Depression. At that time the Canadian government was frightened that all these unemployed young men congregating in the cities would start a revolution, or at least cause great troubles.
So they formed these labour camps called relief camps. All they paid us was 20¢ a day.
I was working for a while as a longshoreman. By then I was a convinced communist and I thought these guys in the relief camps need organizing so I quit and got work in a relief camp in the old fort, the Citadel, in Halifax, Nova Scotia.
WE NEED TO ALL STICK TOGETHER.
We lived in these big barrack rooms they had there for the soldiers. In the long winter evenings there was a big stove going, and we'd talk with the guys.
We'd say to the fellows, UNITY IS STRENGTH!
They didn't take much organizing. They knew they were given a bum deal.
And then it got so bad in the camps in British Columbia that all the inmates decided to go on strike in Vancouver and demand unemployment pay instead of going back to the camps.
I decided to go out west to join the camp strikers in BC.

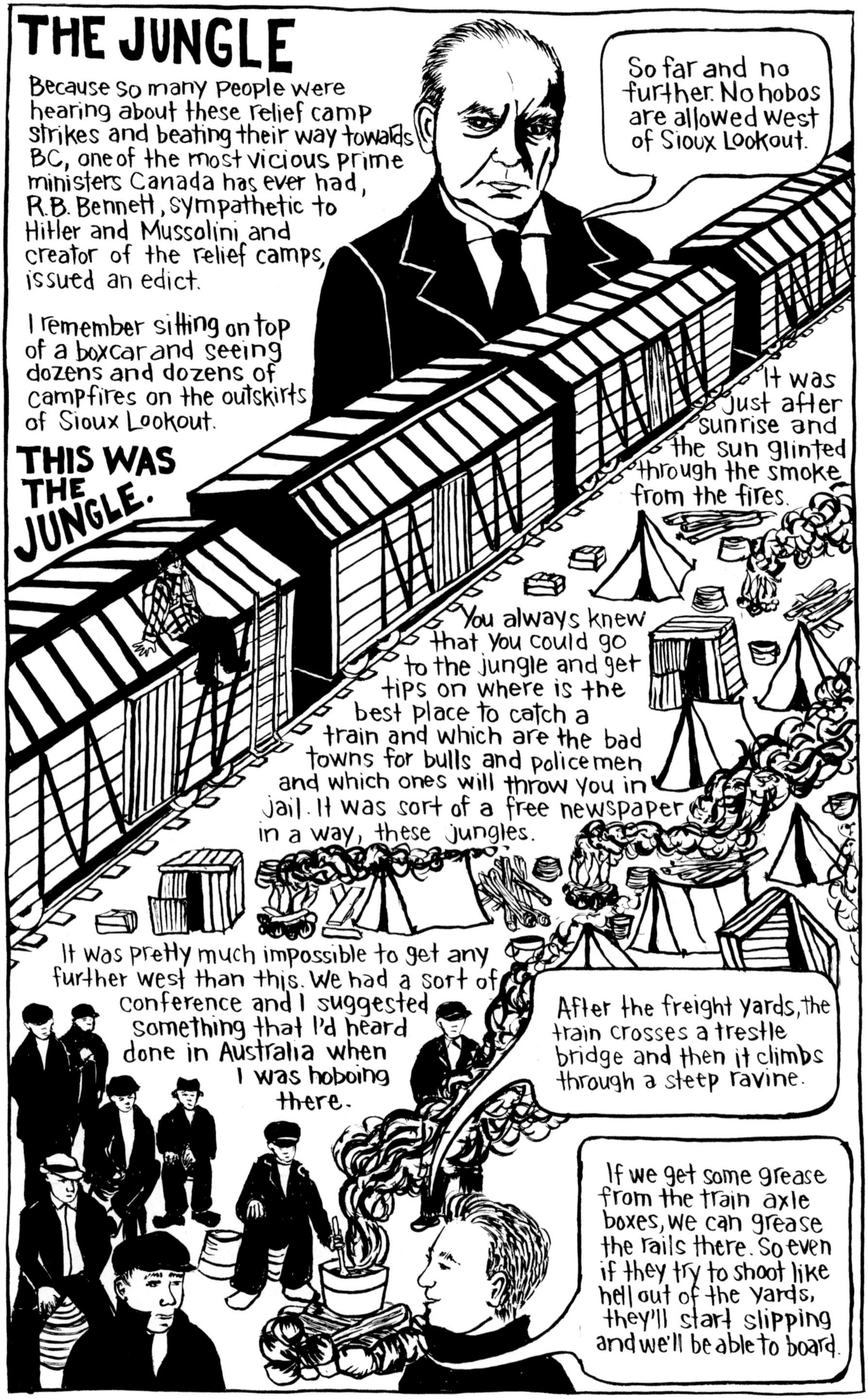
THE JUNGLE
Because so many people were hearing about these relief camp strikes and beating their way towards BC, one of the most vicious prime ministers Canada has ever had, R.B. Bennett, sympathetic to Hitler and Mussolini and creator of the relief camps, issued an edict.
So far and no further. No hobos are allowed west of Sioux Lookout.
I remember sitting on top of a boxcar and seeing dozens and dozens of campfires on the outskirts of Sioux Lookout.
THIS WAS THE JUNGLE.
It was just after sunrise and the sun glinted through the smoke from the fires.
You always knew that you could go to the jungle and get tips on where is the best place to catch a train and which are the bad towns for bulls and policemen and which ones will throw you in jail. It was sort of a free newspaper in a way, these jungles.
It was pretty much impossible to get any further west than this. We had a sort of conference and I suggested something that I'd heard done in Australia when I was hoboing there.
After the freight yards, the train crosses a trestle bridge and then it climbs through a steep ravine.
If we get some grease from the train axle boxes, we can grease the rails there. So even if they try to shoot like hell out of the yards, they'll start slipping and we'll be able to board.

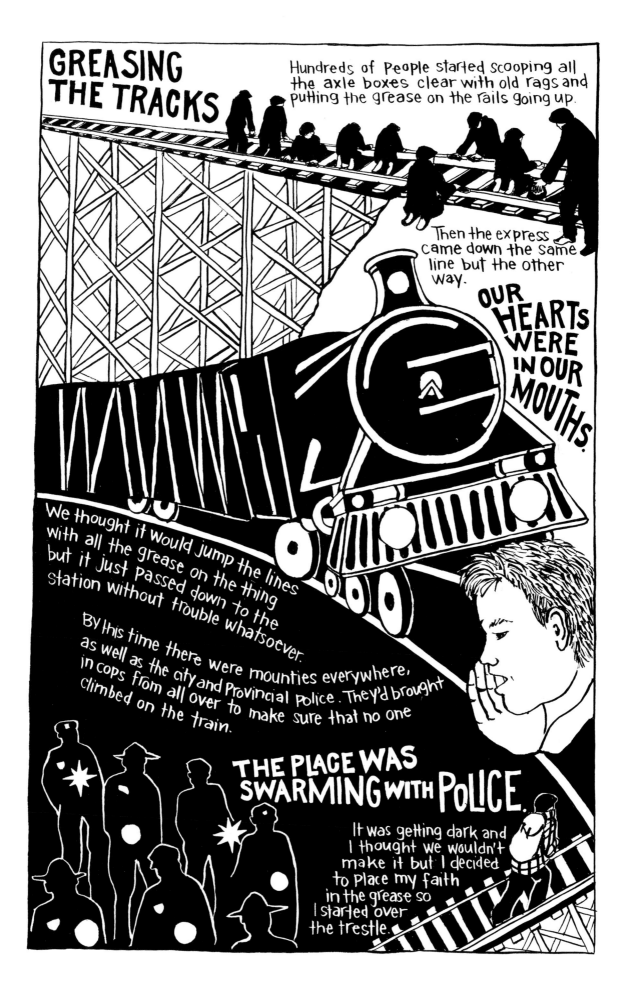

GREASING THE TRACKS

Hundreds of people started scooping all the axle boxes clear with old rags and putting the grease on the rails going up.

Then the express came down the same line but the other way.

OUR HEARTS WERE IN OUR MOUTHS.

We thought it would jump the lines with all the grease on the thing but it just passed down to the station without trouble whatsoever.

By this time there were mounties everywhere, as well as the city and Provincial Police. They'd brought in cops from all over to make sure that no one climbed on the train.

THE PLACE WAS SWARMING WITH POLICE.

It was getting dark and I thought we wouldn't make it but I decided to place my faith in the grease so I started over the trestle.

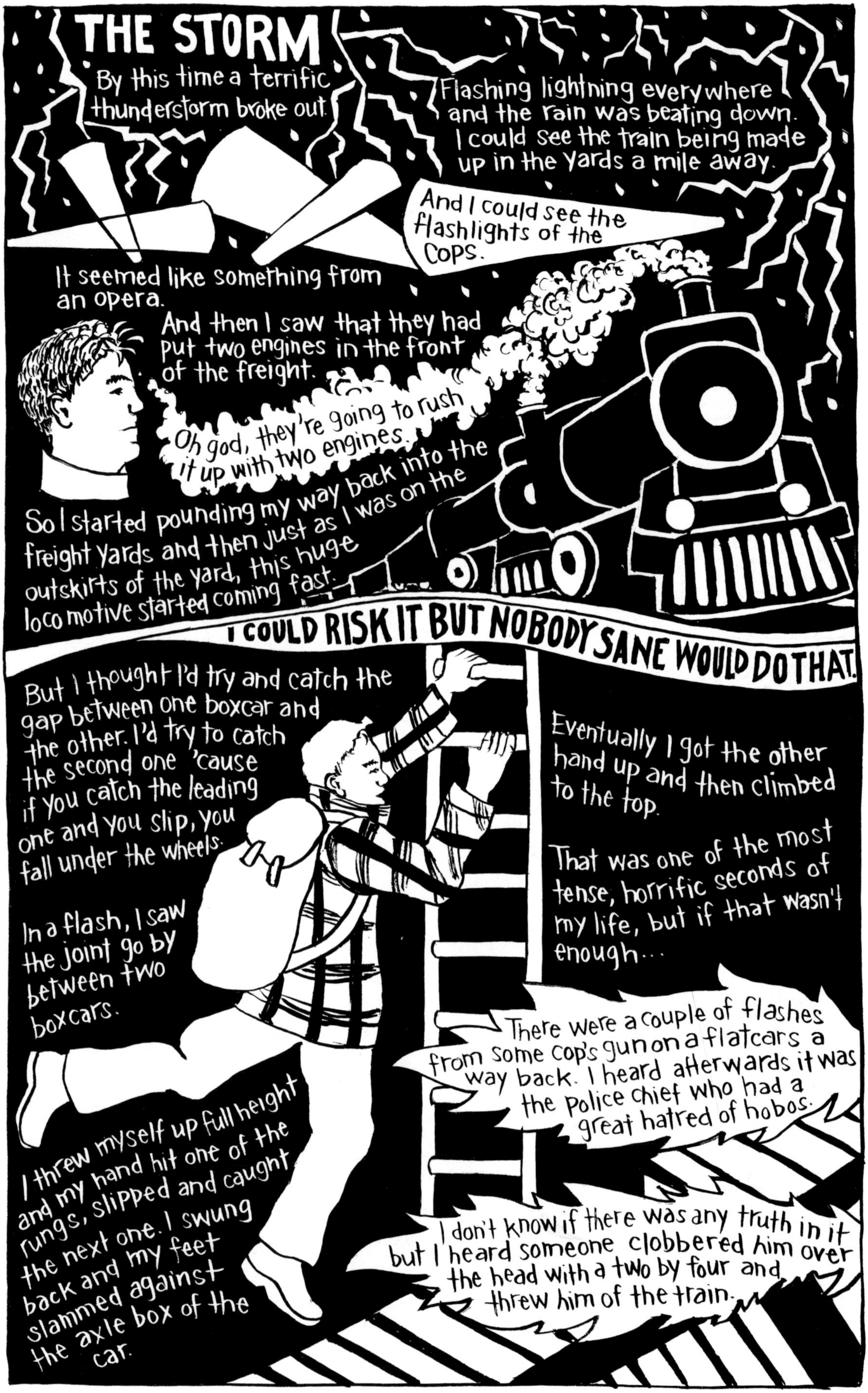
THE STORM
By this time a terrific thunderstorm broke out.
Flashing lightning everywhere and the rain was beating down. I could see the train being made up in the yards a mile away.
And I could see the flashlights of the cops.
It seemed like something from an opera.
And then I saw that they had put two engines in the front of the freight.
Oh god, they're going to rush it up with two engines.
So I started pounding my way back into the freight yards and then just as I was on the outskirts of the yard, this huge locomotive started coming fast.
I COULD RISK IT BUT NOBODY SANE WOULD DO THAT.
But I thought I'd try and catch the gap between one boxcar and the other. I'd try to catch the second one 'cause if you catch the leading one and you slip, you fall under the wheels.
In a flash, I saw the joint go by between two boxcars.
I threw myself up full height and my hand hit one of the rungs, slipped and caught the next one. I swung back and my feet slammed against the axle box of the car.
Eventually I got the other hand up and then climbed to the top.
That was one of the most tense, horrific seconds of my life, but if that wasn't enough...
There were a couple of flashes from some cop's gun on a flatcars a way back. I heard afterwards it was the police chief who had a great hatred of hobos.
I don't know if there was any truth in it but I heard someone clobbered him over the head with a two by four and threw him of the train.

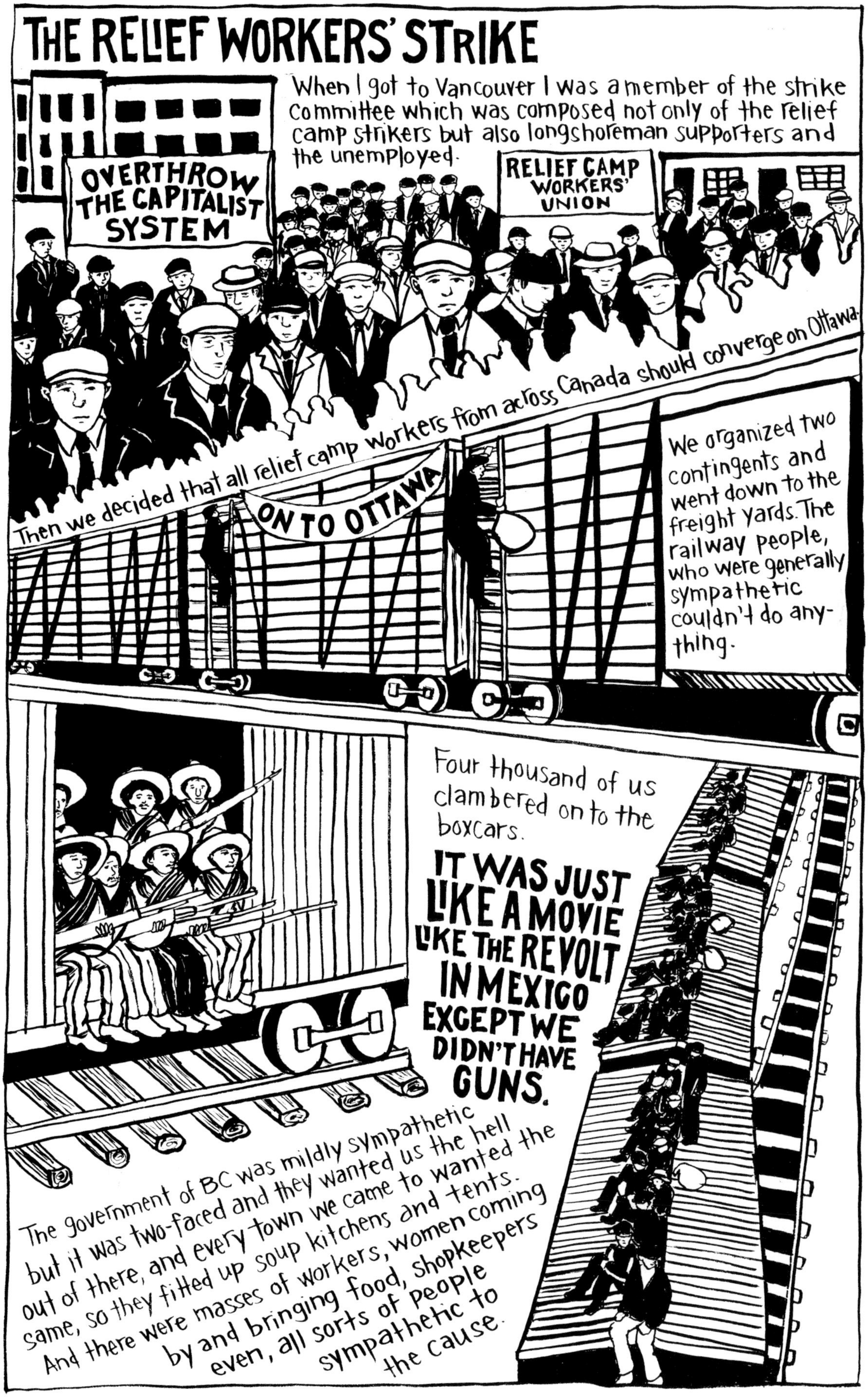
THE RELIEF WORKERS' STRIKE
When I got to Vancouver I was a member of the strike committee which was composed not only of the relief camp strikers but also longshoreman supporters and the unemployed.
OVERTHROW THE CAPITALIST SYSTEM
RELIEF CAMP WORKERS' UNION
Then we decided that all relief camp workers from across Canada should converge on Ottawa.
ON TO OTTAWA
We organized two contingents and went down to the freight yards. The railway people, who were generally sympathetic couldn't do anything.
Four thousand of us clambered on to the boxcars.
IT WAS JUST LIKE A MOVIE LIKE THE REVOLT IN MEXICO EXCEPT WE DIDN'T HAVE GUNS.
The government of BC was mildly sympathetic but it was two-faced and they wanted us the hell out of there, and every town we came to wanted the same, so they fitted up soup kitchens and tents. And there were masses of workers, women coming by and bringing food, shopkeepers even, all sorts of people sympathetic to the cause.

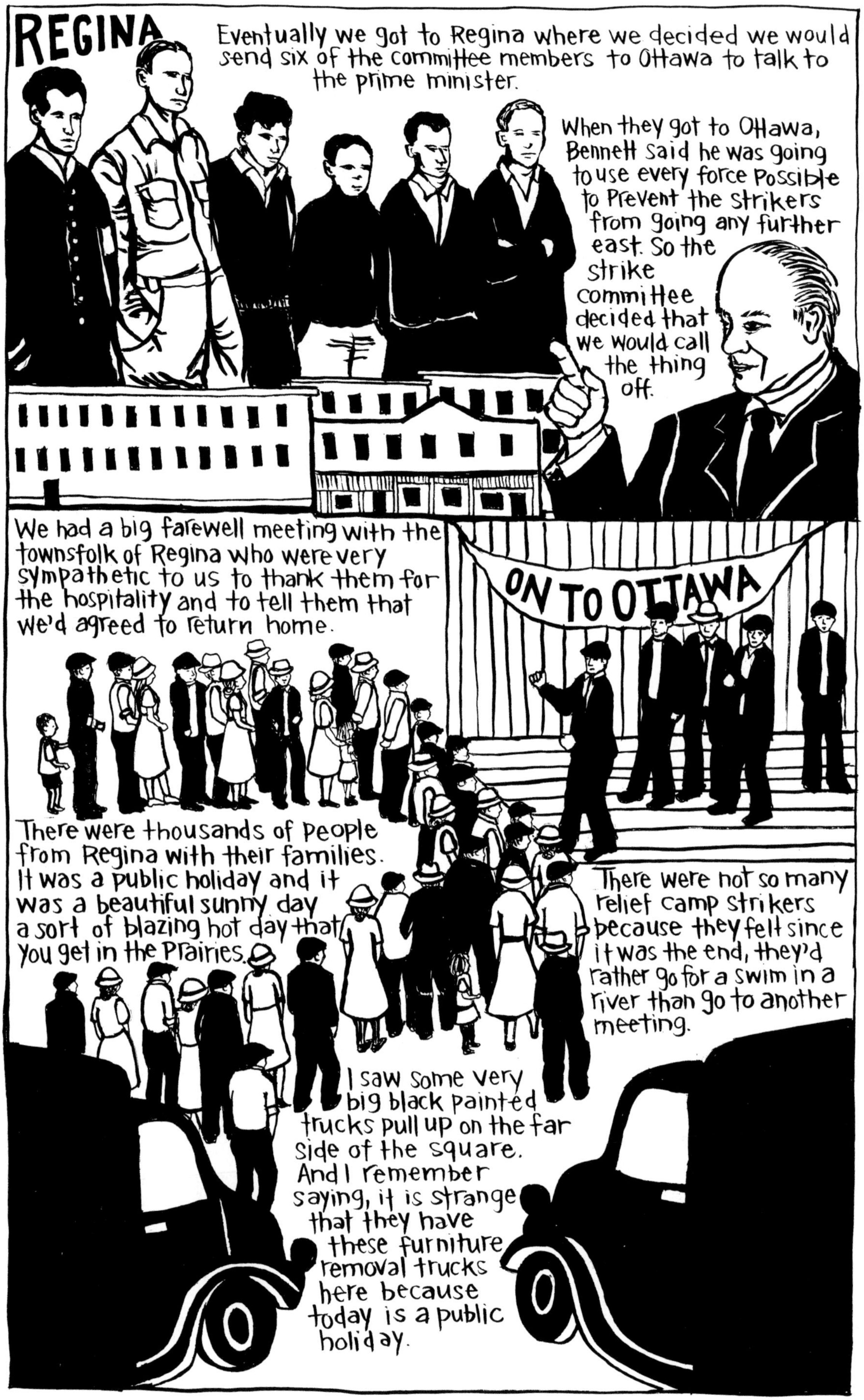
REGINA
Eventually we got to Regina where we decided we would send six of the committee members to Ottawa to talk to the prime minister.
When they got to Ottawa, Bennett said he was going to use every force possible to prevent the strikers from going any further east. So the strike committee decided that we would call the thing off.
We had a big farewell meeting with the townsfolk of Regina who were very sympathetic to us to thank them for the hospitality and to tell them that we'd agreed to return home.
ON TO OTTAWA
There were thousands of people from Regina with their families. It was a public holiday and it was a beautiful sunny day a sort of blazing hot day that you get in the Prairies.
There were not so many relief camp strikers because they felt since it was the end, they'd rather go for a swim in a river than go to another meeting.
I saw some very big black painted trucks pull up on the far side of the square. And I remember saying, it is strange that they have these furniture removal trucks here because today is a public holiday.

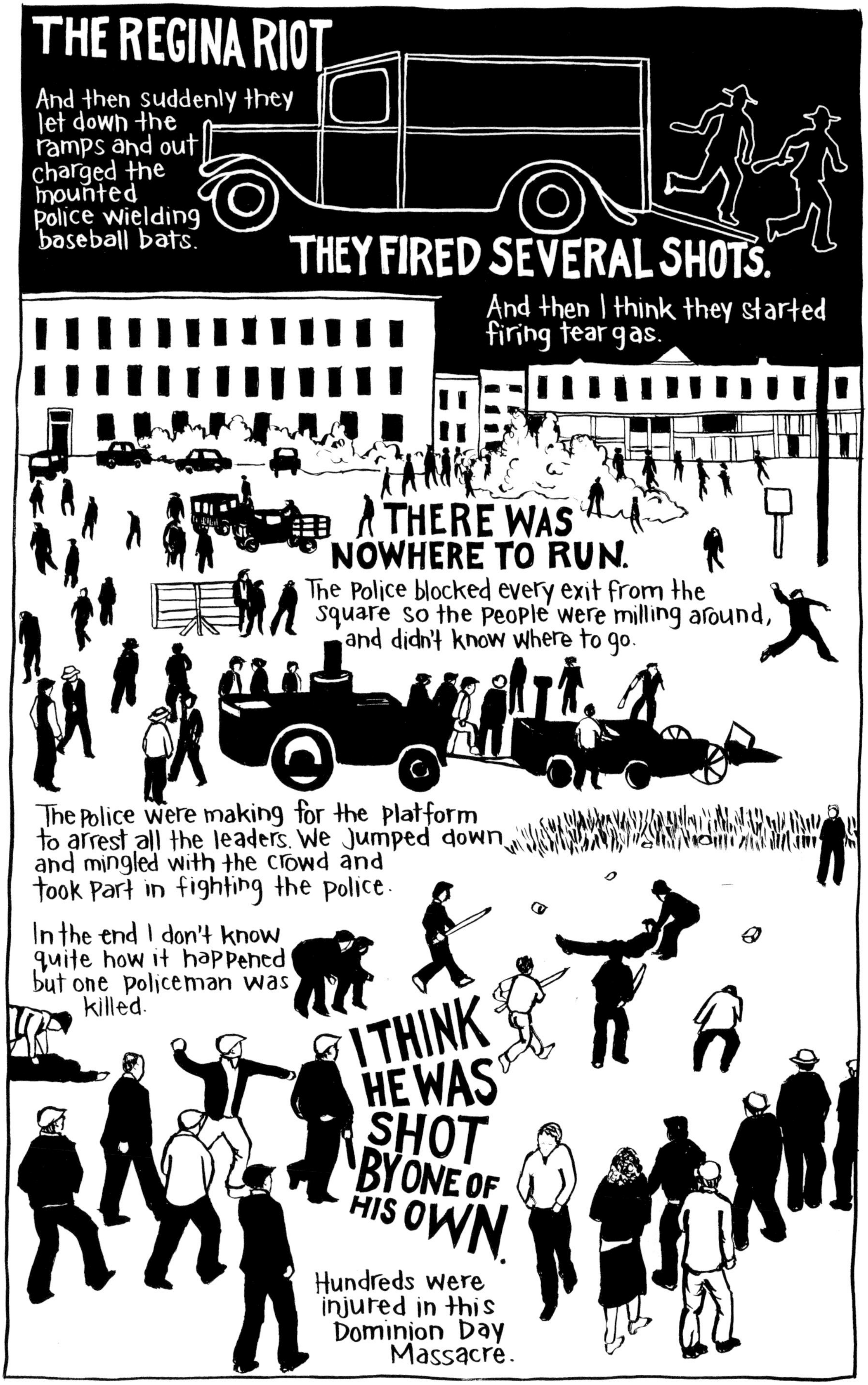

THE REGINA RIOT
And then suddenly they let down the ramps and out charged the mounted police wielding baseball bats.
THEY FIRED SEVERAL SHOTS.
And then I think they started firing tear gas.
THERE WAS NOWHERE TO RUN.
The police blocked every exit from the square so the people were milling around, and didn't know where to go.
The police were making for the platform to arrest all the leaders. We jumped down and mingled with the crowd and took part in fighting the police.
In the end I don't know quite how it happened but one policeman was killed.
I THINK HE WAS SHOT BY ONE OF HIS OWN.
Hundreds were injured in this Dominion Day Massacre.

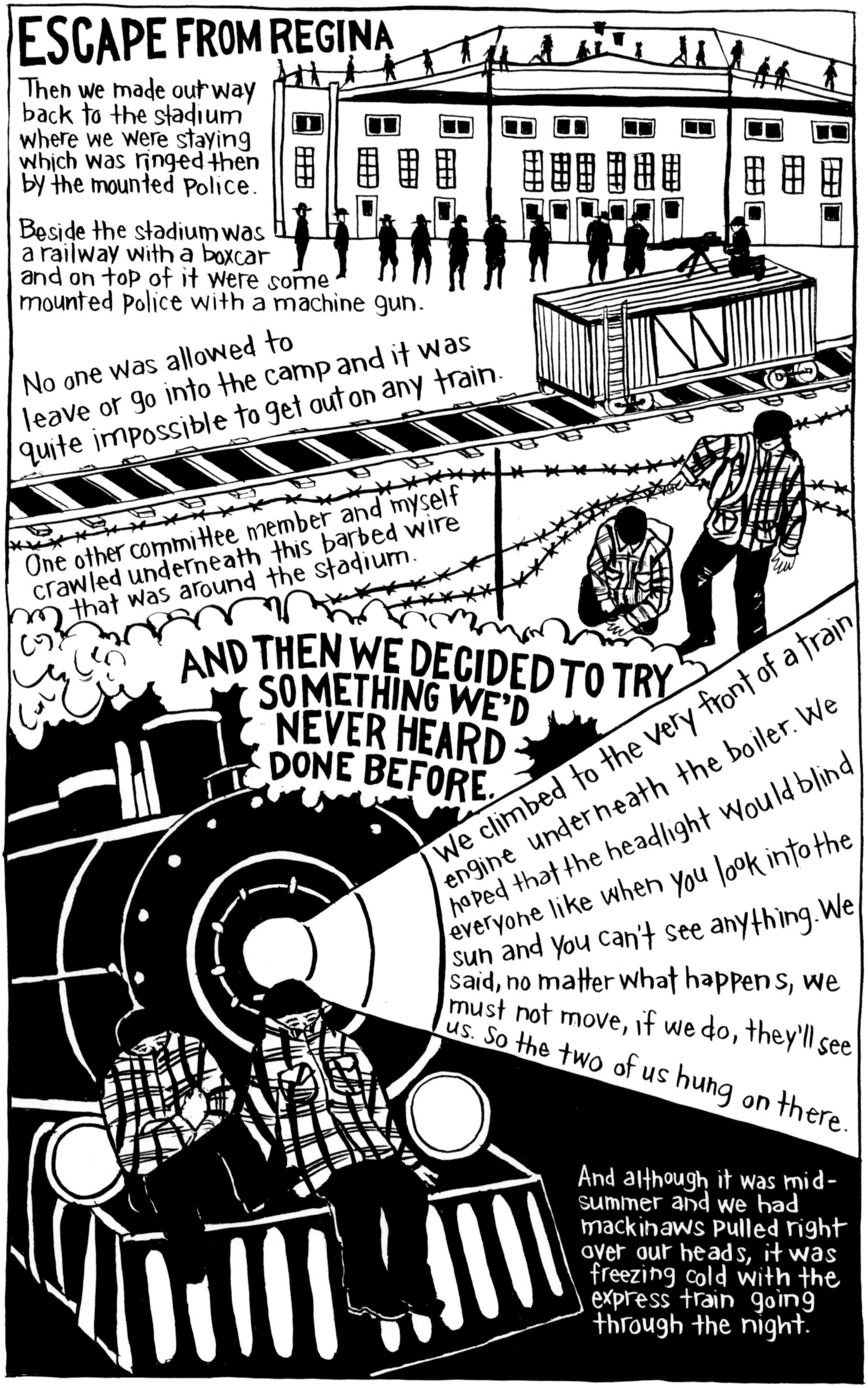
ESCAPE FROM REGINA
Then we made our way back to the stadium where we were staying which was ringed then by the mounted Police.
Beside the stadium was a railway with a boxcar and on top of it were some mounted Police with a machine gun.
No one was allowed to leave or go into the camp and it was quite impossible to get out on any train.
One other committee member and myself crawled underneath this barbed wire that was around the stadium.
AND THEN WE DECIDED TO TRY SOMETHING WE'D NEVER HEARD DONE BEFORE.
We climbed to the very front of a train engine underneath the boiler. We hoped that the headlight would blind everyone like when you look into the sun and you can't see anything. We said, no matter what happens, we must not move, if we do, they'll see us. So the two of us hung on there.
And although it was mid-summer and we had mackinaws pulled right over our heads, it was freezing cold with the express train going through the night.

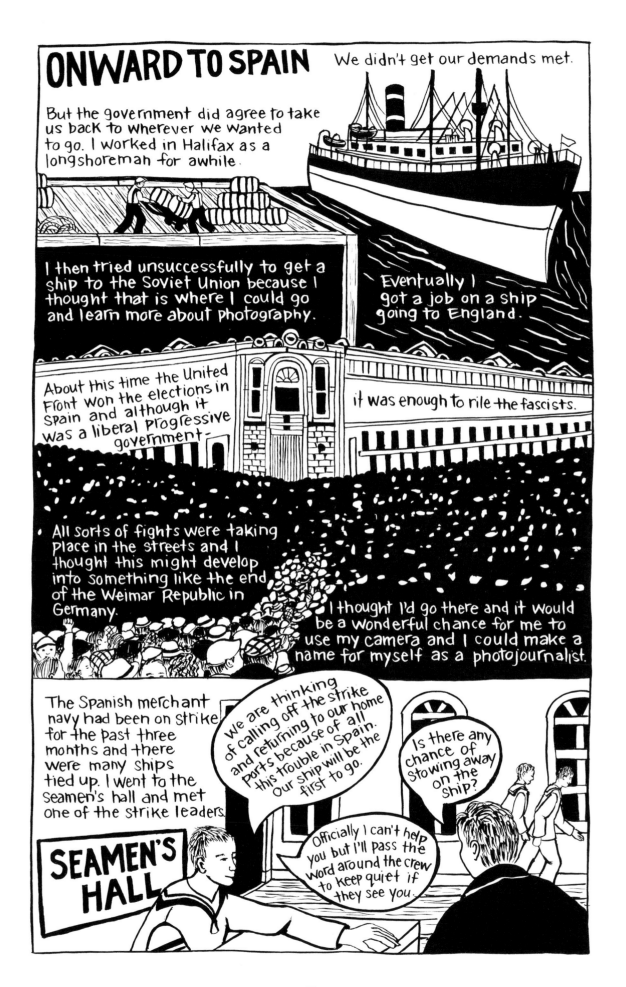

ONWARD TO SPAIN

We didn't get our demands met.

But the government did agree to take us back to wherever we wanted to go. I worked in Halifax as a longshoreman for awhile.

I then tried unsuccessfully to get a ship to the Soviet Union because I thought that is where I could go and learn more about photography.

Eventually I got a job on a ship going to England.

About this time the United Front won the elections in Spain and although it was a liberal progressive government—

it was enough to rile the fascists.

All sorts of fights were taking place in the streets and I thought this might develop into something like the end of the Weimar Republic in Germany.

I thought I'd go there and it would be a wonderful chance for me to use my camera and I could make a name for myself as a photojournalist.

The Spanish merchant navy had been on strike for the past three months and there were many ships tied up. I went to the seamen's hall and met one of the strike leaders.

We are thinking of calling off the strike and returning to our home ports because of all this trouble in Spain. Our ship will be the first to go.

Is there any chance of stowing away on the ship?

Officially I can't help you but I'll pass the word around the crew to keep quiet if they see you.

SEAMEN'S HALL

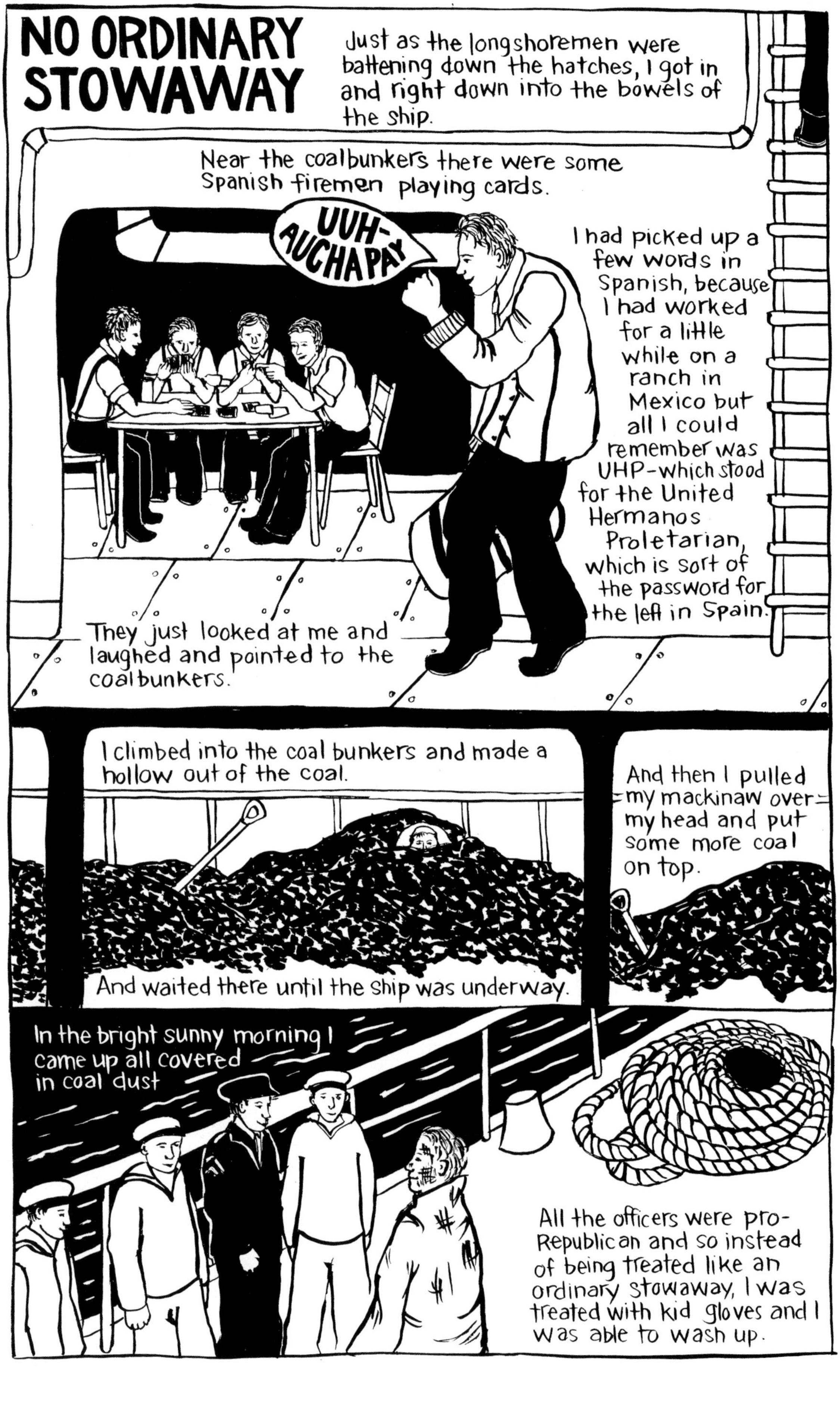
NO ORDINARY STOWAWAY
Just as the longshoremen were battening down the hatches, I got in and right down into the bowels of the ship.
Near the coalbunkers there were some Spanish firemen playing cards.
UUH-AUCHAPAY
I had picked up a few words in Spanish, because I had worked for a little while on a ranch in Mexico but all I could remember was UHP-which stood for the United Hermanos Proletarian, which is sort of the password for the left in Spain.
They just looked at me and laughed and pointed to the coalbunkers.
I climbed into the coal bunkers and made a hollow out of the coal.
And waited there until the ship was underway.
And then I pulled my mackinaw over my head and put some more coal on top.
In the bright sunny morning I came up all covered in coal dust
All the officers were pro-Republican and so instead of being treated like an ordinary stowaway, I was treated with kid gloves and I was able to wash up.

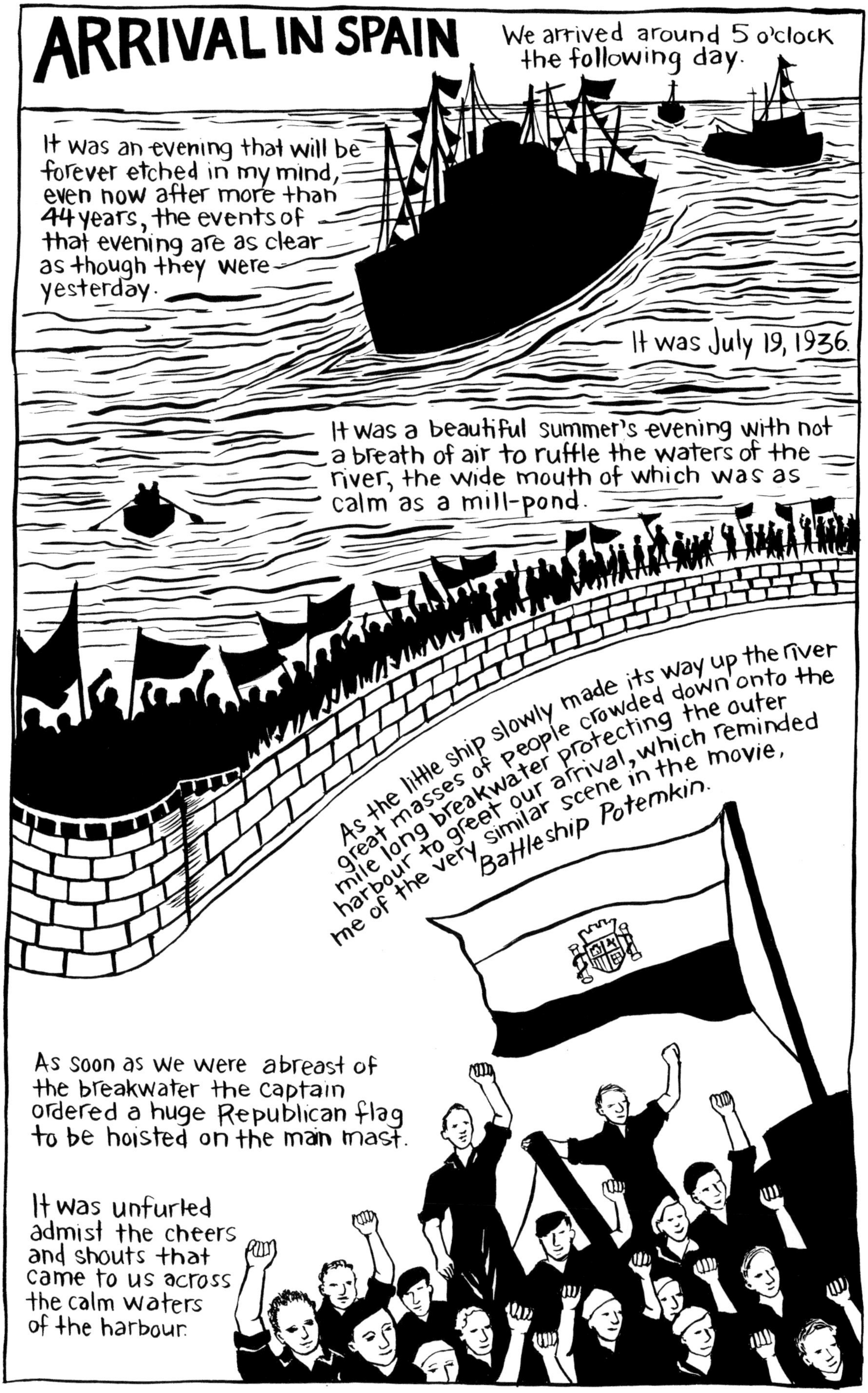
ARRIVAL IN SPAIN
We arrived around 5 o'clock the following day.
It was an evening that will be forever etched in my mind, even now after more than 44 years, the events of that evening are as clear as though they were yesterday.
It was July 19, 1936.
It was a beautiful summer's evening with not a breath of air to ruffle the waters of the river, the wide mouth of which was as calm as a mill-pond.
As the little ship slowly made its way up the river great masses of people crowded down onto the mile long breakwater protecting the outer harbour to greet our arrival, which reminded me of the very similar scene in the movie, Battleship Potemkin.
As soon as we were abreast of the breakwater the captain ordered a huge Republican flag to be hoisted on the main mast.
It was unfurled admist the cheers and shouts that came to us across the calm waters of the harbour.

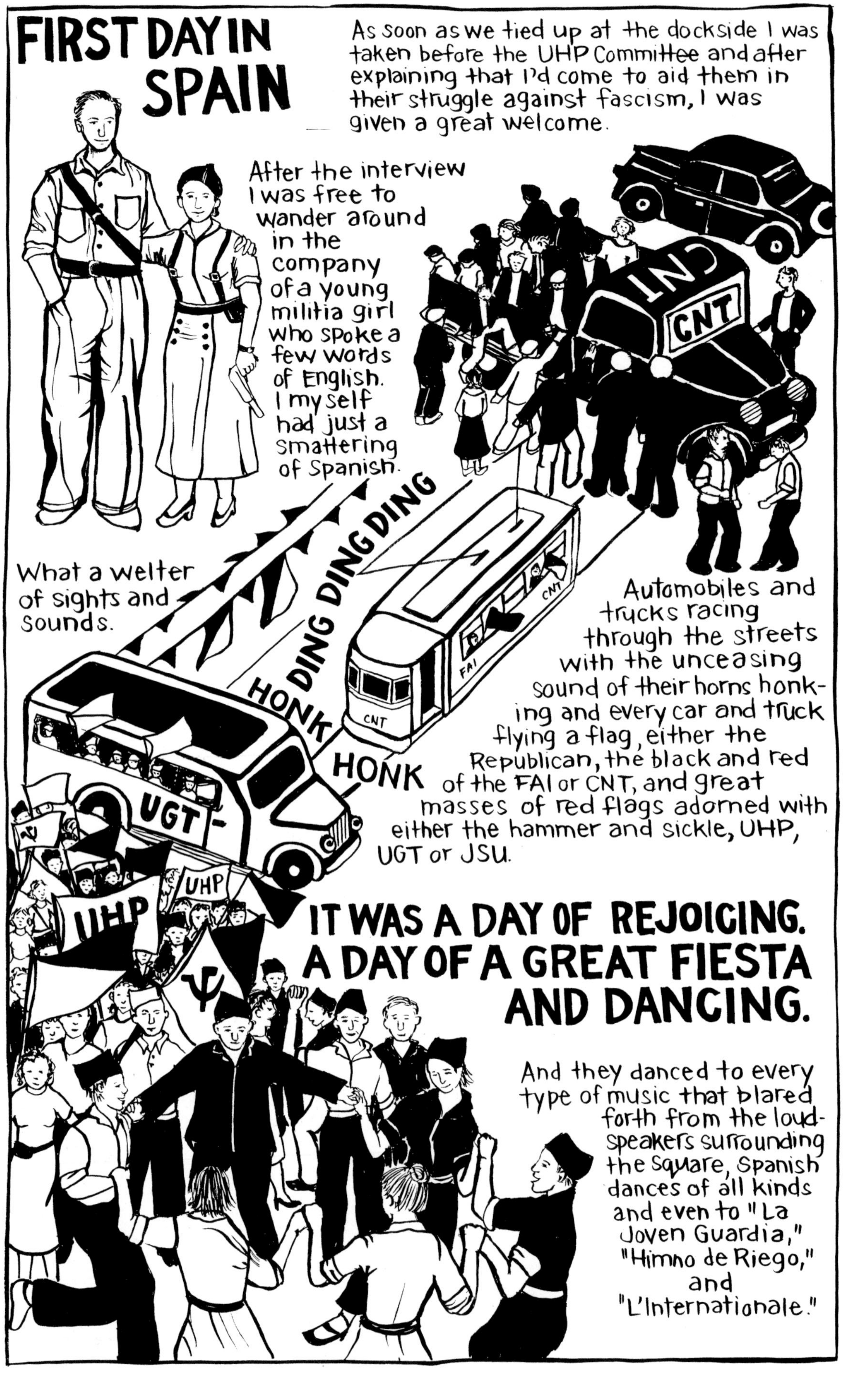
FIRST DAY IN SPAIN
As soon as we tied up at the dockside I was taken before the UHP Committee and after explaining that I'd come to aid them in their struggle against fascism, I was given a great welcome.
After the interview I was free to wander around in the company of a young militia girl who spoke a few words of English. I myself had just a smattering of Spanish.
CNT
CNT
DING DING DING
What a welter of sights and sounds.
CNT
FAI
CNT
HONK HONK
UGT
Automobiles and trucks racing through the streets with the unceasing sound of their horns honking and every car and truck flying a flag, either the Republican, the black and red of the FAI or CNT, and great masses of red flags adorned with either the hammer and sickle, UHP, UGT or JSU.
UHP
UHP
IT WAS A DAY OF REJOICING. A DAY OF A GREAT FIESTA AND DANCING.
And they danced to every type of music that blared forth from the loud-speakers surrounding the square, Spanish dances of all kinds and even to "La Joven Guardia," "Himno de Riego," and "L'Internationale."

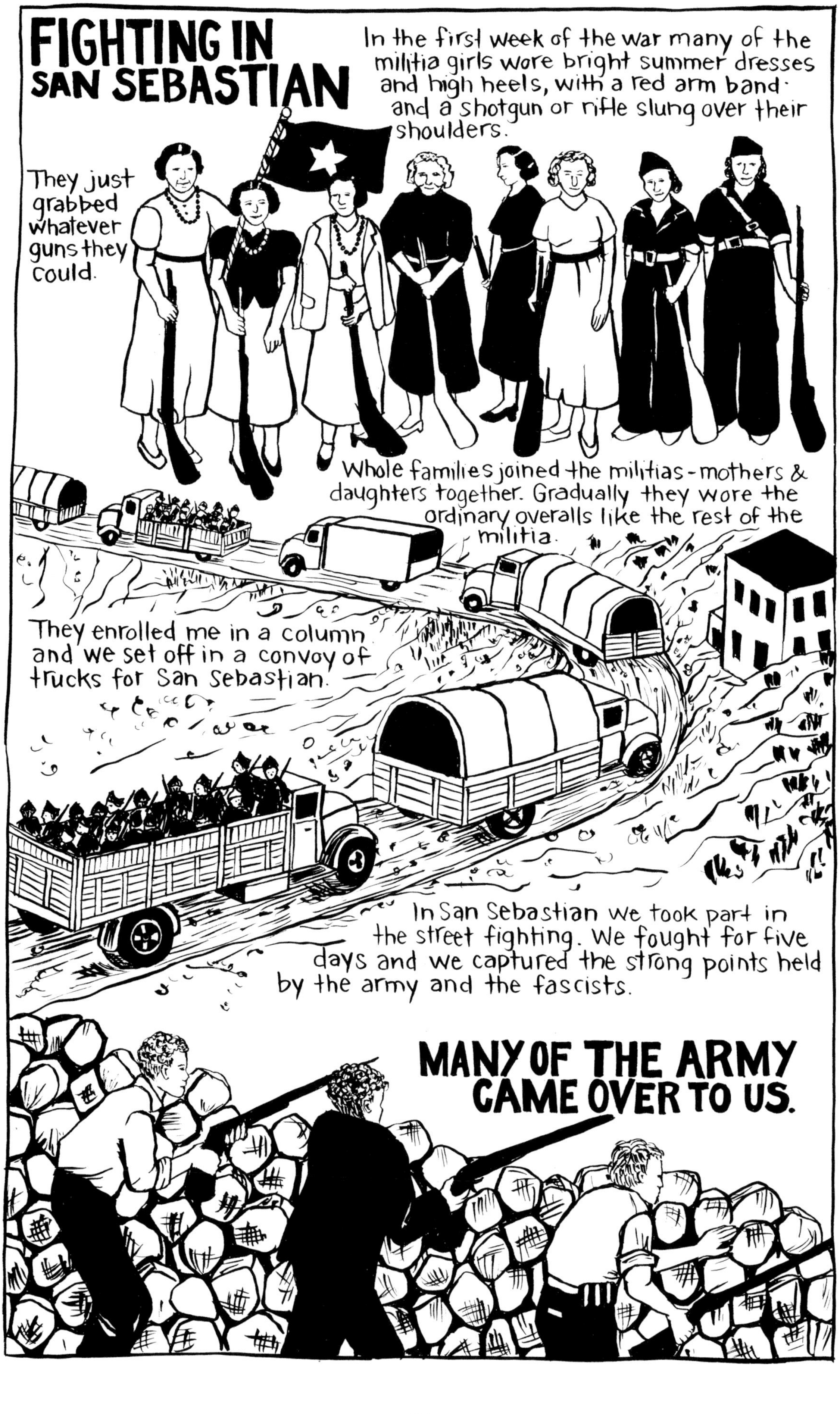
FIGHTING IN SAN SEBASTIAN
In the first week of the war many of the militia girls wore bright summer dresses and high heels, with a red arm band and a shotgun or rifle slung over their shoulders.
They just grabbed whatever guns they could.
Whole families joined the militias - mothers & daughters together. Gradually they wore the ordinary overalls like the rest of the militia.
They enrolled me in a column and we set off in a convoy of trucks for San Sebastian.
In San Sebastian we took part in the street fighting. We fought for five days and we captured the strong points held by the army and the fascists.
MANY OF THE ARMY CAME OVER TO US.

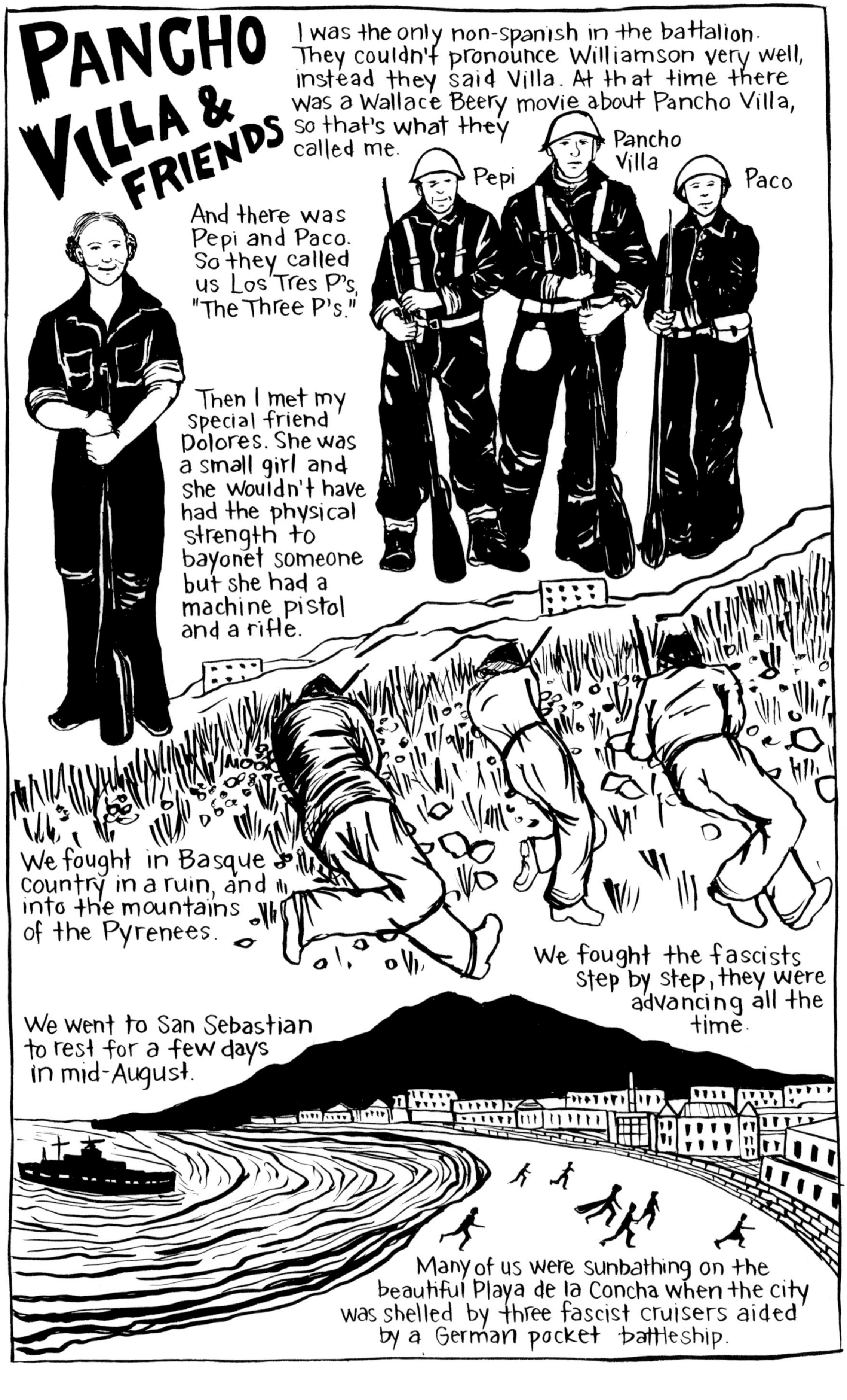
PANCHO VILLA & FRIENDS
I was the only non-spanish in the battalion. They couldn't pronounce Williamson very well, instead they said Villa. At that time there was a Wallace Beery movie about Pancho Villa, so that's what they called me.
Pepi
Pancho Villa
Paco
And there was Pepi and Paco. So they called us Los Tres P's, "The Three P's."
Then I met my special friend Dolores. She was a small girl and she wouldn't have had the physical strength to bayonet someone but she had a machine pistol and a rifle.
We fought in Basque country in a ruin, and into the mountains of the Pyrenees.
We fought the fascists step by step, they were advancing all the time.
We went to San Sebastian to rest for a few days in mid-August.
Many of us were sunbathing on the beautiful Playa de la Concha when the city was shelled by three fascist cruisers aided by a German pocket battleship.

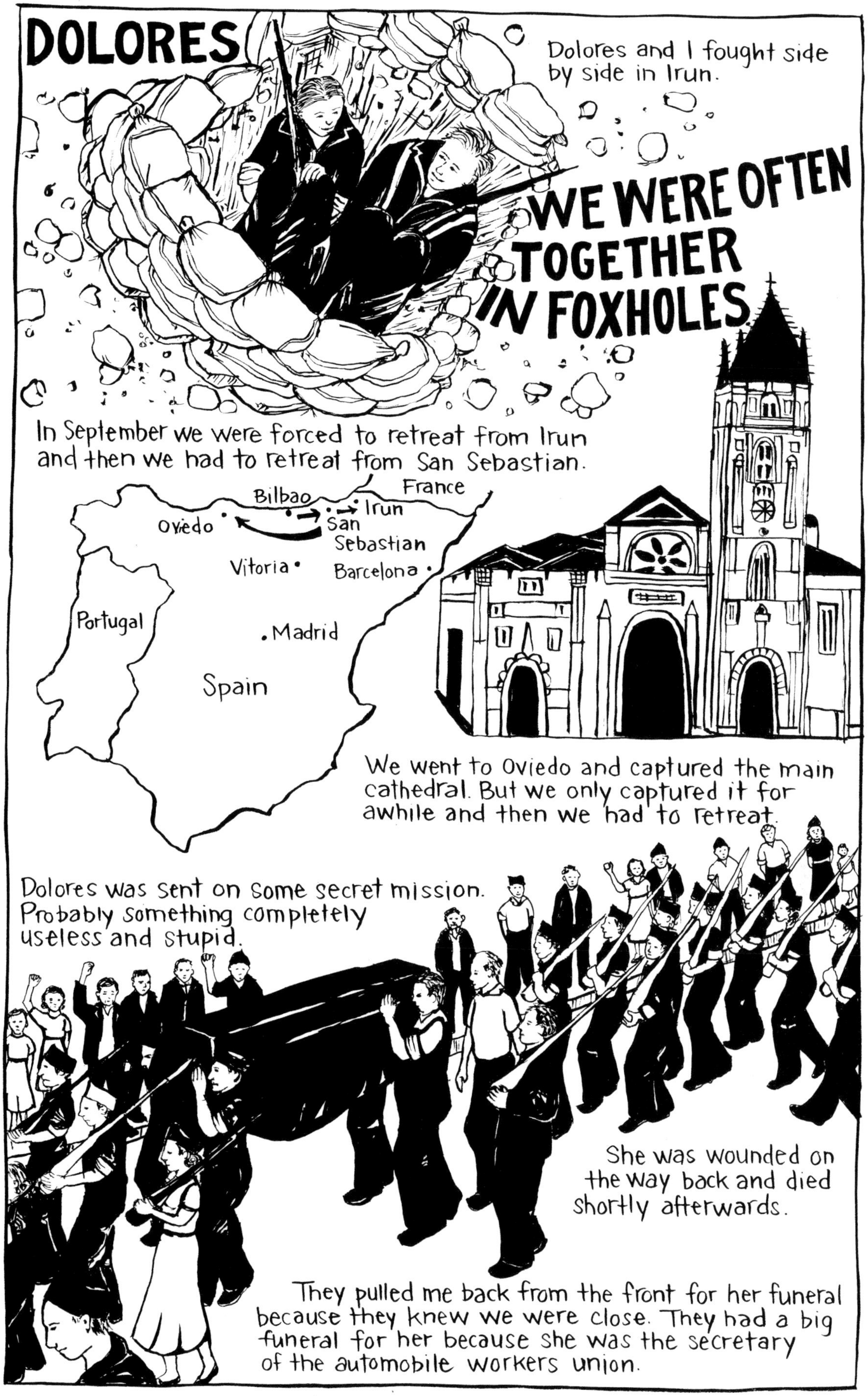
DOLORES
Dolores and I fought side by side in Irun.
WE WERE OFTEN TOGETHER IN FOXHOLES.
In September we were forced to retreat from Irun and then we had to retreat from San Sebastian.
France
Bilbao
Irun
Oviedo
San Sebastian
Vitoria
Barcelona
Portugal
Madrid
Spain
We went to Oviedo and captured the main cathedral. But we only captured it for awhile and then we had to retreat.
Dolores was sent on some secret mission. Probably something completely useless and stupid.
She was wounded on the way back and died shortly afterwards.
They pulled me back from the front for her funeral because they knew we were close. They had a big funeral for her because she was the secretary of the automobile workers union.

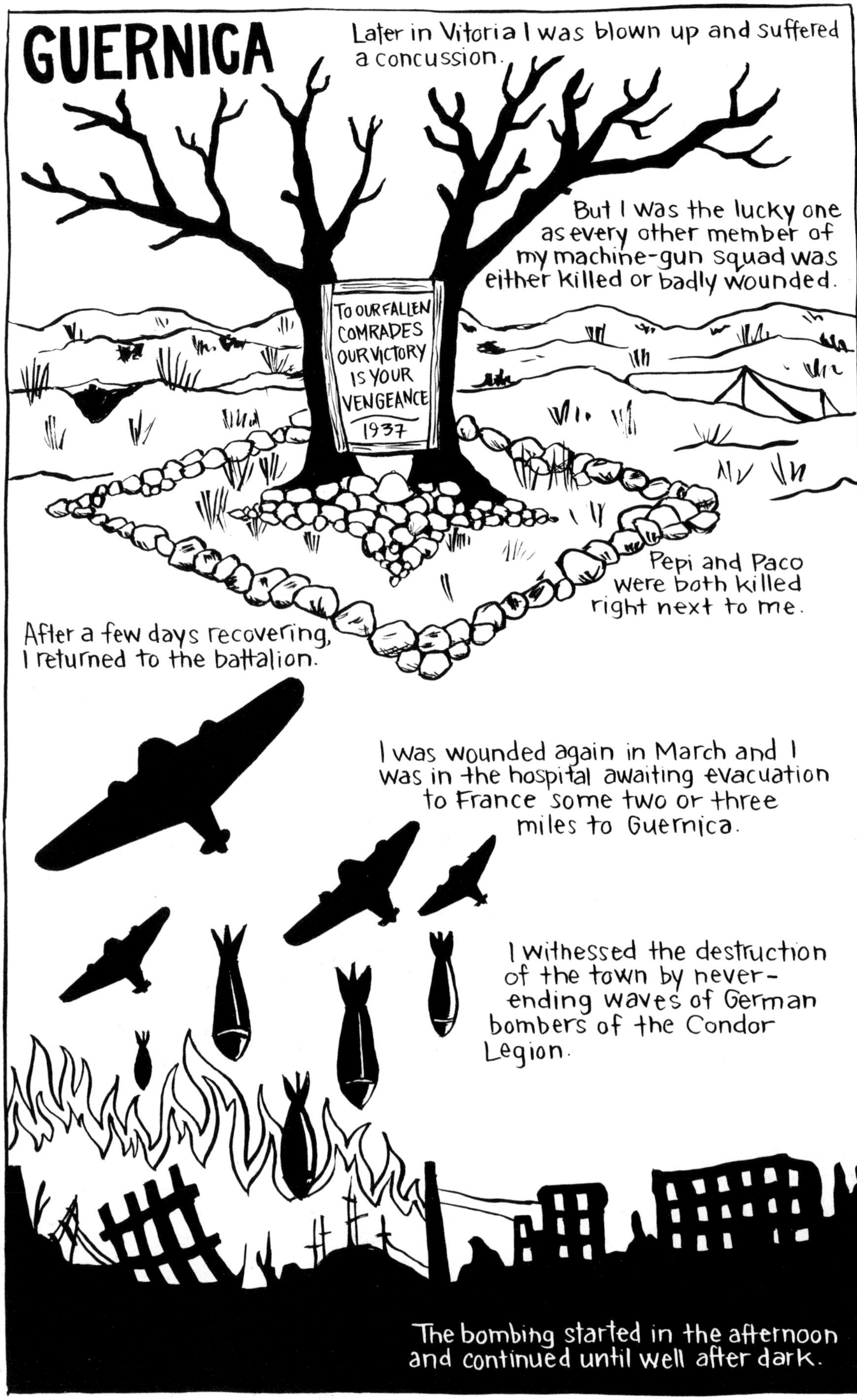
GUERNICA
Later in Vitoria I was blown up and suffered a concussion.
But I was the lucky one as every other member of my machine-gun squad was either killed or badly wounded.
TO OUR FALLEN COMRADES OUR VICTORY IS YOUR VENGEANCE 1937
Pepi and Paco were both killed right next to me.
After a few days recovering, I returned to the battalion.
I was wounded again in March and I was in the hospital awaiting evacuation to France some two or three miles to Guernica.
I witnessed the destruction of the town by never-ending waves of German bombers of the Condor Legion.
The bombing started in the afternoon and continued until well after dark.

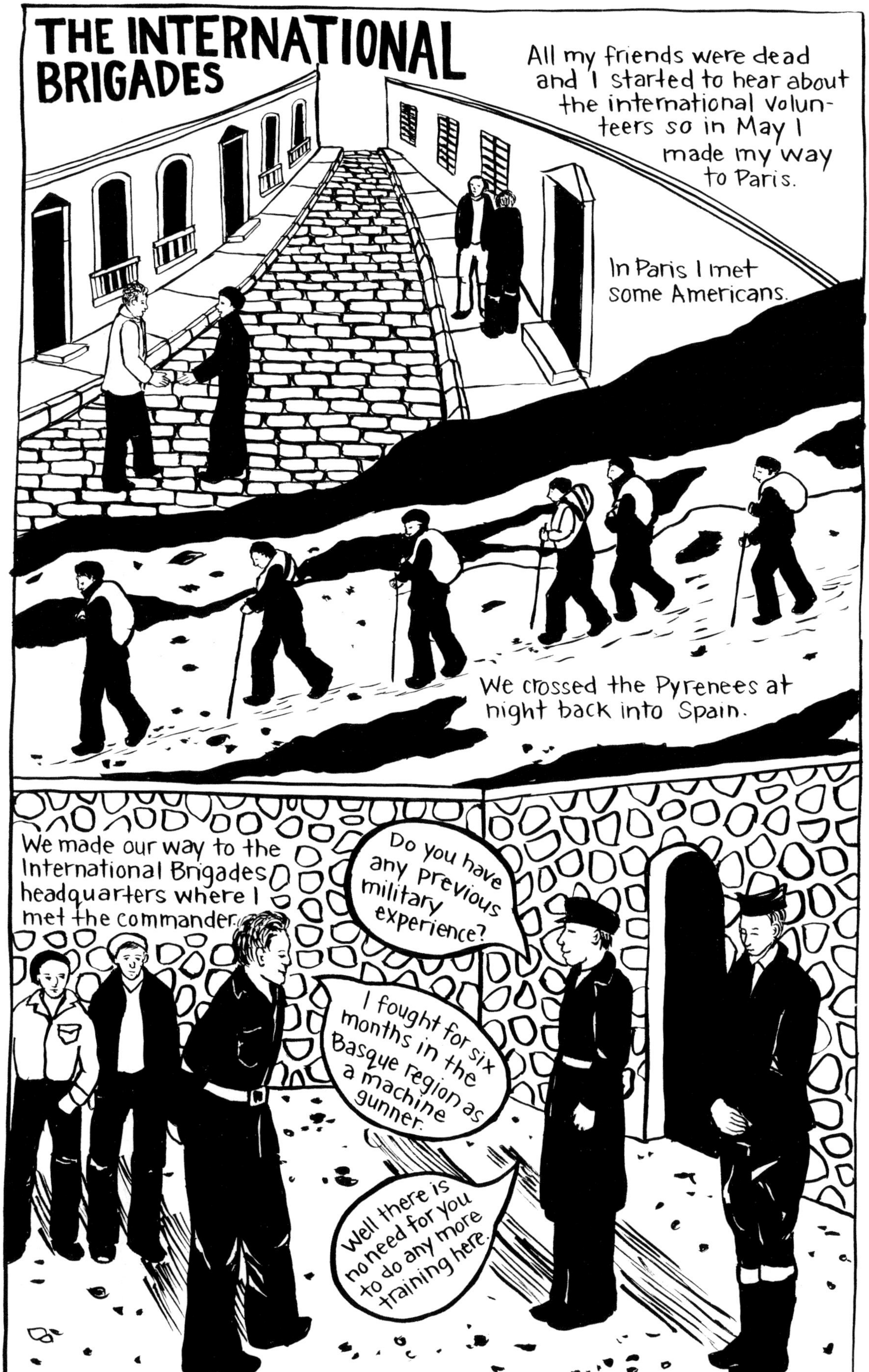
THE INTERNATIONAL BRIGADES
All my friends were dead and I started to hear about the international volunteers so in May I made my way to Paris.
In Paris I met some Americans.
We crossed the Pyrenees at night back into Spain.
We made our way to the International Brigades headquarters where I met the commander.
Do you have any previous military experience?
I fought for six months in the Basque region as a machine gunner.
Well there is no need for you to do any more training here.

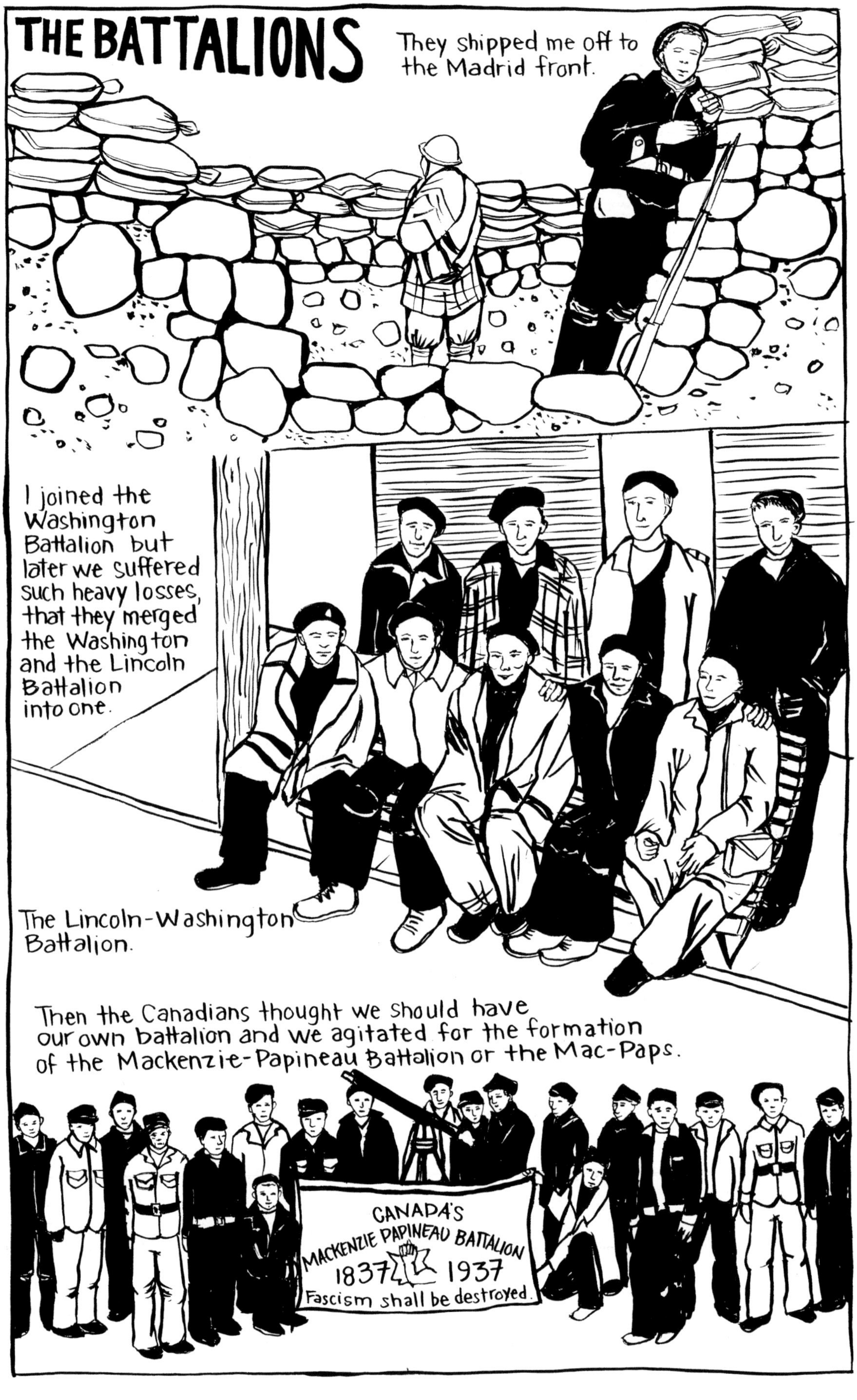
THE BATTALIONS
They shipped me off to the Madrid front.
I joined the Washington Battalion but later we suffered such heavy losses, that they merged the Washington and the Lincoln Battalion into one.
The Lincoln-Washington Battalion.
Then the Canadians thought we should have our own battalion and we agitated for the formation of the Mackenzie-Papineau Battalion or the Mac-Paps.
CANADA'S
MACKENZIE PAPINEAU BATTALION
1837 1937
Fascism shall be destroyed.

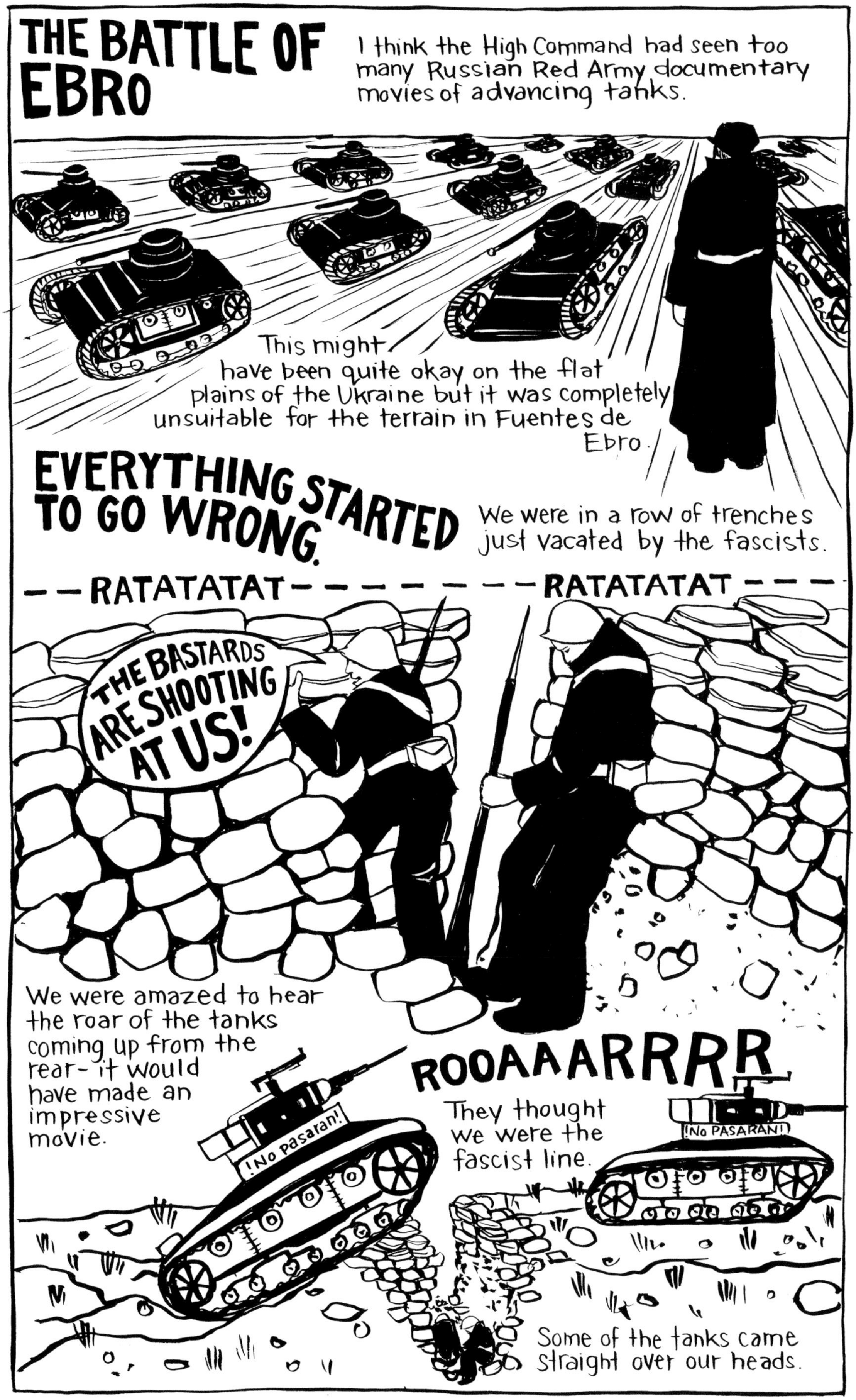

THE BATTLE OF EBRO
I think the High Command had seen too many Russian Red Army documentary movies of advancing tanks.
This might have been quite okay on the flat plains of the Ukraine but it was completely unsuitable for the terrain in Fuentes de Ebro.
EVERYTHING STARTED TO GO WRONG.
We were in a row of trenches just vacated by the fascists.
RATATATAT
RATATATAT
THE BASTARDS ARE SHOOTING AT US!
We were amazed to hear the roar of the tanks coming up from the rear- it would have made an impressive movie.
ROOAAARRRR
!NO PASARAN!
They thought we were the fascist line.
!NO PASARAN!
Some of the tanks came straight over our heads.

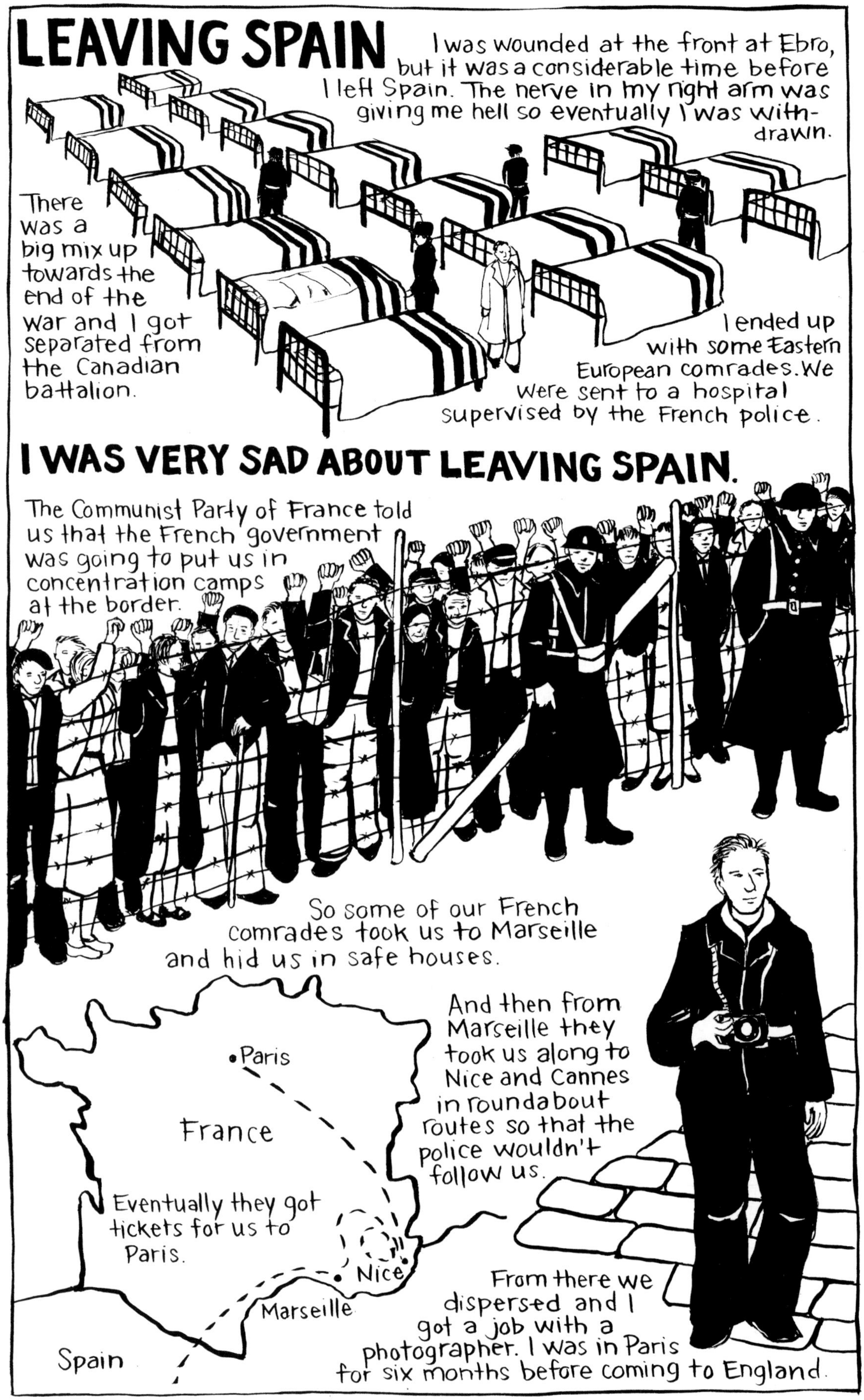
LEAVING SPAIN
I was wounded at the front at Ebro, but it was a considerable time before I left Spain. The nerve in my right arm was giving me hell so eventually I was withdrawn.
There was a big mix up towards the end of the war and I got separated from the Canadian battalion.
I ended up with some Eastern European comrades. We were sent to a hospital supervised by the French police.
I WAS VERY SAD ABOUT LEAVING SPAIN.
The Communist Party of France told us that the French government was going to put us in concentration camps at the border.
So some of our French comrades took us to Marseille and hid us in safe houses.
And then from Marseille they took us along to Nice and Cannes in roundabout routes so that the police wouldn't follow us.
Paris
France
Eventually they got tickets for us to Paris.
Nice
Marseille
Spain
From there we dispersed and I got a job with a photographer. I was in Paris for six months before coming to England.

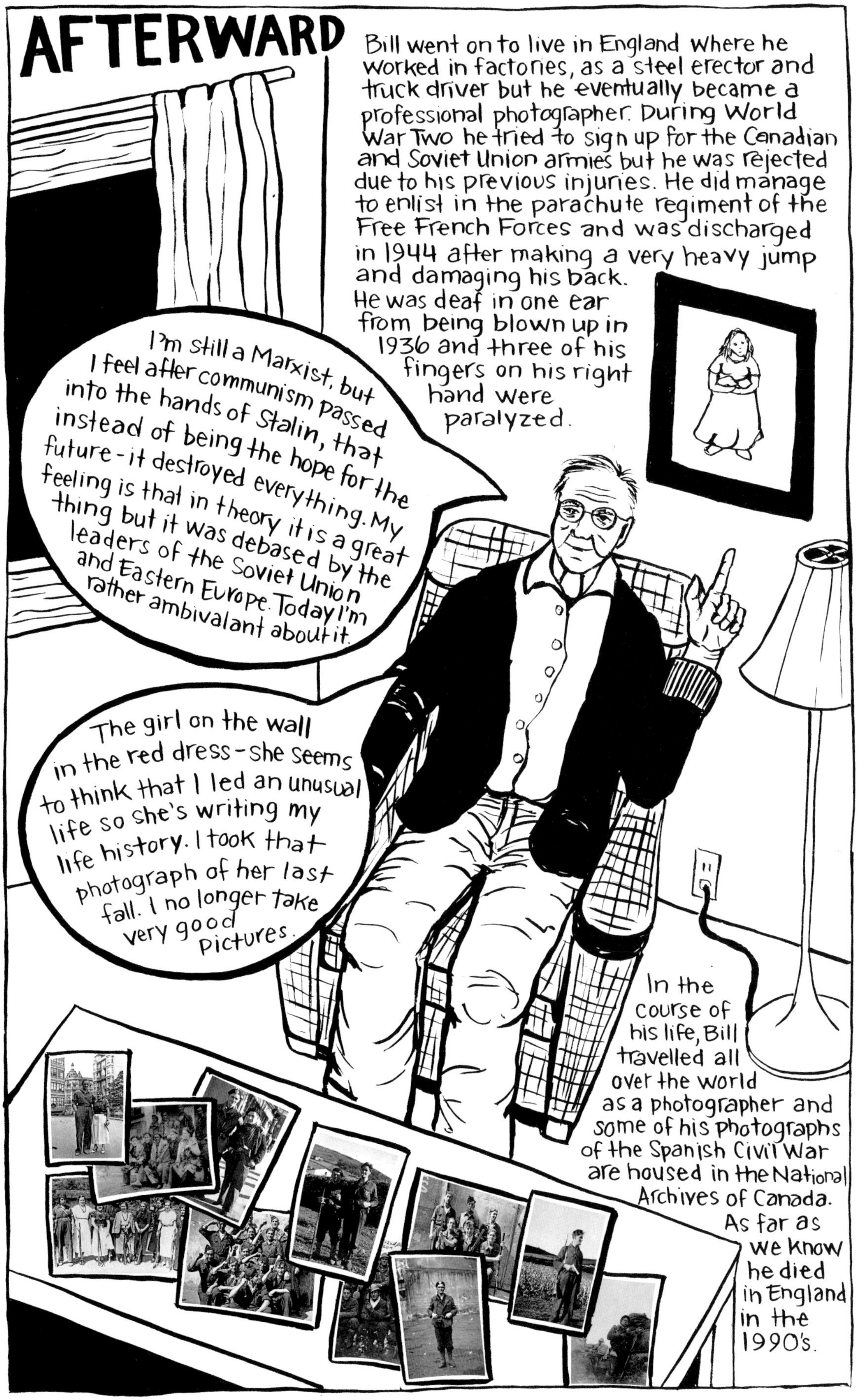
AFTERWARD
Bill went on to live in England where he worked in factories, as a steel erector and truck driver but he eventually became a professional photographer. During World War Two he tried to sign up for the Canadian and Soviet Union armies but he was rejected due to his previous injuries. He did manage to enlist in the parachute regiment of the Free French Forces and was discharged in 1944 after making a very heavy jump and damaging his back.
He was deaf in one ear from being blown up in 1936 and three of his fingers on his right hand were paralyzed.
I'm still a Marxist, but I feel after communism passed into the hands of Stalin, that instead of being the hope for the future - it destroyed everything. My feeling is that in theory it is a great thing but it was debased by the leaders of the Soviet Union and Eastern Europe. Today I'm rather ambivalant about it.
The girl on the wall in the red dress - she seems to think that I led an unusual life so she's writing my life history. I took that photograph of her last fall. I no longer take very good pictures.
In the course of his life, Bill travelled all over the world as a photographer and some of his photographs of the Spanish Civil War are housed in the National Archives of Canada.
As far as we know he died in England in the 1990's.

Acknowledgements

Thank you to David Cunningham for ideas, inspiration, and trips to the archives. Thank you to the Graphic History Collective for all their work on the Graphic History Project, and especially to Sean Carleton for editing and encouragement.

Notes

This story is based on two letters Bill Williamson wrote in the early 1980s that are housed in the Library Archives of Canada in Ottawa (there is also a copy of one of the letters in the Rare Books and Special Collections Division of the University of British Columbia) and two interviews he did with the Imperial War Museum in London, U.K., in 1990. I transcribed some of the audio interviews and combined them with the content of the letters. The words are Bill's, but I have edited them for clarity and for the purpose of the story.

I also consulted many books on Soviet film poster design and tried to incorporate some of the design elements into my pages.

Title Page (Page 65): The background photo is one Bill Williamson took of his comrades during the Spanish Civil War. It is from the Mackenzie-Papineau Battalion collection, R2609-0-0-E, Library and Archives Canada (LAC). The image of Bill is based on another photo from the same collection. The design is inspired by Soviet film posters.

Page 66: Winnipeg. The image of houses is inspired by a photo of Winnipeg streets from Virtual Heritage Winnipeg, www.virtual.heritagewinnipeg. com; a photo from the Archives of Manitoba in Winnipeg; and photos in the Houses and Housing Photo Archive on website of the Manitoba Historical Society, www.mhs.mb.ca/docs/features/timelinks/ imageref/imageref21.shtml. The image of the train yard is inspired by a photo of the Winnipeg Train Yard from The Winnipeg Free Press, www. winnipegfreepress.com/opinion/fyi/bridge-over-troubled-yards-161537775.html.

Page 68: Sydney, Australia. The bottom image is inspired by the poster for Sergei M. Eisenstein's 1925 film, Battleship Potemkin.

Page 69: Battleship Potemkin. All images are inspired by screenshots from Battleship Potemkin.

Bill is referring to Eduard Tisse who was Sergei Eisenstein's cinematographer for many films, including Strike (1924), Battleship Potemkin (1925), October (1928), and ¡Que viva México! (1937).

Page 70: Shanghai, 1932. The historical images of Shanghai are inspired by "Shanghai," Wikipedia, http://en.wikipedia.org/wiki/History_of_Shanghai. You can view the actual park sign that was at the entrance of Huangpu Park online, "Huangpu Park," Wikipedia, http://en.wikipedia.org/wiki/Huangpu_Park.

Page 71: Relief Camps. There are a series of images of the Halifax Relief Camp in Relief Projects No. 1, Canada. Dept. of National Defence, LAC, PA-034516. There is even a photo of Bill in the background of one of the photos.

Page 73: Greasing the Tracks. This page is inspired by a Soviet film poster designed by Georgii and Vladimir Stenberg. More film posters can be viewed at The Guardian, www.theguardian.com/film/gallery/2014/jan/05/silent-cinema-soviet-film-posters-russia?picture=426158824.

Page 75: The Relief Workers Strike. The demonstration is based on a photo from the Saskatchewan Archives that took place before the Regina Riot. The image of the train was inspired by one from The Winnipeg Free Press, http://media.winnipegfreepress.com/images/4980114.jpg.

Page 76: Regina. Images of the On-to-Ottawa Trekkers, www.ontoottawa.ca. The image of R.B. Bennett is based on a photo from The Toronto Star, www.thestar.com/news/canada/2009/03/15/letters_of_desperation_to_a_prime_minister.html.

Page 77: The Regina Riot. The photos of the Regina Riot come from "Regina the Early Years," Saskatchewan Archival Information Network, http://scaa.usask.ca/gallery/regina/central/riot.html. Additional images of the riot and the trek can be found here: http://1935reginariot.blogspot.ca/p/photographs_23.html.

Page 78: Escape from Regina. The image of the stadium is in Bill Waiser, All Hell Can't Stop Us: The On-to-Ottawa Trek and Regina Riot (Calgary: Fifth House, 2003).

Page 79: Onward to Spain. The middle image is inspired by an image of a celebration in Madrid when people heard of the Popular Front victory: http://arlequinsworld.blogspot.ca/2013/07/the-spanish-civil-war-1936-election.html.

Page 81: Arrival in Spain. The top image is inspired by screenshots from *Battleship Potemkin* and from a photo in Raymond Carr's book *Images of the Spanish Civil War* (New York: W.W. Norton & Company, 1989). The bottom image is inspired by the photo, "Tripulació del creuer Libertad de la flota republicana. c. 1936–1937" in *Guerra I Propaganda*.

Page 82: First Day in Spain.

Acronyms:

FAI = Federación Anarquista Ibérica (Iberian Anarchist Federation)

CNT = Confederación Nacional del Trabajo (National Confederation of Labour), a confederation of anarcho-syndicalist labour unions

UHP = Uníos Hermanos Proletarios (United Brothers of the Proletariat)

UGT = Unión General de Trabajadores (General Union of Workers), a major trade union

JSU = Juventudes Socialistas Unificadas (Unified Socialist Youth), a youth organization

The image of Bill and the militia woman is inspired by a photo by Bill: "Bill and Conchita (a militia woman)," Library and Archives Canada. The CNT truck is based on a photo from *Images of the Spanish Civil War*. The streetcars and trains are inspired by a poster by Sindicato Unico Ramo Transporte: "CNT, FAI, AIT Servicios Publicos Urbanos," in *Images of the Spanish Civil War*, p. 67.

Page 83: Fighting in San Sebastian. The image of the militia women is inspired by a photo by Bill: "Columna Ochandiano. Julio 1936. [Group of women holding rifles]," Library and Archives Canada. The image of the convoy is inspired by a photo in the book, *Imágenes inéditas de La Guerra Civil Española (1936–1939)* (Agencia EFE, 2002). The fighters at the barricades are based on the photo "Workers manning the street barricades during the fighting on 19-20 July," in *Images of the Spanish Civil War*, p. 53.

Page 84: Pancho Villa and Friends. The font for the title is based on a film poster for the film *Viva Villa*, starring Wallace Beery. The image of Los Tres P's is a based on a photo by Bill, "Three comrades—

Batallion Perezagoa," Library and Archives Canada. The image of Dolores is also based on a photo by Bill, "Dolores and Carmen—young communists—Dolores was killed two months later." The middle image is based on the photo "Militiawoman and men in the Aragon hills; probably a posed picture," in *Images of the Spanish Civil War*.

Page 86: Guernica. The tree with the memorial is based on a photo by Bill, "Return to Pat [View of grave by tree]." The images of Guernica are from the books *Imágenes inéditas de La Guerra Civil Española*; *La guerra de España en sus fotografías* (Ediciones Marte, 1966); *The Italian Airforce in Spain: 40 Photographs Taken by Mussolini's Observers* (London: United Editorial). English booklet attacking Italian military involvement in Spain. *Images of the Spanish Civil War*

Page 87: The International Brigades. The image of the Pyrenees references the photo "Refugees making their way across the Pyrenees to France," in *Images of the Spanish Civil War*.

Page 88: The Battalions. The top image references a photo by Bill, "Soldier of the Mackenzie-Papineau Battalion in a trench," Library and Archives Canada. The Lincoln-Washington Battalion image is also based on a photo by Bill (though it is captioned "Members of the Mackenzie-Papineau Battalion in the Spanish Civil War"). The Mackenzie-Papineau Battalion is based on the photo "Group photo of Mackenzie-Papineau Battalion, 1837–1937 posing with banner and gun," Library and Archives Canada.

Page 90: Leaving Spain. The concentration camp image references a Getty Image photo, "Pre-World War II, 8th February 1939, Argeles-sur-Mer, France, Spanish refugee soldiers behind a barbed wire enclosure at an internment camp, after their escape into France from Catalonia."

Page 91: Afterward. All these photos are from Library and Archives Canada, and I believe they were taken by Bill. Clockwise from the top left:

"Bill and Conchita (a militia woman)"

"Members of the Mackenzie-Papineau Battalion in the Spanish Civil War"

"Augusto 1936, San Sebastian [two men standing on a street in San Sebastian, Spain]"

"Czech comrade and myself "

"Irun. July 1936 [Group of six posing with rifles]"

"EWW [Juan villa. Fall 1936]"

"Soldier of the Mackenzie-Papineau Batallion in a
 trench"

"San Sebastian, Guipuzcoa. Sept. 1936 [young man
 standing in front of a building]"

"Williamson—2nd from Left. Standing—BTN
 Perezagua. [the two men identified are posing with
 five other men; all have rifles in hand]"

"July and into August 1936 in Irun [group portrait]"

"Columna Ochandiano. Julio 1936. [Group of women
 holding rifles]"

Coal Mountain
The 1935 Corbin Miners' Strike

Holding the Line in Corbin
Ron Verzuh

In *Coal Mountain: The 1935 Corbin Miners' Strike*, artist and author Nicole Marie Burton proves that Canada's labour history is anything but boring. By bringing to life an incident in British Columbia's past that has been obscured for too long, Burton takes a sympathetic yet conscientious approach to her task, one that historian Bryan D. Palmer has described as enabling the labour and social historian to "glimpse the tenacity of common people struggling against increasingly harsh realities."

In that spirit of deep understanding and in stunning detail, Burton tells the story of Corbin, a company town built in the early 1900s by Daniel Chase Corbin of Spokane, Washington, a prospector, railway builder, and founder of the Corbin Coal and Coke Company. As Burton shows with her powerful images and terse narrative, the people of Corbin had big hearts in the 1930s and they needed them to cope with the poor living and working conditions that Corbin offered its workers.

In another innovative approach to recounting labour history, Burton chooses as her narrator a young girl named Gracie to relate descriptions of those conditions. Based partly on the recollections of Grace Roe, a woman who once lived in Corbin, this literary device adds an intimacy to the Corbin story. Drawing on interviews with Grace Roe, Burton looks at history through "a different set of eyes," offering us Gracie's view of the tragic events that led to one of the Canadian mining industry's most brutal attempts to break a strike.

With her stark images of the lives of the miners and their families living in the Crowsnest Pass area of British Columbia, Burton transforms an important event in Canada's labour history into a moving visual documentary, making it come alive with pictures and text.

In her memoir *Right Hand Left Hand*, celebrated Canadian poet Dorothy Livesay also vividly recounts what happened. To illustrate the scene, she quotes one of the strike leaders: "The womenfolk were grouped in the middle and some were up front. Suddenly, as at a signal, the full detachment of police ran out from the hotel and grouped themselves in two squads on either side of the caterpillar, flanking the picket line....Before we could understand anything the caterpillar was moving forward, straight at our women." Seventy-five years later, in 2010, a report in the *People's Voice* reminded readers that "the legs of several women were crushed, and one woman was dragged 300 feet by the bulldozer. Another had to be hospitalized after the machine's blade tore the flesh from her legs. A pregnant woman lost her unborn child after being clubbed across the shoulders and her abdomen."

As Burton explains, fifty people were hurt, including fourteen police officers, and seventeen strikers were arrested, but the mine in Corbin stayed closed. The struggle continued for many months and the company's unconscionable behavior was broadly exposed by labour-friendly politicians like Tom Uphill.

Historian Allen Seager notes that the events at Corbin had "an electric effect" in Blairmore, Alberta, where militant members of the Mine Workers' Union of Canada (MWUC) adopted the radical outlook of the Communist-sponsored Workers' Unity League (WUL). Disgusted with the violent way the Corbin company had responded to the strikers, the MWUC sent money and other forms of support to strikers and their families.

MWUC leaders also led a march uphill for sixteen kilometres to reach the town, singing the great labour anthems of the day, including "The Red Flag," "The Internationale," and Joe Hill's "The

Preacher and the Slave." What they saw when they arrived in the strike-torn and defeated camp was a town that one strike leader described as struck by "police terror."

The WUL's Harvey Murphy, who organized the march, described the aftermath: "The doctor was out of medicine, and all kinds of people were hurt...There was just this narrow roadway and the police had this wired. That's why the doctor was out of medicine for these injured women. They were locked in, and the R.C.M.P. was in charge.... And it was only when we got through that we got those people out of their houses." Secret police reports record the efforts of Murphy and other MWUC leaders to rally the unemployed and miners in Southern Alberta to support the Corbin strikers as they would do for many strikes in the mines and metal smelters of B.C. and Alberta. But despite these attempts, the miners of Coal Mountain eventually moved away to look for work elsewhere.

The company town of Corbin, once boasting a population of six hundred souls, was abandoned in the early 1950s and became an almost forgotten ghost town. Some traditional historians might consider the Corbin coal strike a failure. After all, in its assessment of the dispute, the *Labour Gazette* of June 1935 concluded that "a number of strikers were charged with assault, creating a disturbance on a public highway, and impeding police in the discharge of duty." It further reported that "nine were sentenced to terms in jail of three and six months and thirteen were fined. Appeals from the jail sentences were entered in some cases and the convicted men released on bail."

Others might assess the outcome of the bitter strike in less clinical terms, perhaps seeing what Burton sees: a struggle deserving of our attention because it points to the valour and determination of men and women who were willing to hold the line in their fight for the right to earn a decent living, to not back down.

Historian Irene Howard numbered the Corbin women among "militant participants in labour struggles" in B.C. In her account of the activities of the Mothers' Council of Vancouver, she saw them as akin to the Chartist women in the Great Britain of the 1830s, or the women of the Paris Commune of 1871, or the "revolutionary sisters" of the famed Bread and Roses strike of textile workers in Lawrence, Massachusetts, in 1912. One could easily add the monumental women's victory in the early 1950s during a violent New Mexico miners' strike as depicted in the banned film *Salt of the Earth*.

Like these and other powerful historical occurrences, the Corbin strike should be recognized and celebrated rather than, as Howard remarks, "omitted from 'official' history." Instead of being jettisoned as insignificant, that story deserves to be told, and what better lens through which to view it than Gracie's eyes?

Now with *Coal Mountain* we can do precisely that. By revisiting the tragic events of 1935 through Burton's depiction of the lives of the Corbin miners and their families, we can take a graphic tour of their struggle and witness the courageous actions of the men and women of this company town eighty years ago. Thanks to Burton, Corbin takes its proper place in labour history as a symbol of resistance to oppressive employers everywhere.

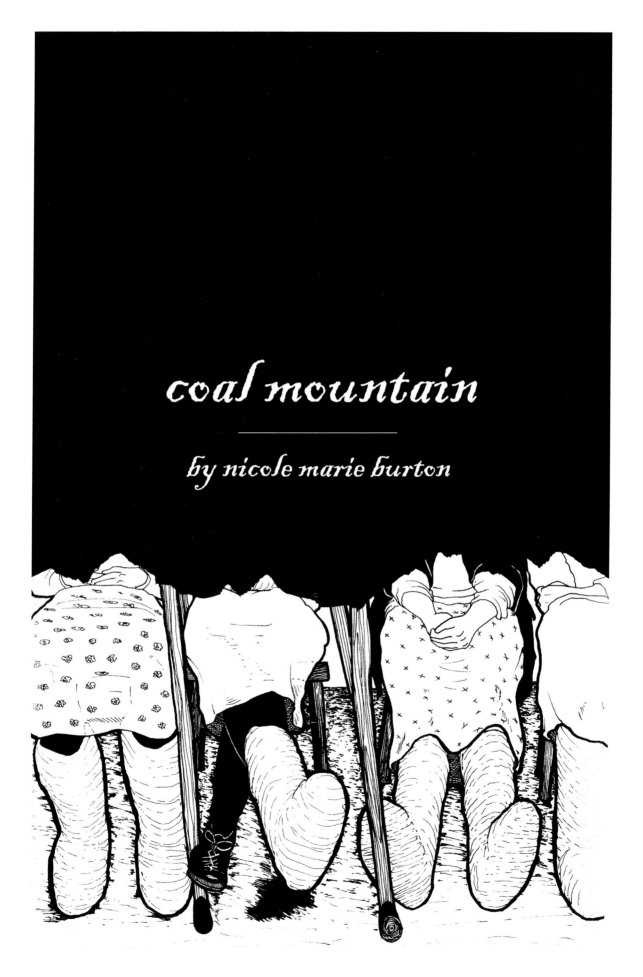

coal mountain

by nicole marie burton

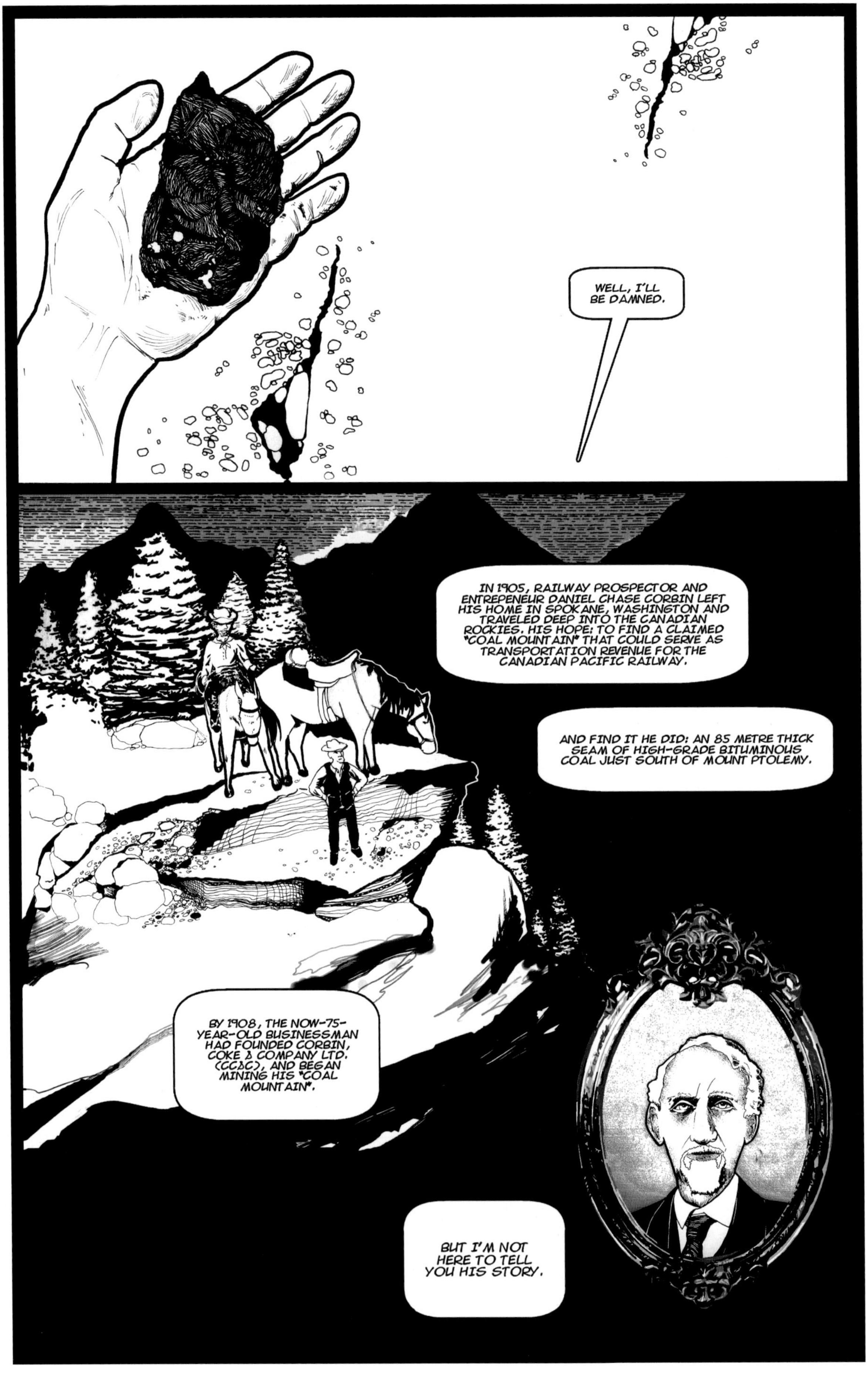
WELL, I'LL BE DAMNED.
IN 1905, RAILWAY PROSPECTOR AND ENTREPENEUR DANIEL CHASE CORBIN LEFT HIS HOME IN SPOKANE, WASHINGTON AND TRAVELED DEEP INTO THE CANADIAN ROCKIES. HIS HOPE: TO FIND A CLAIMED "COAL MOUNTAIN" THAT COULD SERVE AS TRANSPORTATION REVENUE FOR THE CANADIAN PACIFIC RAILWAY.
AND FIND IT HE DID: AN 85 METRE THICK SEAM OF HIGH-GRADE BITUMINOUS COAL JUST SOUTH OF MOUNT PTOLEMY.
BY 1908, THE NOW-75-YEAR-OLD BUSINESSMAN HAD FOUNDED CORBIN, COKE & COMPANY LTD. (CC&C), AND BEGAN MINING HIS "COAL MOUNTAIN".
BUT I'M NOT HERE TO TELL YOU HIS STORY.

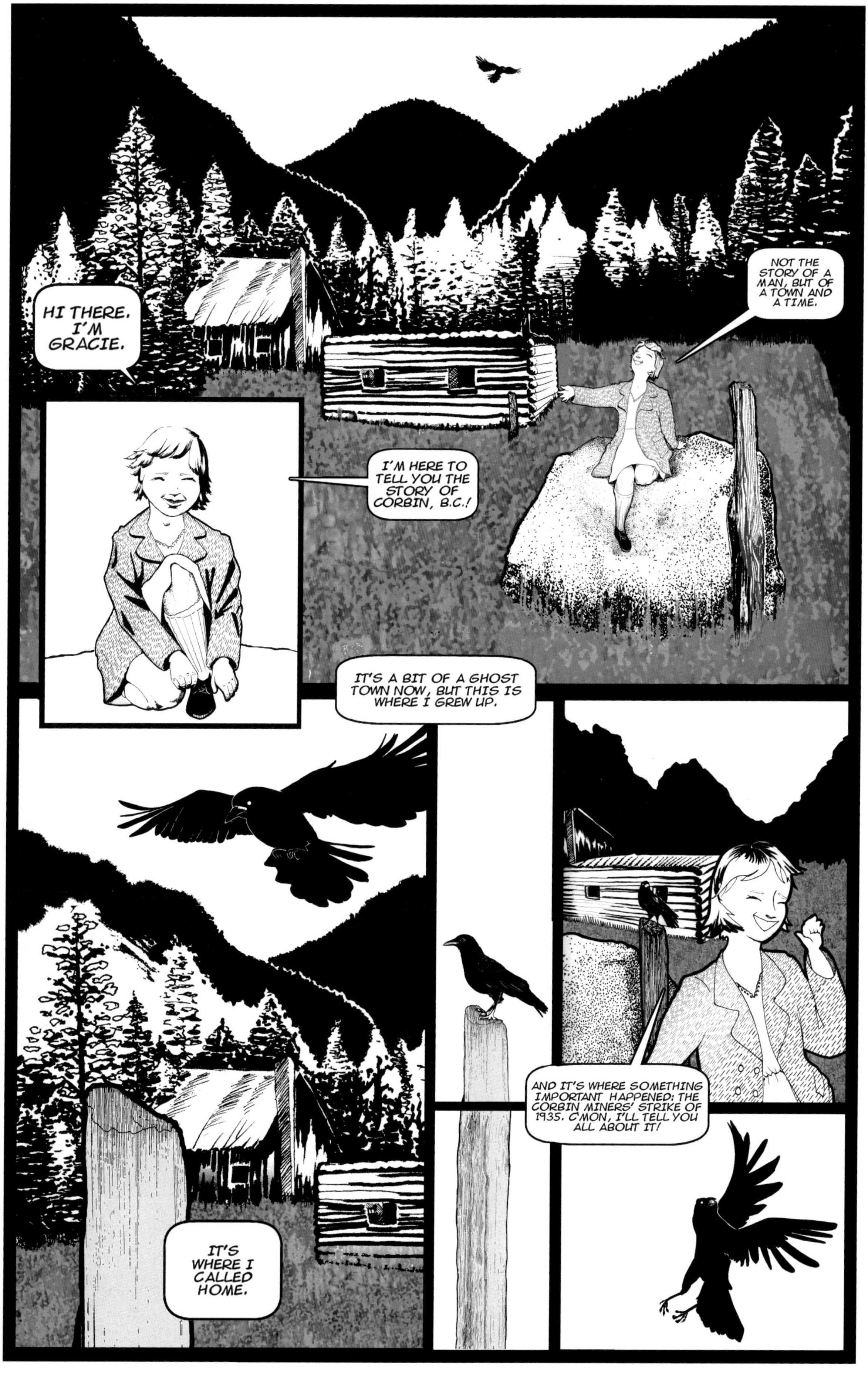
HI THERE. I'M GRACIE.
NOT THE STORY OF A MAN, BUT OF A TOWN AND A TIME.
I'M HERE TO TELL YOU THE STORY OF CORBIN, B.C.!
IT'S A BIT OF A GHOST TOWN NOW, BUT THIS IS WHERE I GREW UP.
IT'S WHERE I CALLED HOME.
AND IT'S WHERE SOMETHING IMPORTANT HAPPENED: THE CORBIN MINERS' STRIKE OF 1935. C'MON, I'LL TELL YOU ALL ABOUT IT!

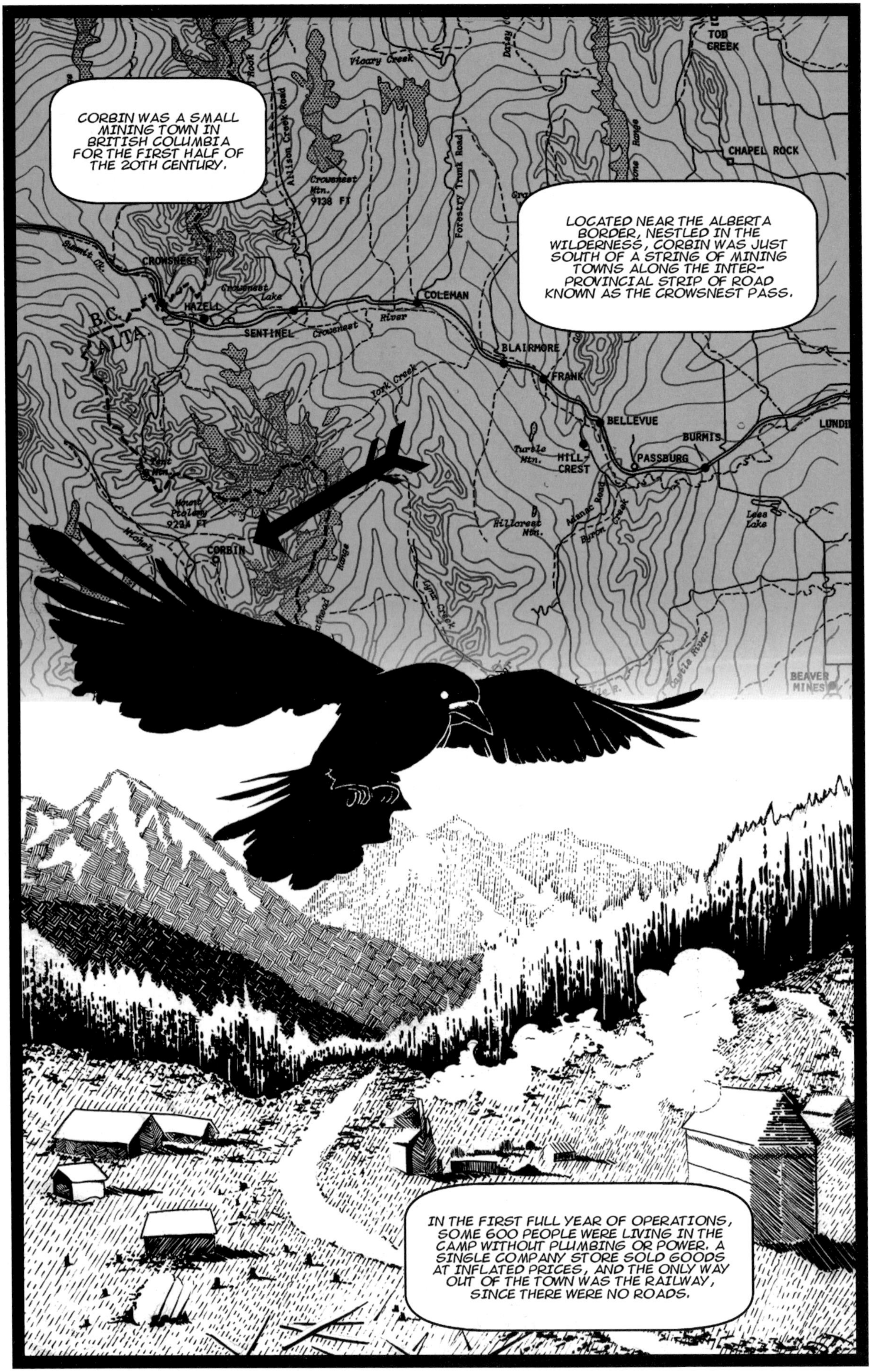
CORBIN WAS A SMALL MINING TOWN IN BRITISH COLUMBIA FOR THE FIRST HALF OF THE 20TH CENTURY.
LOCATED NEAR THE ALBERTA BORDER, NESTLED IN THE WILDERNESS, CORBIN WAS JUST SOUTH OF A STRING OF MINING TOWNS ALONG THE INTER-PROVINCIAL STRIP OF ROAD KNOWN AS THE CROWSNEST PASS.
TOD CREEK
CHAPEL ROCK
CROWSNEST
HAZELL
COLEMAN
SENTINEL
B.C.
ALTA.
BLAIRMORE
FRANK
BELLEVUE
BURMIS
HILL CREST
PASSBURG
CORBIN
BEAVER MINES
IN THE FIRST FULL YEAR OF OPERATIONS, SOME 600 PEOPLE WERE LIVING IN THE CAMP WITHOUT PLUMBING OR POWER. A SINGLE COMPANY STORE SOLD GOODS AT INFLATED PRICES, AND THE ONLY WAY OUT OF THE TOWN WAS THE RAILWAY, SINCE THERE WERE NO ROADS.

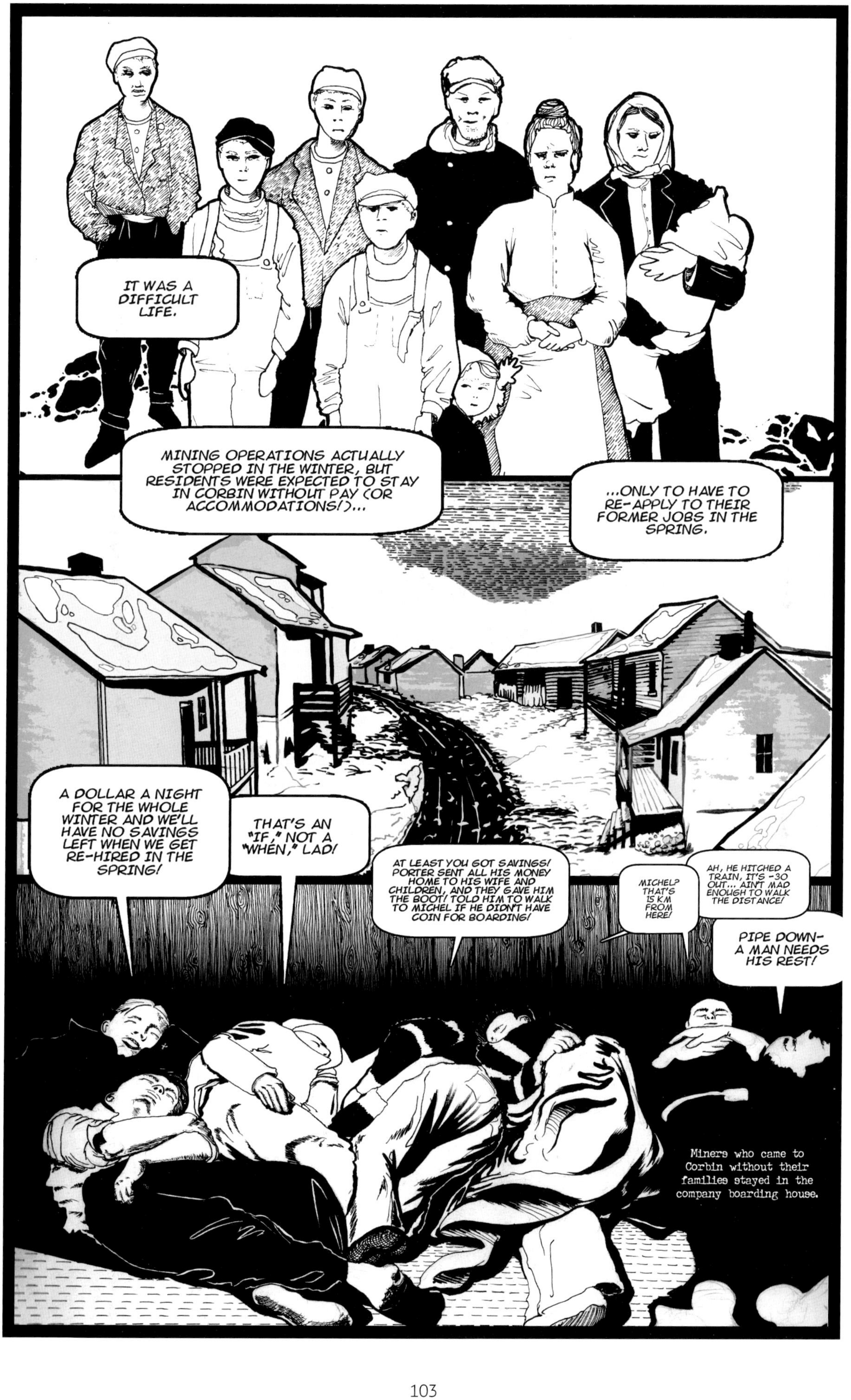
IT WAS A DIFFICULT LIFE.
MINING OPERATIONS ACTUALLY STOPPED IN THE WINTER, BUT RESIDENTS WERE EXPECTED TO STAY IN CORBIN WITHOUT PAY (OR ACCOMMODATIONS!)...
...ONLY TO HAVE TO RE-APPLY TO THEIR FORMER JOBS IN THE SPRING.
A DOLLAR A NIGHT FOR THE WHOLE WINTER AND WE'LL HAVE NO SAVINGS LEFT WHEN WE GET RE-HIRED IN THE SPRING!
THAT'S AN "IF," NOT A "WHEN," LAD!
AT LEAST YOU GOT SAVINGS! PORTER SENT ALL HIS MONEY HOME TO HIS WIFE AND CHILDREN, AND THEY GAVE HIM THE BOOT! TOLD HIM TO WALK TO MICHEL IF HE DIDN'T HAVE COIN FOR BOARDING!
MICHEL? THAT'S 15 KM FROM HERE!
AH, HE HITCHED A TRAIN, IT'S -30 OUT... AIN'T MAD ENOUGH TO WALK THE DISTANCE!
PIPE DOWN- A MAN NEEDS HIS REST!
Miners who came to Corbin without their families stayed in the company boarding house.

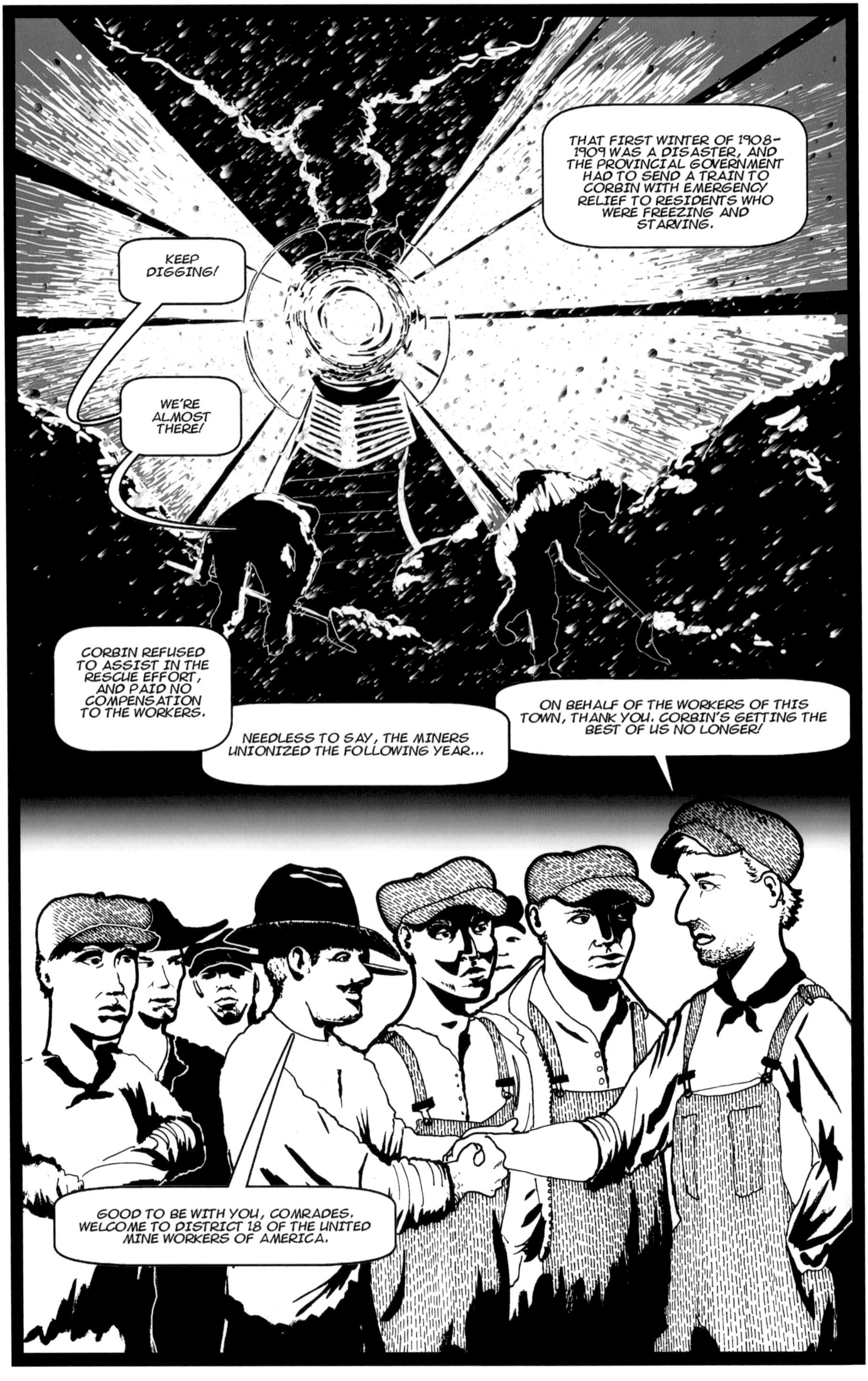
THAT FIRST WINTER OF 1908-1909 WAS A DISASTER, AND THE PROVINCIAL GOVERNMENT HAD TO SEND A TRAIN TO CORBIN WITH EMERGENCY RELIEF TO RESIDENTS WHO WERE FREEZING AND STARVING.
KEEP DIGGING!
WE'RE ALMOST THERE!
CORBIN REFUSED TO ASSIST IN THE RESCUE EFFORT, AND PAID NO COMPENSATION TO THE WORKERS.
NEEDLESS TO SAY, THE MINERS UNIONIZED THE FOLLOWING YEAR...
ON BEHALF OF THE WORKERS OF THIS TOWN, THANK YOU. CORBIN'S GETTING THE BEST OF US NO LONGER!
GOOD TO BE WITH YOU, COMRADES. WELCOME TO DISTRICT 18 OF THE UNITED MINE WORKERS OF AMERICA.

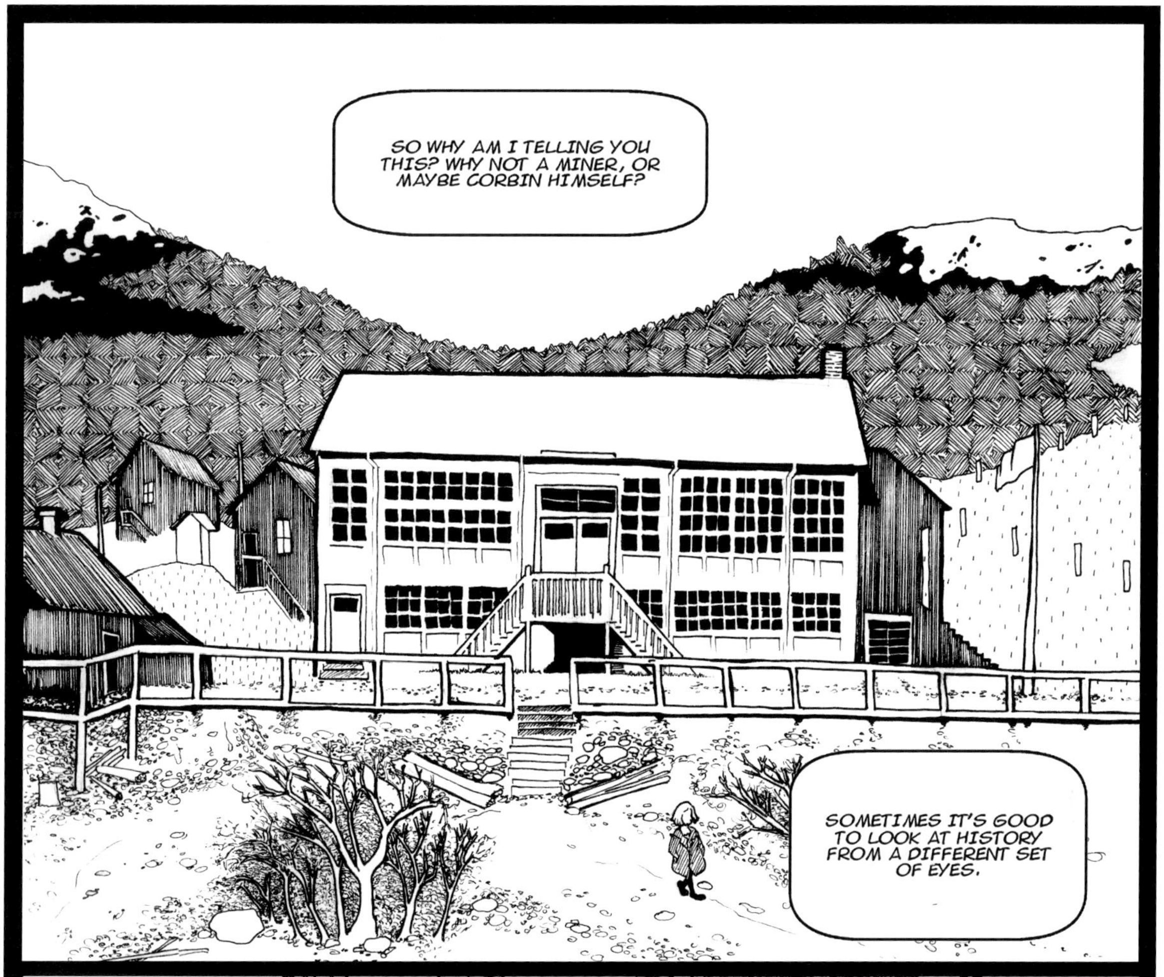
SO WHY AM I TELLING YOU THIS? WHY NOT A MINER, OR MAYBE CORBIN HIMSELF?
SOMETIMES IT'S GOOD TO LOOK AT HISTORY FROM A DIFFERENT SET OF EYES.

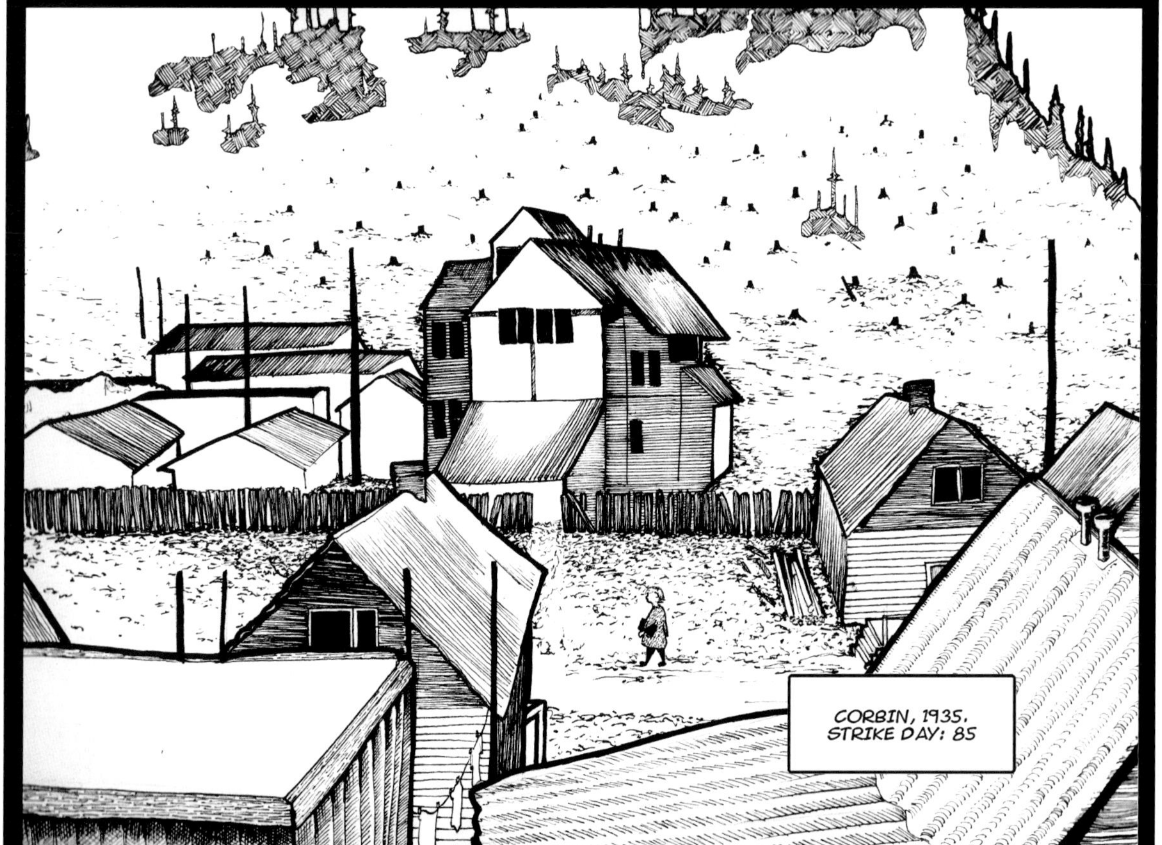
CORBIN, 1935. STRIKE DAY: 85

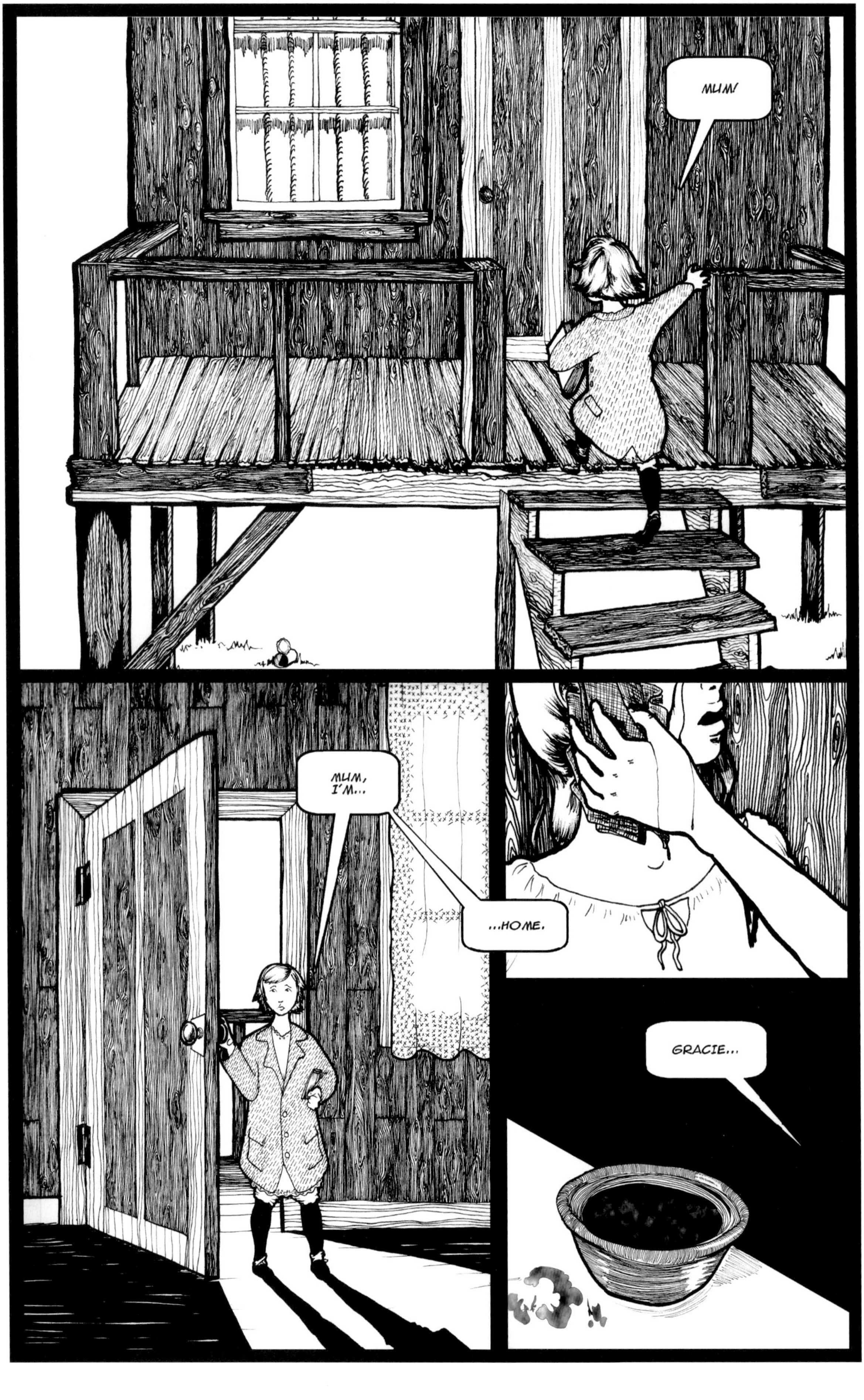
MUM!
MUM, I'M...
...HOME.
GRACIE...

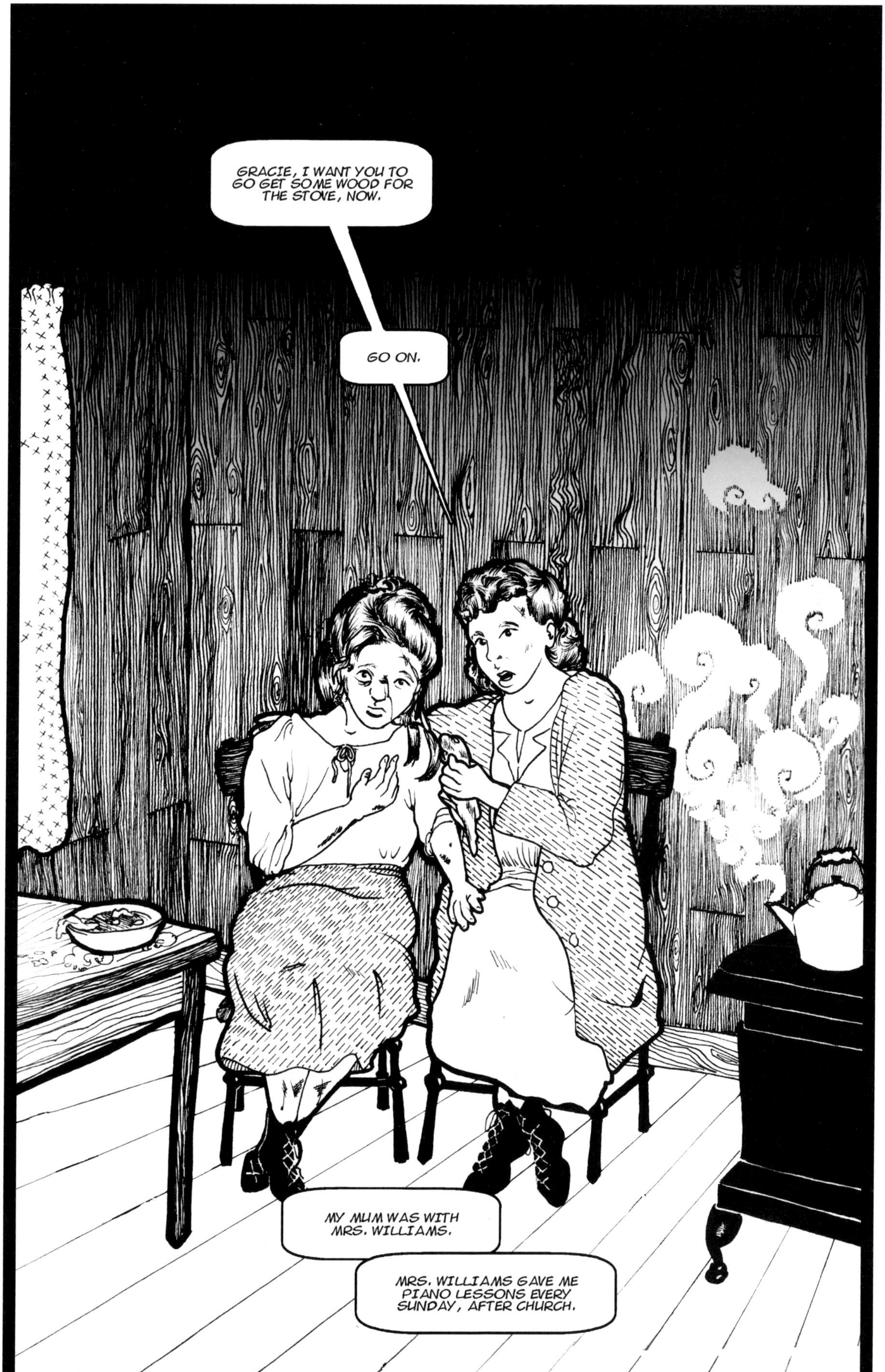
GRACIE, I WANT YOU TO GO GET SOME WOOD FOR THE STOVE, NOW.
GO ON.
MY MUM WAS WITH MRS. WILLIAMS.
MRS. WILLIAMS GAVE ME PIANO LESSONS EVERY SUNDAY, AFTER CHURCH.

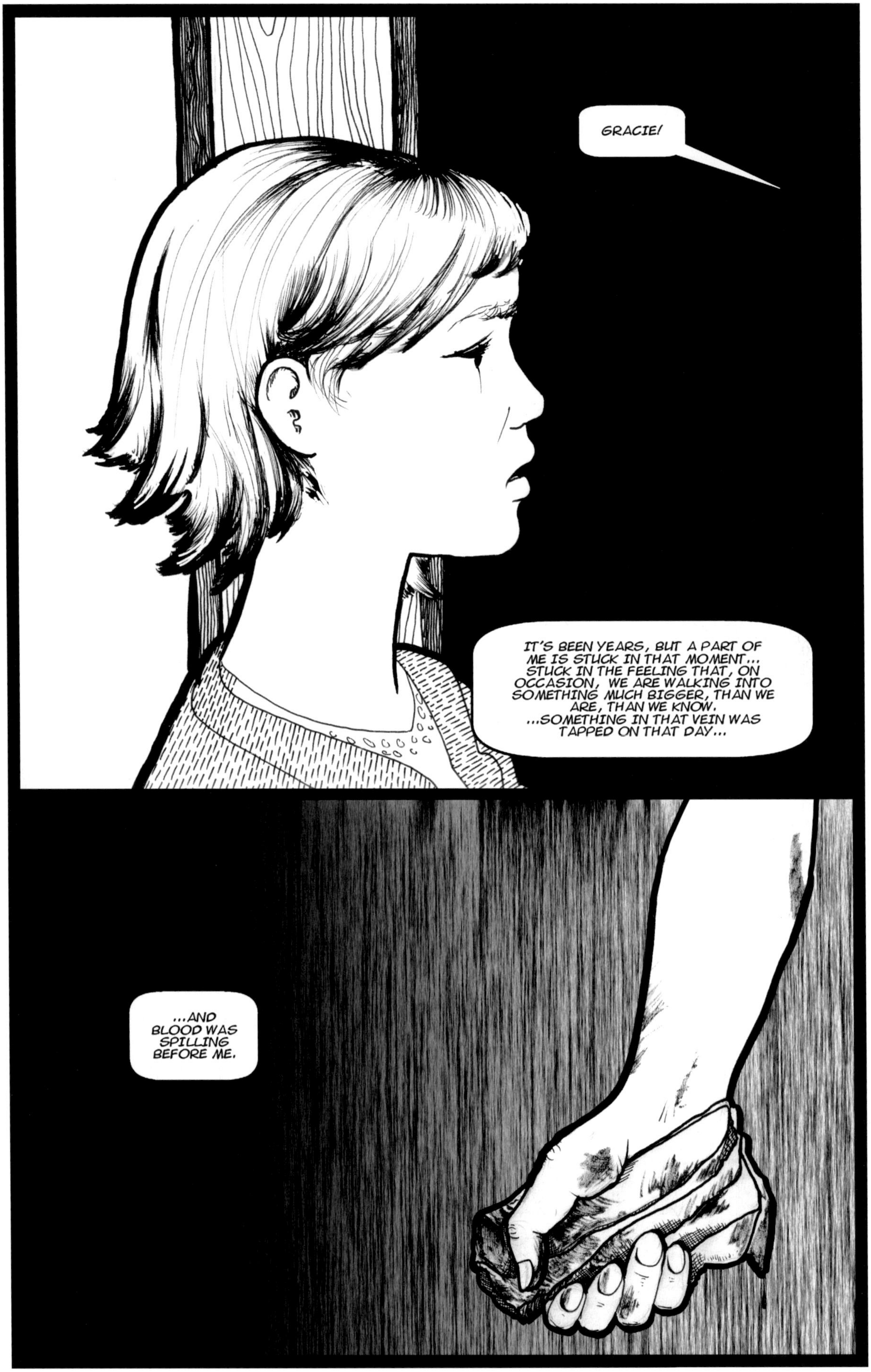
GRACIE!
IT'S BEEN YEARS, BUT A PART OF ME IS STUCK IN THAT MOMENT... STUCK IN THE FEELING THAT, ON OCCASION, WE ARE WALKING INTO SOMETHING MUCH BIGGER, THAN WE ARE, THAN WE KNOW. ...SOMETHING IN THAT VEIN WAS TAPPED ON THAT DAY...
...AND BLOOD WAS SPILLING BEFORE ME.

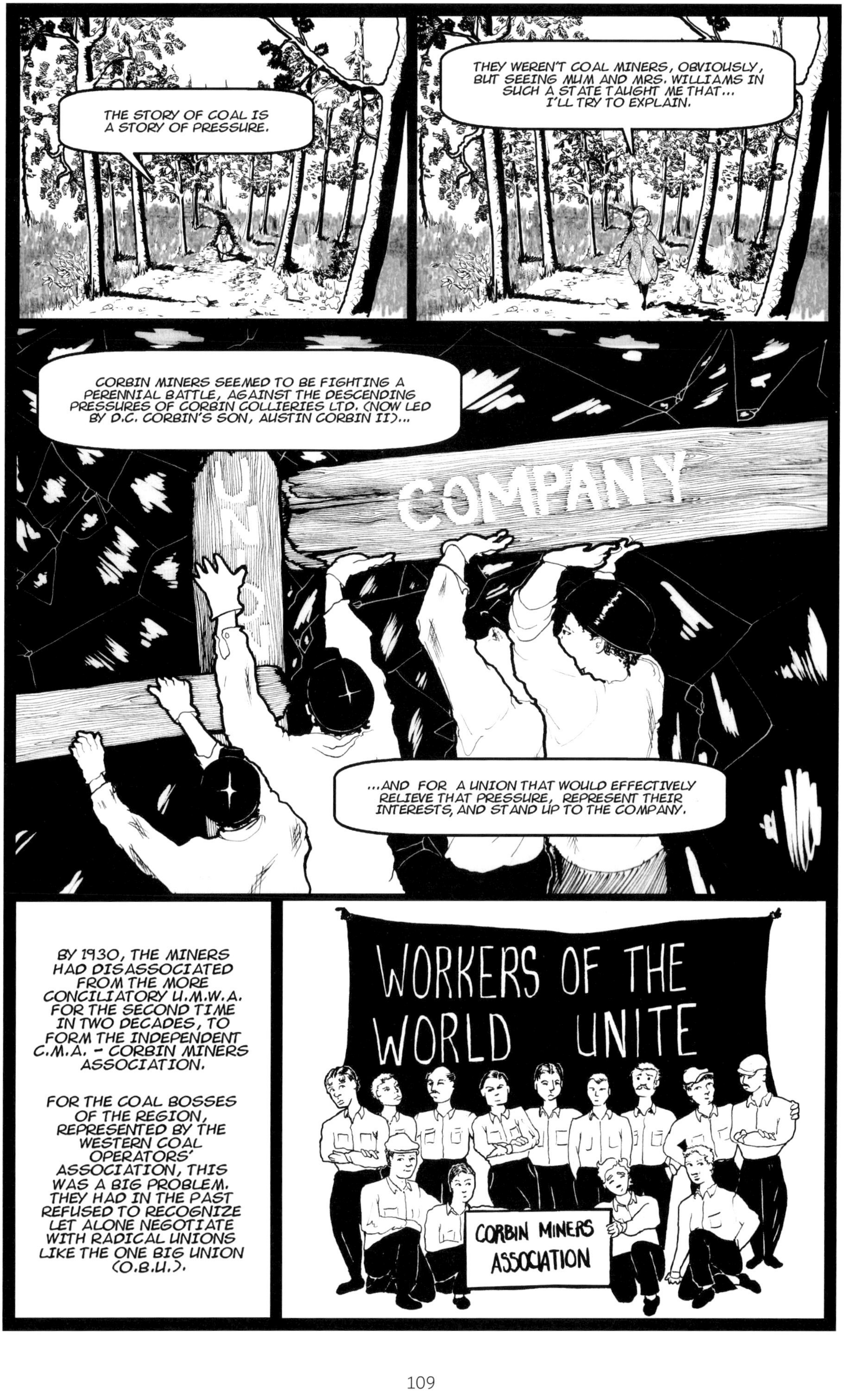
THE STORY OF COAL IS A STORY OF PRESSURE.
THEY WEREN'T COAL MINERS, OBVIOUSLY, BUT SEEING MUM AND MRS. WILLIAMS IN SUCH A STATE TAUGHT ME THAT... I'LL TRY TO EXPLAIN.
CORBIN MINERS SEEMED TO BE FIGHTING A PERENNIAL BATTLE, AGAINST THE DESCENDING PRESSURES OF CORBIN COLLIERIES LTD. (NOW LED BY D.C. CORBIN'S SON, AUSTIN CORBIN II)...
COMPANY
UNION
...AND FOR A UNION THAT WOULD EFFECTIVELY RELIEVE THAT PRESSURE, REPRESENT THEIR INTERESTS, AND STAND UP TO THE COMPANY.
BY 1930, THE MINERS HAD DISASSOCIATED FROM THE MORE CONCILIATORY U.M.W.A. FOR THE SECOND TIME IN TWO DECADES, TO FORM THE INDEPENDENT C.M.A. - CORBIN MINERS ASSOCIATION.
FOR THE COAL BOSSES OF THE REGION, REPRESENTED BY THE WESTERN COAL OPERATORS' ASSOCIATION, THIS WAS A BIG PROBLEM. THEY HAD IN THE PAST REFUSED TO RECOGNIZE LET ALONE NEGOTIATE WITH RADICAL UNIONS LIKE THE ONE BIG UNION (O.B.U.).
WORKERS OF THE WORLD UNITE
CORBIN MINERS ASSOCIATION

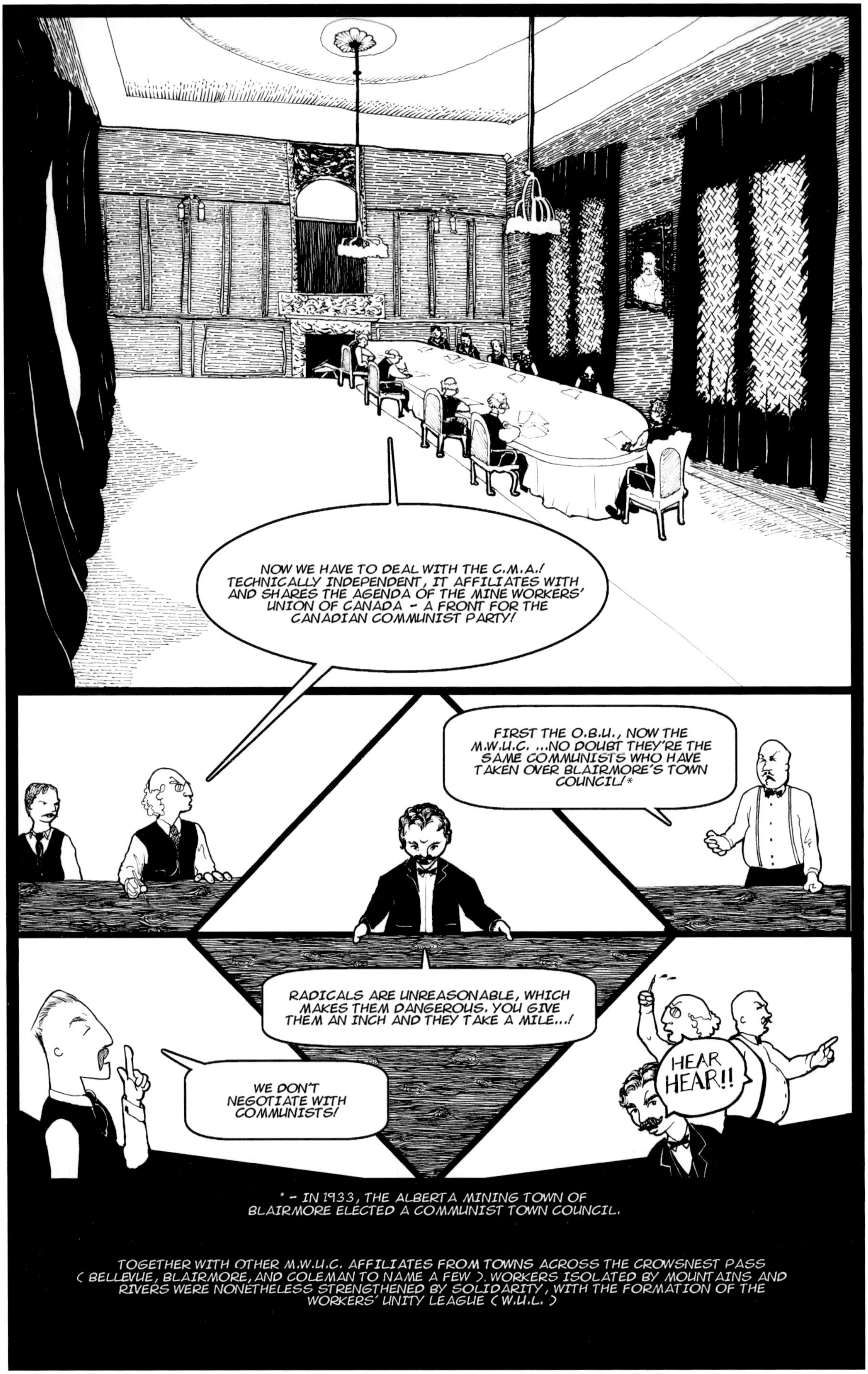
NOW WE HAVE TO DEAL WITH THE C.M.A.! TECHNICALLY INDEPENDENT, IT AFFILIATES WITH AND SHARES THE AGENDA OF THE MINE WORKERS' UNION OF CANADA - A FRONT FOR THE CANADIAN COMMUNIST PARTY!
FIRST THE O.B.U., NOW THE M.W.U.C. ...NO DOUBT THEY'RE THE SAME COMMUNISTS WHO HAVE TAKEN OVER BLAIRMORE'S TOWN COUNCIL!*
RADICALS ARE UNREASONABLE, WHICH MAKES THEM DANGEROUS. YOU GIVE THEM AN INCH AND THEY TAKE A MILE...!
WE DON'T NEGOTIATE WITH COMMUNISTS!
HEAR HEAR!!
* - IN 1933, THE ALBERTA MINING TOWN OF BLAIRMORE ELECTED A COMMUNIST TOWN COUNCIL.
TOGETHER WITH OTHER M.W.U.C. AFFILIATES FROM TOWNS ACROSS THE CROWSNEST PASS (BELLEVUE, BLAIRMORE, AND COLEMAN TO NAME A FEW), WORKERS ISOLATED BY MOUNTAINS AND RIVERS WERE NONETHELESS STRENGTHENED BY SOLIDARITY, WITH THE FORMATION OF THE WORKERS' UNITY LEAGUE (W.U.L.)

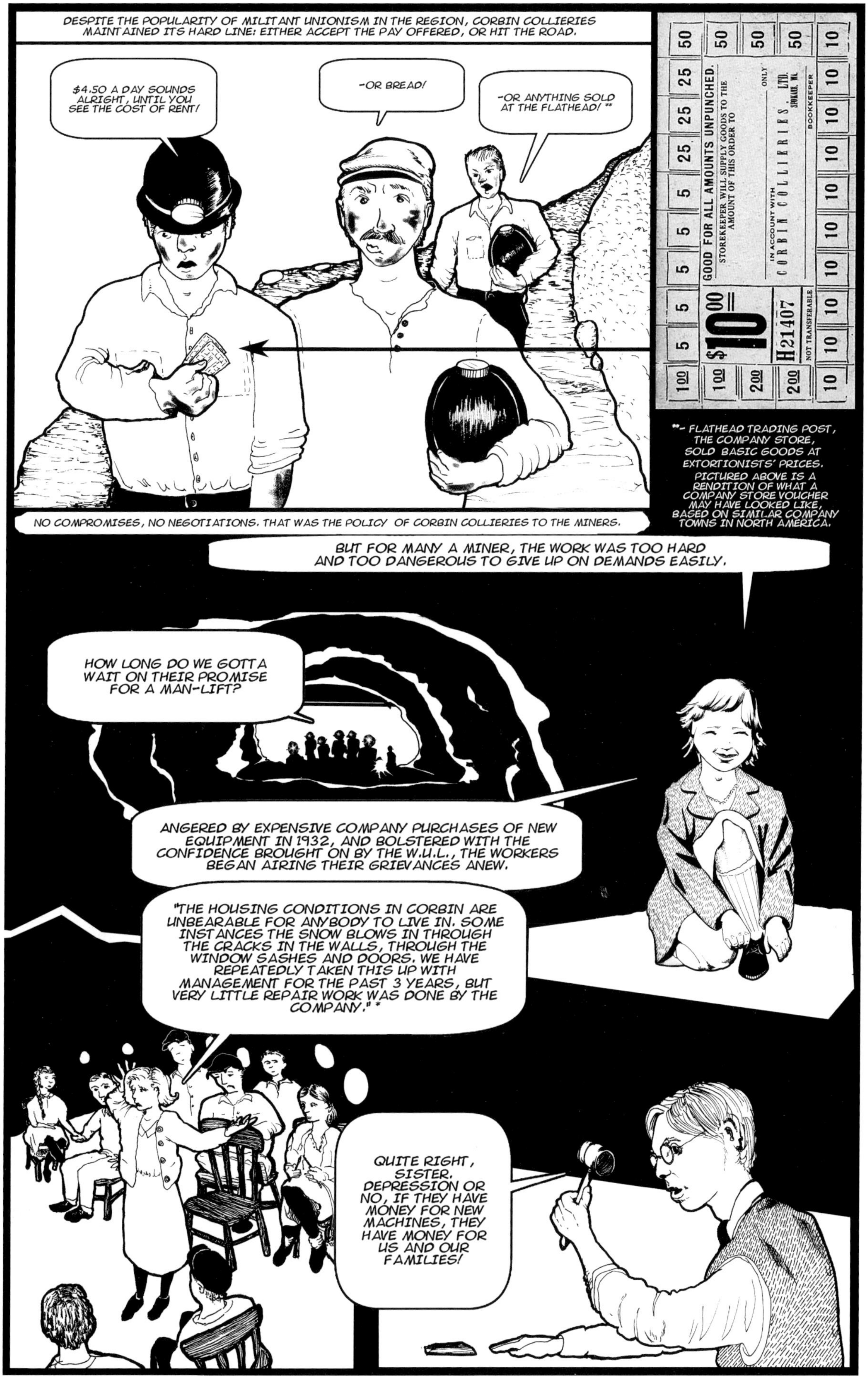
DESPITE THE POPULARITY OF MILITANT UNIONISM IN THE REGION, CORBIN COLLIERIES MAINTAINED ITS HARD LINE: EITHER ACCEPT THE PAY OFFERED, OR HIT THE ROAD.
$4.50 A DAY SOUNDS ALRIGHT, UNTIL YOU SEE THE COST OF RENT!
-OR BREAD!
-OR ANYTHING SOLD AT THE FLATHEAD! **
GOOD FOR ALL AMOUNTS UNPUNCHED.
STOREKEEPER WILL SUPPLY GOODS TO THE AMOUNT OF THIS ORDER TO
ONLY
IN ACCOUNT WITH CORBIN COLLIERIES, LTD.
BOOKKEEPER
$10.00
H21407
NOT TRANSFERABLE
NO COMPROMISES, NO NEGOTIATIONS. THAT WAS THE POLICY OF CORBIN COLLIERIES TO THE MINERS.
**- FLATHEAD TRADING POST, THE COMPANY STORE, SOLD BASIC GOODS AT EXTORTIONISTS' PRICES. PICTURED ABOVE IS A RENDITION OF WHAT A COMPANY STORE VOUCHER MAY HAVE LOOKED LIKE, BASED ON SIMILAR COMPANY TOWNS IN NORTH AMERICA.
BUT FOR MANY A MINER, THE WORK WAS TOO HARD AND TOO DANGEROUS TO GIVE UP ON DEMANDS EASILY.
HOW LONG DO WE GOTTA WAIT ON THEIR PROMISE FOR A MAN-LIFT?
ANGERED BY EXPENSIVE COMPANY PURCHASES OF NEW EQUIPMENT IN 1932, AND BOLSTERED WITH THE CONFIDENCE BROUGHT ON BY THE W.U.L., THE WORKERS BEGAN AIRING THEIR GRIEVANCES ANEW.
"THE HOUSING CONDITIONS IN CORBIN ARE UNBEARABLE FOR ANYBODY TO LIVE IN. SOME INSTANCES THE SNOW BLOWS IN THROUGH THE CRACKS IN THE WALLS, THROUGH THE WINDOW SASHES AND DOORS. WE HAVE REPEATEDLY TAKEN THIS UP WITH MANAGEMENT FOR THE PAST 3 YEARS, BUT VERY LITTLE REPAIR WORK WAS DONE BY THE COMPANY." *
QUITE RIGHT, SISTER. DEPRESSION OR NO, IF THEY HAVE MONEY FOR NEW MACHINES, THEY HAVE MONEY FOR US AND OUR FAMILIES!

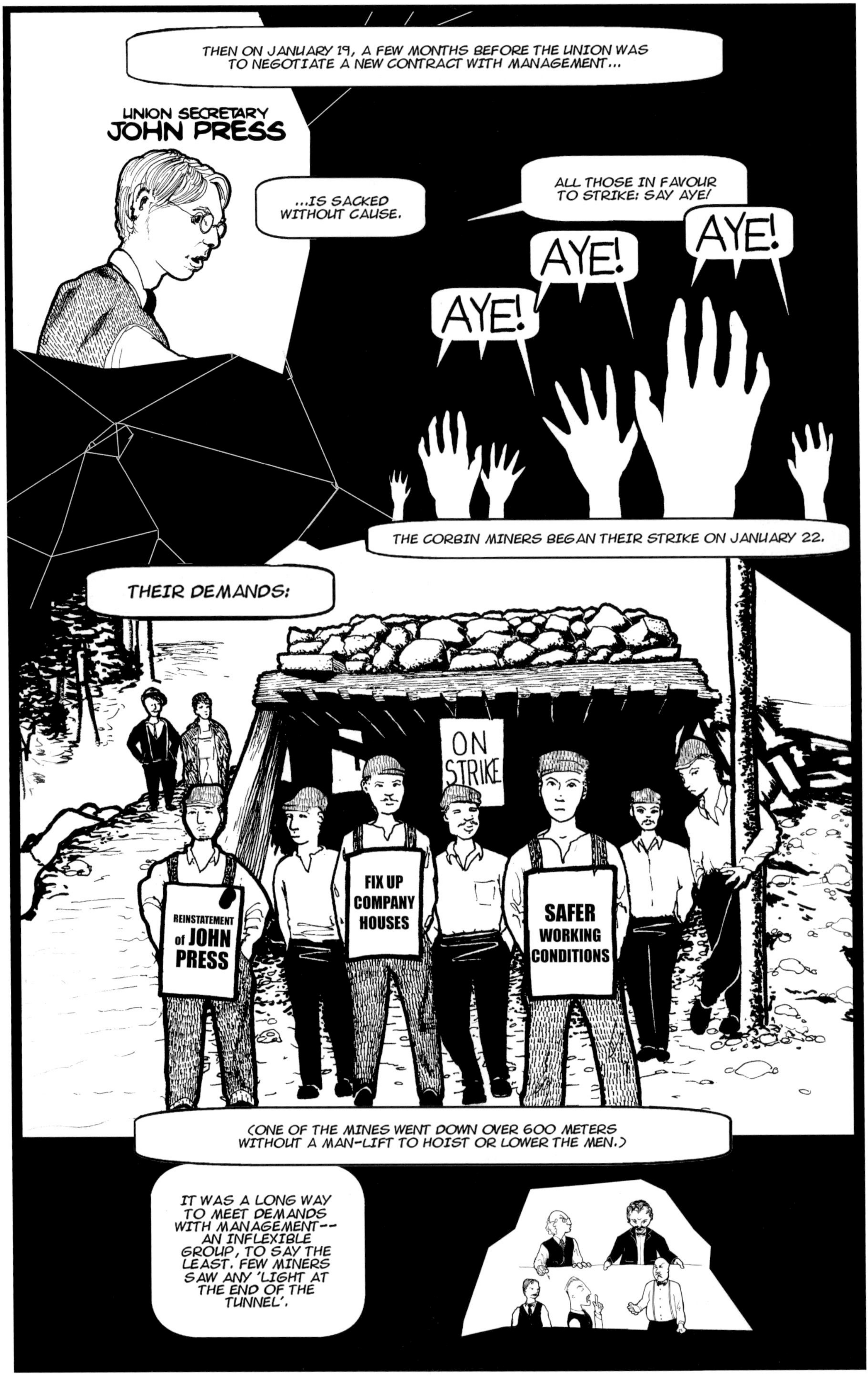
THEN ON JANUARY 19, A FEW MONTHS BEFORE THE UNION WAS TO NEGOTIATE A NEW CONTRACT WITH MANAGEMENT...
UNION SECRETARY JOHN PRESS
...IS SACKED WITHOUT CAUSE.
ALL THOSE IN FAVOUR TO STRIKE: SAY AYE!
AYE!
AYE!
AYE!
THE CORBIN MINERS BEGAN THEIR STRIKE ON JANUARY 22.
THEIR DEMANDS:
ON STRIKE
REINSTATEMENT of JOHN PRESS
FIX UP COMPANY HOUSES
SAFER WORKING CONDITIONS
(ONE OF THE MINES WENT DOWN OVER 600 METERS WITHOUT A MAN-LIFT TO HOIST OR LOWER THE MEN.)
IT WAS A LONG WAY TO MEET DEMANDS WITH MANAGEMENT-- AN INFLEXIBLE GROUP, TO SAY THE LEAST. FEW MINERS SAW ANY 'LIGHT AT THE END OF THE TUNNEL'.

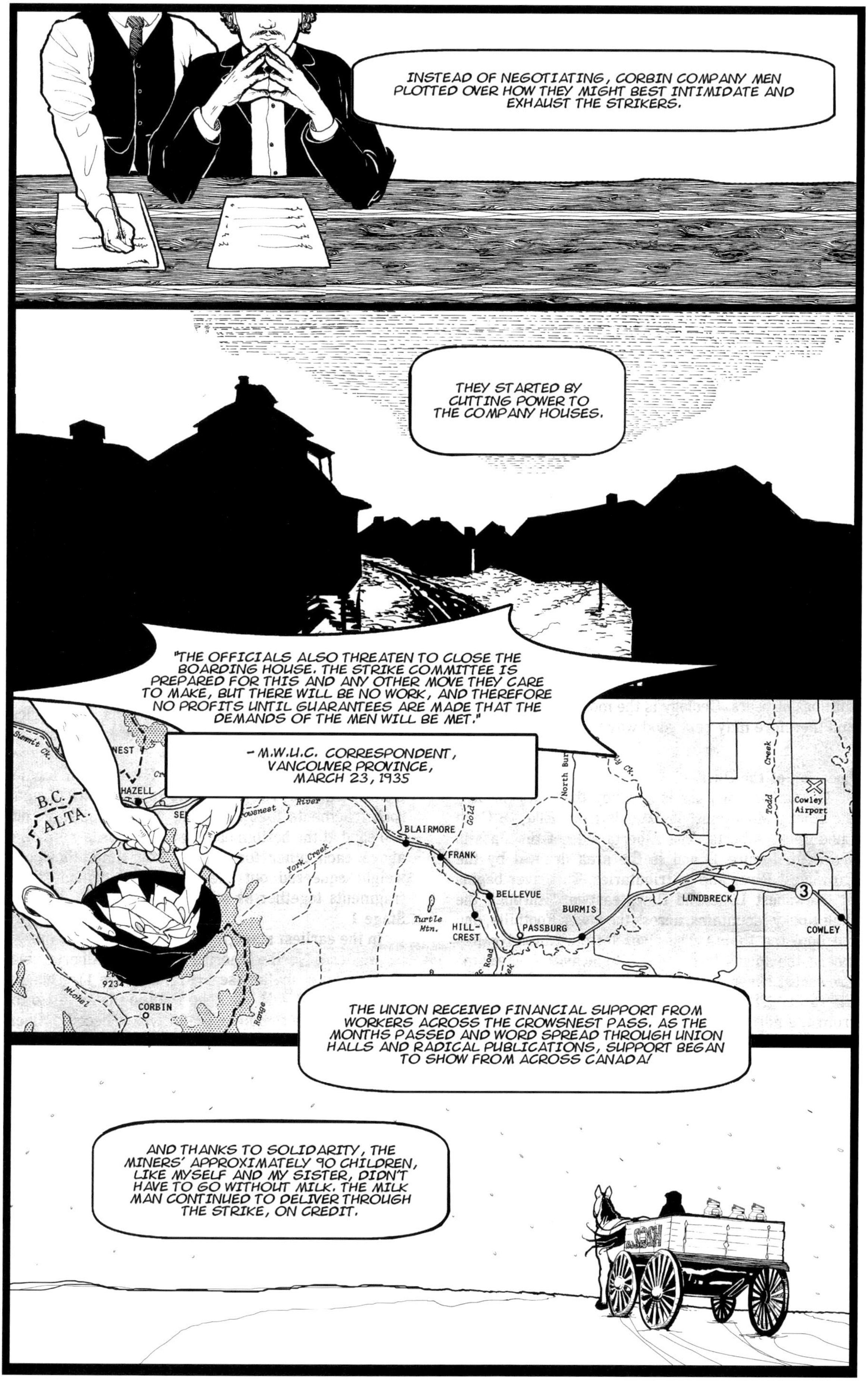
INSTEAD OF NEGOTIATING, CORBIN COMPANY MEN PLOTTED OVER HOW THEY MIGHT BEST INTIMIDATE AND EXHAUST THE STRIKERS.
THEY STARTED BY CUTTING POWER TO THE COMPANY HOUSES.
"THE OFFICIALS ALSO THREATEN TO CLOSE THE BOARDING HOUSE. THE STRIKE COMMITTEE IS PREPARED FOR THIS AND ANY OTHER MOVE THEY CARE TO MAKE, BUT THERE WILL BE NO WORK, AND THEREFORE NO PROFITS UNTIL GUARANTEES ARE MADE THAT THE DEMANDS OF THE MEN WILL BE MET."
-M.W.U.C. CORRESPONDENT, VANCOUVER PROVINCE, MARCH 23, 1935
HAZELL
B.C.
ALTA.
BLAIRMORE
FRANK
York Creek
BELLEVUE
Turtle Mtn.
HILLCREST
PASSBURG
BURMIS
LUNDBRECK
Cowley Airport
COWLEY
CORBIN
THE UNION RECEIVED FINANCIAL SUPPORT FROM WORKERS ACROSS THE CROWSNEST PASS. AS THE MONTHS PASSED AND WORD SPREAD THROUGH UNION HALLS AND RADICAL PUBLICATIONS, SUPPORT BEGAN TO SHOW FROM ACROSS CANADA!
AND THANKS TO SOLIDARITY, THE MINERS' APPROXIMATELY 90 CHILDREN, LIKE MYSELF AND MY SISTER, DIDN'T HAVE TO GO WITHOUT MILK. THE MILK MAN CONTINUED TO DELIVER THROUGH THE STRIKE, ON CREDIT.

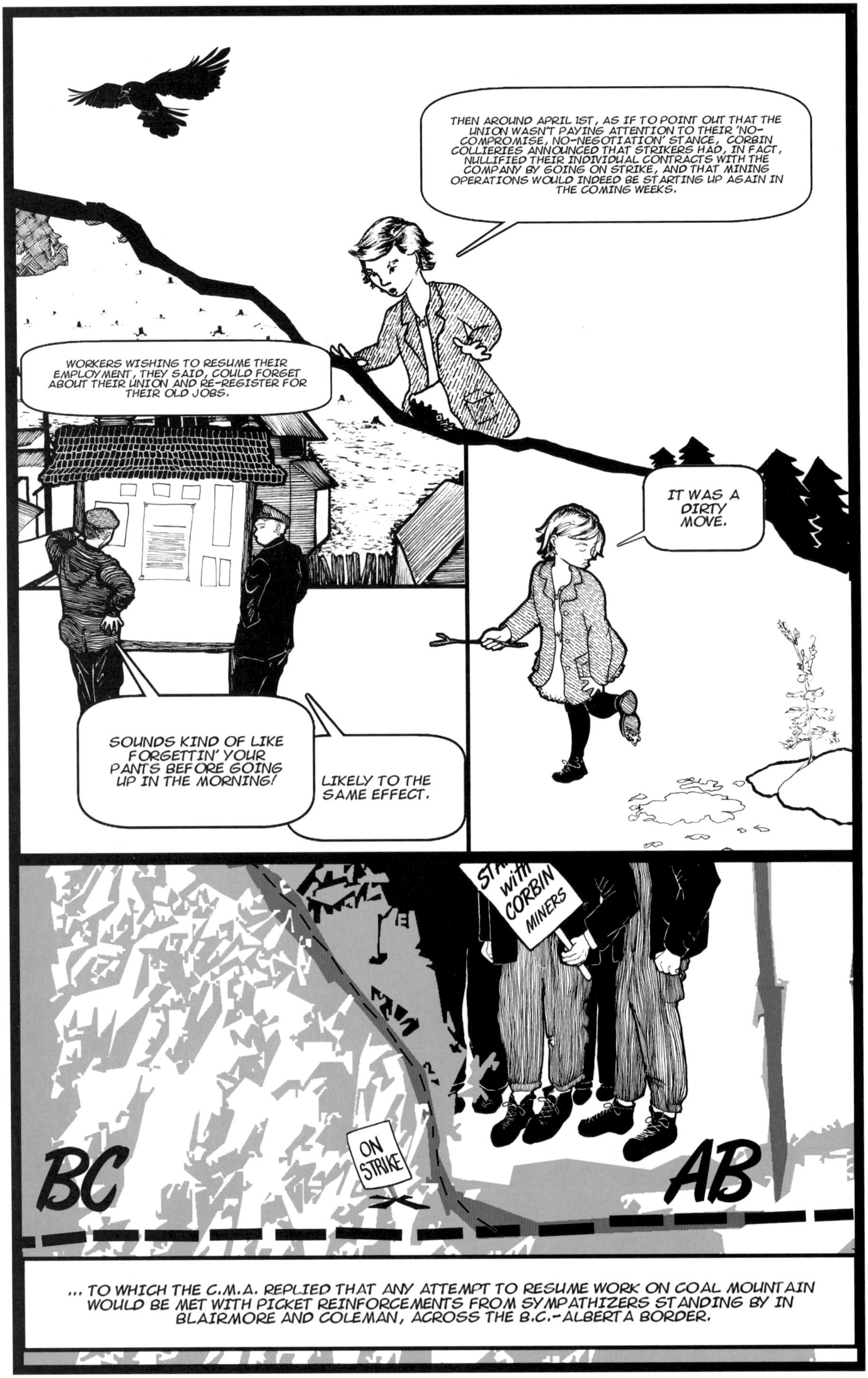
THEN AROUND APRIL 1ST, AS IF TO POINT OUT THAT THE UNION WASN'T PAYING ATTENTION TO THEIR 'NO-COMPROMISE, NO-NEGOTIATION' STANCE, CORBIN COLLIERIES ANNOUNCED THAT STRIKERS HAD, IN FACT, NULLIFIED THEIR INDIVIDUAL CONTRACTS WITH THE COMPANY BY GOING ON STRIKE, AND THAT MINING OPERATIONS WOULD INDEED BE STARTING UP AGAIN IN THE COMING WEEKS.
WORKERS WISHING TO RESUME THEIR EMPLOYMENT, THEY SAID, COULD FORGET ABOUT THEIR UNION AND RE-REGISTER FOR THEIR OLD JOBS.
SOUNDS KIND OF LIKE FORGETTIN' YOUR PANTS BEFORE GOING UP IN THE MORNING!
LIKELY TO THE SAME EFFECT.
IT WAS A DIRTY MOVE.
WITH CORBIN MINERS
ON STRIKE
BC
AB
... TO WHICH THE C.M.A. REPLIED THAT ANY ATTEMPT TO RESUME WORK ON COAL MOUNTAIN WOULD BE MET WITH PICKET REINFORCEMENTS FROM SYMPATHIZERS STANDING BY IN BLAIRMORE AND COLEMAN, ACROSS THE B.C.-ALBERTA BORDER.

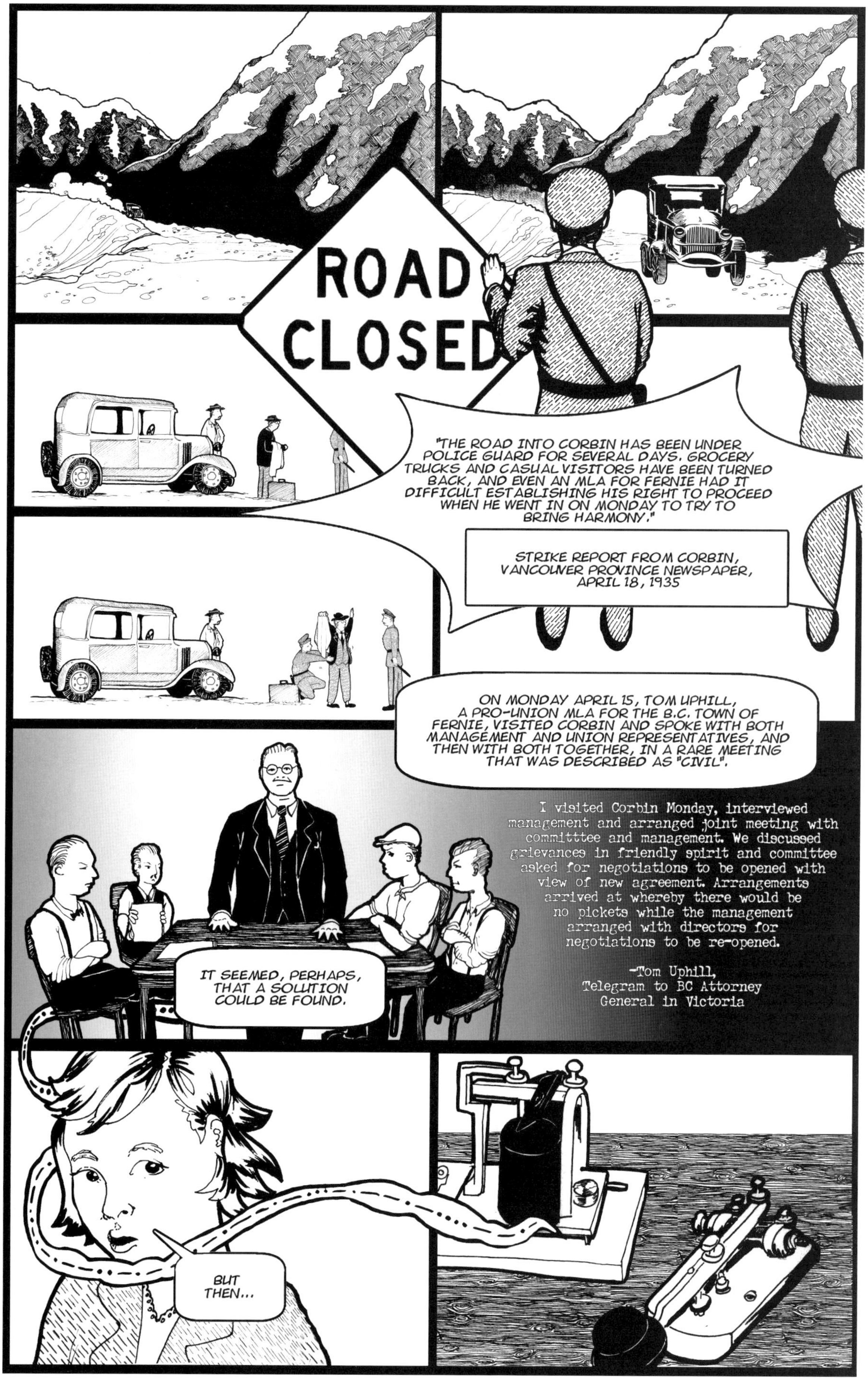
ROAD CLOSED
"THE ROAD INTO CORBIN HAS BEEN UNDER POLICE GUARD FOR SEVERAL DAYS. GROCERY TRUCKS AND CASUAL VISITORS HAVE BEEN TURNED BACK, AND EVEN AN MLA FOR FERNIE HAD IT DIFFICULT ESTABLISHING HIS RIGHT TO PROCEED WHEN HE WENT IN ON MONDAY TO TRY TO BRING HARMONY."
STRIKE REPORT FROM CORBIN, VANCOUVER PROVINCE NEWSPAPER, APRIL 18, 1935
ON MONDAY APRIL 15, TOM UPHILL, A PRO-UNION MLA FOR THE B.C. TOWN OF FERNIE, VISITED CORBIN AND SPOKE WITH BOTH MANAGEMENT AND UNION REPRESENTATIVES, AND THEN WITH BOTH TOGETHER, IN A RARE MEETING THAT WAS DESCRIBED AS "CIVIL".
I visited Corbin Monday, interviewed management and arranged joint meeting with committtee and management. We discussed grievances in friendly spirit and committee asked for negotiations to be opened with view of new agreement. Arrangements arrived at whereby there would be no pickets while the management arranged with directors for negotiations to be re-opened.
-Tom Uphill, Telegram to BC Attorney General in Victoria
IT SEEMED, PERHAPS, THAT A SOLUTION COULD BE FOUND.
BUT THEN...

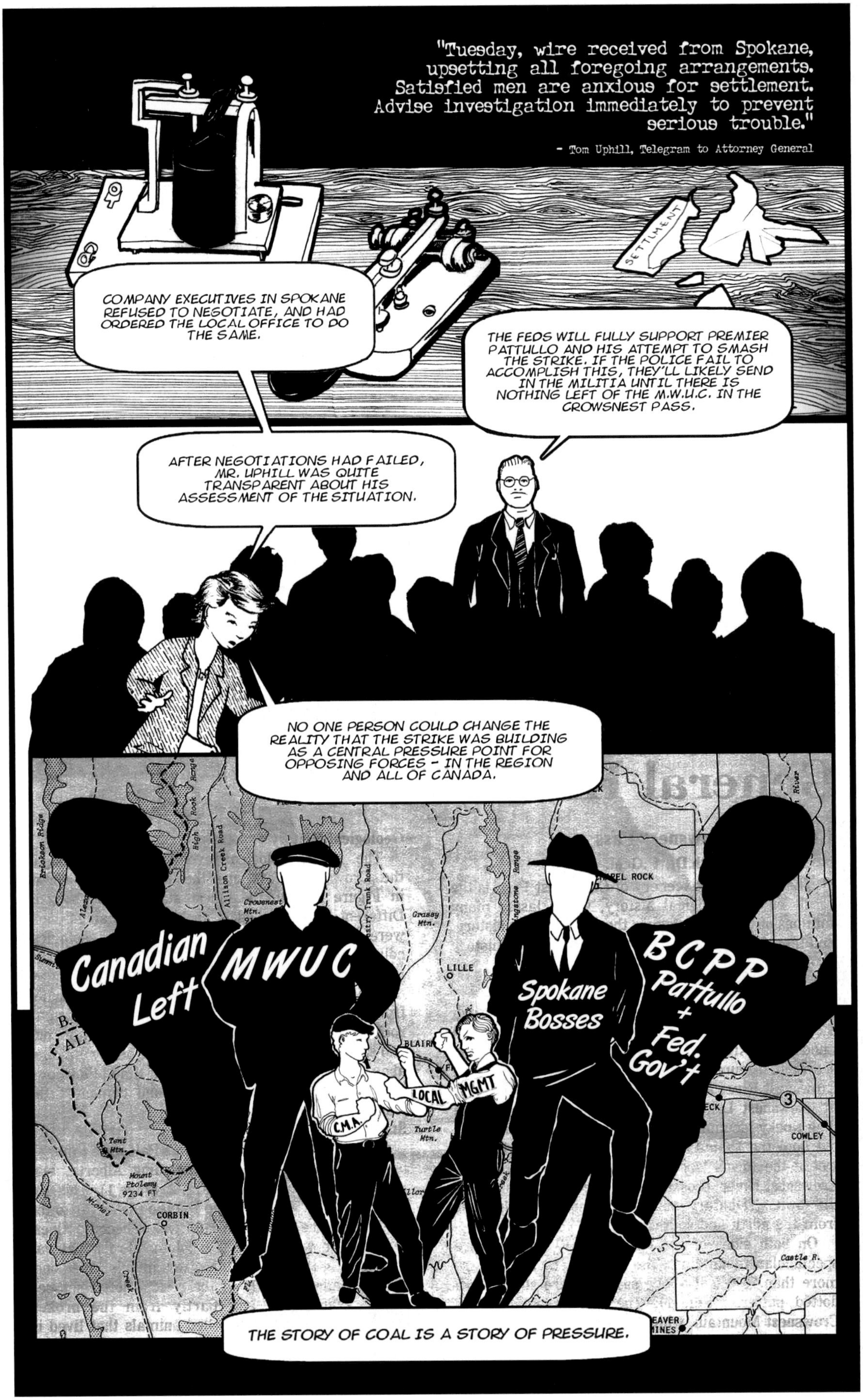
"Tuesday, wire received from Spokane, upsetting all foregoing arrangements. Satisfied men are anxious for settlement. Advise investigation immediately to prevent serious trouble."
- Tom Uphill, Telegram to Attorney General
SETTLEMENT
COMPANY EXECUTIVES IN SPOKANE REFUSED TO NEGOTIATE, AND HAD ORDERED THE LOCAL OFFICE TO DO THE SAME.
THE FEDS WILL FULLY SUPPORT PREMIER PATTULLO AND HIS ATTEMPT TO SMASH THE STRIKE. IF THE POLICE FAIL TO ACCOMPLISH THIS, THEY'LL LIKELY SEND IN THE MILITIA UNTIL THERE IS NOTHING LEFT OF THE M.W.U.C. IN THE CROWSNEST PASS.
AFTER NEGOTIATIONS HAD FAILED, MR. UPHILL WAS QUITE TRANSPARENT ABOUT HIS ASSESSMENT OF THE SITUATION.
NO ONE PERSON COULD CHANGE THE REALITY THAT THE STRIKE WAS BUILDING AS A CENTRAL PRESSURE POINT FOR OPPOSING FORCES - IN THE REGION AND ALL OF CANADA.
Canadian Left
MWUC
Spokane Bosses
BCPP Pattullo + Fed. Gov't
C.M.A.
LOCAL
MGMT
LILLE
BLAIRMORE
COWLEY
CORBIN
Turtle Mtn.
Tent Mtn.
Mount Ptolemy 9234 FT
Crowsnest Mtn.
Grassy Mtn.
CHAPEL ROCK
THE STORY OF COAL IS A STORY OF PRESSURE.

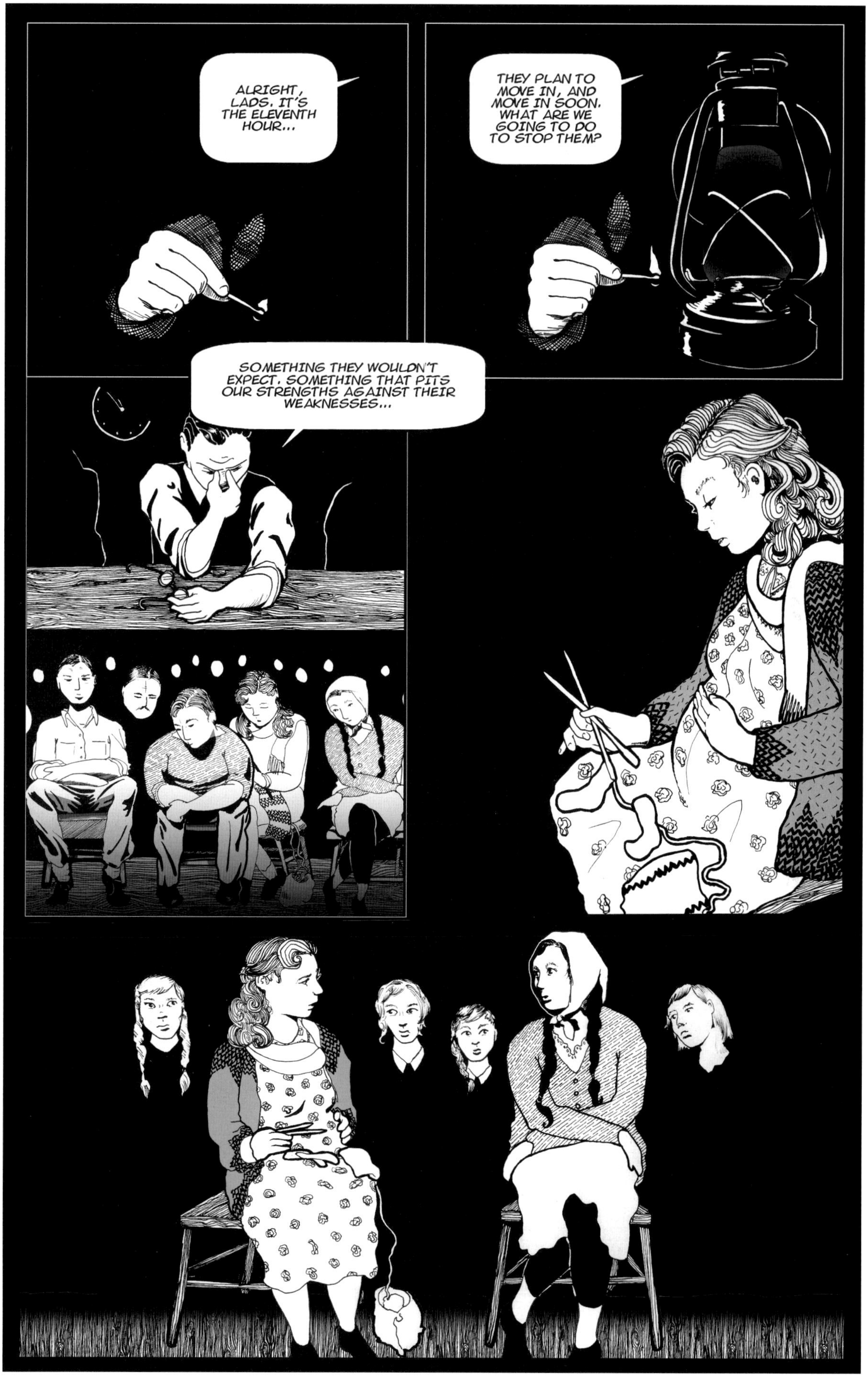
ALRIGHT, LADS. IT'S THE ELEVENTH HOUR...
THEY PLAN TO MOVE IN, AND MOVE IN SOON. WHAT ARE WE GOING TO DO TO STOP THEM?
SOMETHING THEY WOULDN'T EXPECT. SOMETHING THAT PITS OUR STRENGTHS AGAINST THEIR WEAKNESSES...

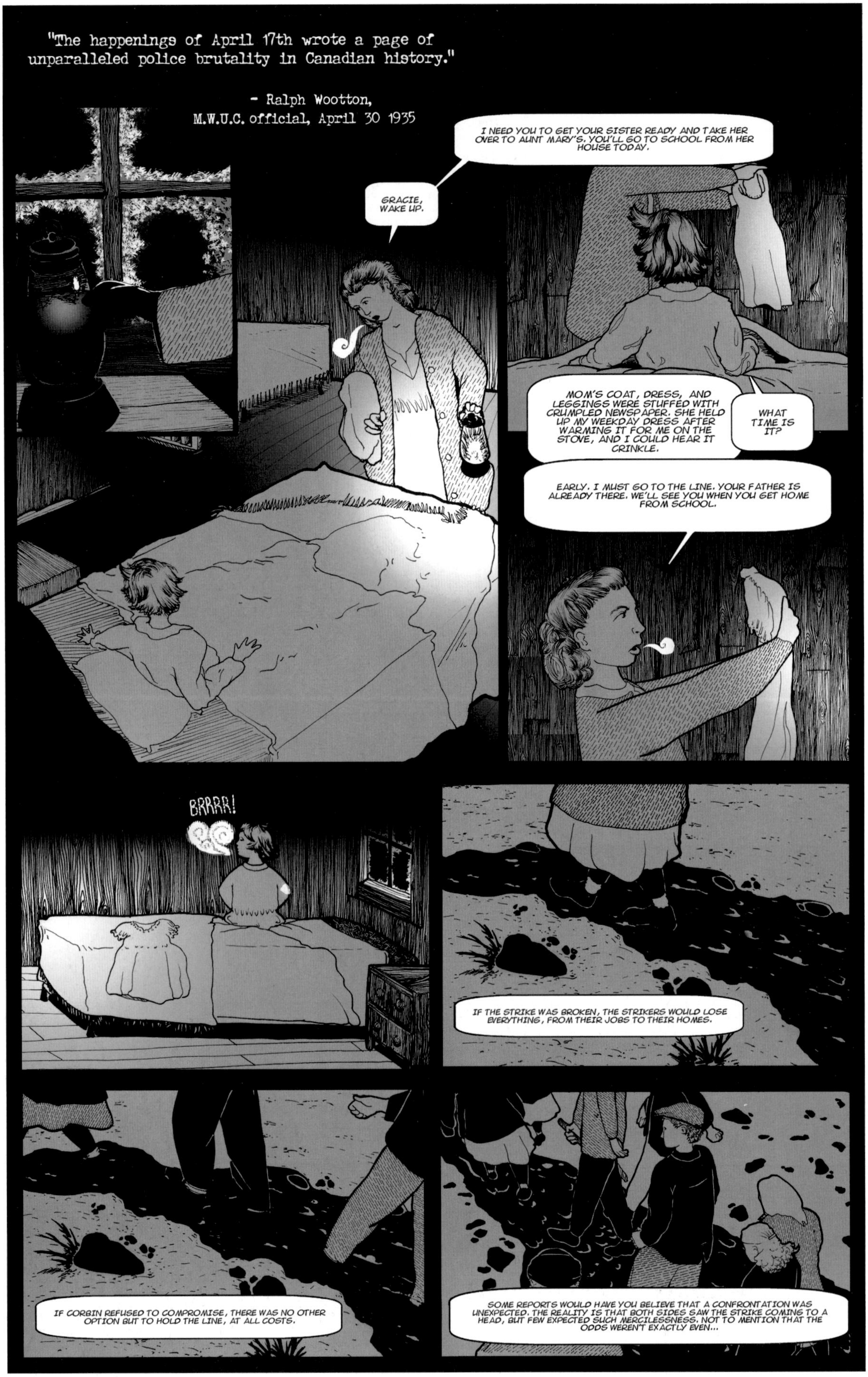
"The happenings of April 17th wrote a page of unparalleled police brutality in Canadian history."
- Ralph Wootton, M.W.U.C. official, April 30 1935
GRACIE, WAKE UP.
I NEED YOU TO GET YOUR SISTER READY AND TAKE HER OVER TO AUNT MARY'S. YOU'LL GO TO SCHOOL FROM HER HOUSE TODAY.
MOM'S COAT, DRESS, AND LEGGINGS WERE STUFFED WITH CRUMPLED NEWSPAPER. SHE HELD UP MY WEEKDAY DRESS AFTER WARMING IT FOR ME ON THE STOVE, AND I COULD HEAR IT CRINKLE.
WHAT TIME IS IT?
EARLY. I MUST GO TO THE LINE. YOUR FATHER IS ALREADY THERE. WE'LL SEE YOU WHEN YOU GET HOME FROM SCHOOL.
BRRRR!
IF THE STRIKE WAS BROKEN, THE STRIKERS WOULD LOSE EVERYTHING, FROM THEIR JOBS TO THEIR HOMES.
IF CORBIN REFUSED TO COMPROMISE, THERE WAS NO OTHER OPTION BUT TO HOLD THE LINE, AT ALL COSTS.
SOME REPORTS WOULD HAVE YOU BELIEVE THAT A CONFRONTATION WAS UNEXPECTED. THE REALITY IS THAT BOTH SIDES SAW THE STRIKE COMING TO A HEAD, BUT FEW EXPECTED SUCH MERCILESSNESS. NOT TO MENTION THAT THE ODDS WEREN'T EXACTLY EVEN...

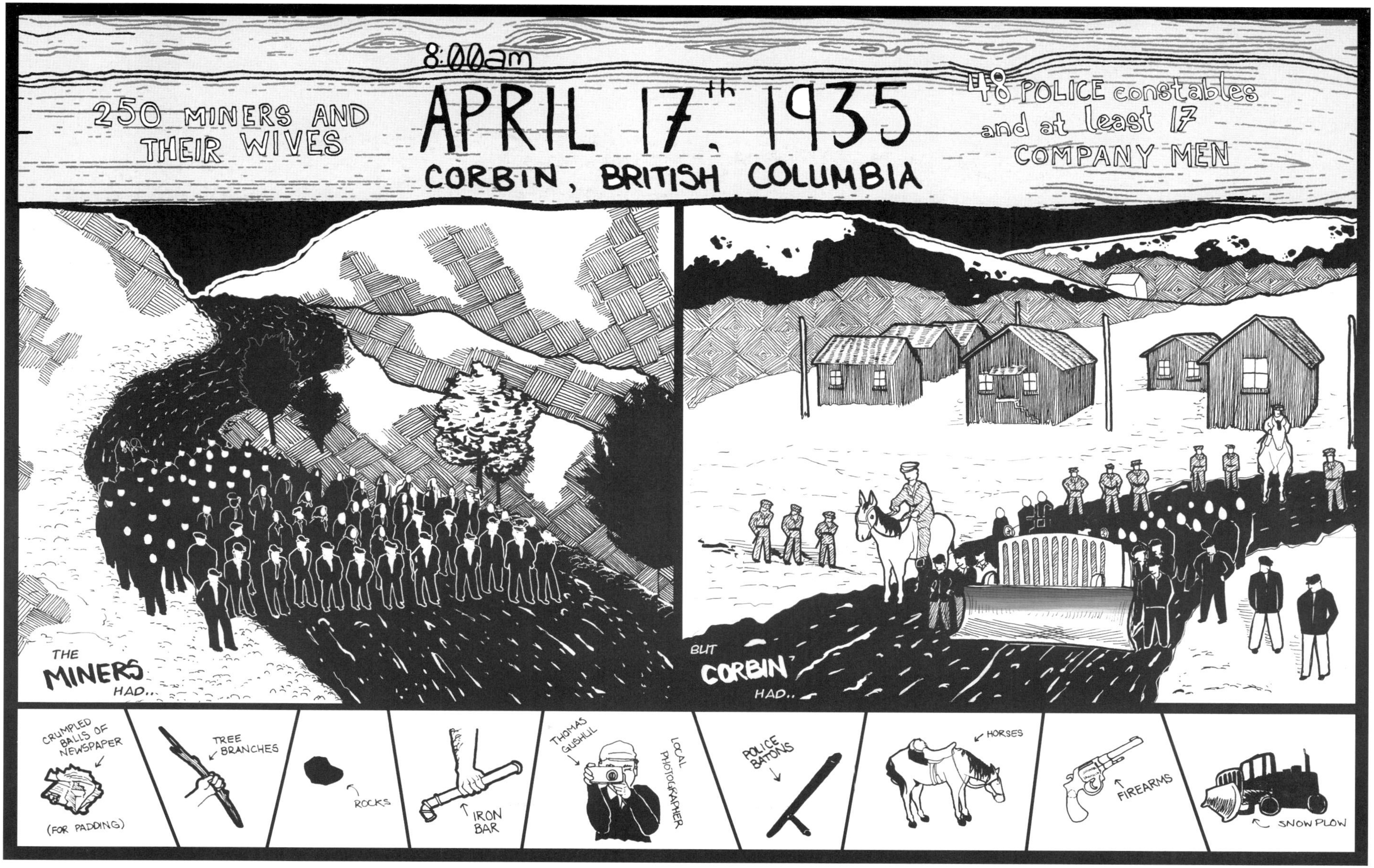
8:00am
APRIL 17th, 1935
CORBIN, BRITISH COLUMBIA
250 MINERS AND THEIR WIVES
48 POLICE constables and at least 17 COMPANY MEN
THE MINERS HAD..
BUT CORBIN HAD..
CRUMPLED BALLS OF NEWSPAPER (FOR PADDING)
TREE BRANCHES
ROCKS
IRON BAR
THOMAS GUSHUL LOCAL PHOTOGRAPHER
POLICE BATONS
HORSES
FIREARMS
SNOWPLOW

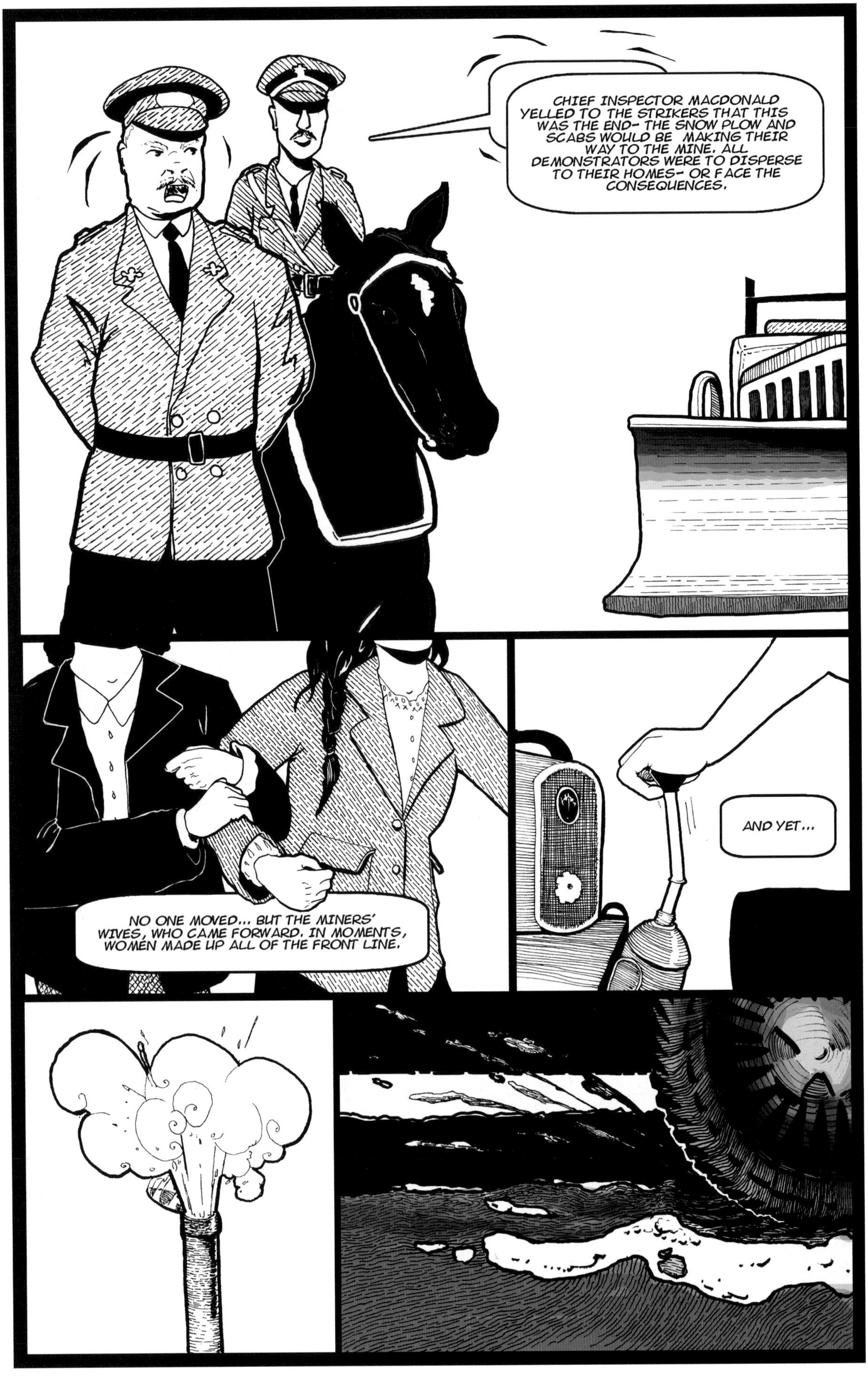
CHIEF INSPECTOR MACDONALD YELLED TO THE STRIKERS THAT THIS WAS THE END- THE SNOW PLOW AND SCABS WOULD BE MAKING THEIR WAY TO THE MINE. ALL DEMONSTRATORS WERE TO DISPERSE TO THEIR HOMES- OR FACE THE CONSEQUENCES.
NO ONE MOVED... BUT THE MINERS' WIVES, WHO CAME FORWARD. IN MOMENTS, WOMEN MADE UP ALL OF THE FRONT LINE.
AND YET...

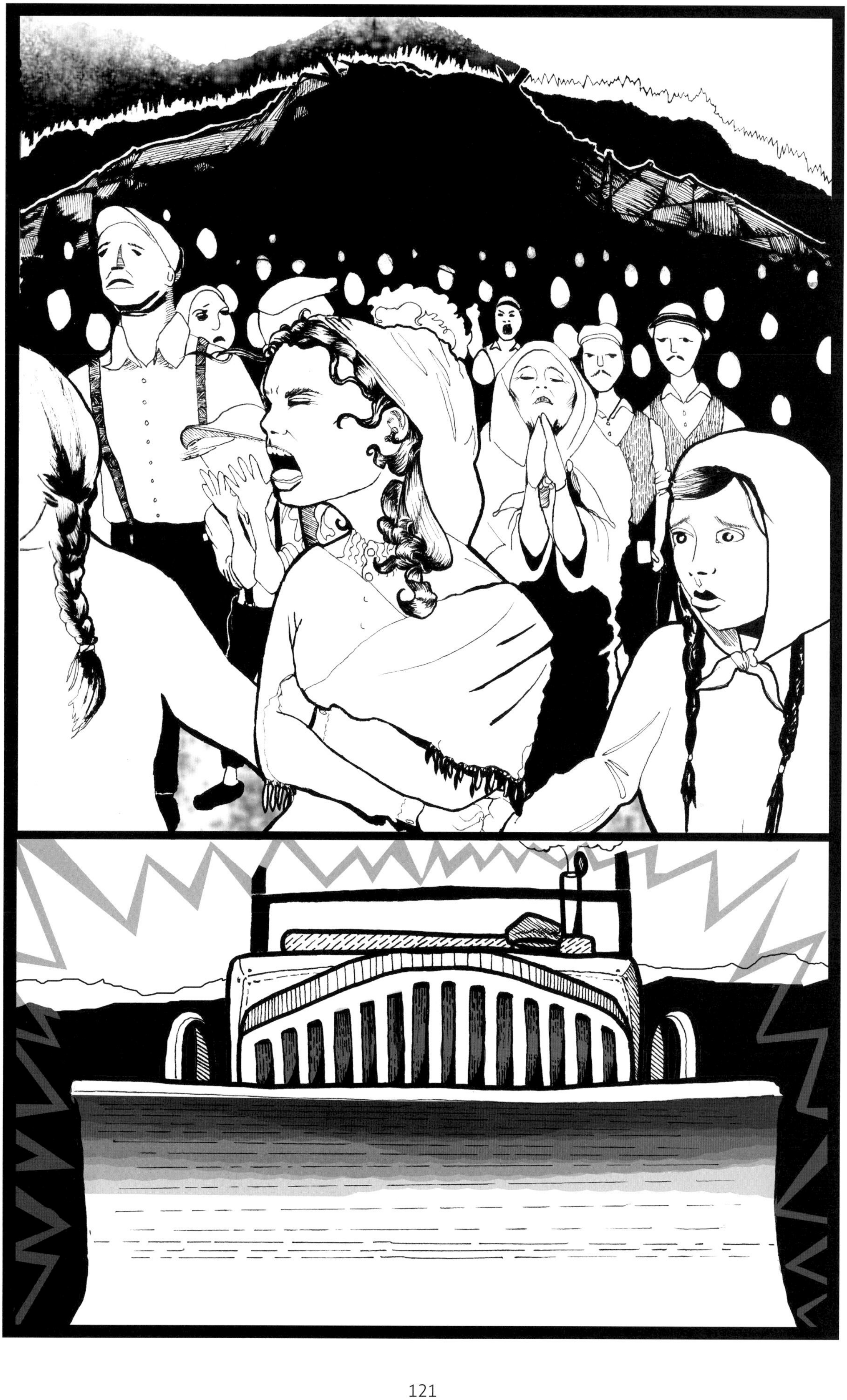

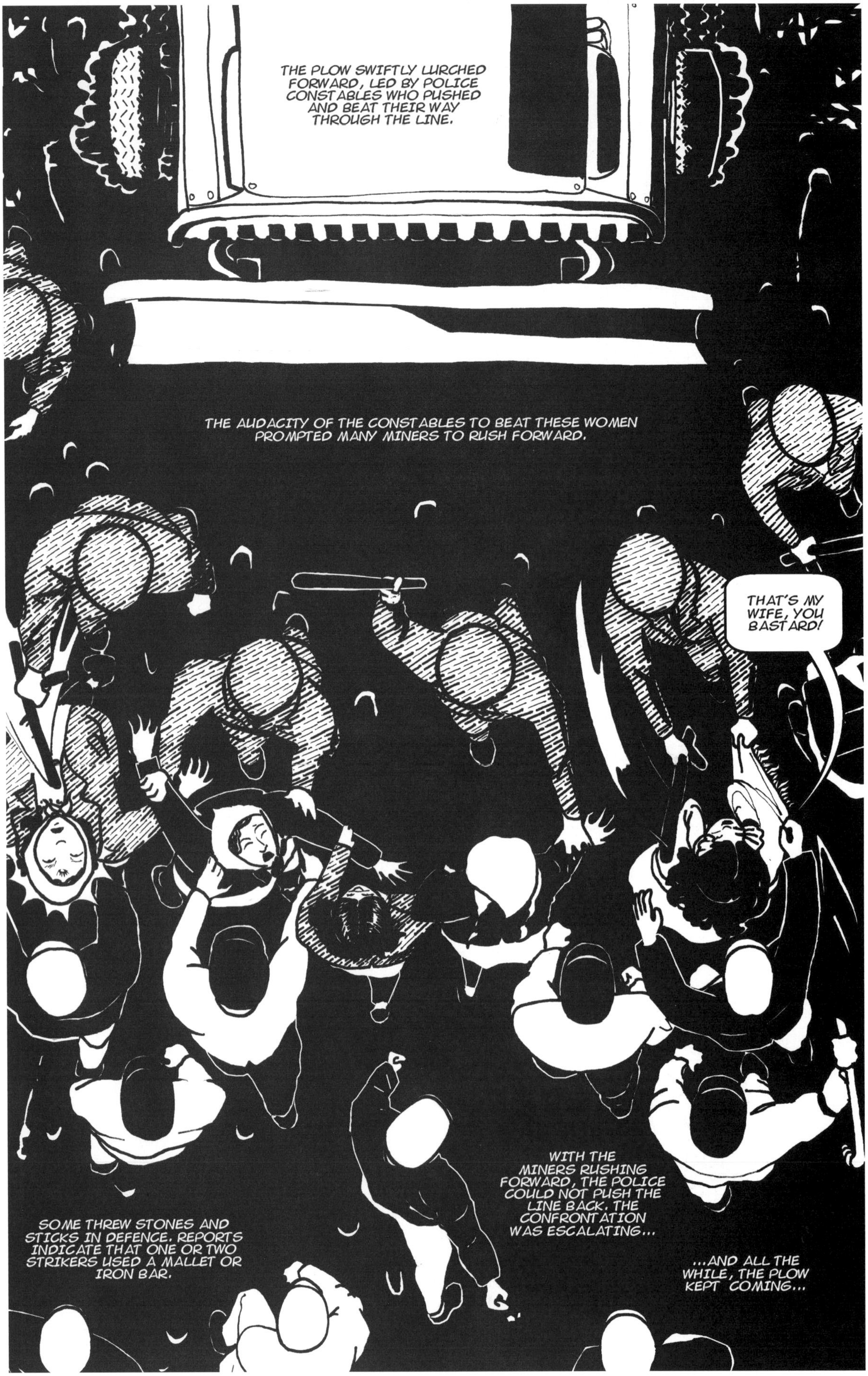
THE PLOW SWIFTLY LURCHED FORWARD, LED BY POLICE CONSTABLES WHO PUSHED AND BEAT THEIR WAY THROUGH THE LINE.
THE AUDACITY OF THE CONSTABLES TO BEAT THESE WOMEN PROMPTED MANY MINERS TO RUSH FORWARD.
THAT'S MY WIFE, YOU BASTARD!
SOME THREW STONES AND STICKS IN DEFENCE. REPORTS INDICATE THAT ONE OR TWO STRIKERS USED A MALLET OR IRON BAR.
WITH THE MINERS RUSHING FORWARD, THE POLICE COULD NOT PUSH THE LINE BACK. THE CONFRONTATION WAS ESCALATING...
...AND ALL THE WHILE, THE PLOW KEPT COMING...

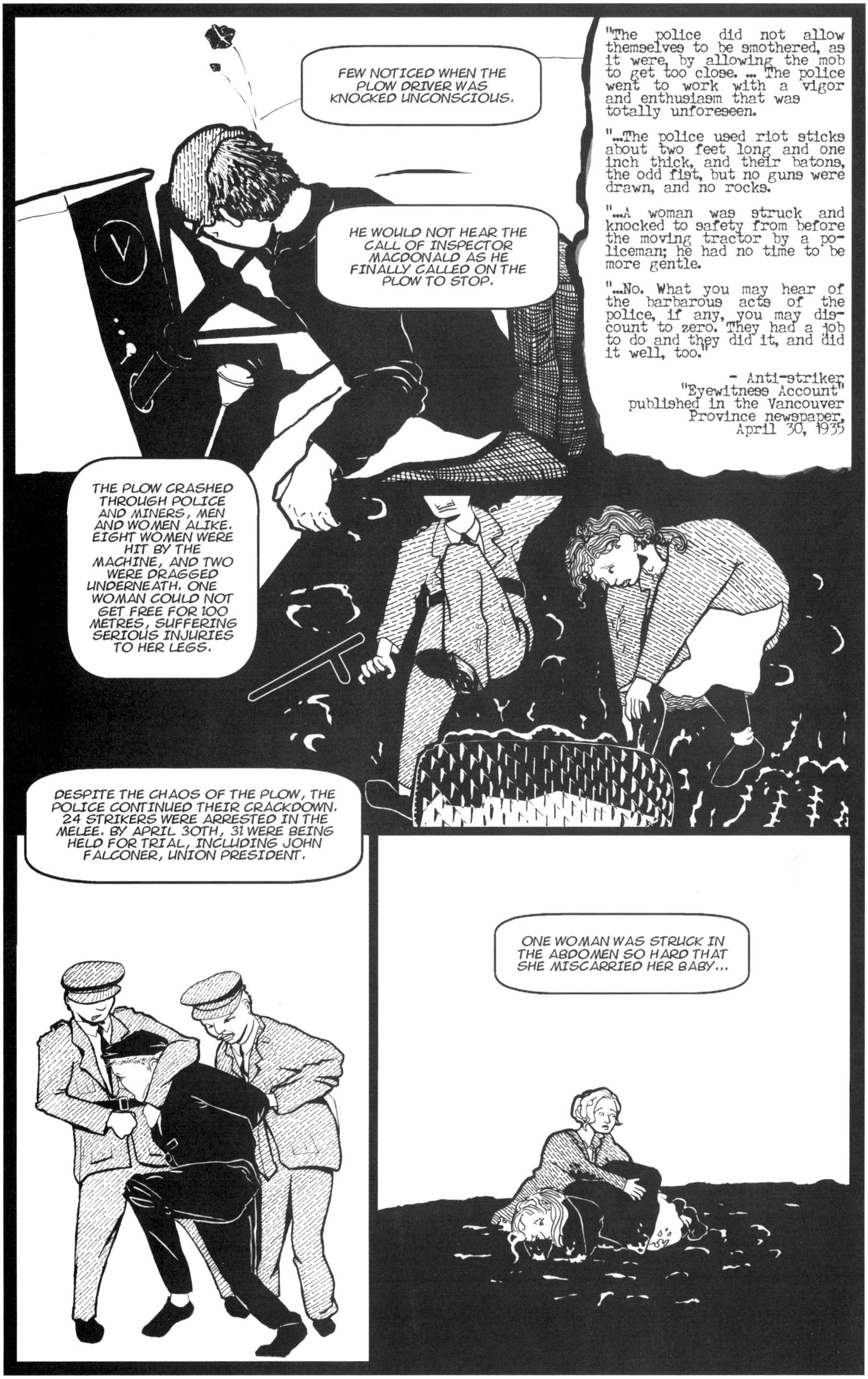
FEW NOTICED WHEN THE PLOW DRIVER WAS KNOCKED UNCONSCIOUS.
HE WOULD NOT HEAR THE CALL OF INSPECTOR MACDONALD AS HE FINALLY CALLED ON THE PLOW TO STOP.
"The police did not allow themselves to be smothered, as it were, by allowing the mob to get too close. ... The police went to work with a vigor and enthusiasm that was totally unforeseen.
"...The police used riot sticks about two feet long and one inch thick, and their batons, the odd fist, but no guns were drawn, and no rocks.
"...A woman was struck and knocked to safety from before the moving tractor by a policeman; he had no time to be more gentle.
"...No. What you may hear of the barbarous acts of the police, if any, you may discount to zero. They had a job to do and they did it, and did it well, too."
- Anti-striker "Eyewitness Account" published in the Vancouver Province newspaper, April 30, 1935
THE PLOW CRASHED THROUGH POLICE AND MINERS, MEN AND WOMEN ALIKE. EIGHT WOMEN WERE HIT BY THE MACHINE, AND TWO WERE DRAGGED UNDERNEATH. ONE WOMAN COULD NOT GET FREE FOR 100 METRES, SUFFERING SERIOUS INJURIES TO HER LEGS.
DESPITE THE CHAOS OF THE PLOW, THE POLICE CONTINUED THEIR CRACKDOWN. 24 STRIKERS WERE ARRESTED IN THE MELEE. BY APRIL 30TH, 31 WERE BEING HELD FOR TRIAL, INCLUDING JOHN FALCONER, UNION PRESIDENT.
ONE WOMAN WAS STRUCK IN THE ABDOMEN SO HARD THAT SHE MISCARRIED HER BABY...

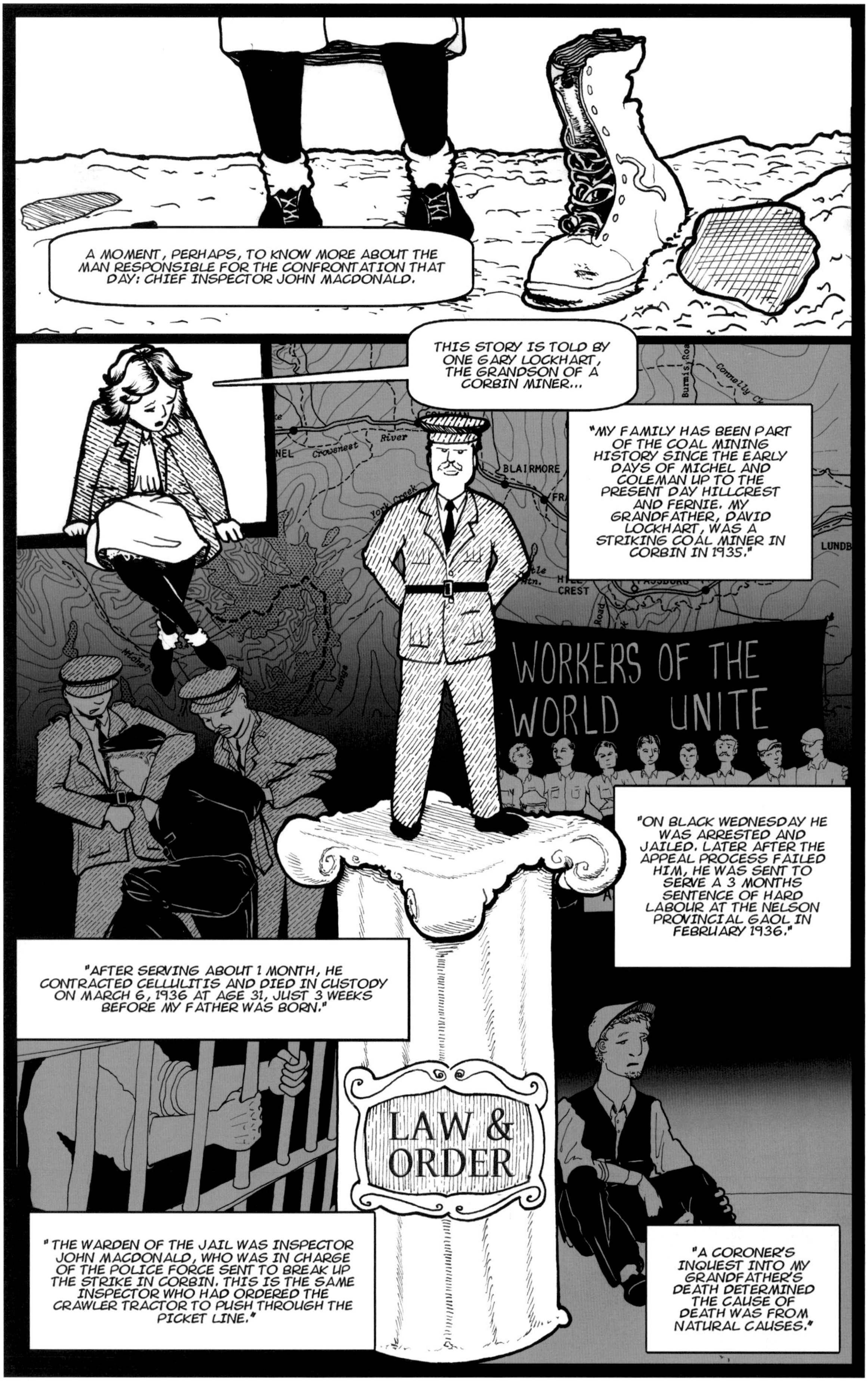
A MOMENT, PERHAPS, TO KNOW MORE ABOUT THE MAN RESPONSIBLE FOR THE CONFRONTATION THAT DAY: CHIEF INSPECTOR JOHN MACDONALD.
THIS STORY IS TOLD BY ONE GARY LOCKHART, THE GRANDSON OF A CORBIN MINER...
"MY FAMILY HAS BEEN PART OF THE COAL MINING HISTORY SINCE THE EARLY DAYS OF MICHEL AND COLEMAN UP TO THE PRESENT DAY HILLCREST AND FERNIE. MY GRANDFATHER, DAVID LOCKHART, WAS A STRIKING COAL MINER IN CORBIN IN 1935."
BLAIRMORE
Crowsnest River
HILLCREST
WORKERS OF THE WORLD UNITE
"ON BLACK WEDNESDAY HE WAS ARRESTED AND JAILED. LATER AFTER THE APPEAL PROCESS FAILED HIM, HE WAS SENT TO SERVE A 3 MONTHS SENTENCE OF HARD LABOUR AT THE NELSON PROVINCIAL GAOL IN FEBRUARY 1936."
"AFTER SERVING ABOUT 1 MONTH, HE CONTRACTED CELLULITIS AND DIED IN CUSTODY ON MARCH 6, 1936 AT AGE 31, JUST 3 WEEKS BEFORE MY FATHER WAS BORN."
LAW & ORDER
"THE WARDEN OF THE JAIL WAS INSPECTOR JOHN MACDONALD, WHO WAS IN CHARGE OF THE POLICE FORCE SENT TO BREAK UP THE STRIKE IN CORBIN. THIS IS THE SAME INSPECTOR WHO HAD ORDERED THE CRAWLER TRACTOR TO PUSH THROUGH THE PICKET LINE."
"A CORONER'S INQUEST INTO MY GRANDFATHER'S DEATH DETERMINED THE CAUSE OF DEATH WAS FROM NATURAL CAUSES."

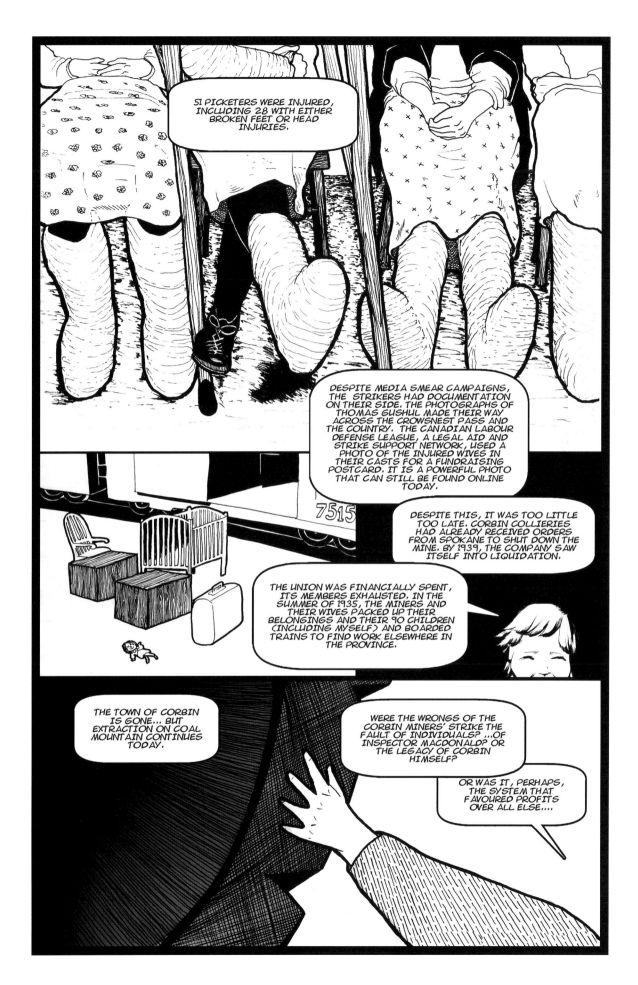

51 PICKETERS WERE INJURED, INCLUDING 28 WITH EITHER BROKEN FEET OR HEAD INJURIES.

DESPITE MEDIA SMEAR CAMPAIGNS, THE STRIKERS HAD DOCUMENTATION ON THEIR SIDE. THE PHOTOGRAPHS OF THOMAS GUSHUL MADE THEIR WAY ACROSS THE CROWSNEST PASS AND THE COUNTRY. THE CANADIAN LABOUR DEFENSE LEAGUE, A LEGAL AID AND STRIKE SUPPORT NETWORK, USED A PHOTO OF THE INJURED WIVES IN THEIR CASTS FOR A FUNDRAISING POSTCARD. IT IS A POWERFUL PHOTO THAT CAN STILL BE FOUND ONLINE TODAY.

DESPITE THIS, IT WAS TOO LITTLE TOO LATE. CORBIN COLLIERIES HAD ALREADY RECEIVED ORDERS FROM SPOKANE TO SHUT DOWN THE MINE. BY 1939, THE COMPANY SAW ITSELF INTO LIQUIDATION.

THE UNION WAS FINANCIALLY SPENT, ITS MEMBERS EXHAUSTED. IN THE SUMMER OF 1935, THE MINERS AND THEIR WIVES PACKED UP THEIR BELONGINGS AND THEIR 90 CHILDREN (INCLUDING MYSELF) AND BOARDED TRAINS TO FIND WORK ELSEWHERE IN THE PROVINCE.

THE TOWN OF CORBIN IS GONE... BUT EXTRACTION ON COAL MOUNTAIN CONTINUES TODAY.

WERE THE WRONGS OF THE CORBIN MINERS' STRIKE THE FAULT OF INDIVIDUALS? ...OF INSPECTOR MACDONALD? OR THE LEGACY OF CORBIN HIMSELF?

OR WAS IT, PERHAPS, THE SYSTEM THAT FAVOURED PROFITS OVER ALL ELSE....

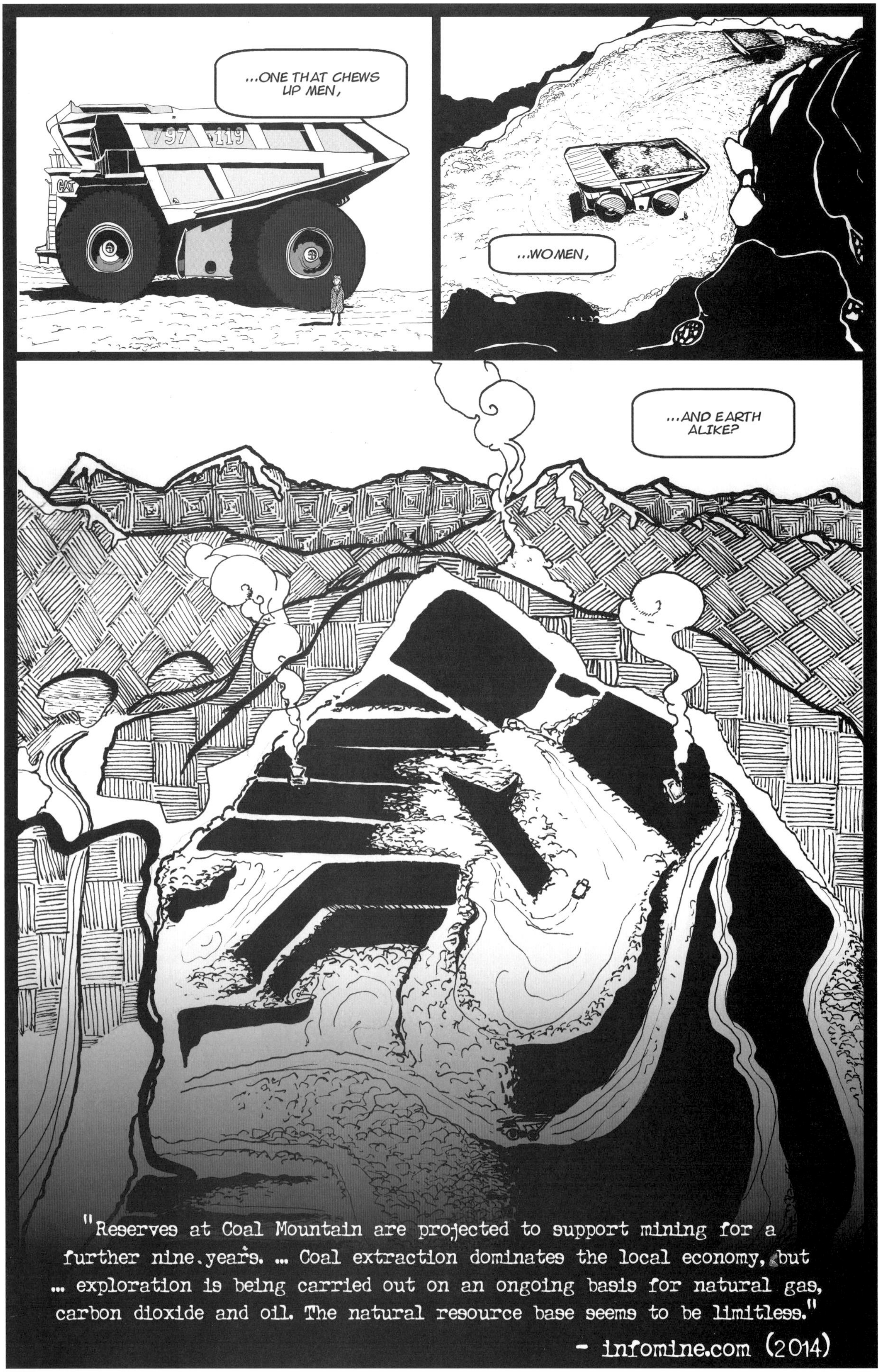
...ONE THAT CHEWS UP MEN,
797 119
CAT
...WOMEN,
...AND EARTH ALIKE?
"Reserves at Coal Mountain are projected to support mining for a further nine years. ... Coal extraction dominates the local economy, but ... exploration is being carried out on an ongoing basis for natural gas, carbon dioxide and oil. The natural resource base seems to be limitless."
- infomine.com (2014)

Acknowledgements

I would like to thank the Graphic History Collective, and Robin Folvik especially, for supporting me through this effort.

Finally, this work would not have been possible without the contribution of Grace Roe. As a child during the Corbin Miners' Strike, Grace helped to convey important visual and sensory information about life in Corbin in the 1930s. Her childhood self was the inspiration for Gracie, the story's narrator. *Coal Mountain* is inspired by true events, as seen through her eyes.

Notes

Page 100: Daniel Chase Corbin/Northwest Museum of Arts and Culture.

Page 103: Homeless coalminers in makeshift sleeping accommodations, Crowsnest Pass. Glenbow Archives/NC-54-4078.

Page 104: Miners in Corbin before 1930. Fernie and District Historical Society.

Page 120: Chief of Police, Crowsnest Pass, Alberta. Glenbow Archives/NC-54-2569.

Page 122: Corbin Riot. Gary Lockhart Collection.

Page 125: Injured wives of striking coal miners; snowplow used against Corbin miners and families. Glenbow Museum/NA-3479-2 (Combined photograph).

Additional images used for historic Corbin landscape illustrations available online: www.flickr.com/photos/pams17.

Additional images used for contemporary illustrations of Corbin available online: ghosttownpix.com/bc/corbin.html.

A number of photos used as reference for accurate representation of the buildings and scenery in Corbin are courtesy of the Grieve Family.

Madeleine Parent
A Life of Struggle and Solidarity

A Fearless Activist

Andrée Lévesque

When Madeleine Parent left us on March 12, 2012, at the age of ninety-three, the media praised her sense of justice and passion for labour struggles. Most people had forgotten that she had once been called a "witch" and a "communist." An activist since her youth, Madeleine left her mark on some of the most momentous Canadian social struggles of the 20th century. To the end, she never abandoned the fight.

At McGill University, which she attended between 1936 and 1939, she joined the campaign for scholarships for needy students. At a meeting of the Civil Liberties Union, she met union organizer Lea Roback, fifteen years her senior, who inspired her and became her mentor and her lifelong friend. After graduation, Madeleine got a job at the Montréal Labour Union Council, organized workers in the war industries, and subsequently in the textile mills in the Montréal districts of Saint-Henri and Hochelaga. In 1941, she married labour organizer Valdimar Bjarnasson, who was soon to leave for military service overseas.

Between 1943 and 1946, Madeleine helped her fellow trade unionist Kent Rowley, who was organizing textile workers at the Montréal Cotton plant, part of the Dominion Textile cotton empire, in Valleyfield, some sixty kilometres southwest of Montréal. Faced with the refusal of the company to negotiate with its employees, over three thousand workers went on strike, led by twenty-eight-year-old Madeleine Parent. Attorney-General and Premier Maurice Duplessis quickly declared the strike illegal. After a hundred days marked by police violence, clerical support for the scabs, and tremendous solidarity on the part of the population, the company agreed to sign an agreement with the United Textile Workers of America (UTWA) Canadian directors.

Parent went on organizing in the textile industry, leading another strike in 1947, when she and Rowley were arrested for seditious conspiracy, and in 1952, when the UTWA let them down and expelled the now famous couple. Feeling betrayed yet undeterred, the couple set up its own Canadian Textile and Chemical Workers Union. This step marks the beginning Madeleine's commitment to Canadian nationalism, which was to explode in the left in the 1960s. In short, Parent felt that big American unions, like the UTWA, were not providing Canadian members with the attention and support needed to resolve local issues.

Madeleine and Kent consistently opposed capitalism and imperialism. During the Cold War, this was enough to be considered a member of a seditious organization. Her first marriage having ended soon after the war, Madeleine married Kent in 1953. He had then moved to Brantford, Ontario, but they commuted back and forth to Montréal until Madeleine joined him in 1967. They kept campaigning for the Canadianization of the labour movement and, in opposition to American-affiliated unionism, in 1969 they founded the Confederation of Canadian Unions (CCU).

For the next fifteen years, Madeleine carried on Canadian union struggles in Ontario, with special attention to women's issues, such as pay equity and childcare. Parent and Rowley are associated with landmarks of labour militancy: the Texpack strike in Brantford in 1971, involving mainly women workers, and the 1973 Artistic Woodwork strike in Toronto, marked by police brutality and widespread solidarity. Unfortunately, it was at this time that Kent suffered a stroke and had to stay away from the picket line.

Since her early union organizing in the war industries and in the textile plants, Madeleine was sensitive to women's issues, first in the workplace, where unequal pay was the rule, and outside, where she endorsed the campaigns for child care centres and the right to abortion. She was a founding member for the National Action Committee on the Status of Women, where her main battles were for pay equity and Indigenous women's rights.

Kent Rowley died of a heart attack in February 1978; Madeleine remained in Ontario until 1983, when she returned to Montréal. Retired from the union, she never stopped being involved in politics and protest movements. Never wavering in her denunciation of American political and economic imperialism, she was a staunch opponent of the free trade agreement, she opposed cuts in social services, and she campaigned for Québec's independence during both referendum campaigns. As a pacifist, she opposed both Iraq wars as well as Canada's involvement in Afghanistan.

In Québec, Madeleine pursued her activism in the feminist movement. As a member of the Federation of Québec Women, she was in the streets with the Women's World March for Bread and Roses of 1995, and with the March to End Poverty and Violence against Women in 2005. She supported the struggle for the rights of Indigenous women in Québec, of immigrants, and especially of Southeast Asian women.

In the last years of her life, Parkinson's disease confined her to her home, but she never remained inactive and continued her struggle for women's rights and social justice. As long as she could, she went on reading the newspaper, signing petitions, phoning politicians, and answering those who solicited her opinion.

She never held back; she remained critical of injustices of all kinds and, most importantly, Madeleine Parent never lost hope for a better world. And she never took anything for granted.

In 2002, filmmaker Sophie Bissonette made a documentary on her life, *Tisserande de solidarités*, and since 1997 the headquarters of Quebec women's organizations was named the Maison Parent-Roback. Since 2014, the bridge that crosses the Beauharnois Canal, some 25 miles upstream from Valleyfield, bears the name Madeleine-Parent. The southwest borough of Montréal is planning a Madeleine Parent Park along the Lachine Canal, a stone's throw from the old Dominion Textile plants that Madeleine started organizing in the 1940s. Madeleine will be remembered as a lifelong fighter on behalf of all those on the margin and at the bottom of society.

Madeleine Parent

a life of struggle & solidarity

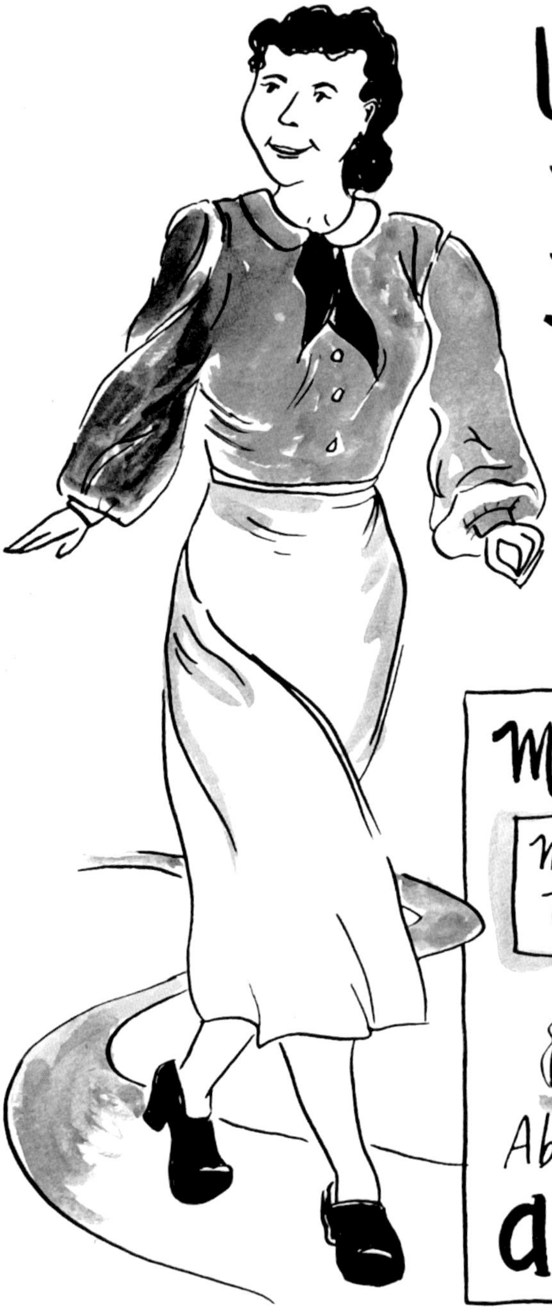

UNION ORGANIZER
agitator
friend · lover
Teacher
FEMINIST
advocate

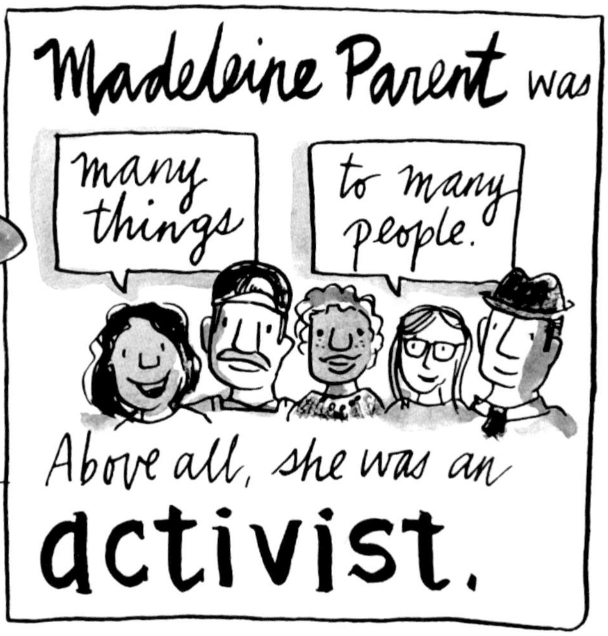
Madeleine Parent was
many things
to many people.
Above all, she was an
activist.

Illustrated by Sam Bradd and co-authored by
Sean Carleton, Robin Folvik and Julia Smith

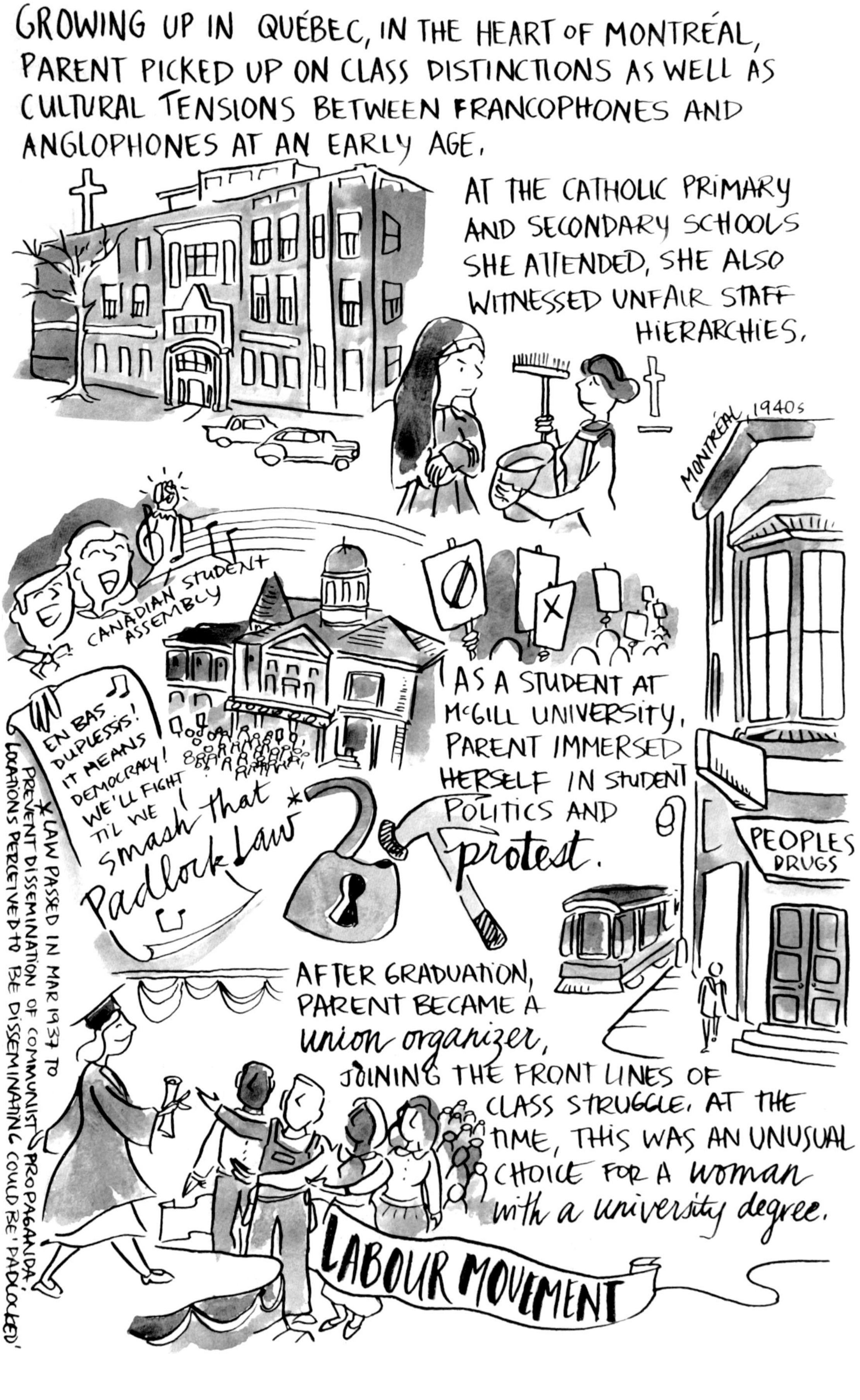
GROWING UP IN QUÉBEC, IN THE HEART OF MONTRÉAL, PARENT PICKED UP ON CLASS DISTINCTIONS AS WELL AS CULTURAL TENSIONS BETWEEN FRANCOPHONES AND ANGLOPHONES AT AN EARLY AGE.
AT THE CATHOLIC PRIMARY AND SECONDARY SCHOOLS SHE ATTENDED, SHE ALSO WITNESSED UNFAIR STAFF HIERARCHIES.
MONTRÉAL, 1940s
CANADIAN STUDENT ASSEMBLY
EN BAS DUPLESSIS! IT MEANS DEMOCRACY! WE'LL FIGHT 'TIL WE
smash that Padlock Law*
AS A STUDENT AT McGILL UNIVERSITY, PARENT IMMERSED HERSELF IN STUDENT POLITICS AND protest.
PEOPLES DRUGS
*LAW PASSED IN MAR 1937 TO PREVENT DISSEMINATION OF COMMUNIST PROPAGANDA; LOCATIONS PERCEIVED TO BE DISSEMINATING COULD BE 'PADLOCKED'
AFTER GRADUATION, PARENT BECAME A union organizer, JOINING THE FRONT LINES OF CLASS STRUGGLE. AT THE TIME, THIS WAS AN UNUSUAL CHOICE FOR A woman with a university degree.
LABOUR MOVEMENT

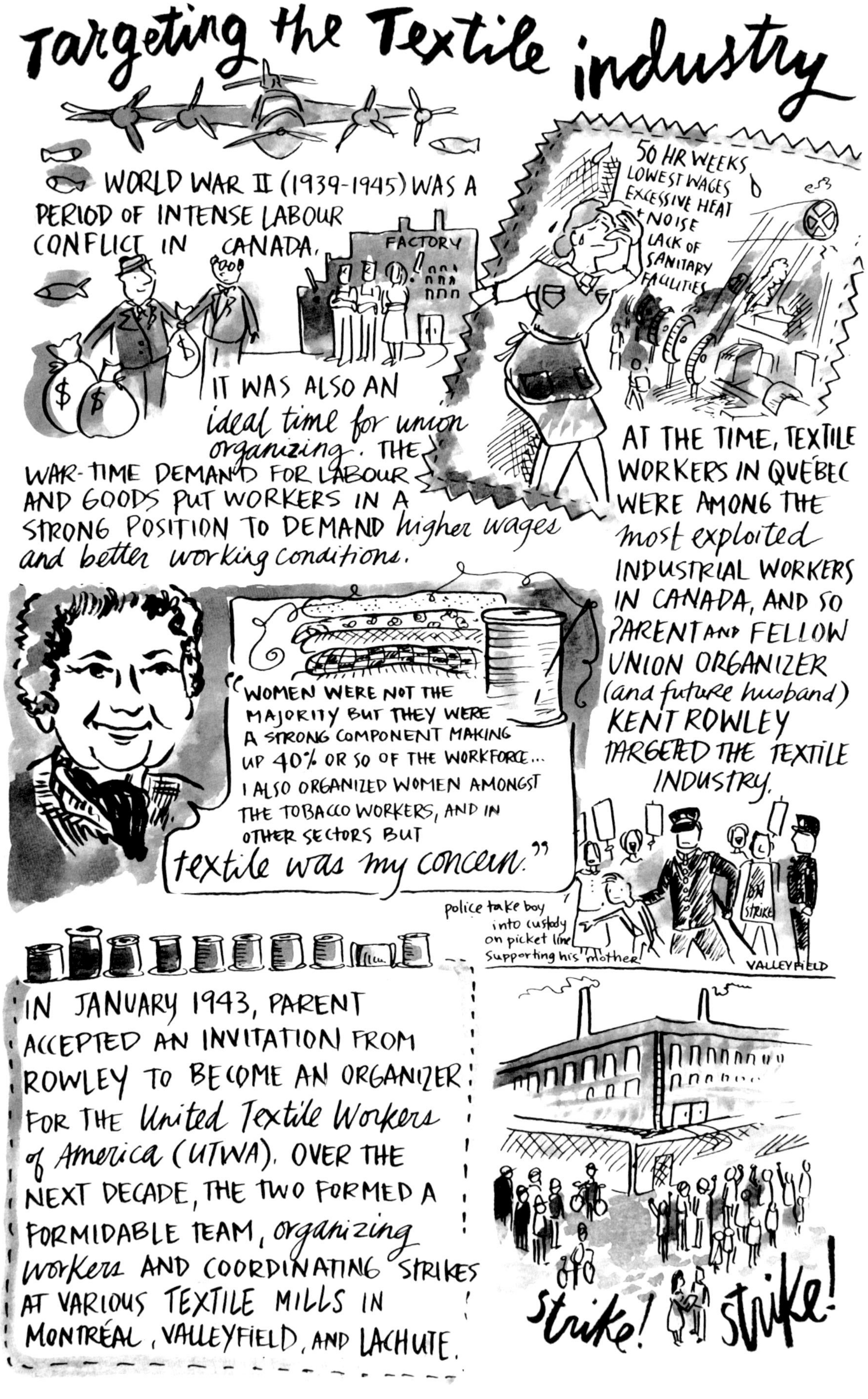
Targeting the Textile industry
WORLD WAR II (1939-1945) WAS A PERIOD OF INTENSE LABOUR CONFLICT IN CANADA.
FACTORY
IT WAS ALSO AN ideal time for union organizing. THE WAR-TIME DEMAND FOR LABOUR AND GOODS PUT WORKERS IN A STRONG POSITION TO DEMAND higher wages and better working conditions.
50 HR WEEKS
LOWEST WAGES
EXCESSIVE HEAT + NOISE
LACK OF SANITARY FACILITIES
AT THE TIME, TEXTILE WORKERS IN QUÉBEC WERE AMONG THE most exploited INDUSTRIAL WORKERS IN CANADA, AND SO PARENT AND FELLOW UNION ORGANIZER (and future husband) KENT ROWLEY TARGETED THE TEXTILE INDUSTRY.
"WOMEN WERE NOT THE MAJORITY BUT THEY WERE A STRONG COMPONENT MAKING UP 40% OR SO OF THE WORKFORCE... I ALSO ORGANIZED WOMEN AMONGST THE TOBACCO WORKERS, AND IN OTHER SECTORS BUT textile was my concern."
ON STRIKE
police take boy into custody on picket line supporting his mother
VALLEYFIELD
IN JANUARY 1943, PARENT ACCEPTED AN INVITATION FROM ROWLEY TO BECOME AN ORGANIZER FOR THE United Textile Workers of America (UTWA). OVER THE NEXT DECADE, THE TWO FORMED A FORMIDABLE TEAM, organizing workers AND COORDINATING STRIKES AT VARIOUS TEXTILE MILLS IN MONTRÉAL, VALLEYFIELD, AND LACHUTE.
Strike! Strike!

Anti-Communism

PARENT QUICKLY EARNED THE TRUST OF TEXTILE WORKERS AND DEVELOPED A REPUTATION AS A SUCCESSFUL UNION ORGANIZER.

PRESSE
SOVIET SPY?
SOVIET SPY ON THE GASPÉ?

However, SOME SAW PARENT AS A THREAT AND TRIED TO DISCREDIT HER BY LABELLING HER AS A RABBLE-ROUSER AND A COMMUNIST.

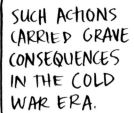

SUCH ACTIONS CARRIED GRAVE CONSEQUENCES IN THE COLD WAR ERA.

IN THE CLIMATE OF ANTI-COMMUNISM, EVEN LABOUR UNIONS WERE BRANDING *militant leaders* COMMUNISTS AS AN EXCUSE TO EXPEL THEM.

"It was a period of general attack on union rights."

Photo of Rowley

AFTER A PARTICULARLY BITTER STRIKE IN LACHUTE IN 1947, PARENT AND ROWLEY WERE CHARGED WITH *Seditious conspiracy*, A CHARGE THAT TOOK EIGHT YEARS TO BEAT.

"Every labour battle teaches a worker how to fight. Nothing is ever completely lost."

THOUGH THE COLD WAR ERA MADE UNION ORGANIZING DIFFICULT, PARENT AND ROWLEY'S WORK WITH THE UTWA IN THE 1940s and 1950s *drastically improved* wages and working conditions IN THE Textile INDUSTRY

Moving on from Québec

PARENT and ROWLEY SOON TURNED THEIR ATTENTION TO STRUGGLES OUTSIDE OF QUÉBEC. IN THE EARLY 1950s, PARENT VISITED SUDBURY, ONTARIO TO SUPPORT MILL WORKERS.

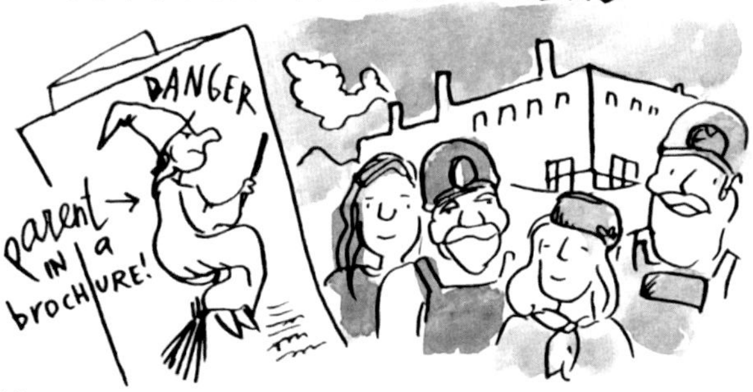

DANGER
parent → IN a brochure!

SHE HELPED MINE MILL LOCAL 598 MEMBERS AND THEIR WIVES REBUFF A RAID* BY THE UNITED STEELWORKERS OF AMERICA.

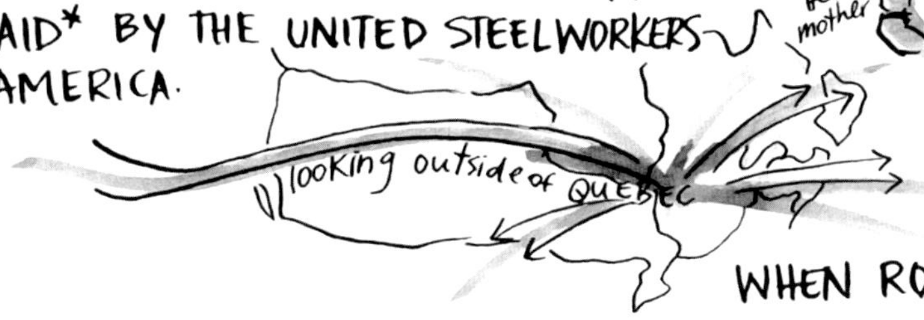

looking outside of QUÉBEC

IN THE 1970s, PARENT JOINED ROWLEY IN BRANTFORD, ONTARIO TO ORGANIZE WORKERS AT THE TEXPACK TEXTILE MILL.

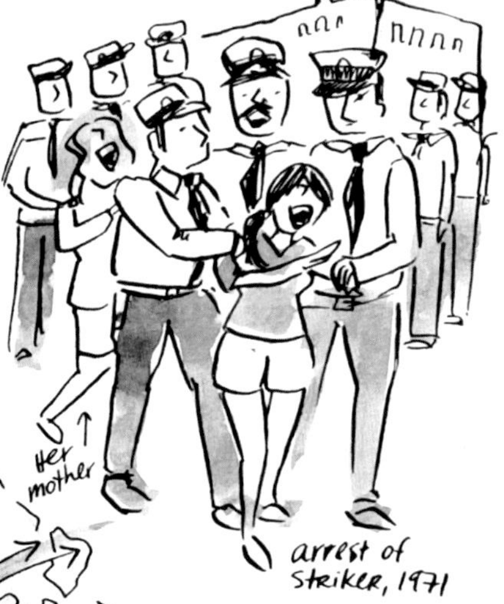

Her mother
arrest of striker, 1971

IN 1971, THE TWO HELPED COORDINATE A BITTER STRIKE THAT HIGHLIGHTED NATIONALISTIC TENSIONS WITHIN THE LABOUR MOVEMENT

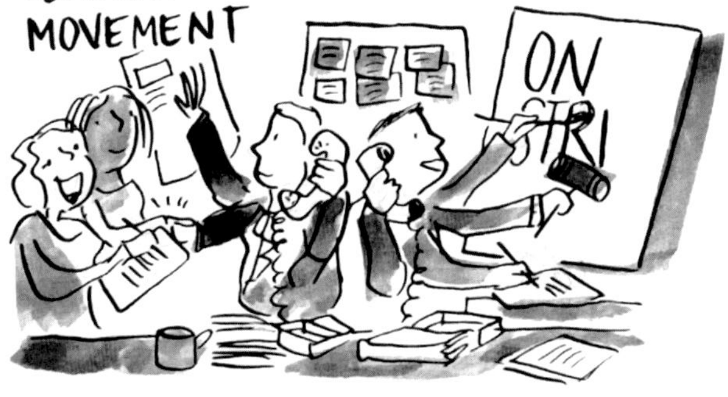

ON STRI

AS WELL AS THE NEED TO ORGANIZE WOMEN WORKERS.

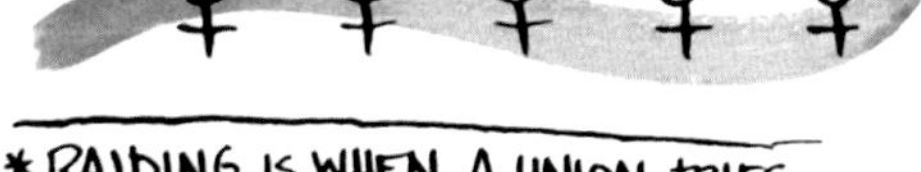

* RAIDING IS WHEN A UNION TRIES TO SIGN UP WORKERS ALREADY REPRESENTED BY ANOTHER UNION.

WHEN ROWLEY DIED IN 1978, PARENT TRAVELLED TO CAPE BRETON.

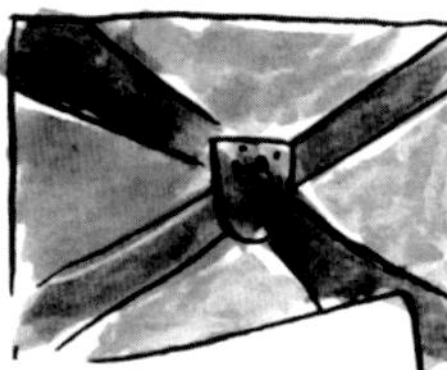

WHILE IN NOVA SCOTIA PARENT HELPED COAL MINERS WHO WANTED TO BREAK WITH THE UNITED MINE WORKERS OF AMERICA

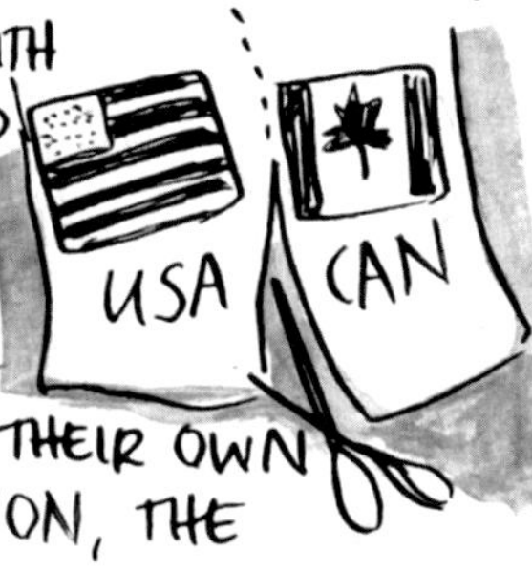

USA
CAN

AND SET UP THEIR OWN ORGANIZATION, THE *Canadian Mineworkers Union.*

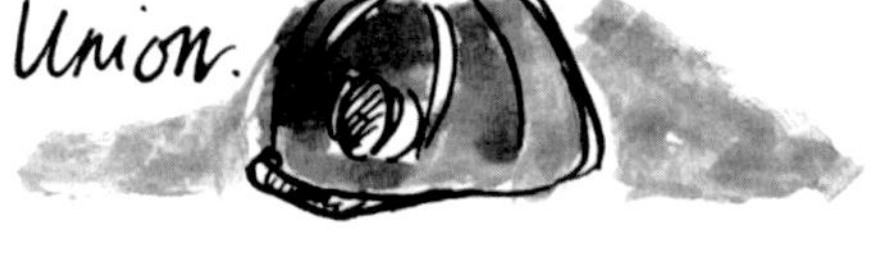

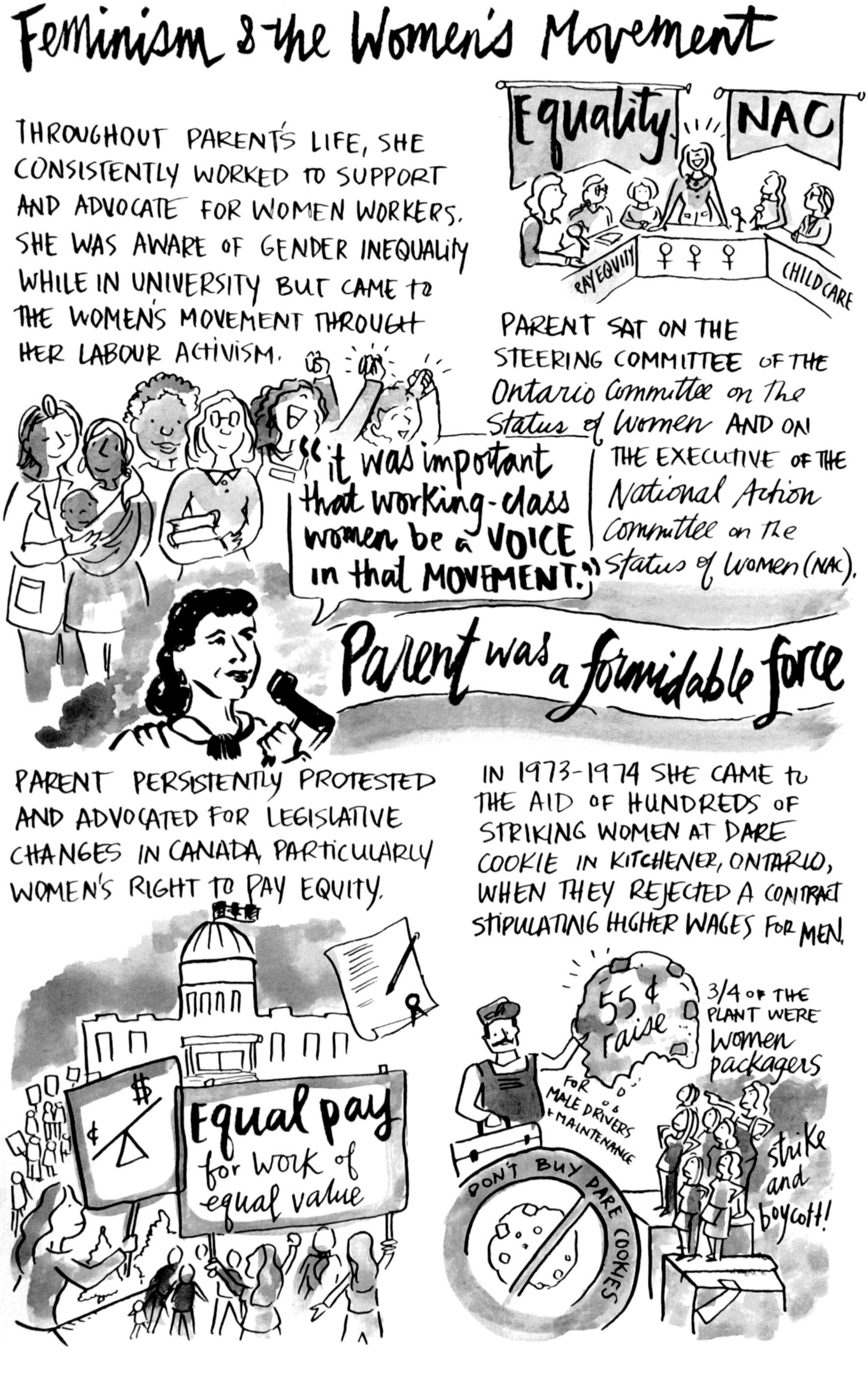
Feminism & the Women's Movement
THROUGHOUT PARENT'S LIFE, SHE CONSISTENTLY WORKED TO SUPPORT AND ADVOCATE FOR WOMEN WORKERS. SHE WAS AWARE OF GENDER INEQUALITY WHILE IN UNIVERSITY BUT CAME TO THE WOMEN'S MOVEMENT THROUGH HER LABOUR ACTIVISM.
Equality
NAC
PAY EQUITY
CHILD CARE
PARENT SAT ON THE STEERING COMMITTEE OF THE Ontario Committee on the Status of Women AND ON THE EXECUTIVE OF THE National Action Committee on the Status of Women (NAC).
"it was important that working-class women be a VOICE in that MOVEMENT."
Parent was a formidable force
PARENT PERSISTENTLY PROTESTED AND ADVOCATED FOR LEGISLATIVE CHANGES IN CANADA, PARTICULARLY WOMEN'S RIGHT TO PAY EQUITY.
¢
$
Equal pay for work of equal value
IN 1973-1974 SHE CAME TO THE AID OF HUNDREDS OF STRIKING WOMEN AT DARE COOKIE IN KITCHENER, ONTARIO, WHEN THEY REJECTED A CONTRACT STIPULATING HIGHER WAGES FOR MEN.
55¢ raise
FOR MALE DRIVERS + MAINTENANCE
3/4 OF THE PLANT WERE women packagers
strike and boycott!
DON'T BUY DARE COOKIES

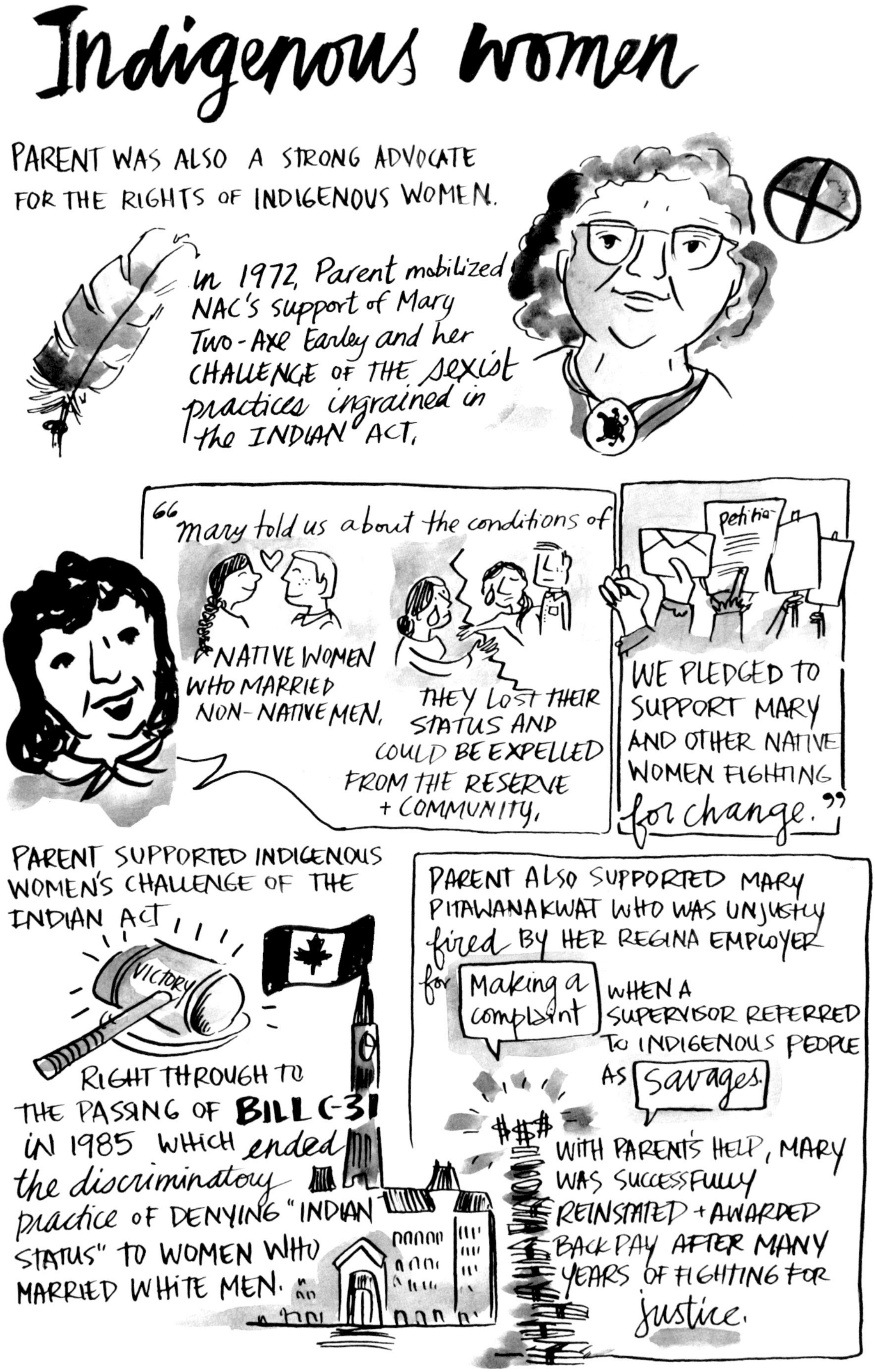
Indigenous women
PARENT WAS ALSO A STRONG ADVOCATE FOR THE RIGHTS OF INDIGENOUS WOMEN.
In 1972, Parent mobilized NAC's support of Mary Two-Axe Earley and her CHALLENGE OF THE sexist practices ingrained in the INDIAN ACT.
"mary told us about the conditions of
NATIVE WOMEN WHO MARRIED NON-NATIVE MEN.
THEY LOST THEIR STATUS AND COULD BE EXPELLED FROM THE RESERVE + COMMUNITY.
petition
WE PLEDGED TO SUPPORT MARY AND OTHER NATIVE WOMEN FIGHTING for change."
PARENT SUPPORTED INDIGENOUS WOMEN'S CHALLENGE OF THE INDIAN ACT
VICTORY
RIGHT THROUGH TO THE PASSING OF BILL C-31 in 1985 WHICH ended the discriminatory practice of DENYING "INDIAN STATUS" TO WOMEN WHO MARRIED WHITE MEN.
PARENT ALSO SUPPORTED MARY PITAWANAKWAT WHO WAS UNJUSTLY fired BY HER REGINA EMPLOYER for
Making a complaint
WHEN A SUPERVISOR REFERRED TO INDIGENOUS PEOPLE AS
savages.
WITH PARENT'S HELP, MARY WAS SUCCESSFULLY REINSTATED + AWARDED BACK PAY AFTER MANY YEARS OF FIGHTING FOR justice.

Conclusion

PARENT LIVED AN INSPIRING LIFE OF STRUGGLE AND SOLIDARITY AS SHE SOUGHT TO BUILD CONNECTIONS BETWEEN DIFFERENT MOVEMENTS FOR SOCIAL JUSTICE.

Childcare NOW

SHE REMAINED ACTIVE IN THE Women's movement

CAMPAIGNED FOR QUEBEC'S INDEPENDENCE

AND WAS AN ARDENT PACIFIST.

"Labor unity is further enhanced by solidarity... We must defend the right OF ALL PEOPLE to clean air and drinking water... We must STRENGTHEN SOLIDARITIES with the Native peoples, still and always threatened with betrayal of their RIGHTS, we must WORK MORE CLOSELY PROVINCE to PROVINCE to defend our democratic rights and statutory FREEDOMS. "

The struggle for a **better world** like Parent's **legacy**, lives on.

MADELEINE PARENT, 1918-2012

Acknowledgements

The Graphic History Collective would like to thank Andrée Lévesque for her assistance with this project. We also acknowledge the activists and academics, including Lévesque, who have previously studied Parent's life and whose insights assisted us in producing this comic book.

Notes

Most of the photos and sources we used to produce the comic book can be found in Andrée Lévesque, ed., *Madeleine Parent: Activist* (Toronto: Sumach Press, 2005).

Page 133: The opening image depicts Madeleine Parent at a Labour Day celebration in Valleyfield, Québec, circa 1948. Library and Archives Canada, PA 17841.

Page 134: The song lyrics come from Margaret Gillett, *We Walked Very Warily: A History of Women at McGill* (Montréal: Eden Press, 1981), 267.

Page 134: The image of Parent on stage is based on "Graduation photo," Studio Rice.

Page 135: The image of the young boy taken into custody during the 1946 Montréal Cotton strike in Valleyfield comes from the collection of Madeleine Parent.

Page 136: The Kent Rowley photo is based on an image of him displayed at the third assembly of the Canadian Textile Council in 1947. Library and Archives Canada, PA 93878.

Page 136: The portrait of Parent is based on an image of her at the St. Jerome court after her conviction for "seditious conspiracy" in 1948. Library and Archives Canada, PA 120397.

Page 137: The image of the arrest of a Texpack striker in 1971 is based on a photo of the incident. Collection of Madeleine Parent.

Page 139: The image of Mary Two-Axe Early is based on an online photo: www.newfederation.org/Native_Leaders/Bios/Two-Axe-Early.htm.

Page 140: The image of Parent speaking is based on a photo of her addressing protesters at Sauvé Park after a march. Library and Archives Canada, PA 120397.

Page 140: The concluding image is based on a photo of Parent in 2002 at the 50th anniversary celebration of Paul Robeson's concert at the Peace Arch in British Columbia. Collection of Madeline Parent.

Page 140: The quote is from "Keynote Address, 18 May 2002, 50th Anniversary of Paul Robeson's Concert at the Peace Arch, Blaine, Washington/Douglas, British Columbia," *Labour/Le Travail* 70 (Fall 2012), 199–202.

An "Entirely Different" Kind of Labour Union
The Service, Office, and Retail Workers' Union of Canada

Socialist-Feminist Union Organizing in Canada

Joan Sangster

The fact that the Service, Office, and Retail Workers' Union of Canada (SORWUC) no longer exists may have contributed to a regrettable amnesia about its history. This is unfortunate, since SORWUC's successes and failures still offer timely lessons for the contemporary labour movement, despite the very different economic and social context we face today. SORWUC was a unique experiment in grassroots organizing, a militant attempt to unionize marginalized service workers, and a social or community-based union dedicated to radical social change. The socialist and feminist vision of a more equitable society that animated its founders may seem hopelessly utopian in today's neo-liberal climate, but it remains relevant to those committed to building a labour movement as one pathway to social transformation.

The history of SORWUC stands at the crossroads of a number of forces of social change in 1970s Canada: the increasing post–World War II participation of women in the labour force, the growth in service and white-collar jobs, the revitalization of a feminist movement, and radical, left-wing challenges to the politics and practices of the existing trade union movement.

SORWUC's dedication to organizing workers in white-collar, retail, and service sector jobs was one response to the changing gender makeup of the labour force in the post–World War II period. While women were discouraged from continuing in skilled, better-paid jobs at the end of the war in order to concentrate on raising families, the long-term pattern of female work for pay was actually quite the opposite. Between 1941 and 1971, the percentage of women in the paid labour force nearly doubled. Women were pushed into the labour force by families' need for two earners to make ends meet, and they were pulled in by employer demand for workers in expanding areas of the economy, particularly jobs resolutely typecast as "female" in nature, including clerical work, retail selling, and serving labour.

In other areas, such as bank telling, women had been slowly increasing their presence for decades. New jobs in hospitals, child care centres, schools, and government offices emerged in the expanding public sector, but the bureaucratization and professionalization of large enterprises in the private sector were also factors in this expansion. Women's increased labour force participation rate may have been ideologically obscured in the 1950s and 1960s by the prevailing "June Cleaver" images of female domesticity in popular culture, but the actual changes taking place would have a significant, long-term impact on ideas about appropriate gender roles, the nature of the family, and social institutions such as the labour movement

By the 1970s and 1980s, women were more likely to remain in the labour force for life; they also increased their educational attainment. Women born after World War II—the famous baby boomers—were more likely to secure a secondary school education, and a minority also began to break through the existing gender barriers and secure a university education. Due both to a limited democratization of secondary and university education for all (as it became available to more children of working families) and changing expectations for females, young women in the 1960s and 1970s began to question the rigidly structured gendered division of labour and lack of job options which they faced upon graduation. If they were to be confined to white-collar and service work, women wanted to know how they could improve their workplaces and working conditions.

These social and economic changes stimulated and supported political and ideological change. The women in Vancouver's Women Working Women's Workshop who founded SORWUC had already been "schooled" in radical ideas as part of the New Left and the student movement of the late 1960s and early 1970s. They subsequently moved away from university politics into the community, setting up an organization dedicated to organizing women as workers, particularly women whom they believed had been ignored by existing unions.

Like the revitalized New Left, SORWUC women questioned old, Cold War fears of communist and socialist labels: they were not afraid to articulate their view that capitalism needed a major makeover and that socialist ideas of co-operation and equality were preferable to exploitation and competition. Influenced by both old and new socialist texts, and by New Left organizing, they developed new definitions of socialism that incorporated ideas about grassroots decision making, rank and file democracy, and also gender equality.

Feminism was also part of this heady mix of political change. Feminist organizations and ideas had existed in Canada since the 19th century, and the movement was never unitary and singular in its politics: it had always been divided by different goals, strategies, and visions of what feminism meant. Since the earliest socialist and labour parties emerged in the 19th century to later communist women's organizing in the Depression, socialist-feminists had very different solutions to inequality in mind from feminists who believed that lobbying and integration into Liberal and Conservative organizations and parties were the answers. Feminism also went through periods of revival, retreat, and reinvigoration; sometimes these coincided with periods when feminists created coalitions across political differences, built around key issues like suffrage or reproductive rights.

All of these forces produced an explosion of new ideas about organizing, in which socialism, feminism, and democracy figured prominently. The latter was a key element of SORWUC's new thinking. The existing labour movement was both male-dominated and dominated by large, industrial (often international) unions. The postwar "accord" between labour and capital—an unstated, informal accommodation that led to enhanced legal rights for unions and labour peace and stability for employers—did provide some stability to large, industrial unions, and, in 1956, two major union organizations combined to create the Canadian Labour Congress (CLC), minus expelled communist-led unions. Although the percentage of female union membership was increasing through this period, women were still a minority, only 16 per cent in the 1960s, though their number grew to 30 per cent by the 1980s. This impressive growth was in large part due to public sector organizing and the growth of unions like the Canadian Union of Public Employees and the Public Service Alliance of Canada, which significantly changed the landscape of labour.

However, when SORWUC was founded, many women felt deeply pessimistic about the interest of the labour movement in new organizing, and indeed, there was a prevailing view within the union movement that women, perceived to be more "transient" workers in and out of the workforce, often working in smaller service or white-collar workplaces, were simply hard to organize. Despite some attempts by the Canadian Labour Congress to set up white-collar organizing campaigns in the 1950s and 1960s, few significant gains were made. Questions were also raised in the late 1960s and 1970s about the dominating power of American international unions on the Canadian movement; head offices, research budgets, and priorities, socialist and nationalist critics argued, were American-centred and reflected American political priorities. A Canadianization movement was afoot, and though the number of new, independent Canadian unions created was small, they had history on their side: increasingly, Canadian-based unions became more powerful within the CLC, in part because of the growth of public sector unions.

These intersecting critiques, of labour's apathy about organizing women workers, the highly bureaucratized nature of the labour movement, and the need for Canadian perspectives, convinced

SORWUC members that workers had to experiment with something new: a union committed to equality, grassroots democracy, and independence. SORWUC union officials were not paid more than workers, members were encouraged to make and shape union policies, and the union reached out extensively to other community groups for support.

That SORWUC was able to organize so many locals of child care workers, bank tellers, waitresses—and more—speaks to both their dedication to workplace organizing and the success of their grassroots strategies. SORWUC not only showed that these women could be organized, and in fact that they *wanted* to be organized, but it also promoted a broader view of unions as vehicles for social change, a means to better the lives of working people through improved child care for society, enhanced dignity in the workplace, and especially equality for women.

Like many upstart organizations, however, SORWUC faced immense obstacles: the lack of understanding and hostility of the existing labour movement toward their project resulted in attempts to raid SORWUC locals, and later, better-funded parallel organizing efforts. The regulatory power of the state, through Labour Relations Boards and other state machinery, was immense and seldom favoured the interests of small units trying to establish first contracts. And never should we forget employer opposition to union organizing: SORWUC was a threat on many levels. While all these factors eventually led to its demise, considering the forces arrayed against it, SORWUC might also be considered a resounding success.

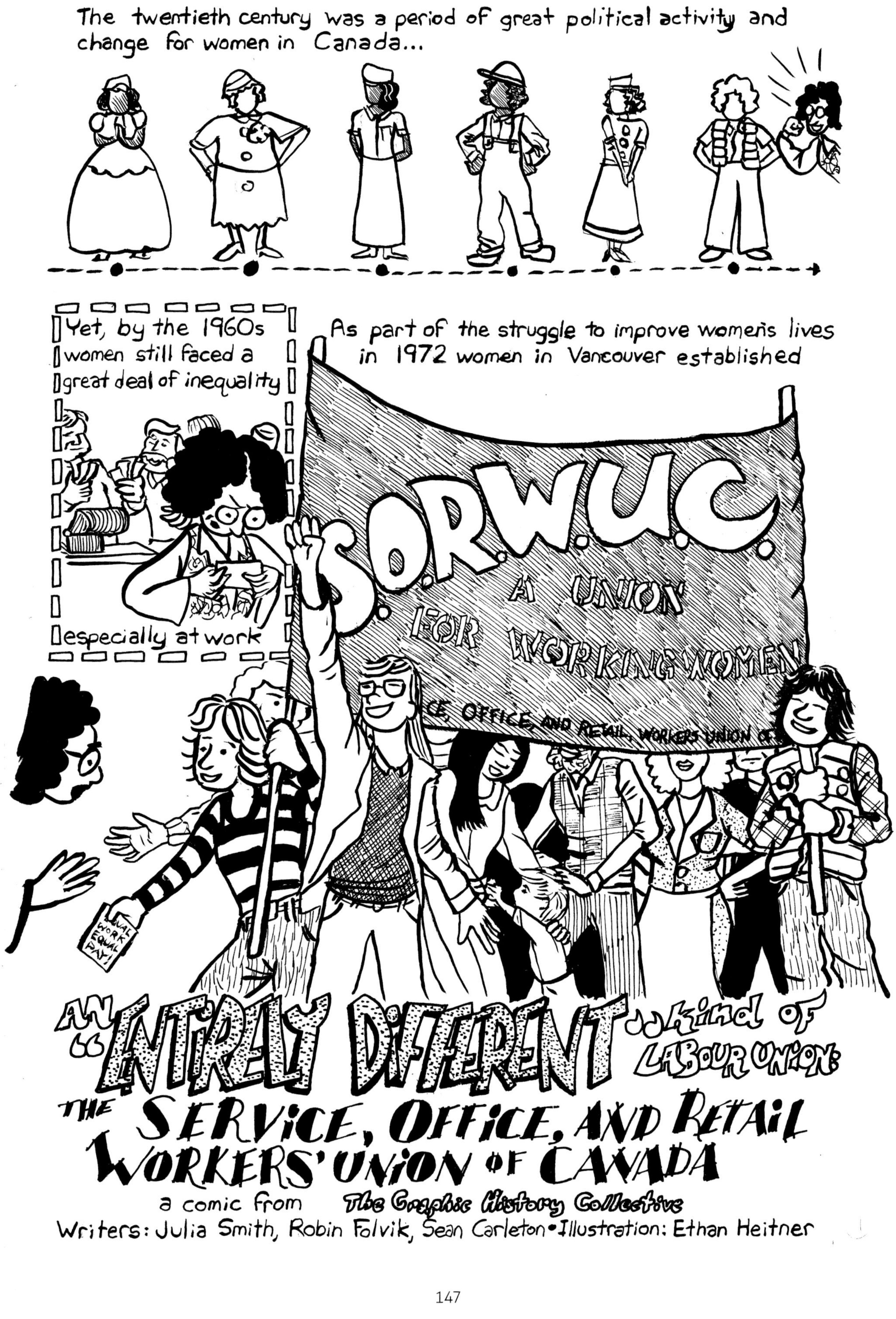
The twentieth century was a period of great political activity and change for women in Canada...
Yet, by the 1960s women still faced a great deal of inequality
especially at work
As part of the struggle to improve women's lives in 1972 women in Vancouver established
S.O.R.W.U.C.
A UNION FOR WORKING WOMEN
CE, OFFICE, AND RETAIL WORKERS UNION OF C
EQUAL WORK EQUAL PAY!
AN "ENTIRELY DIFFERENT" KIND OF LABOUR UNION:
THE SERVICE, OFFICE, AND RETAIL WORKERS' UNION OF CANADA
a comic from The Graphic History Collective
Writers: Julia Smith, Robin Folvik, Sean Carleton • Illustration: Ethan Heitner

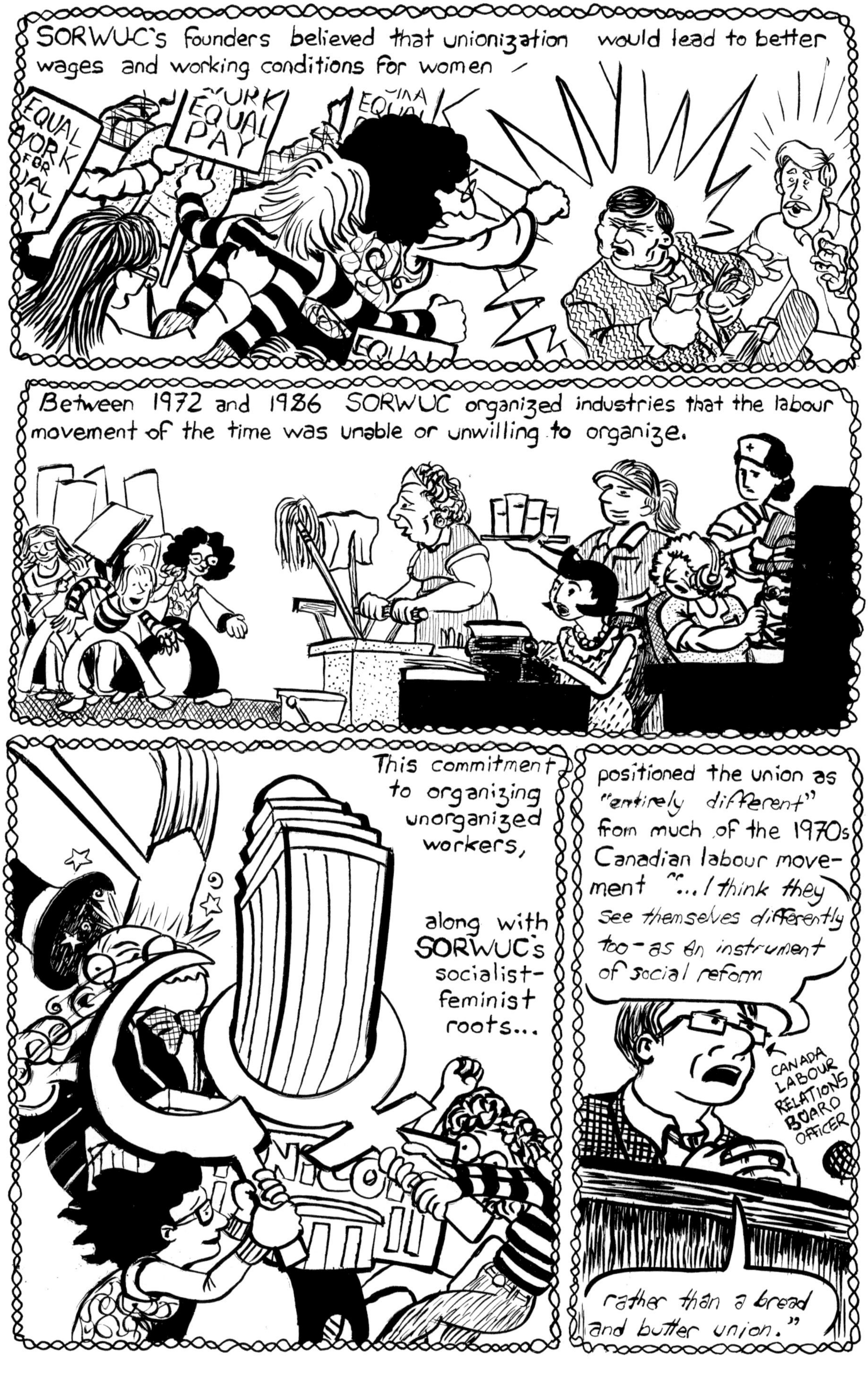
SORWUC's founders believed that unionization would lead to better wages and working conditions for women
EQUAL PAY
Between 1972 and 1986 SORWUC organized industries that the labour movement of the time was unable or unwilling to organize.
This commitment to organizing unorganized workers,
along with SORWUC's socialist-feminist roots...
positioned the union as "entirely different" from much of the 1970s Canadian labour movement
"...I think they see themselves differently too - as an instrument of social reform
CANADA LABOUR RELATIONS BOARD OFFICER
rather than a bread and butter union."

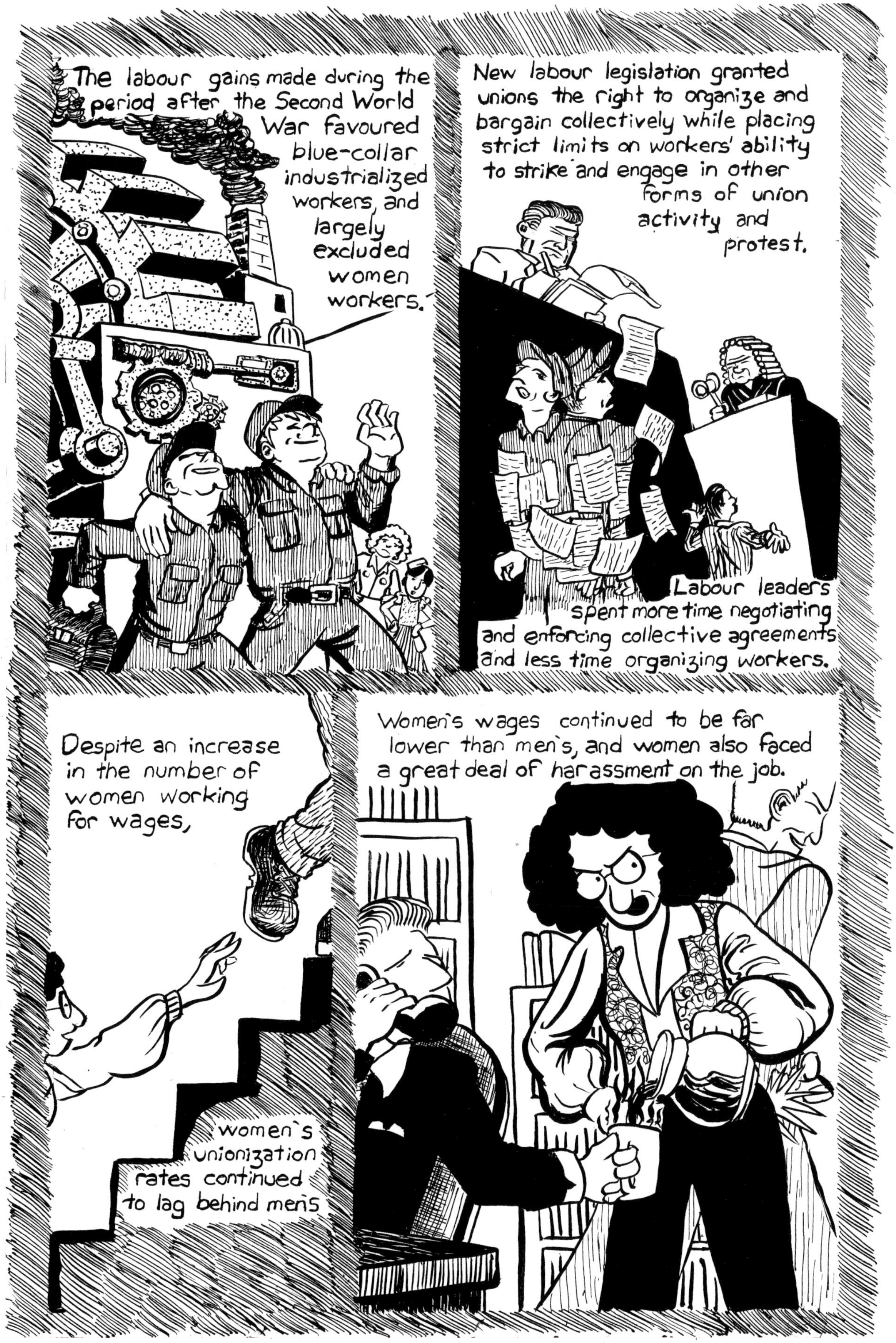
The labour gains made during the period after the Second World War favoured blue-collar industrialized workers, and largely excluded women workers.
New labour legislation granted unions the right to organize and bargain collectively while placing strict limits on workers' ability to strike and engage in other forms of union activity and protest.
Labour leaders spent more time negotiating and enforcing collective agreements and less time organizing workers.
Despite an increase in the number of women working for wages,
women's unionization rates continued to lag behind men's
Women's wages continued to be far lower than men's, and women also faced a great deal of harassment on the job.

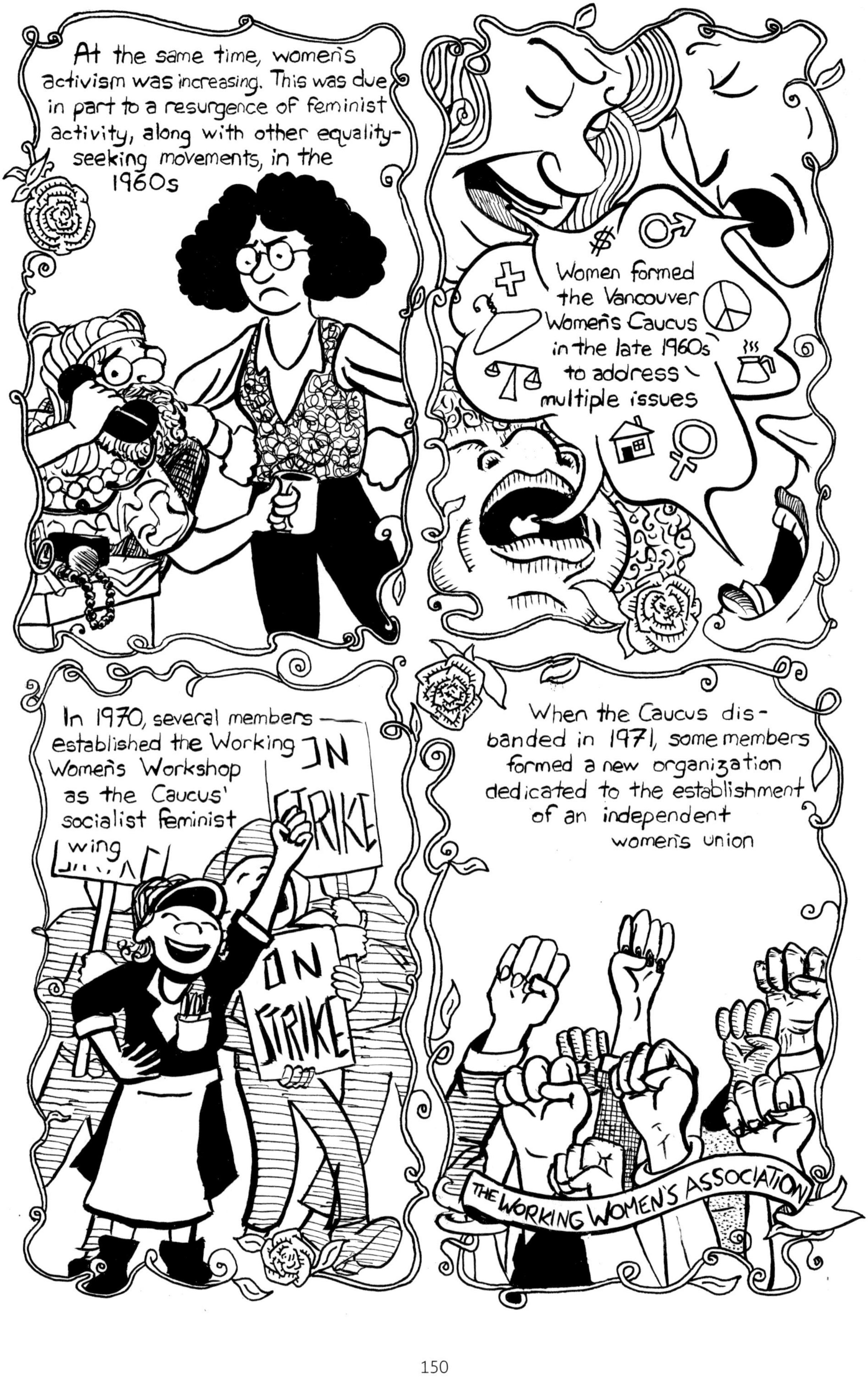
At the same time, women's activism was increasing. This was due in part to a resurgence of feminist activity, along with other equality-seeking movements, in the 1960s
Women formed the Vancouver Women's Caucus in the late 1960s to address multiple issues
In 1970, several members established the Working Women's Workshop as the Caucus' socialist feminist wing
ON STRIKE
ON STRIKE
When the Caucus disbanded in 1971, some members formed a new organization dedicated to the establishment of an independent women's union
THE WORKING WOMEN'S ASSOCIATION

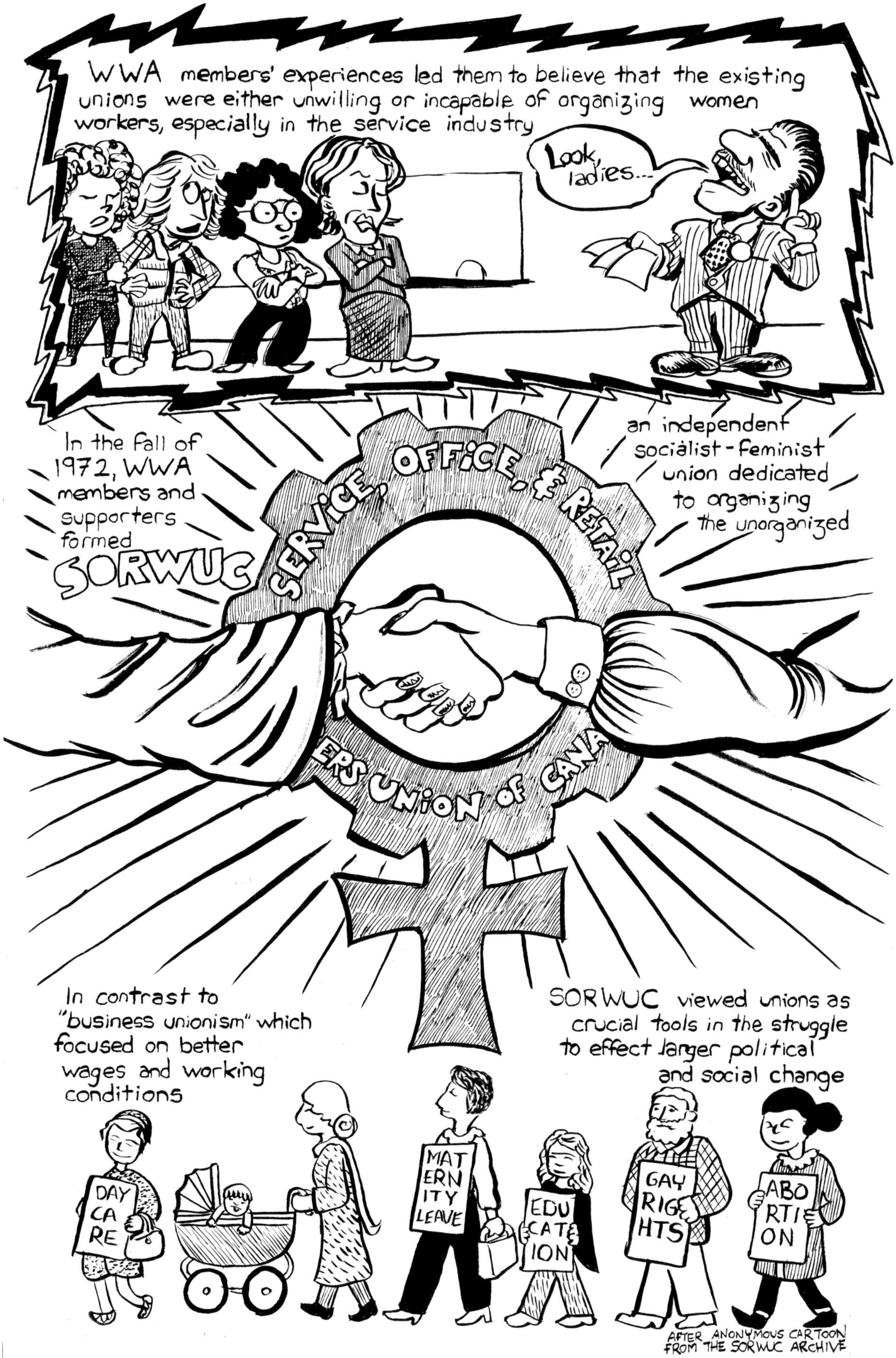
WWA members' experiences led them to believe that the existing unions were either unwilling or incapable of organizing women workers, especially in the service industry
Look, ladies...
In the fall of 1972, WWA members and supporters formed SORWUC
SERVICE, OFFICE, & RETAIL
ERS UNION OF CANA
an independent socialist-feminist union dedicated to organizing the unorganized
In contrast to "business unionism" which focused on better wages and working conditions
SORWUC viewed unions as crucial tools in the struggle to effect larger political and social change
DAY CA RE
MAT ERN ITY LEAVE
EDU CAT ION
GAY RIG HTS
ABO RTI ON
AFTER ANONYMOUS CARTOON FROM THE SORWUC ARCHIVE

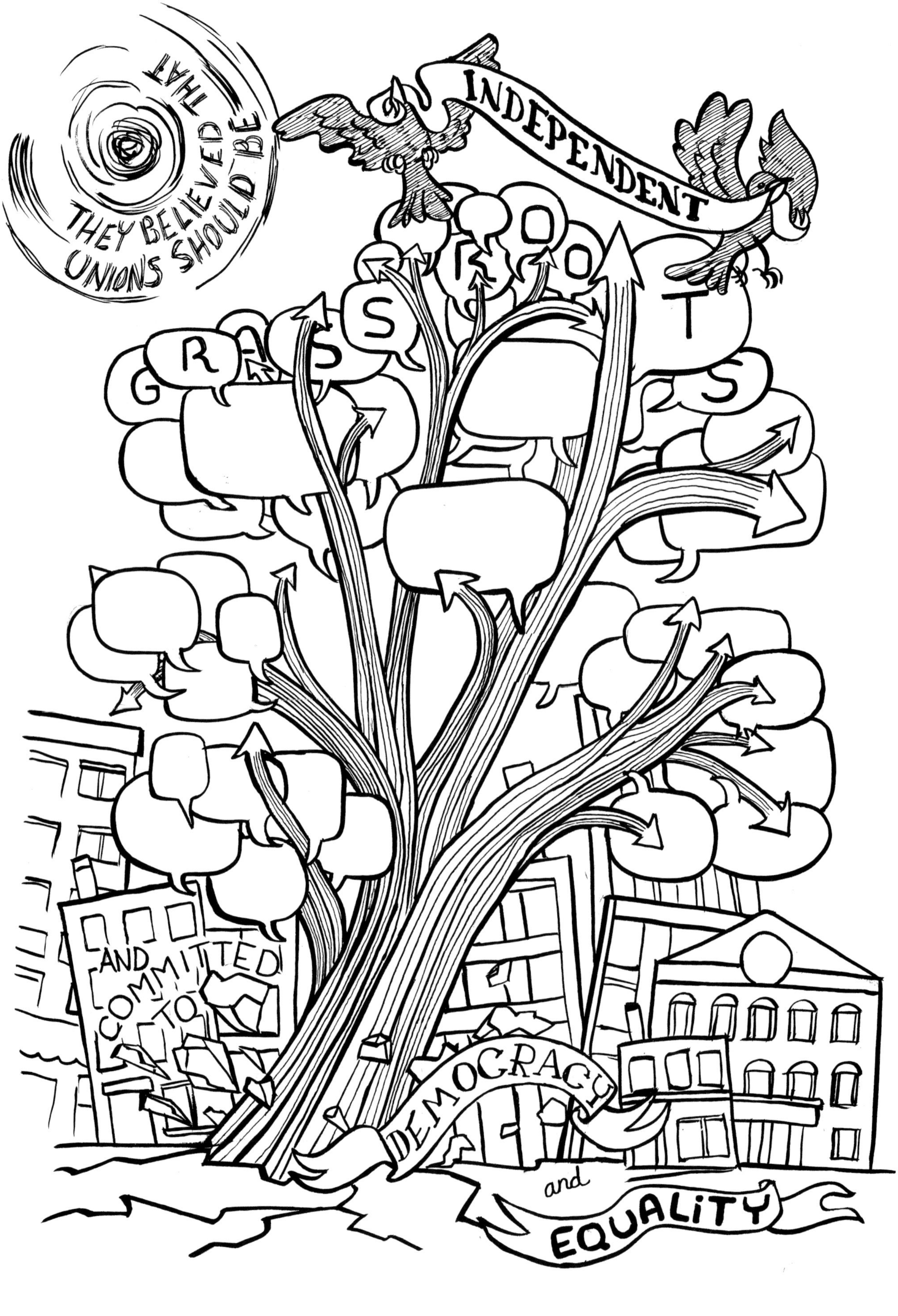
THEY BELIEVED UNIONS SHOULD BE THAT
INDEPENDENT
GRASSROOTS
AND COMMITTED TO
DEMOCRACY
and
EQUALITY

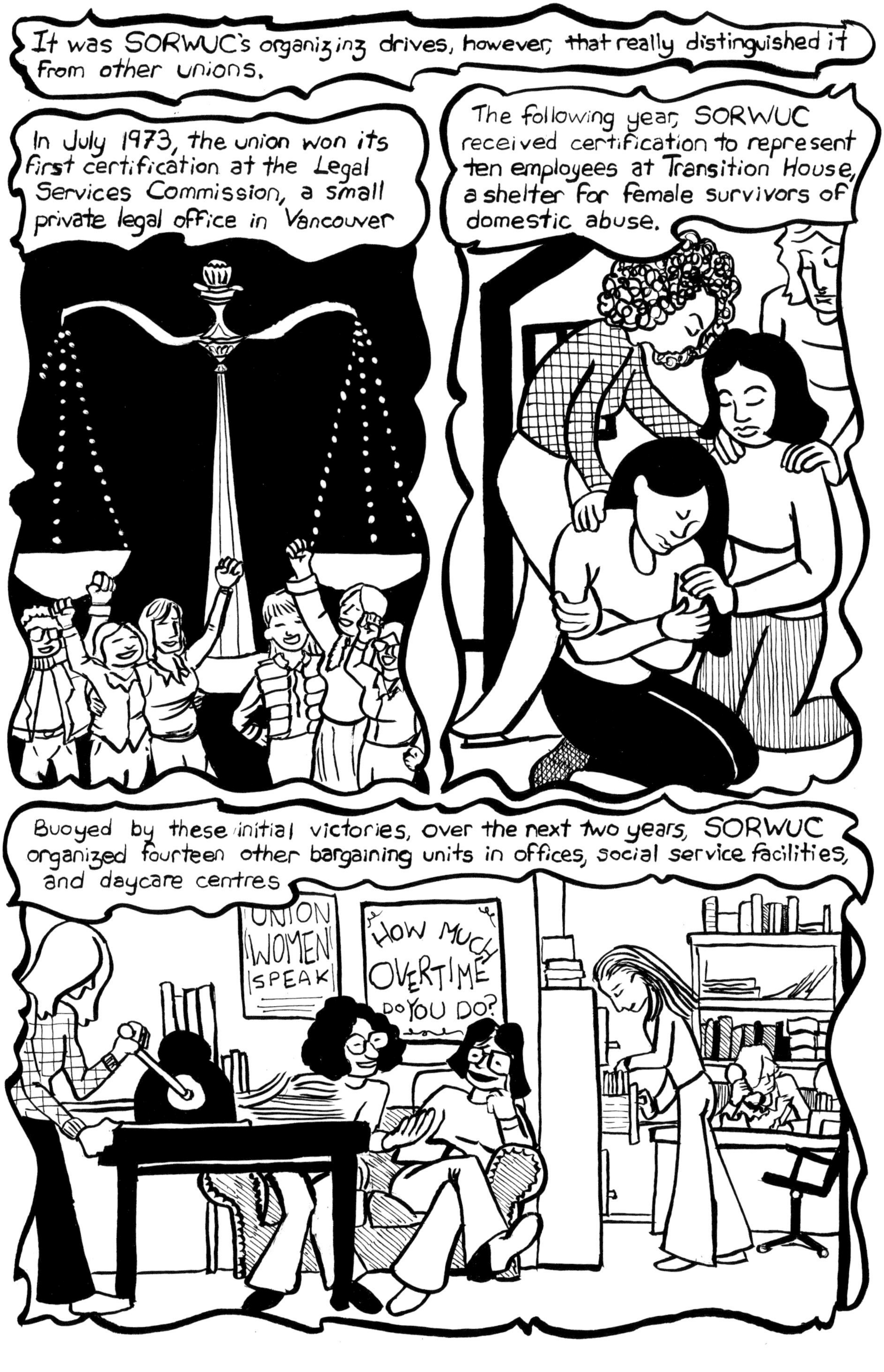
It was SORWUC's organizing drives, however, that really distinguished it from other unions.
In July 1973, the union won its first certification at the Legal Services Commission, a small private legal office in Vancouver
The following year, SORWUC received certification to represent ten employees at Transition House, a shelter for female survivors of domestic abuse.
Buoyed by these initial victories, over the next two years, SORWUC organized fourteen other bargaining units in offices, social service facilities, and daycare centres
UNION WOMEN SPEAK
HOW MUCH OVERTIME DO YOU DO?

SORWUC achieved a number of important organizing victories.

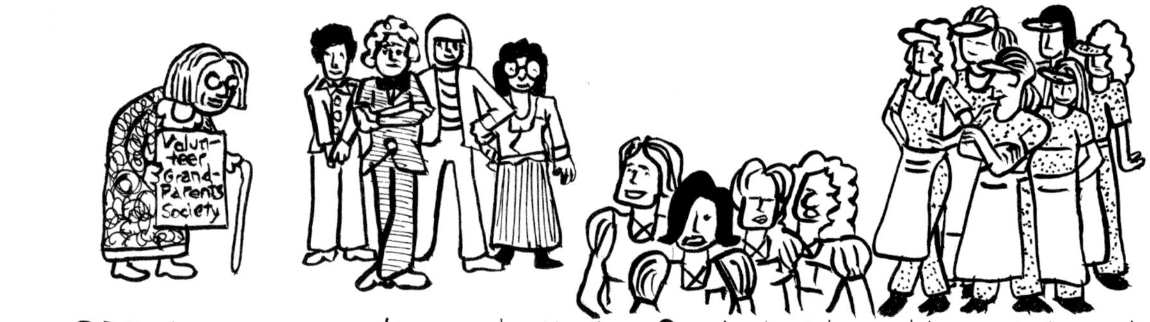
Volun-teer Grand-Parents Society

SORWUC recieved the most attention for its highly-publicized drive to organize bank workers.

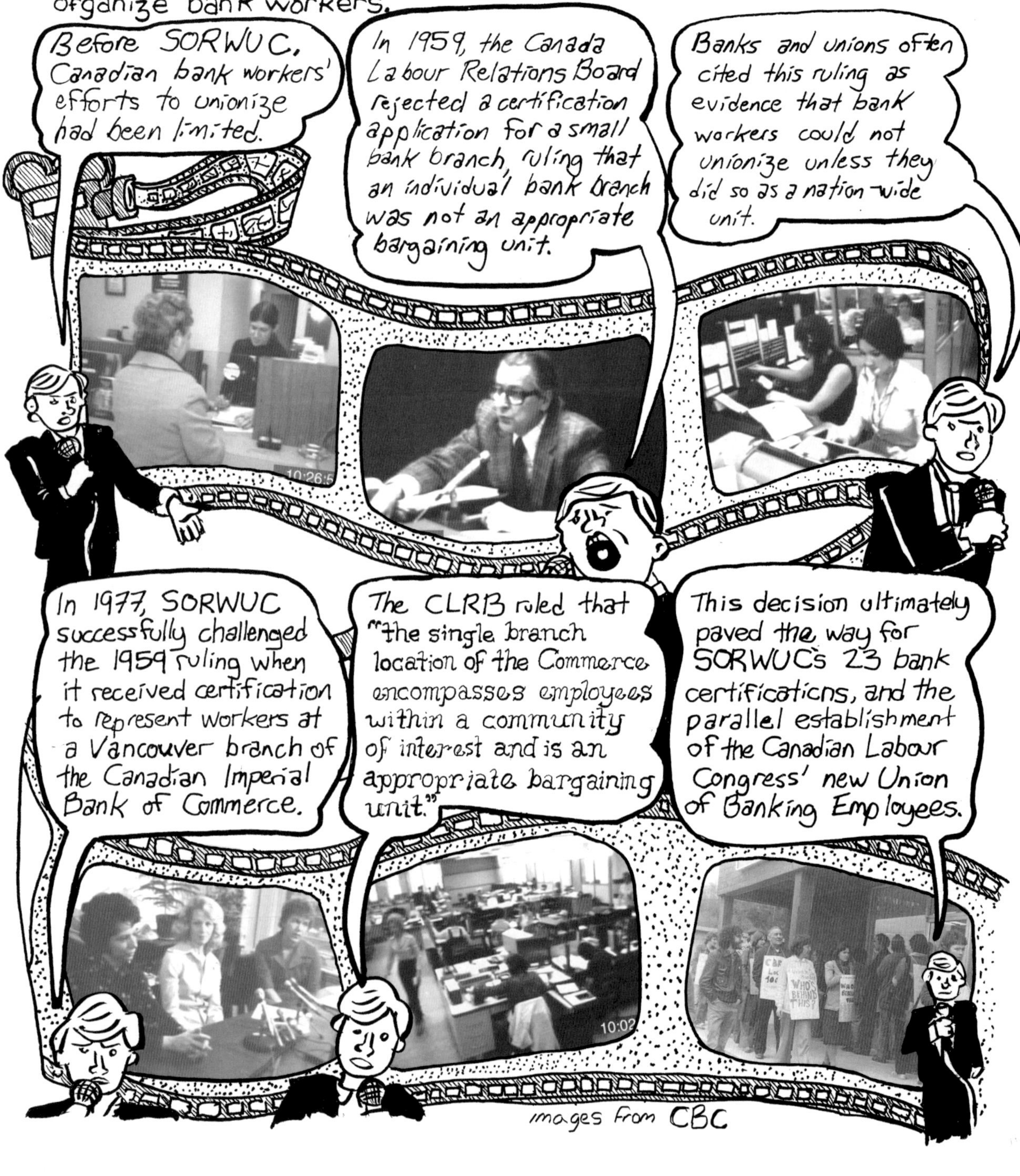
Before SORWUC, Canadian bank workers' efforts to unionize had been limited.
In 1959, the Canada Labour Relations Board rejected a certification application for a small bank branch, ruling that an individual bank branch was not an appropriate bargaining unit.
Banks and unions often cited this ruling as evidence that bank workers could not unionize unless they did so as a nation-wide unit.
In 1977, SORWUC successfully challenged the 1959 ruling when it received certification to represent workers at a Vancouver branch of the Canadian Imperial Bank of Commerce.
The CLRB ruled that "the single branch location of the Commerce encompasses employees within a community of interest and is an appropriate bargaining unit."
This decision ultimately paved the way for SORWUC's 23 bank certifications, and the parallel establishment of the Canadian Labour Congress' new Union of Banking Employees.

images from CBC

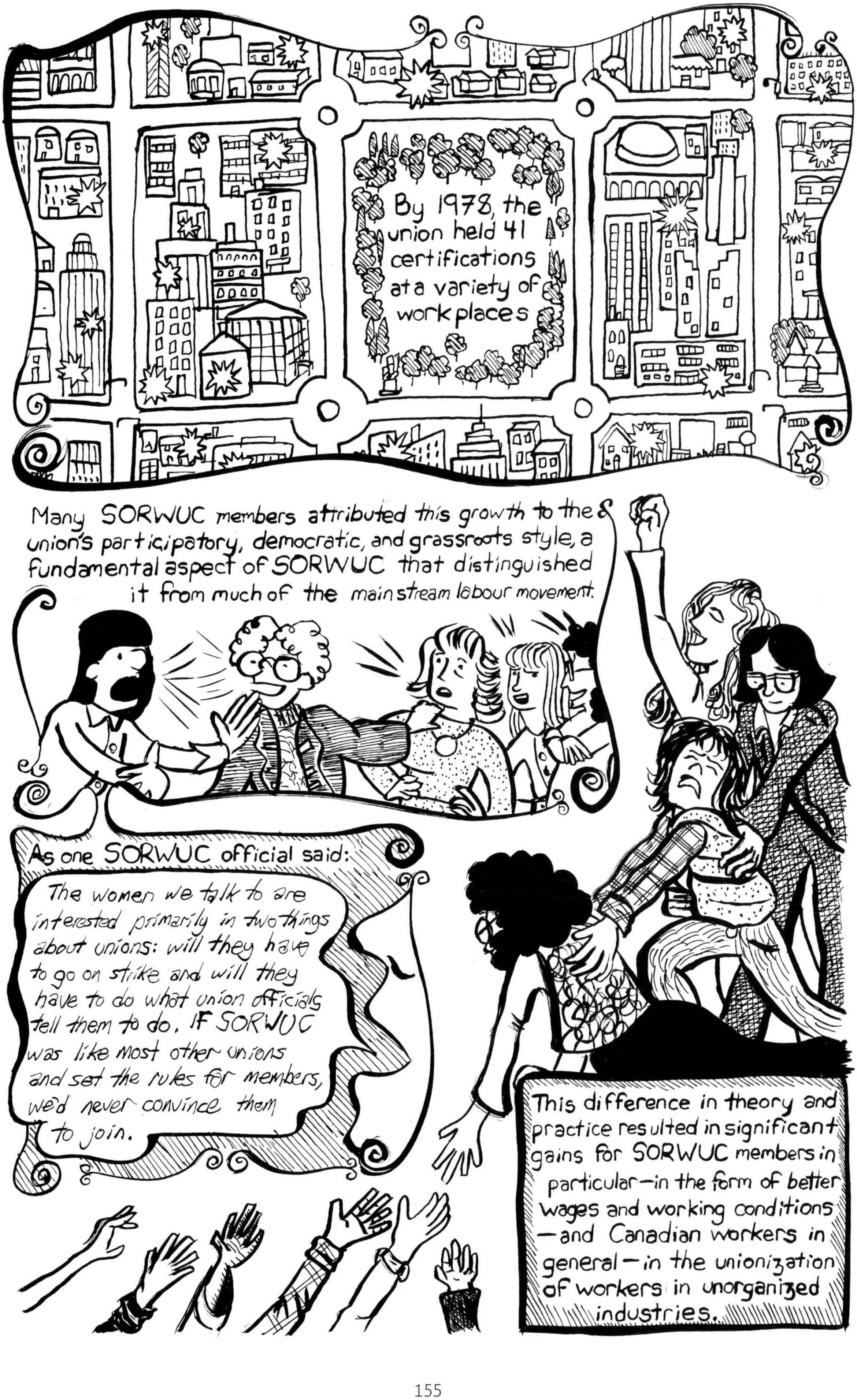
By 1978, the union held 41 certifications at a variety of workplaces
Many SORWUC members attributed this growth to the union's participatory, democratic, and grassroots style, a fundamental aspect of SORWUC that distinguished it from much of the mainstream labour movement.
As one SORWUC official said:
The women we talk to are interested primarily in two things about unions: will they have to go on strike and will they have to do what union officials tell them to do. If SORWUC was like most other unions and set the rules for members, we'd never convince them to join.
This difference in theory and practice resulted in significant gains for SORWUC members in particular—in the form of better wages and working conditions—and Canadian workers in general—in the unionization of workers in unorganized industries.

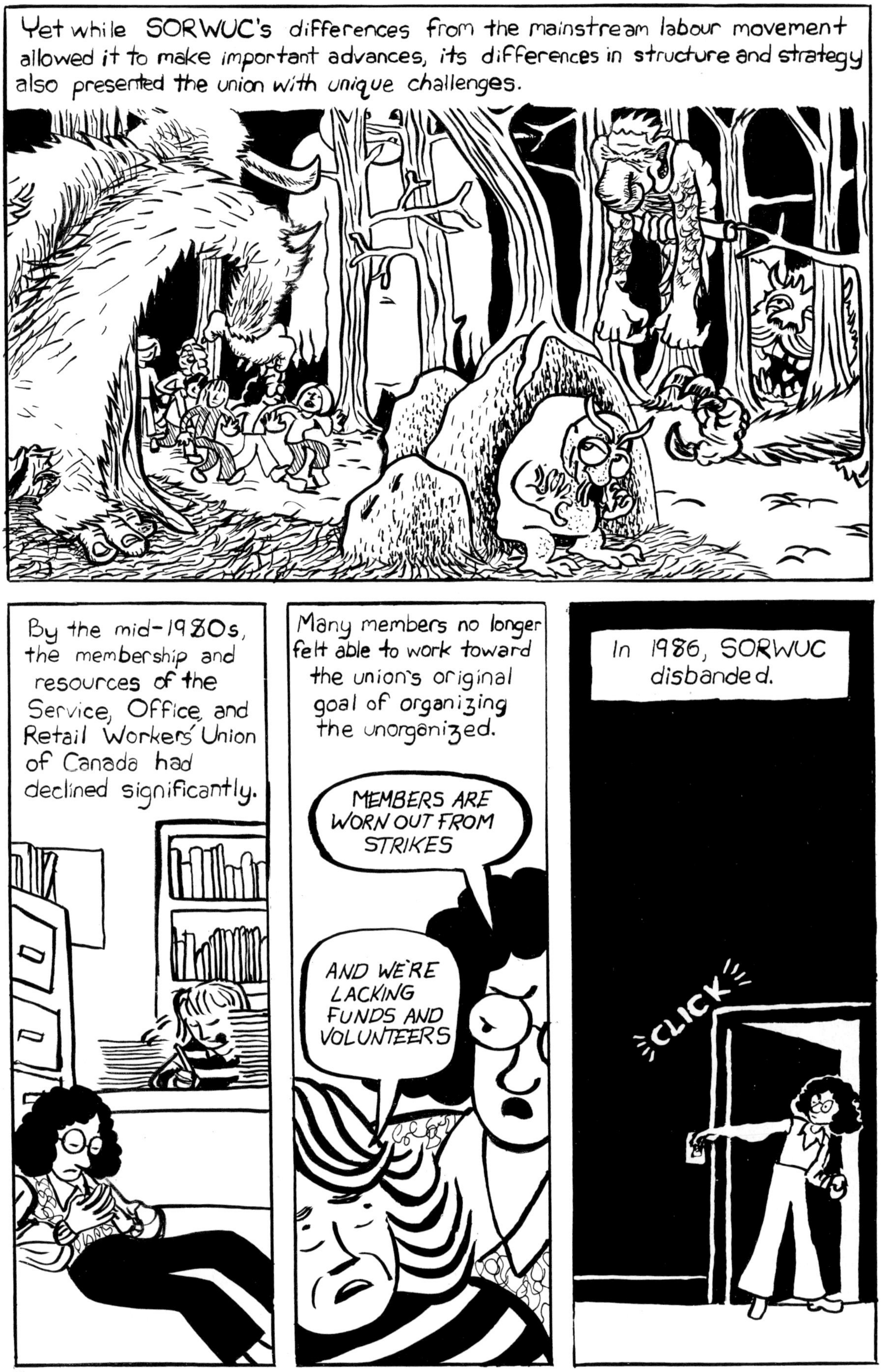
Yet while SORWUC's differences from the mainstream labour movement allowed it to make important advances, its differences in structure and strategy also presented the union with unique challenges.
By the mid-1980s, the membership and resources of the Service, Office, and Retail Workers' Union of Canada had declined significantly.
Many members no longer felt able to work toward the union's original goal of organizing the unorganized.
MEMBERS ARE WORN OUT FROM STRIKES
AND WE'RE LACKING FUNDS AND VOLUNTEERS
In 1986, SORWUC disbanded.
CLICK

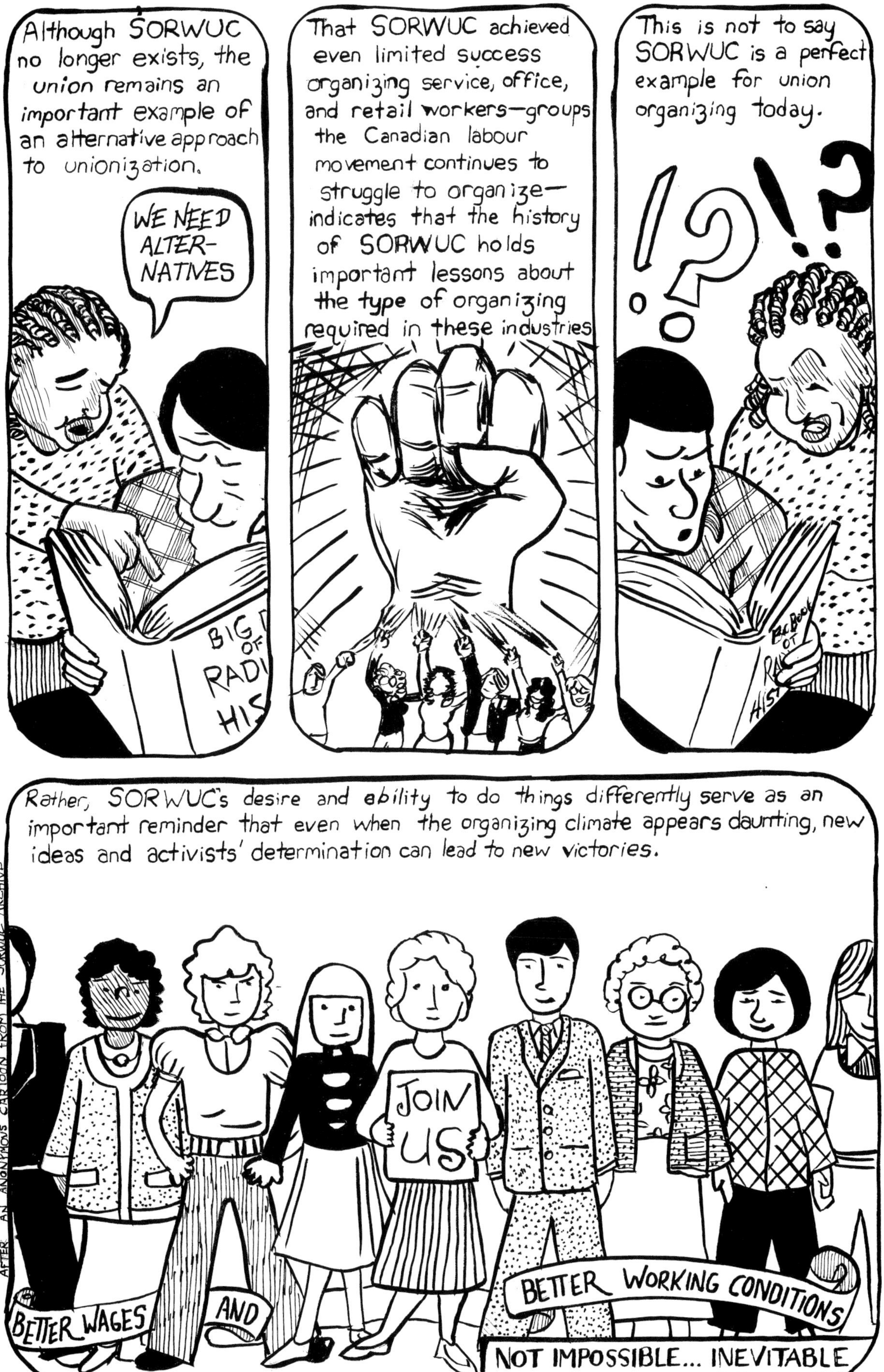
Although SORWUC no longer exists, the union remains an important example of an alternative approach to unionization.
WE NEED ALTERNATIVES
That SORWUC achieved even limited success organizing service, office, and retail workers—groups the Canadian labour movement continues to struggle to organize—indicates that the history of SORWUC holds important lessons about the type of organizing required in these industries
This is not to say SORWUC is a perfect example for union organizing today.
Rather, SORWUC's desire and ability to do things differently serve as an important reminder that even when the organizing climate appears daunting, new ideas and activists' determination can lead to new victories.
AFTER AN ANONYMOUS CARTOON FROM THE SORWUC ARCHIVE
JOIN US
BETTER WAGES
AND
BETTER WORKING CONDITIONS
NOT IMPOSSIBLE... INEVITABLE

Acknowledgements

We are grateful to the many people and organizations who assisted us with the production of this comic book. The Simon Fraser University Labour Studies Program and the Morgan Centre for Labour Research provided crucial financial support. The staff at the University of British Columbia Library Rare Books and Special Collections assisted us with archival research. The Canadian Broadcasting Corporation allowed us to reproduce images from their archives, and Colin Preston at CBC Vancouver assisted with this matter. Former SORWUC members shared their knowledge and resources with us. We thank all of these people for their support and encouragement.

We also acknowledge the activists and academics who have previously studied the Service, Office, and Retail Workers' Union of Canada and whose works assisted us in producing our comic book.

Notes

Page 147: The image of the banner was inspired by a photograph of SORWUC members holding a banner. The original photograph is in University of British Columbia Library Rare Books and Special Collections, Service, Office and Retail Workers Union of Canada fonds, Box 6, File 8.

Page 151: The image of the picket line was inspired by a cartoon in The Bank Book Collective, *An Account to Settle: The Story of the United Bank Workers (SORWUC)* (Vancouver: Press Gang Publishers, 1979).

Page 154: The film images came from the Canadian Broadcasting Corporation (CBC) coverage of SORWUC. These images have been reproduced with permission from CBC Vancouver.

Page 157: The image of the picket line was inspired by a cartoon in The Bank Book Collective, *An Account to Settle.*

The Days of Action
The Character of Class Struggle in 1990s Ontario

Looking Back at the Ontario Days of Action
David Camfield

A quirk of how we deal with history in our society is that we often hear more about events that took place fifty or one hundred years ago than momentous happenings in the not-too-distant past. When it comes to working-class history in Canada, some people have at least heard of the Winnipeg General Strike of 1919 or the strike of Ford workers in Windsor in 1946 that led to the Rand Formula (or automatic union dues checkoff). But how many people who began to become politically aware at some point in the 21st century know anything about the Ontario Days of Action?

In 1995, the Ontario NDP government of Bob Rae—vilified by the corporate media even though it had abandoned its initial agenda of minor social reforms, moved against public sector unions, and initiated a crackdown on "welfare fraud," and facing a racist backlash against its employment equity law fostered by both the Tories and Liberals—went down to defeat in the provincial election. The new Tory government headed by Mike Harris implemented a decisive turn to neoliberal policy in the province, much as the Liberal government headed by Prime Minister Jean Chrétien had just done at the federal level of the state. Without delay, the Tories brought in major cuts to public sector services and jobs. They slashed social assistance payments by 21.6 per cent and repealed the *Employment Equity Act*. They also revoked several pro-worker elements of labour law while adding a few employer-friendly provisions. University and college tuition fees were increased. In September 1995, Dudley George was shot and killed when police moved against a group of Indigenous people occupying Ipperwash Provincial Park. All this created a highly polarized political situation in which anti-Tory sentiment was strong. As *The Days of Action* shows so well, there followed several years of protest and resistance, sometimes on a large scale. The city-wide mobilizations known as Days of Action were at the centre of this popular upsurge.

Very little has been written about the Days of Action, so this comic book by Orion Keresztesi, Doug Nesbitt, and Sean Carleton is most welcome. Its pages ably recount the key events of the fight-back movement in Ontario between 1995 and 1998. *The Days of Action* reminds us that hundreds of thousands of people took part in the anti-Tory protests of the time in one way or another. These deserve to be recognized as one of the most important episodes of extra-parliamentary political action by workers in the last several decades, alongside the Common Front strikes in Québec in 1972 and, more recently, the anti-austerity protests and highly politicized strikes by ferry workers, health support workers, and teachers in British Columbia between 2002 and 2005 and the 2012 student/popular movement in Québec.

There was more to the Days of Action than large—in a few cases, huge—Saturday marches in the streets to protest the actions of the provincial government. What set the Days of Action apart from most anti-austerity protests in Canada and Québec was that they also included mass direct action, in the form of political strikes. By walking off the job on a Friday to protest the government's attacks (and, in many cases, their employers' support for the government), tens of thousands of people disrupted "business as usual" and defied the tight restrictions on when and how workers are permitted to withdraw their labour that have been central to labour law since the mid-1940s.

It is important to underscore that this strike action was made possible by the efforts of many union activists. It required many conversations with co-workers about what the government was doing and why people should not just go to a rally on a Saturday but stay away from work the day before, even though doing this fell outside the law. For many workers, participating in political strike action meant defying their bosses and losing a day's pay (there were also cases in which union officials arranged with employers that the day's production would be made up on another day or that workers would work a holiday in exchange for a day off on the Friday). The activity that went into mobilizing workers for a kind of action that had not been seen in Ontario since the pan-Canadian one-day strike against federal government wage controls in 1976 was important as political education on a mass scale. The strike action itself was a valuable learning experience.

It is also worth emphasizing that the Days of Action were class struggle. Even though most of their organizers and many of the people who took part would not have described what they were doing in that way (a consequence of the long-term decline of working-class politics in Canada), class struggle is what was happening. Mobilizing under the banner of "labour" and "community" against Harris, organizing through union locals, city-wide bodies like labour councils and coalitions for social justice, student groups, and many other organizations, and carrying placards or wearing buttons with messages about the harm being inflicted on women, students, the poor, union members, people of colour, people with disabilities, and others, the working class in Ontario moved against what capital—acting through its state—was doing to them.

The movement certainly had many weaknesses, as do all mass movements. As this comic book makes clear, the top leaders of Ontario's unions were divided. Some (the "Pinks") were outright opposed to the Days of Action, seeing them as a distraction and an obstacle to replacing the Tories with the NDP at the next election. Others supported the Days of Action. They also saw re-electing the NDP as the goal, but thought that the protests would help do that as well as build the capacity of unions to influence government. Loyalty to bureaucratic protocol that treats a union's members as the property of its top officials meant that they never appealed to members of the "Pink" unions to support the Days of Action. Theirs was not the strategy advocated by the radical wing of the movement (perhaps most notably the Ontario Coalition Against Poverty, but also including some union activists): trying to build protest into resistance that could block particular Tory measures and escalate resistance to such a level that the government would be forced from office.

This alternative was not merely the vision of a marginal fringe; the demand for a province-wide general strike and chants like "City by city is much too slow, let's shut down Ontario!" were popular at many Days of Action. Unfortunately, supporters of this "fight to win" strategy were too few and insufficiently organized to have an impact on the direction of the movement. No organized opposition with these politics cohered within Ontario's unions. Other weaknesses included a general failure to deepen much of the anti-Tory sentiment into anti-neo-liberal consciousness (in contrast to what the 2012 "Red Square" movement in Québec accomplished) or foster a widely shared basic anti-racist and feminist understanding of the Tory assault. Nor did even the beginnings of a left political alternative to the NDP emerge from the experience.

Despite the weakness of the Days of Action, there is no doubt that the government would have pushed through even worse neo-liberal measures if it had not faced such mass protests. This is worth bearing in mind today, as governments of all stripes implement austerity programs—more neoliberal restructuring in response to the crisis of capitalism that since 2008 has mired the global economy in slump.

Looking back at the Days of Action reminds us that mass working-class struggle isn't something that only happens in other parts of the world—it happened here, and it can happen again (though it can't simply be conjured up by radicals, and we shouldn't expect future upsurges to be just like what took place in Ontario). This history also reminds us that it is a mistake to think that the left wing of the union officialdom will adopt a strategy based on trying to escalate resistance to the level needed to defeat a determined government. It is also wrong to expect that, faced with inadequate leadership, rank and file activists will spontaneously come together to take a movement in a more promising direction. To push for an alternative direction with the possibility of winning takes a lot of grassroots organizing. The success of such efforts will be affected by how much has previously been done by activists who have patiently been trying to foster democratic, militant, and solidaristic unionism. These are some of the lessons that we can learn from *The Days of Action.*

Notes

1 I discuss the reasons for this in "What Is Trade Union Bureaucracy? A Theoretical Account," *Alternate Routes* 24 (2013) (available at alternateroutes.ca).

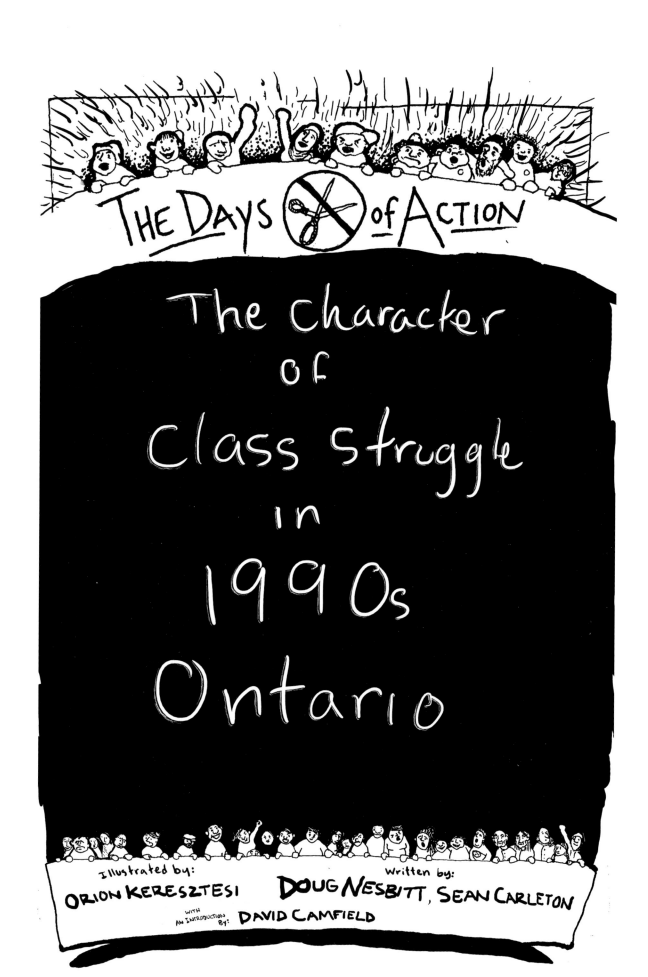

THE DAYS of ACTION

The Character of Class Struggle in 1990s Ontario

Illustrated by:
ORION KERESZTESI

Written by:
DOUG NESBITT, SEAN CARLETON

with an introduction by: DAVID CAMFIELD

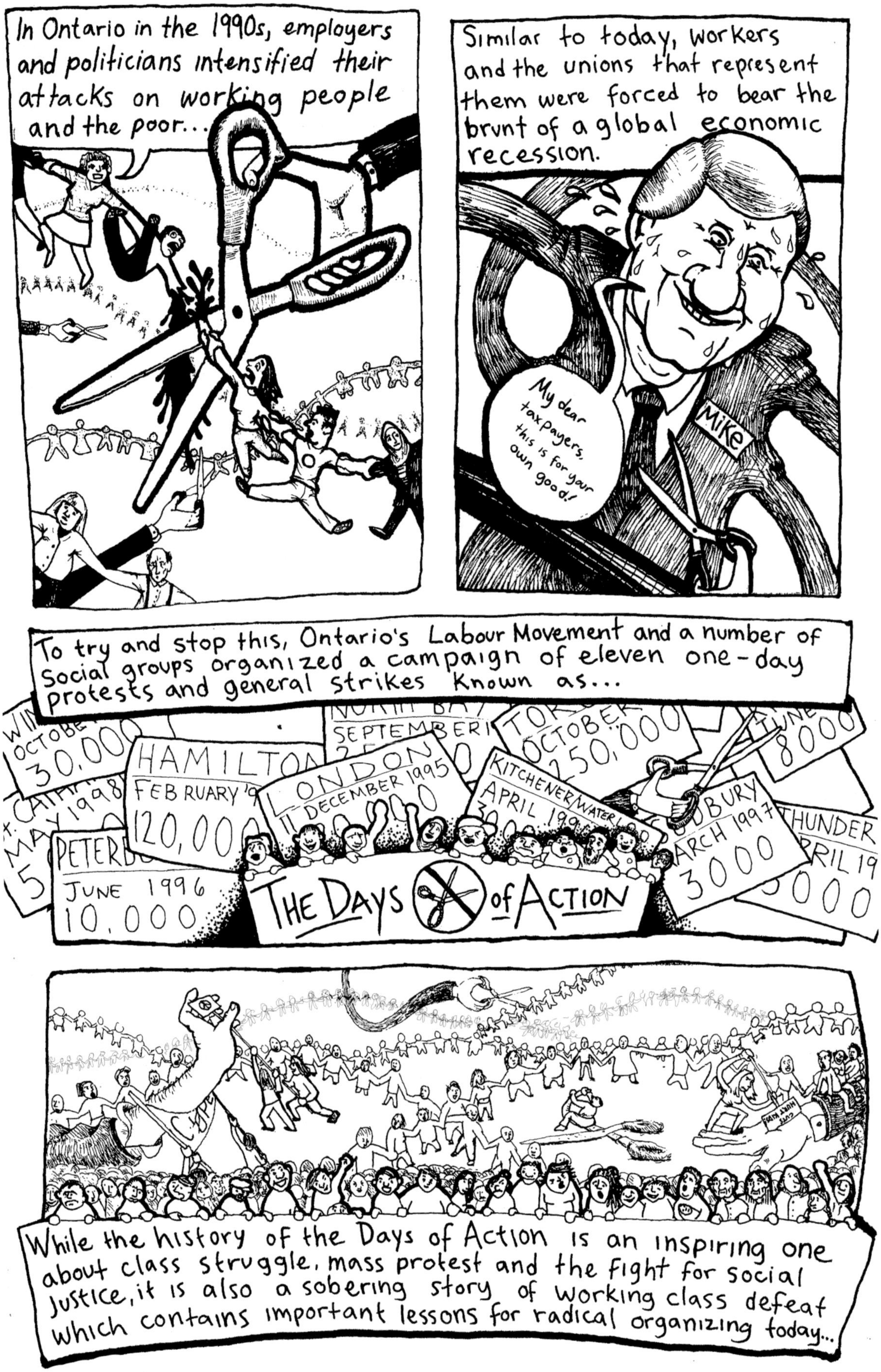
In Ontario in the 1990s, employers and politicians intensified their attacks on working people and the poor...
Similar to today, workers and the unions that represent them were forced to bear the brunt of a global economic recession.
My dear taxpayers, this is for your own good!
MIKE
To try and stop this, Ontario's Labour Movement and a number of social groups organized a campaign of eleven one-day protests and general strikes known as...
30,000
SEPTEMBER
OCTOBER
8000
LONDON
11 DECEMBER 1995
KITCHENER/WATER
JUNE 1996
10,000
3000
THE DAYS OF ACTION
While the history of the Days of Action is an inspiring one about class struggle, mass protest and the fight for social justice, it is also a sobering story of working class defeat which contains important lessons for radical organizing today...

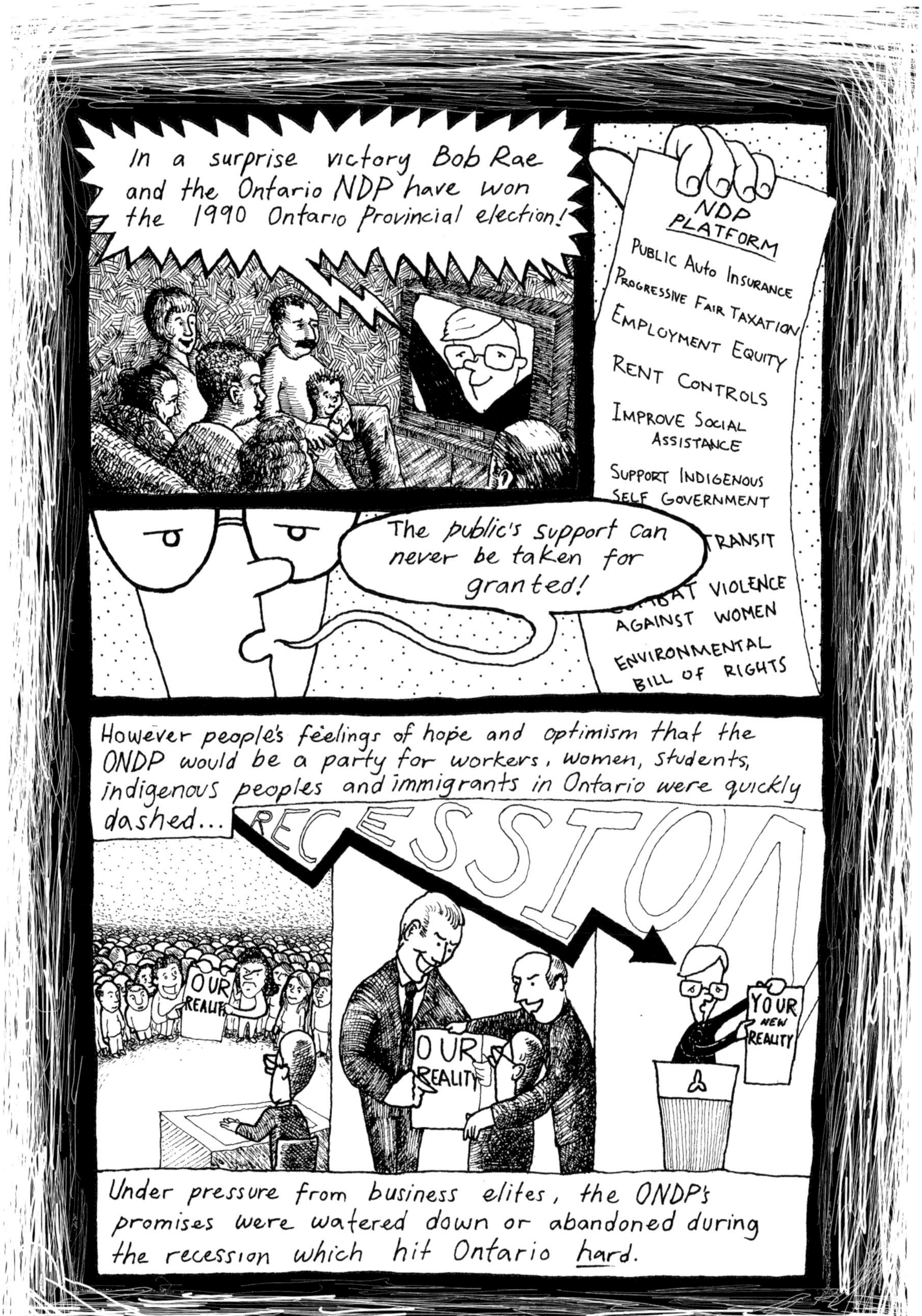

In a surprise victory Bob Rae and the Ontario NDP have won the 1990 Ontario Provincial election!
NDP PLATFORM
PUBLIC AUTO INSURANCE
PROGRESSIVE FAIR TAXATION
EMPLOYMENT EQUITY
RENT CONTROLS
IMPROVE SOCIAL ASSISTANCE
SUPPORT INDIGENOUS SELF GOVERNMENT
TRANSIT
VIOLENCE AGAINST WOMEN
ENVIRONMENTAL BILL OF RIGHTS
The public's support can never be taken for granted!
However people's feelings of hope and optimism that the ONDP would be a party for workers, women, students, indigenous peoples and immigrants in Ontario were quickly dashed...
RECESSION
OUR REALITY
OUR REALITY
YOUR NEW REALITY
Under pressure from business elites, the ONDP's promises were watered down or abandoned during the recession which hit Ontario hard.

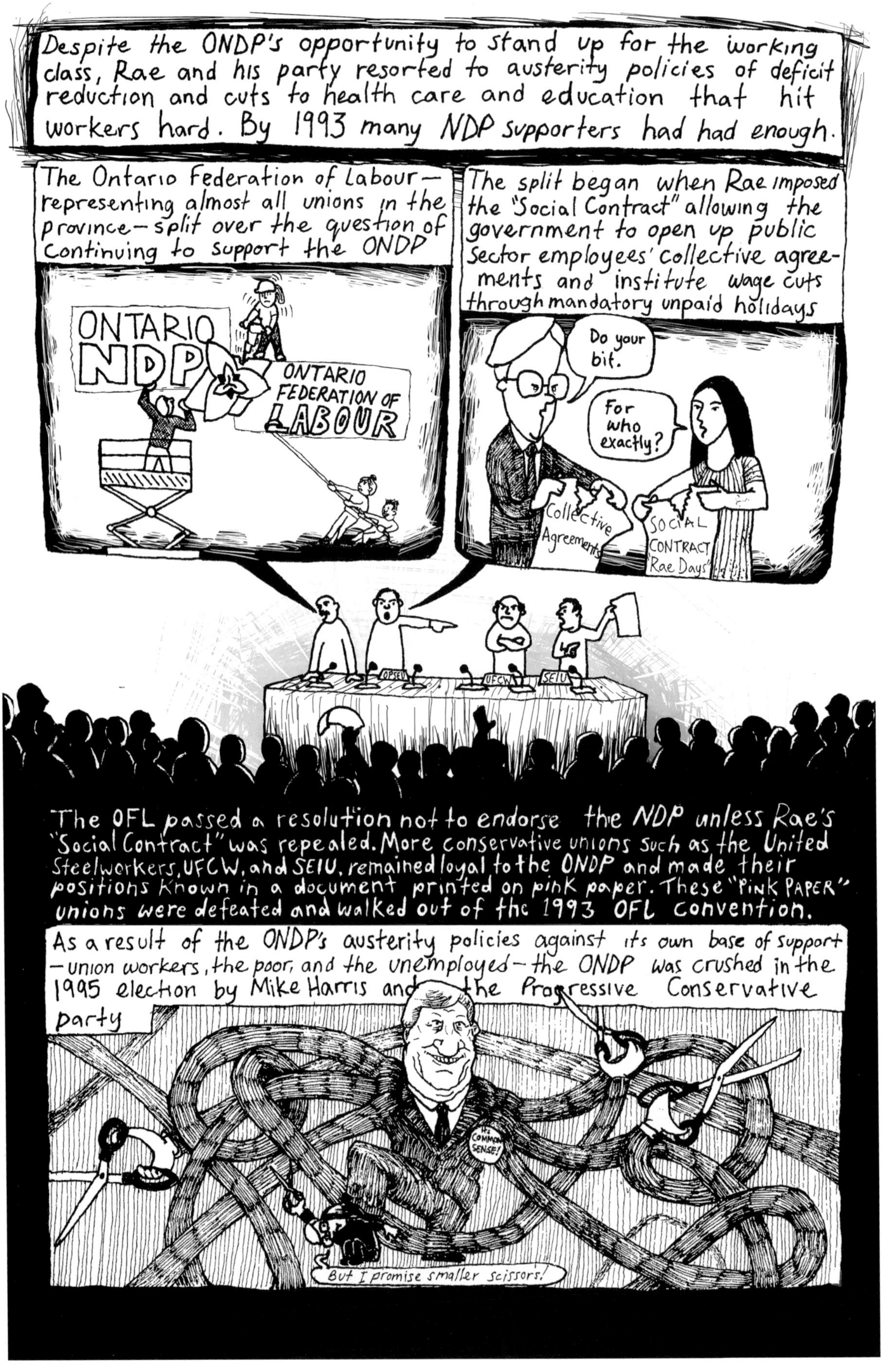
Despite the ONDP's opportunity to stand up for the working class, Rae and his party resorted to austerity policies of deficit reduction and cuts to health care and education that hit workers hard. By 1993 many NDP supporters had had enough.
The Ontario Federation of Labour—representing almost all unions in the province—split over the question of continuing to support the ONDP
ONTARIO NDP
ONTARIO FEDERATION OF LABOUR
The split began when Rae imposed the "Social Contract" allowing the government to open up public sector employees' collective agreements and institute wage cuts through mandatory unpaid holidays
Do your bit.
For who exactly?
Collective Agreements
SOCIAL CONTRACT "Rae Days"
OPSEU
UFCW
SEIU
The OFL passed a resolution not to endorse the NDP unless Rae's "Social Contract" was repealed. More conservative unions such as the United Steelworkers, UFCW, and SEIU, remained loyal to the ONDP and made their positions known in a document printed on pink paper. These "PINK PAPER" unions were defeated and walked out of the 1993 OFL convention.
As a result of the ONDP's austerity policies against its own base of support—union workers, the poor, and the unemployed—the ONDP was crushed in the 1995 election by Mike Harris and the Progressive Conservative party
It's COMMON SENSE!
But I promise smaller scissors!

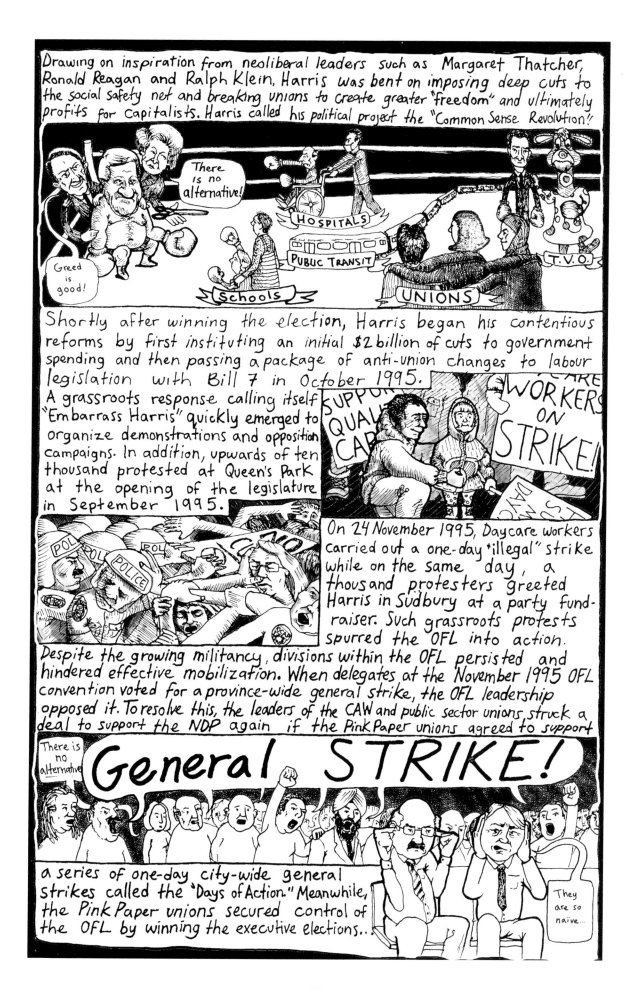

Drawing on inspiration from neoliberal leaders such as Margaret Thatcher, Ronald Reagan and Ralph Klein, Harris was bent on imposing deep cuts to the social safety net and breaking unions to create greater "freedom" and ultimately profits for capitalists. Harris called his political project the "Common Sense Revolution."

There is no alternative!

Greed is good!

HOSPITALS

PUBLIC TRANSIT

Schools

UNIONS

T.V.O.

Shortly after winning the election, Harris began his contentious reforms by first instituting an initial $2 billion of cuts to government spending and then passing a package of anti-union changes to labour legislation with Bill 7 in October 1995.

A grassroots response calling itself "Embarrass Harris" quickly emerged to organize demonstrations and opposition campaigns. In addition, upwards of ten thousand protested at Queen's Park at the opening of the legislature in September 1995.

SUPPORT QUALITY CARE

WORKERS ON STRIKE!

On 24 November 1995, Daycare workers carried out a one-day "illegal" strike while on the same day, a thousand protesters greeted Harris in Sudbury at a party fundraiser. Such grassroots protests spurred the OFL into action.

POLICE

Despite the growing militancy, divisions within the OFL persisted and hindered effective mobilization. When delegates at the November 1995 OFL convention voted for a province-wide general strike, the OFL leadership opposed it. To resolve this, the leaders of the CAW and public sector unions struck a deal to support the NDP again if the Pink Paper unions agreed to support

There is no alternative

General STRIKE!

a series of one-day city-wide general strikes called the "Days of Action." Meanwhile, the Pink Paper unions secured control of the OFL by winning the executive elections...

They are so naïve...

167

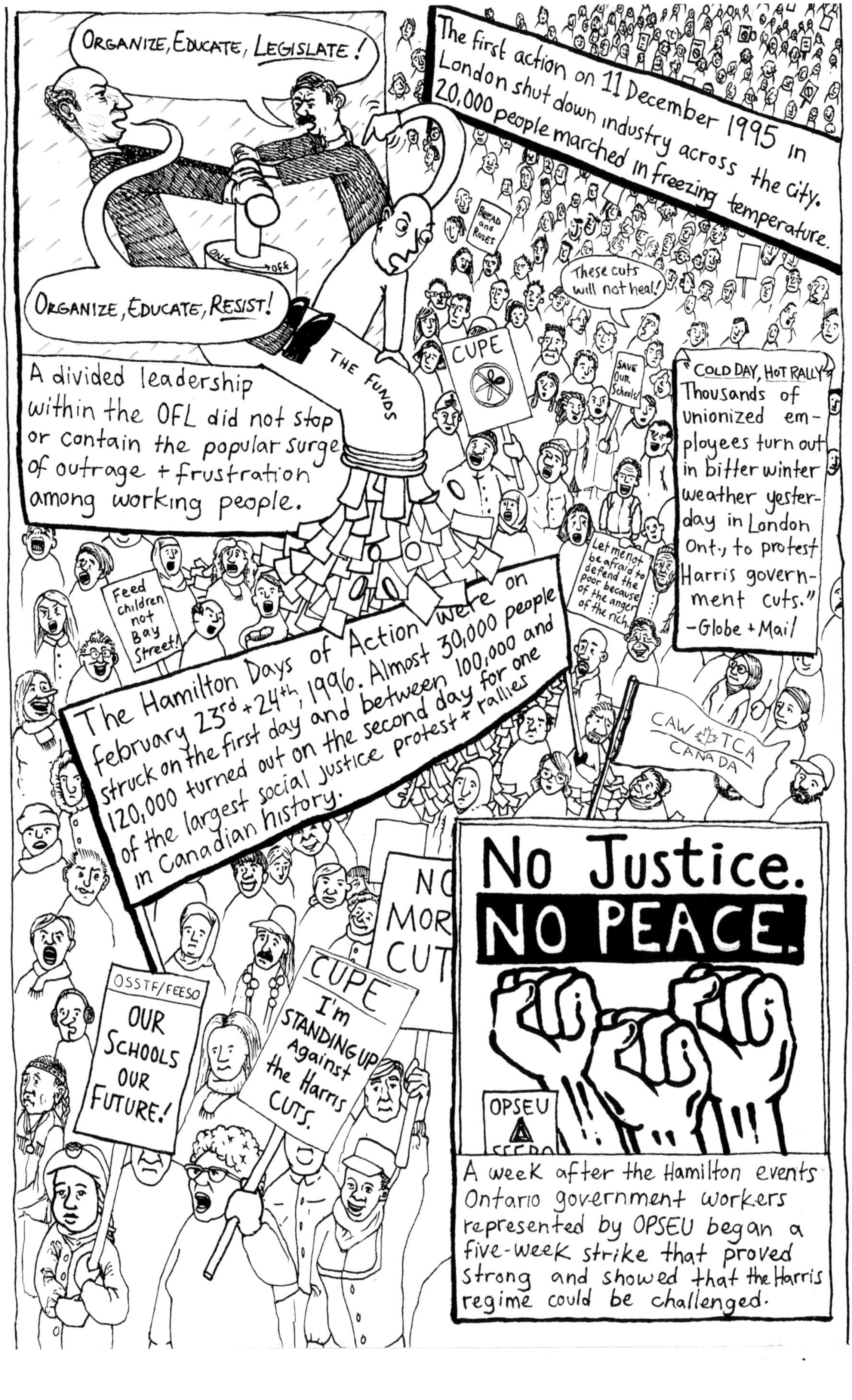
ORGANIZE, EDUCATE, LEGISLATE!
ORGANIZE, EDUCATE, RESIST!
ON OFF
THE FUNDS
A divided leadership within the OFL did not stop or contain the popular surge of outrage + frustration among working people.
The first action on 11 December 1995 in London shut down industry across the city. 20,000 people marched in freezing temperature.
BREAD and ROSES
These cuts will not heal!
CUPE
SAVE OUR Schools!
"COLD DAY, HOT RALLY" Thousands of unionized employees turn out in bitter winter weather yesterday in London Ont., to protest Harris government cuts." -Globe + Mail
Feed children not Bay Street!
Let me not be afraid to defend the poor because of the anger of the rich.
The Hamilton Days of Action were on February 23rd + 24th, 1996. Almost 30,000 people struck on the first day and between 100,000 and 120,000 turned out on the second day for one of the largest social justice protest + rallies in Canadian history.
CAW TCA CANADA
NO MORE CUT
No Justice. NO PEACE.
OPSEU
OSSTF/FEESO OUR SCHOOLS OUR FUTURE!
CUPE I'm STANDING UP Against the Harris CUTS.
A week after the Hamilton events Ontario government workers represented by OPSEU began a five-week strike that proved strong and showed that the Harris regime could be challenged.

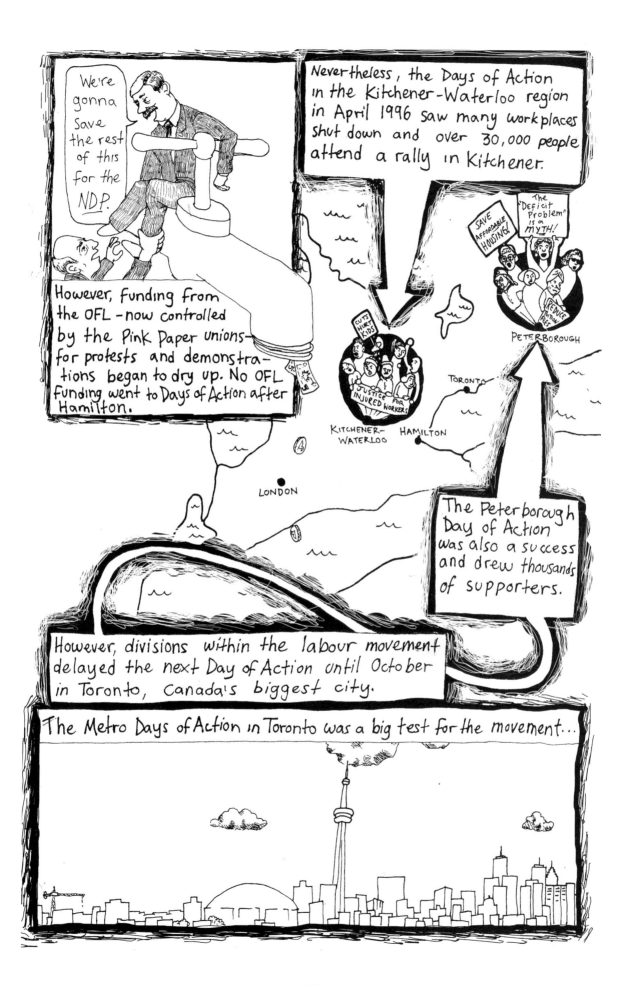

We're gonna save the rest of this for the N.D.P.

Nevertheless, the Days of Action in the Kitchener-Waterloo region in April 1996 saw many workplaces shut down and over 30,000 people attend a rally in Kitchener.

However, funding from the OFL - now controlled by the Pink Paper unions - for protests and demonstrations began to dry up. No OFL funding went to Days of Action after Hamilton.

SAVE AFFORDABLE HOUSING!

The "DEFICIT Problem" is a MYTH!

REDUCE TUITION FEES

PETERBOROUGH

CUTS HURT KIDS

JUSTICE FOR INJURED WORKERS

TORONTO

KITCHENER-WATERLOO

HAMILTON

LONDON

The Peterborough Day of Action was also a success and drew thousands of supporters.

However, divisions within the labour movement delayed the next Day of Action until October in Toronto, Canada's biggest city.

The Metro Days of Action in Toronto was a big test for the movement...

169

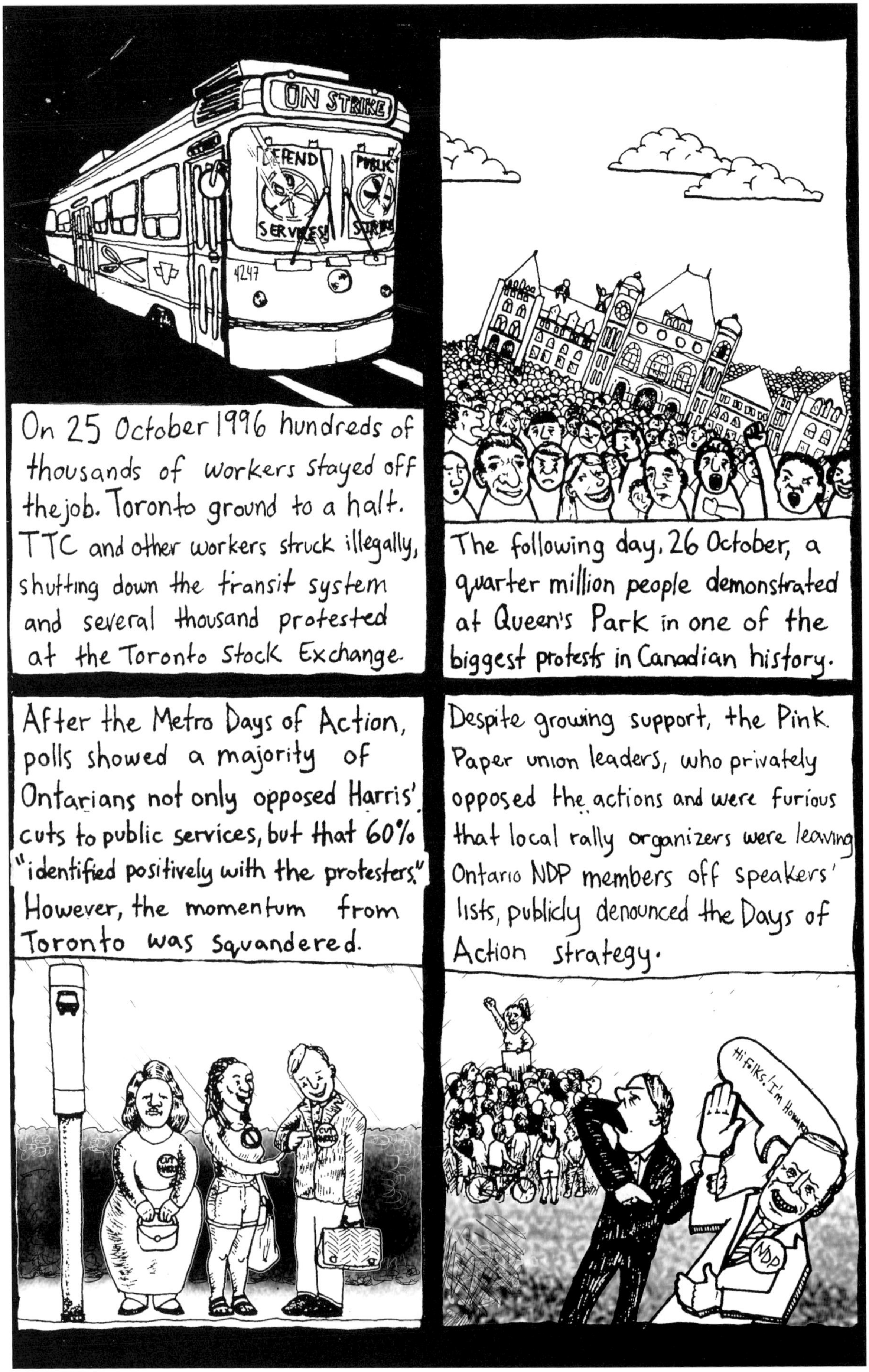
ON STRIKE
DEFEND PUBLIC SERVICES!
PUBLIC STRIKE
4247
On 25 October 1996 hundreds of thousands of workers stayed off the job. Toronto ground to a halt. TTC and other workers struck illegally, shutting down the transit system and several thousand protested at the Toronto Stock Exchange.
The following day, 26 October, a quarter million people demonstrated at Queen's Park in one of the biggest protests in Canadian history.
After the Metro Days of Action, polls showed a majority of Ontarians not only opposed Harris' cuts to public services, but that 60% "identified positively with the protesters." However, the momentum from Toronto was squandered.
CUT HARRIS
Despite growing support, the Pink Paper union leaders, who privately opposed the actions and were furious that local rally organizers were leaving Ontario NDP members off speakers' lists, publicly denounced the Days of Action strategy.
Hi folks! I'm Howard
NDP

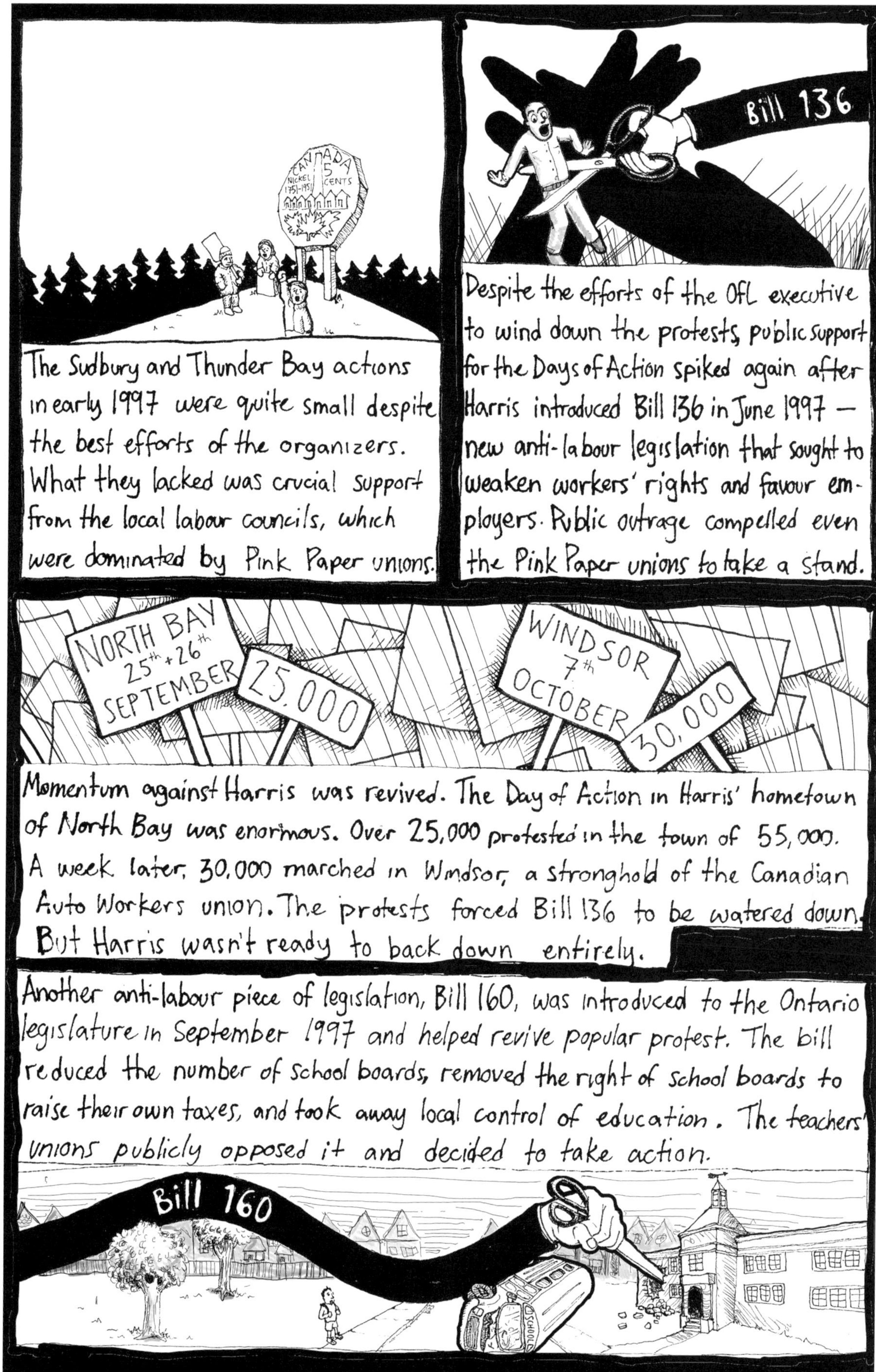
CANADA 5 CENTS NICKEL 1751-1951
The Sudbury and Thunder Bay actions in early 1997 were quite small despite the best efforts of the organizers. What they lacked was crucial support from the local labour councils, which were dominated by Pink Paper unions.
Bill 136
Despite the efforts of the OFL executive to wind down the protests, public support for the Days of Action spiked again after Harris introduced Bill 136 in June 1997 — new anti-labour legislation that sought to weaken workers' rights and favour employers. Public outrage compelled even the Pink Paper unions to take a stand.
NORTH BAY 25th + 26th SEPTEMBER
25,000
WINDSOR 7th OCTOBER
30,000
Momentum against Harris was revived. The Day of Action in Harris' hometown of North Bay was enormous. Over 25,000 protested in the town of 55,000. A week later, 30,000 marched in Windsor, a stronghold of the Canadian Auto Workers union. The protests forced Bill 136 to be watered down. But Harris wasn't ready to back down entirely.
Another anti-labour piece of legislation, Bill 160, was introduced to the Ontario legislature in September 1997 and helped revive popular protest. The bill reduced the number of school boards, removed the right of school boards to raise their own taxes, and took away local control of education. The teachers' unions publicly opposed it and decided to take action.
Bill 160
SCHOOL

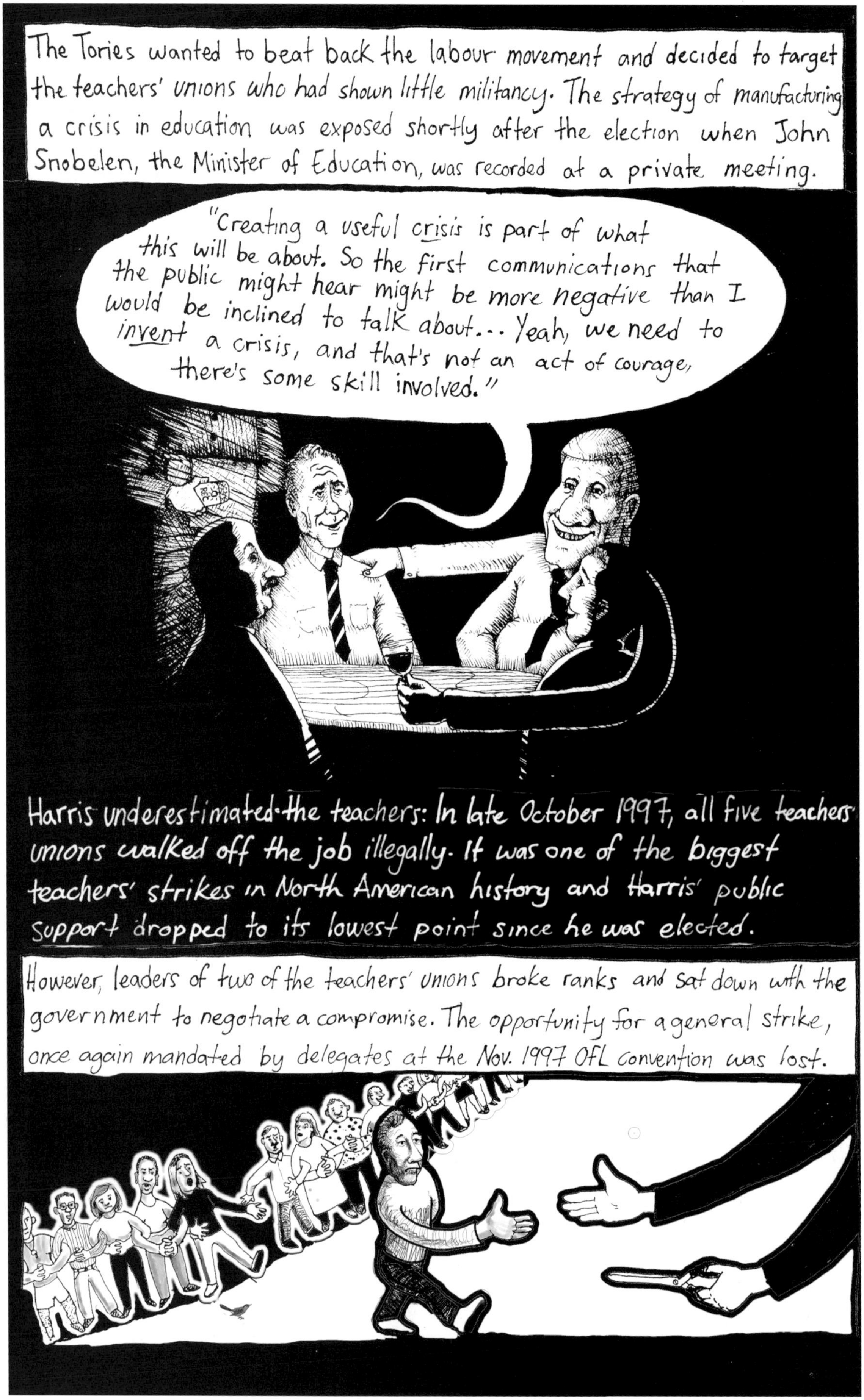
The Tories wanted to beat back the labour movement and decided to target the teachers' unions who had shown little militancy. The strategy of manufacturing a crisis in education was exposed shortly after the election when John Snobelen, the Minister of Education, was recorded at a private meeting.
"Creating a useful crisis is part of what this will be about. So the first communications that the public might hear might be more negative than I would be inclined to talk about... Yeah, we need to invent a crisis, and that's not an act of courage, there's some skill involved."
Harris underestimated the teachers: In late October 1997, all five teachers' unions walked off the job illegally. It was one of the biggest teachers' strikes in North American history and Harris' public support dropped to its lowest point since he was elected.
However, leaders of two of the teachers' unions broke ranks and sat down with the government to negotiate a compromise. The opportunity for a general strike, once again mandated by delegates at the Nov. 1997 OFL convention was lost.

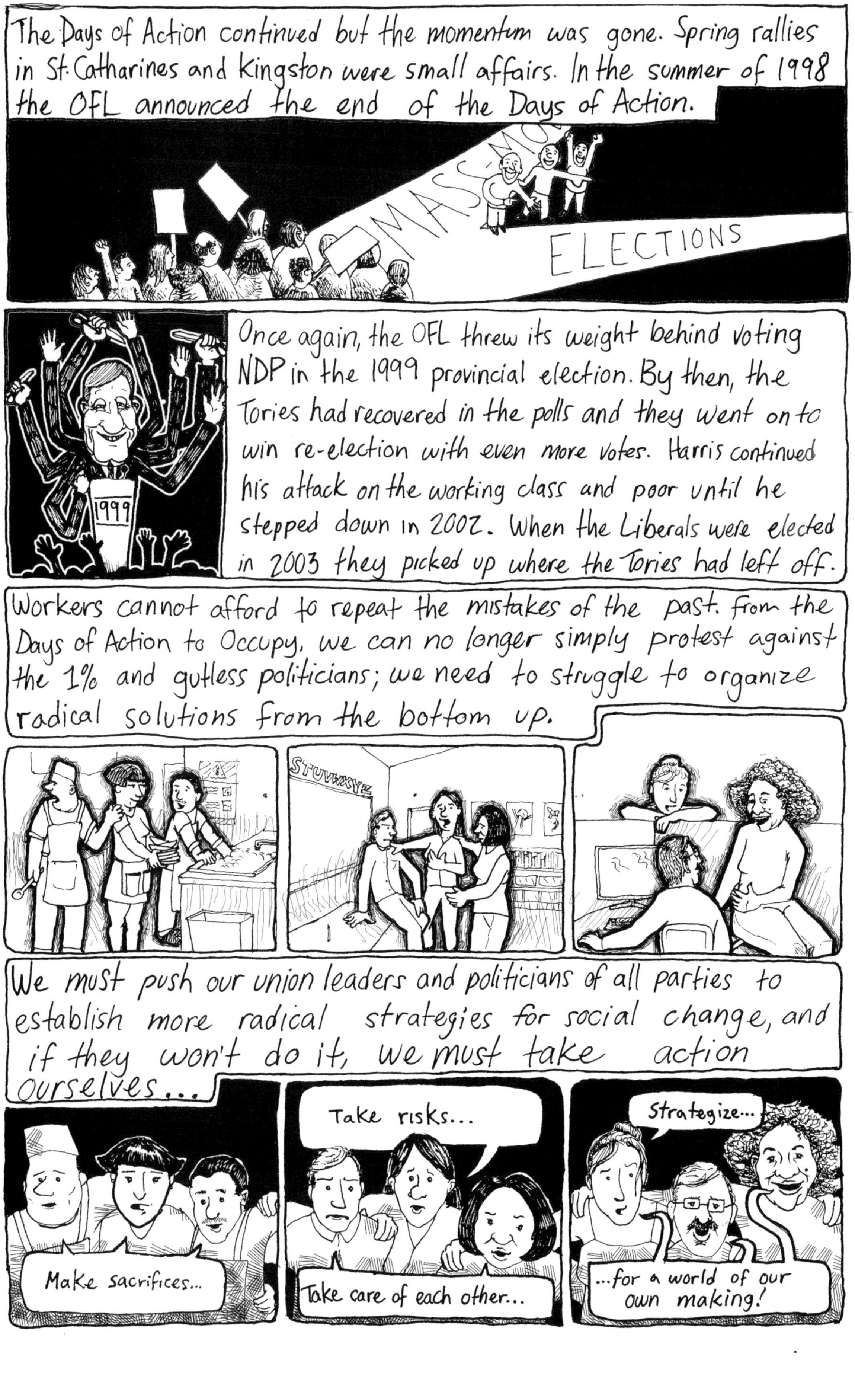
The Days of Action continued but the momentum was gone. Spring rallies in St. Catharines and Kingston were small affairs. In the summer of 1998 the OFL announced the end of the Days of Action.
ELECTIONS
1999
Once again, the OFL threw its weight behind voting NDP in the 1999 provincial election. By then, the Tories had recovered in the polls and they went on to win re-election with even more votes. Harris continued his attack on the working class and poor until he stepped down in 2002. When the Liberals were elected in 2003 they picked up where the Tories had left off.
Workers cannot afford to repeat the mistakes of the past. From the Days of Action to Occupy, we can no longer simply protest against the 1% and gutless politicians; we need to struggle to organize radical solutions from the bottom up.
We must push our union leaders and politicians of all parties to establish more radical strategies for social change, and if they won't do it, we must take action ourselves...
Make sacrifices...
Take risks...
Take care of each other...
Strategize...
...for a world of our own making!

Acknowledgements

We are grateful for the encouragement and financial support we received from Local 3908 of the Canadian Union of Public Employees. We also thank the people who have previously studied the character of class struggle in 1990s Ontario.

Notes

For artistic inspiration, we drew on newspaper articles and images from the period as well as the excellent collection of photographs by Vincenzo Pietropaolo, *Celebration of Resistance: Ontario's Days of Action* (Toronto: Between the Lines, 1999).

Kwentong Bayan
Labour of Love

Celebrating Filipin@ Community Artivism in Toronto

Conely de Leon

When I first learned that the majority of migrant workers who came to Canada to perform domestic and care work in the early 1980s and 1990s were Filipin@,[1] I turned to community leaders, educators, and advocates to understand why. Since then, my involvement in Filipin@ community organizing, researching, and publishing on issues related to gender, migration, and labour has meant that I have gotten a chance to meet passionate and inspiring people like the creators of *Kwentong Bayan: A Labour of Love*, Althea Balmes and Jo Alcampo.

Kwentong Bayan visually traces four decades of community struggle. It is a graphic historical archive of live-in caregivers' community leadership and organizing efforts from 1971 to the present day. It recognizes that migrant domestic workers and caregivers' fight for permanent residency and professional accreditation has been an ongoing and pressing issue—one that preceded and, in fact, prompted the enactment of the 1981 Foreign Domestic Movement Scheme and, later, key changes to the 1992 Live-in Caregiver Program. The "Good Enough to Work, Good Enough to Stay!" campaign (depicted in the graphic novel in the form of a placard) encapsulates efforts to raise awareness around this issue. Set against the current climate of retrograde policy implementation, it serves as an important reminder of battles fought for and won.

The community stories here are punctuated by important victories, most notably the "Juana Tejada Law," which removed the second mandatory medical examination for caregivers applying for permanent residency in Canada. It also highlights key landmarks in the city of Toronto, like Seaton Park and Earl Bales Park, where caregivers have come together to rally, hold meetings, share ideas, and support one another. It is no coincidence that Althea, Jo, and I had one of our very first conversations about *Kwentong Bayan* at an International Women's Day march. Holding a banner alongside Filipin@ community leaders and members, we proudly marched to honour and celebrate the lives and labour of Filipin@ caregivers. It is also no coincidence that we walked the streets of St. James Town together—my childhood home and one of the most densely populated high-rise complexes in Canada with a significantly large Filipino population—and chronicled the history of Filipin@ migration to the area.

Kwentong Bayan is a rich and textured narrative of Filipin@ caregivers' lives in Toronto. Given the recent changes to Canada's Caregiver Program, *Kwentong Bayan* comes at an important time when we need the stories of Toronto's Filipin@ community to be heard. In fact, Jo and Althea urge us to tell *more* stories. This is therefore a community-based arts project with a vision—one that brings to life the stories of Filipin@ caregivers in Toronto and intervenes in dominant spaces like the academy by urging more critical and nuanced stories to be told by, for, and about caregivers. It is a project that traces histories and forges futures. *Kwentong Bayan* puts passion into politics, and art into "artivism."

Notes

1 Filipin@ (pronounced fi-li-pi-na/no) is used here
to highlight the importance of gender in our political
understanding of Filipina/o lives in Canada.

The Transformative Possibilities of the Visual Storytelling of Resistance and Community Organizing

Zenee May Maceda

Kwentong Bayan: Labour of Love serves as a significant community resource for organizing and awareness raising about the working and living conditions of racialized migrant careworkers in Canada. It also portrays how we can care for and love one another, despite the oppressive structures of work and migration that isolate us from our communities and ourselves.

This project is structured in a way that conveys a coherent story detailing the shared experiences of struggle and resistance among migrant workers and caregivers. Notably, the panels depict the shared experiences of Filipin@ migrant workers with other racialized and marginalized workers. More importantly, this comic book project radically disrupts the hierarchies between academic and arts-based knowledge production, celebrates lived experiences of migrant women as a source of knowledge and truth, and exemplifies the transformative possibilities of collaborative knowledge production.

A significant component of this project is the weaving together of the historical emergence and changes to the Live-in Caregiver Program, and how caregivers and activists have responded to these changes within their communities. One of their frames, titled "Community," depicts two women overlooking the annual Philippine National Day Picnic at Seaton Park. The story serves as a reflection of the rich activism carried out by both Filipina and Jamaican domestic workers over the last few decades. The dialogue between the two women is significant because it portrays the different histories and relationships between Filipina and Jamaican domestic workers, and it also reveals their shared histories of resistance. In this way, the use of comics is not just a medium to relay the lived experiences of caregivers, but also an important resource for informing readers about the emergence of the program and of existing networks of political resistance that attempts to blur the distinction between domestic work and political space.

Kwentong Bayan provides creative channels in which the voices of migrant care workers are presented in a manner that is unmediated, and helps to shape the overall character of their activism/movement. It creates space for vibrant discussions around the politics of solidarity and highlights the racialization of gender, class, and citizenship status. This complex articulation of the lived experiences of women of colour draws attention to interlocking systems of oppression, central to their experiences and their modes of resistance. *Kwentong Bayan: Labour of Love* offers a transformative form of storytelling that ruptures the dominance of academia as a preeminent site of knowledge production.

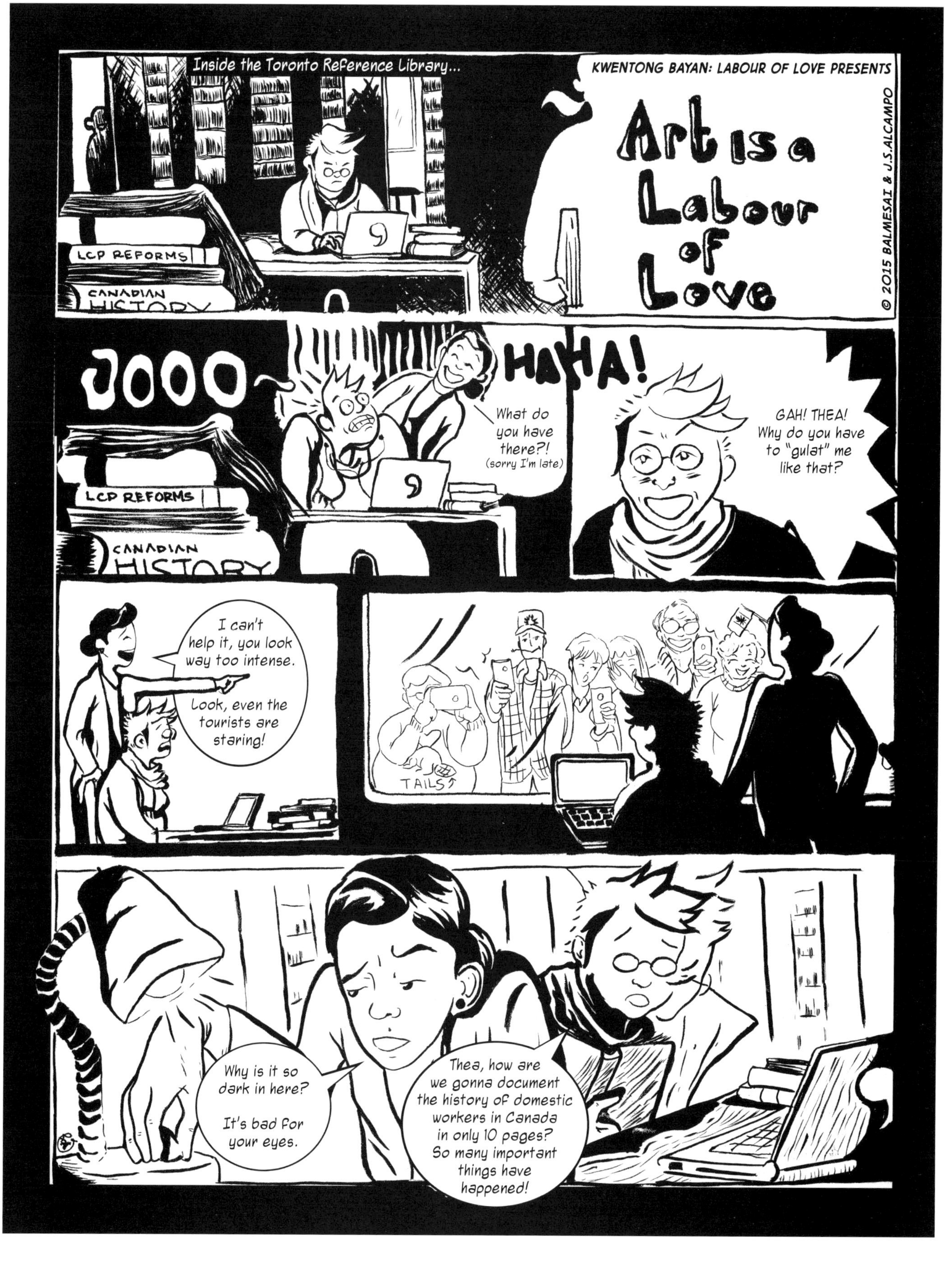

Inside the Toronto Reference Library...
KWENTONG BAYAN: LABOUR OF LOVE PRESENTS
Art is a Labour of Love
© 2015 BALMESAI & J.S.ALCAMPO
LCP REFORMS
CANADIAN HISTORY
JOOO-HAHA!
What do you have there?! (sorry I'm late)
GAH! THEA! Why do you have to "gulat" me like that?
I can't help it, you look way too intense.
Look, even the tourists are staring!
TAILS
Why is it so dark in here?
It's bad for your eyes.
Thea, how are we gonna document the history of domestic workers in Canada in only 10 pages? So many important things have happened!

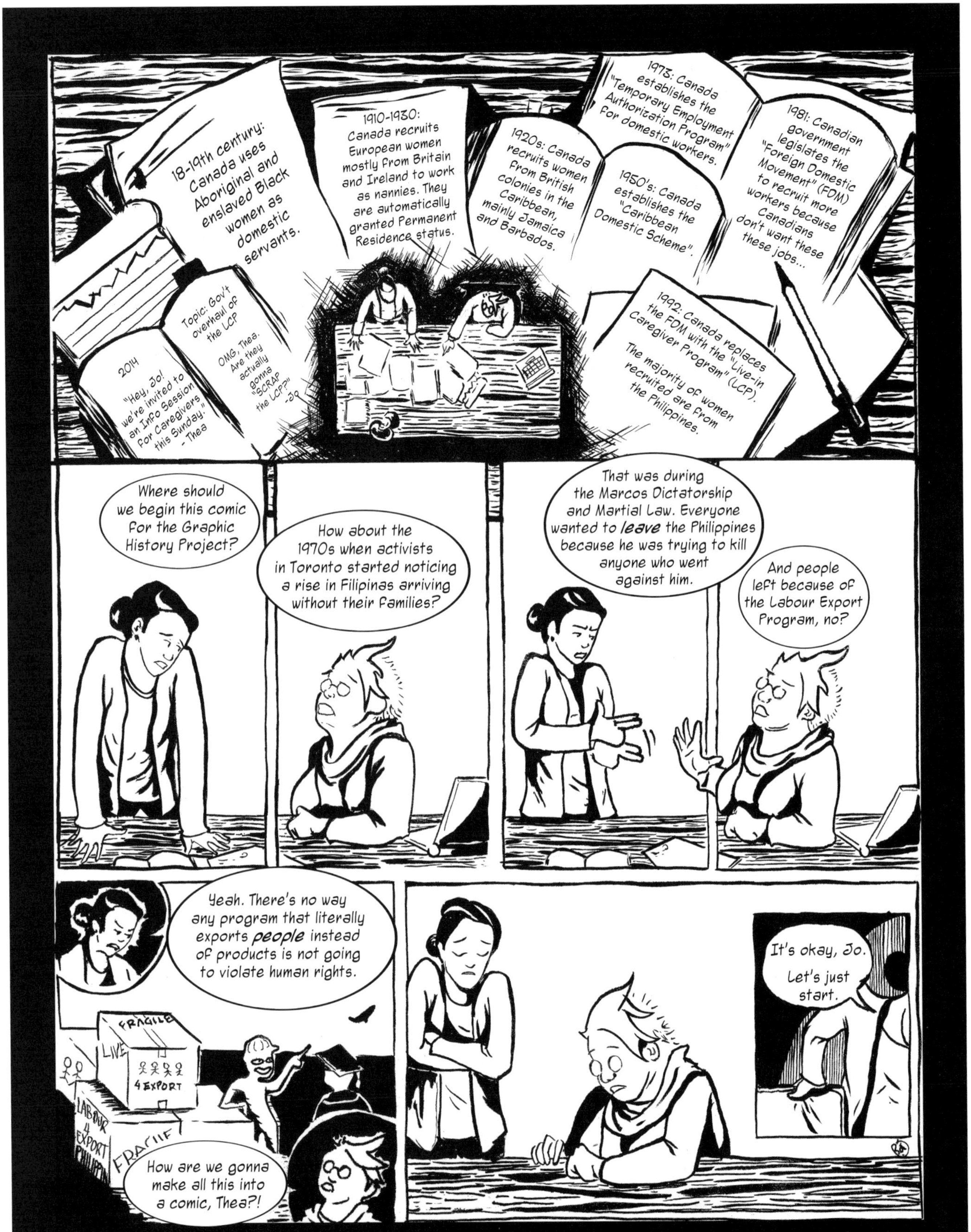
18-19th century: Canada uses Aboriginal and enslaved Black women as domestic servants.
1910-1930: Canada recruits European women mostly from Britain and Ireland to work as nannies. They are automatically granted Permanent Residence status.
1920s: Canada recruits women from British colonies in the Caribbean, mainly Jamaica and Barbados.
1950's: Canada establishes the "Caribbean Domestic Scheme".
1973: Canada establishes the "Temporary Employment Authorization Program" for domestic workers.
1981: Canadian government legislates the "Foreign Domestic Movement" (FDM) to recruit more workers because Canadians don't want these jobs...
Topic: Gov't overhaul of the LCP
2014
"Hey, Jo! we're invited to an Info Session for Caregivers this Sunday." - Thea
OMG, Thea. Are they actually gonna "SCRAP the LCP?" -Jo
1992: Canada replaces the FDM with the "Live-in Caregiver Program" (LCP).
The majority of women recruited are from the Philippines.
Where should we begin this comic for the Graphic History Project?
How about the 1970s when activists in Toronto started noticing a rise in Filipinas arriving without their families?
That was during the Marcos Dictatorship and Martial Law. Everyone wanted to *leave* the Philippines because he was trying to kill anyone who went against him.
And people left because of the Labour Export Program, no?
Yeah. There's no way any program that literally exports *people* instead of products is not going to violate human rights.
FRAGILE
LIVE
4 EXPORT
LABOUR 4 EXPORT
FRAGILE
How are we gonna make all this into a comic, Thea?!
It's okay, Jo.
Let's just start.

In 1973, the Canadian federal government introduced the Temporary Employment Authorization Program. It permitted domestic workers to come to Canada as short-term migrant labourers. But unlike European domestics, they were not granted landed immigrant status, so had to leave their families to work abroad.

By the late 70s, Filipino community leaders in Toronto began to notice more and more young Filipinas arriving without their families. They met at churches and malls on their days off. These informal gatherings sparked the creation of the first social support and advocacy groups. It began with caregivers reaching out to each other.

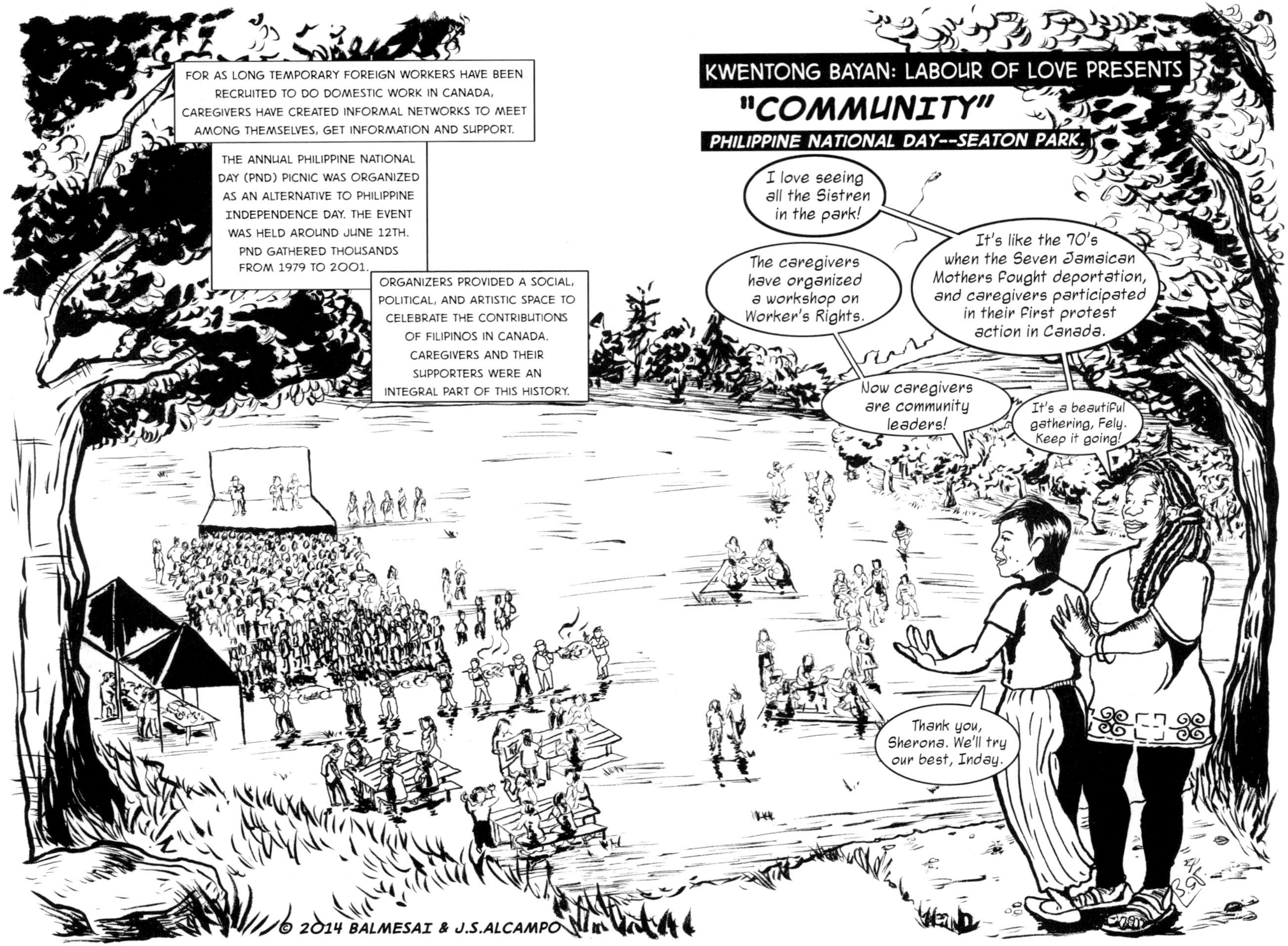
KWENTONG BAYAN: LABOUR OF LOVE PRESENTS
"COMMUNITY"
PHILIPPINE NATIONAL DAY--SEATON PARK.
FOR AS LONG TEMPORARY FOREIGN WORKERS HAVE BEEN RECRUITED TO DO DOMESTIC WORK IN CANADA, CAREGIVERS HAVE CREATED INFORMAL NETWORKS TO MEET AMONG THEMSELVES, GET INFORMATION AND SUPPORT.
THE ANNUAL PHILIPPINE NATIONAL DAY (PND) PICNIC WAS ORGANIZED AS AN ALTERNATIVE TO PHILIPPINE INDEPENDENCE DAY. THE EVENT WAS HELD AROUND JUNE 12TH. PND GATHERED THOUSANDS FROM 1979 TO 2001.
ORGANIZERS PROVIDED A SOCIAL, POLITICAL, AND ARTISTIC SPACE TO CELEBRATE THE CONTRIBUTIONS OF FILIPINOS IN CANADA. CAREGIVERS AND THEIR SUPPORTERS WERE AN INTEGRAL PART OF THIS HISTORY.
I love seeing all the Sistren in the park!
It's like the 70's when the Seven Jamaican Mothers fought deportation, and caregivers participated in their first protest action in Canada.
The caregivers have organized a workshop on Worker's Rights.
Now caregivers are community leaders!
It's a beautiful gathering, Fely. Keep it going!
Thank you, Sherona. We'll try our best, Inday.
© 2014 BALMESAI & J.S.ALCAMPO

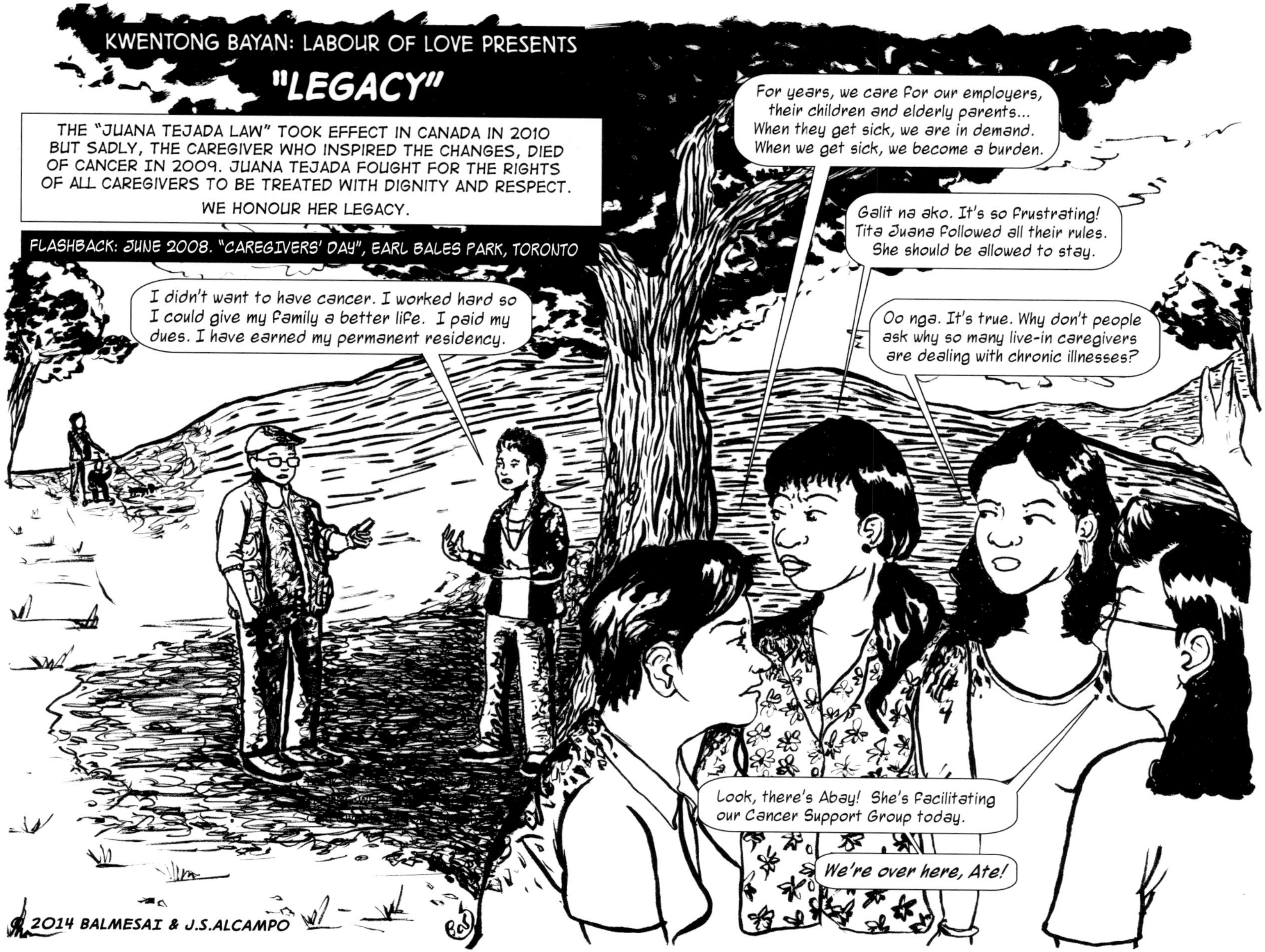
KWENTONG BAYAN: LABOUR OF LOVE PRESENTS
"LEGACY"
THE "JUANA TEJADA LAW" TOOK EFFECT IN CANADA IN 2010 BUT SADLY, THE CAREGIVER WHO INSPIRED THE CHANGES, DIED OF CANCER IN 2009. JUANA TEJADA FOUGHT FOR THE RIGHTS OF ALL CAREGIVERS TO BE TREATED WITH DIGNITY AND RESPECT.
WE HONOUR HER LEGACY.
FLASHBACK: JUNE 2008. "CAREGIVERS' DAY", EARL BALES PARK, TORONTO
I didn't want to have cancer. I worked hard so I could give my family a better life. I paid my dues. I have earned my permanent residency.
For years, we care for our employers, their children and elderly parents... When they get sick, we are in demand. When we get sick, we become a burden.
Galit na ako. It's so frustrating! Tita Juana followed all their rules. She should be allowed to stay.
Oo nga. It's true. Why don't people ask why so many live-in caregivers are dealing with chronic illnesses?
Look, there's Abay! She's facilitating our Cancer Support Group today.
We're over here, Ate!
©2014 BALMESAI & J.S.ALCAMPO

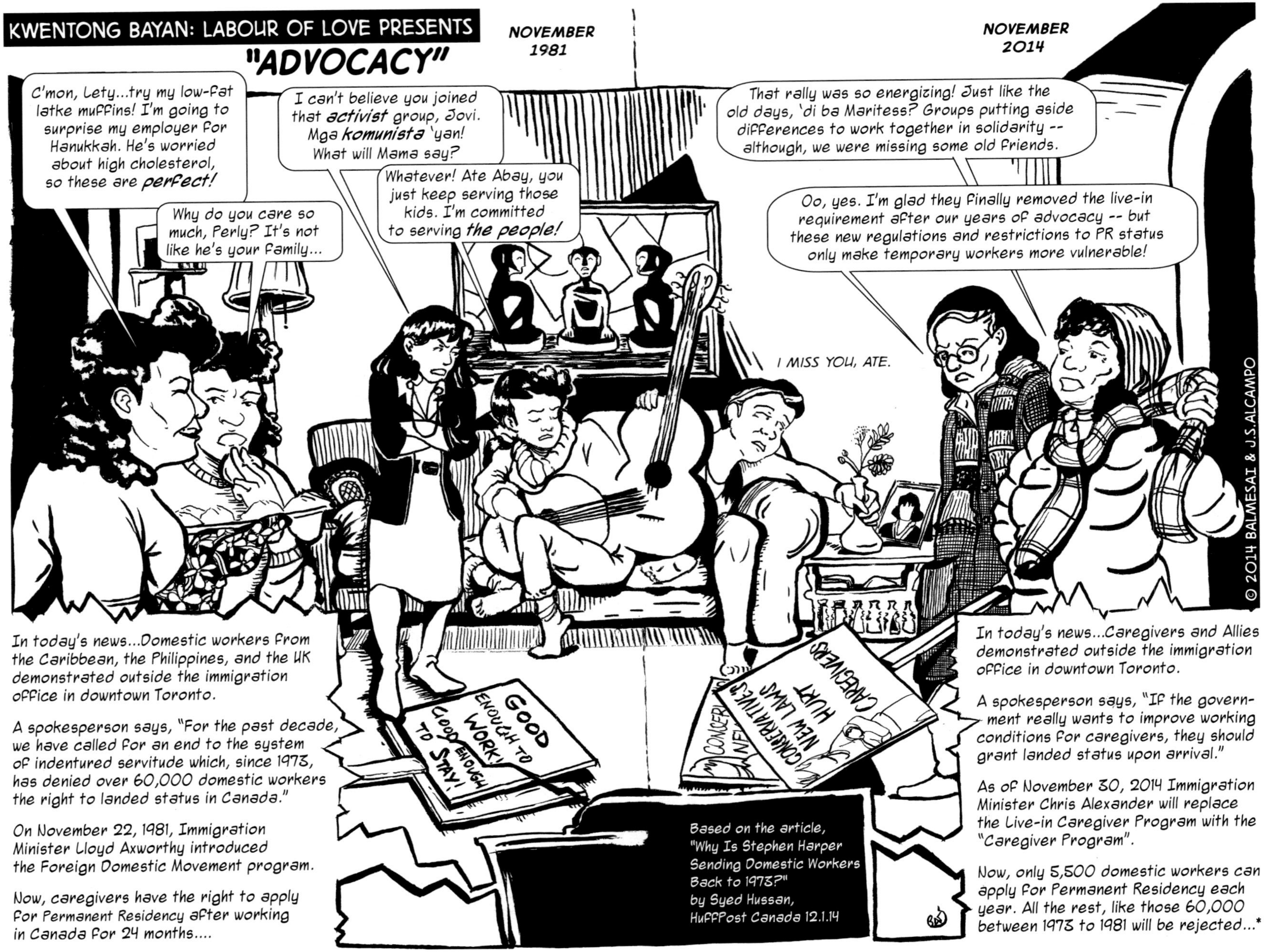
KWENTONG BAYAN: LABOUR OF LOVE PRESENTS
"ADVOCACY"
NOVEMBER 1981
NOVEMBER 2014
C'mon, Lety...try my low-fat latke muffins! I'm going to surprise my employer for Hanukkah. He's worried about high cholesterol, so these are *perfect!*
Why do you care so much, Perly? It's not like he's your family...
I can't believe you joined that *activist* group, Jovi. Mga *komunista* 'yan! What will Mama say?
Whatever! Ate Abay, you just keep serving those kids. I'm committed to serving *the people!*
That rally was so energizing! Just like the old days, 'di ba Maritess? Groups putting aside differences to work together in solidarity -- although, we were missing some old friends.
Oo, yes. I'm glad they finally removed the live-in requirement after our years of advocacy -- but these new regulations and restrictions to PR status only make temporary workers more vulnerable!
I MISS YOU, ATE.
GOOD ENOUGH TO WORK! GOOD ENOUGH TO STAY!
CONSERVATIVE'S NEW LAWS HURT CAREGIVERS
© 2014 BALMESAI & J.S. ALCAMPO
In today's news...Domestic workers from the Caribbean, the Philippines, and the UK demonstrated outside the immigration office in downtown Toronto.
A spokesperson says, "For the past decade, we have called for an end to the system of indentured servitude which, since 1973, has denied over 60,000 domestic workers the right to landed status in Canada."
On November 22, 1981, Immigration Minister Lloyd Axworthy introduced the Foreign Domestic Movement program.
Now, caregivers have the right to apply for Permanent Residency after working in Canada for 24 months....
Based on the article, "Why Is Stephen Harper Sending Domestic Workers Back to 1973?" by Syed Hussan, HuffPost Canada 12.1.14
In today's news...Caregivers and Allies demonstrated outside the immigration office in downtown Toronto.
A spokesperson says, "If the government really wants to improve working conditions for caregivers, they should grant landed status upon arrival."
As of November 30, 2014 Immigration Minister Chris Alexander will replace the Live-in Caregiver Program with the "Caregiver Program".
Now, only 5,500 domestic workers can apply for Permanent Residency each year. All the rest, like those 60,000 between 1973 to 1981 will be rejected...*

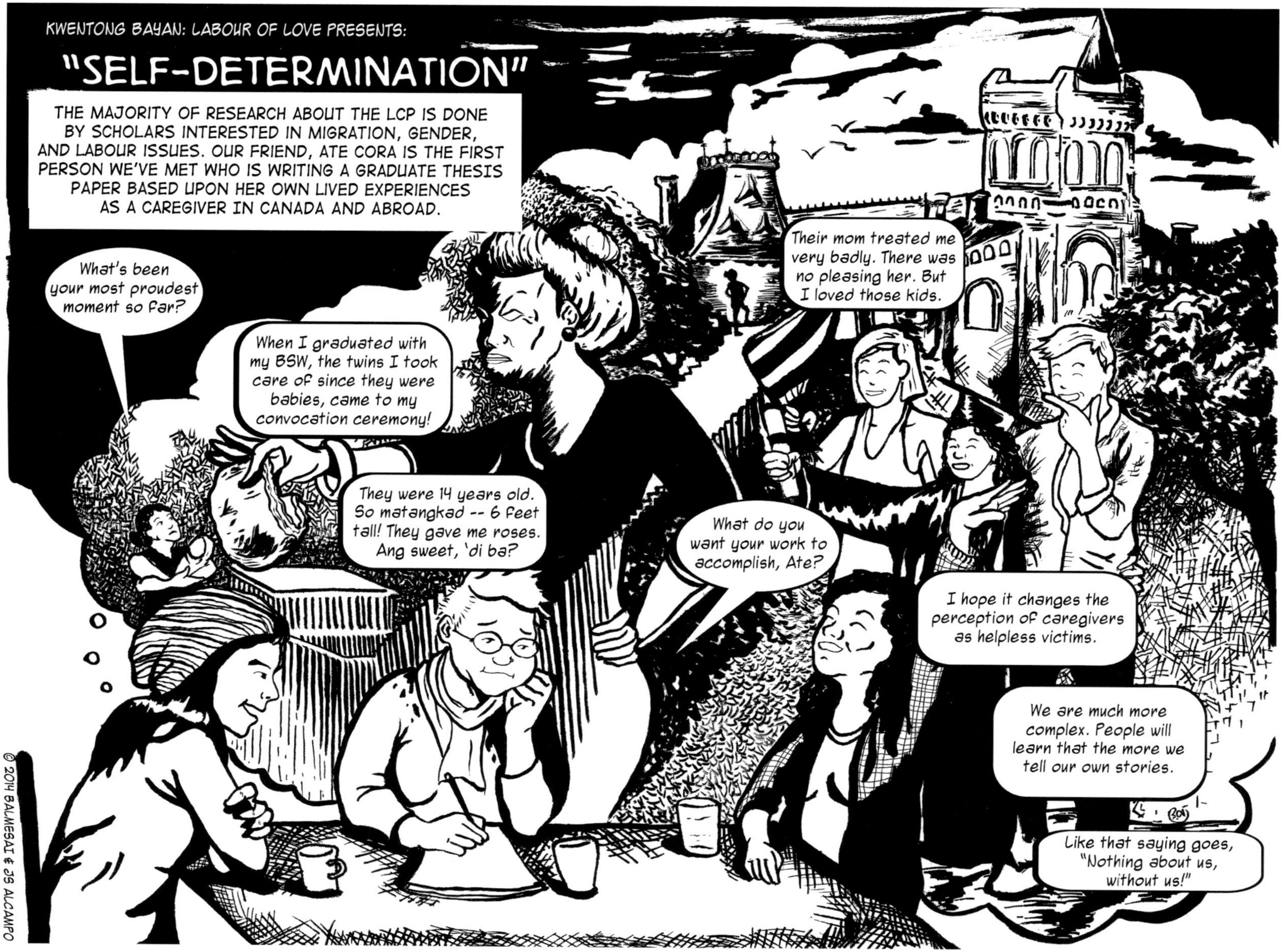
KWENTONG BAYAN: LABOUR OF LOVE PRESENTS:
"SELF-DETERMINATION"
THE MAJORITY OF RESEARCH ABOUT THE LCP IS DONE BY SCHOLARS INTERESTED IN MIGRATION, GENDER, AND LABOUR ISSUES. OUR FRIEND, ATE CORA IS THE FIRST PERSON WE'VE MET WHO IS WRITING A GRADUATE THESIS PAPER BASED UPON HER OWN LIVED EXPERIENCES AS A CAREGIVER IN CANADA AND ABROAD.
What's been your most proudest moment so far?
When I graduated with my BSW, the twins I took care of since they were babies, came to my convocation ceremony!
They were 14 years old. So matangkad -- 6 feet tall! They gave me roses. Ang sweet, 'di ba?
Their mom treated me very badly. There was no pleasing her. But I loved those kids.
What do you want your work to accomplish, Ate?
I hope it changes the perception of caregivers as helpless victims.
We are much more complex. People will learn that the more we tell our own stories.
Like that saying goes, "Nothing about us, without us!"
© 2014 BALMESAI & JS ALCAMPO

KWENTONG BAYAN: LABOUR OF LOVE PRESENTS "ART IS A LABOUR OF LOVE" PART II

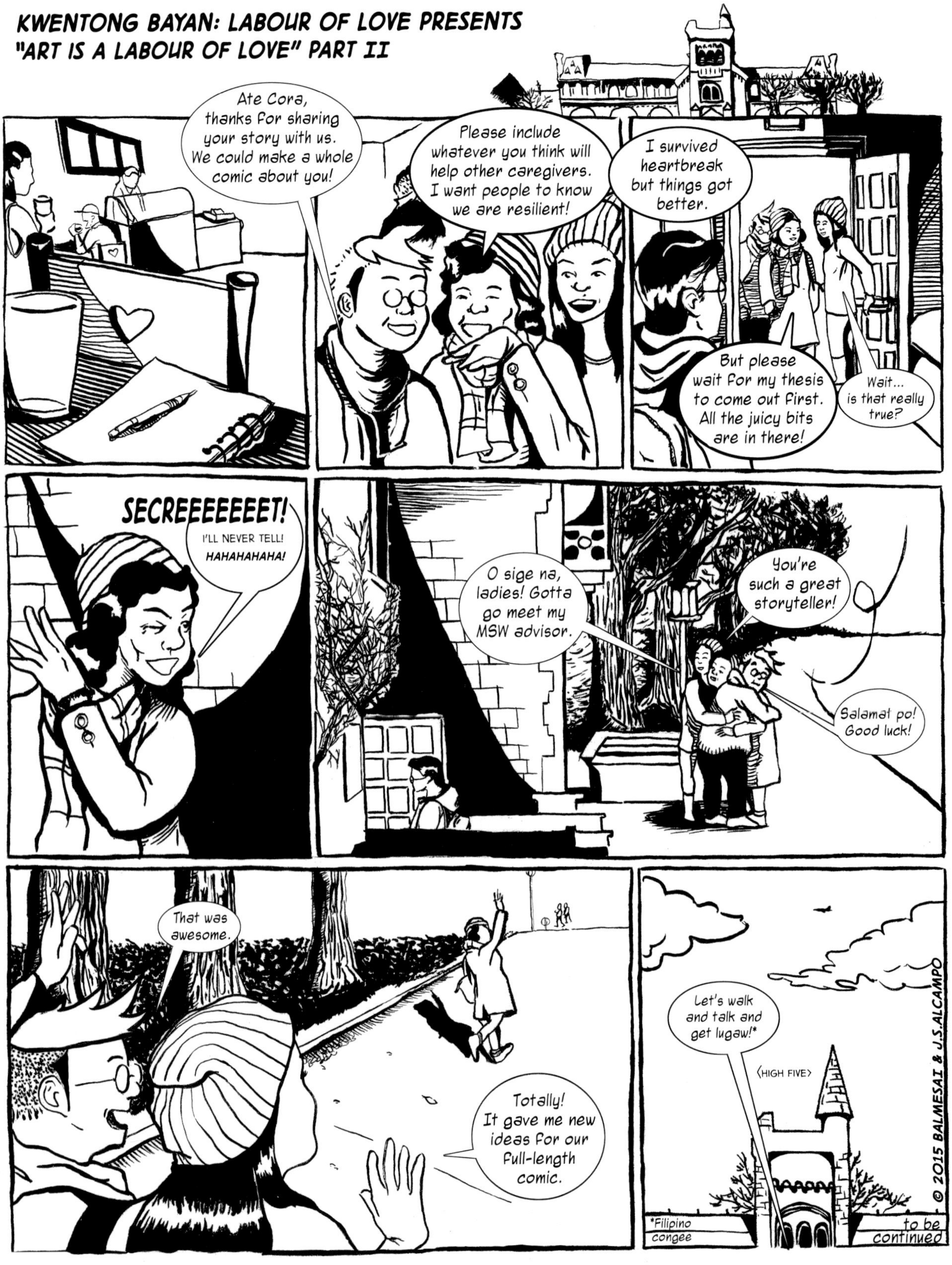
Ate Cora, thanks for sharing your story with us. We could make a whole comic about you!
Please include whatever you think will help other caregivers. I want people to know we are resilient!
I survived heartbreak but things got better.
But please wait for my thesis to come out first. All the juicy bits are in there!
Wait... is that really true?
SECREEEEEEEET!
I'LL NEVER TELL! HAHAHAHAHA!
O sige na, ladies! Gotta go meet my MSW advisor.
You're such a great storyteller!
Salamat po! Good luck!
That was awesome.
Totally! It gave me new ideas for our full-length comic.
Let's walk and talk and get lugaw!*
<HIGH FIVE>
*Filipino congee
to be continued
© 2015 BALMESAI & J.S.ALCAMPO

Acknowledgements

We would like to extend our deepest gratitude to the people who have supported us from the beginning: the Agas-Balmes Family, the Alcampo Family, Christine Balmes, Conely de Leon, Philip Kelly, Zenee May Maceda, Martha Ocampo, Pinky Paglingayen, Dakila Tomas, Geoffrey Louie, Marissa Largo, Miwa Takeuchi, Julia Smith, the Graphic History Collective, and Mayworks Festival of Working People and the Arts. We thank all the artists, labour activists, educators, scholars, and others who have supported our work. It is gratifying that many people care about the struggles of caregivers and migrant workers alike.

Special thanks to our friends at Caregiver Connections Education and Support Organization (CCESO) and all community leaders who fight for the rights of domestic workers and caregivers to be treated with dignity and respect, including the late Felicita (Fely) O. Villasin, Sherona Hall, and Juana Tejada.

We continue to be inspired by the comic style and stories of the Komik masters of the Philippines and other comic artists who embed political consciousness in their work.

Our project is based upon stories shared with us by caregivers, advocates, and community allies. With any acknowledgement *Kwentong Bayan* receives, we are mindful of those who work long hours with little recognition. We thank them for making our work possible.

We honour your labour. May you be surrounded by love.

Notes

This project is based on stories shared with us by caregivers, advocates, and community allies.

Bibliography

The Graphic History Collective sees the study of history as an important part of activism. We believe that changing the world today requires a solid historical understanding of the tactics and strategies that people in the past have used to fight for social change.

As part of our creative process, we—like many of the contributors to this anthology—consult historical books and articles written about the stories we transform into comics as well as primary source materials from the period under study, including photographs, quotes, song lyrics, and more.

Below is a selected list of further reading on Canadian labour and working-class history. We have also included lists of further reading for each comic book in the collection.

Canadian labour and working-class history

Heron, Craig. *The Canadian Labour Movement: A Short History*. 3rd ed. Toronto: James Lorimer & Company, 2012.

Morton, Desmond. *Working People: An Illustrated History of the Canadian Labour Movement*. 5th ed. Montréal and Kingston: McGill-Queen's University Press, 2007.

Palmer, Bryan D. *Working Class Experience: Rethinking the History of Canadian Labour, 1800–1991*. Toronto: McClelland & Stewart, 1992.

Palmer, Bryan D. and Joan Sangster, eds. *Labouring Canada: Class, Gender, and Race in Canadian Working-Class History*. Don Mills, Ontario: Oxford University Press, 2008.

Ross, Stephanie, Larry Savage, Errol Black, and Jim Silver. *Building a Better World: An Introduction to Trade Unionism in Canada*. 3rd ed. Halifax: Fernwood Publishing, 2015.

Sefton MacDowell, Laurel and Ian Radforth, eds. *Canadian Working-Class History: Selected Readings*. Toronto: Canadian Scholars' Press, 2006.

"Dreaming of What Might Be: The Knights of Labor in Canada 1800–1900"

Burr, Christina. *Spreading the Light: Work and Labour Reform in Late Nineteenth-Century Toronto*. Toronto: University of Toronto Press, 1999.

Fink, Leon. *Workingmen's Democracy: The Knights of Labor and American Politics*. Urbana: University of Illinois Press, 1983.

Gerteis, Joseph. *Class and the Color Line: Interracial Class Coalition in the Knights of Labor and the Populist Movement*. Durham: Duke University Press, 2007.

Kealey, Gregory S. and Bryan D. Palmer. *Dreaming of What Might Be: The Knights of Labor in Ontario, 1880–1900*. New York: Cambridge Press, 1982.

———. "The Bonds of Unity: The Knights of Labor in Ontario, 1880–1900." *Histoire Sociale/Social History* 14 (November 1981), 369–411.

Kennedy, Douglas Ross. *The Knights of Labor in Canada*. London: University of Western Ontario, 1956.

Marks, Lynne. "The Knights of Labor and the Salvation Army: Religion and Working-Class Culture in Ontario, 1882–1890." *Labour/Le Travail* 28 (Fall 1991), 89–127.

Weir, Robert E. *Beyond Labor's Veil: The Culture of the Knights of Labor*. University Park: Pennsylvania State University Press, 1996.

"Working on the Water, Fighting for the Land: Indigenous Labour on Burrard Inlet"

Adams, Howard. *Prison of Grass: Canada from the Native Perspective.* Toronto: General Publishing, 1975.

Baker, Simon. *Khot-La-Cha: The Autobiography of Chief Simon Baker.* Edited by Verna J. Kirkness. Vancouver: Douglas & McIntyre, 1994.

Barman, Jean. *The West beyond the West: A History of British Columbia.* Toronto: University of Toronto Press, 2007.

Brownlie, Robin Jarvis. "'Living the Same as the White People': Mohawk and Anishinabe Women's Labour in Southern Ontario, 1920–1940." *Labour/Le Travail* 61 (Spring 2008), 41–68.

Carlson, Keith. "Sto'lo People and the Development of the B.C. Wage Labour Economy." In *You Are Asked to Witness: The Sto'lo in Canada's Pacific Coast History*, edited by Keith Carlson, 109–124. Chilliwack: Sto'lo Heritage Trust, 1997.

Fisher, Robin. *Contact and Conflict: Indian-European Relations in British Columbia, 1774–1890.* Vancouver: University of British Columbia Press, 1977.

Fiske, Jo-Anne. "Fishing Is Women's Business: Changing Economic Role of Carrier Women." In *Native Peoples, Native Lands: Canadian Indians, Inuit and Métis*, edited by Bruce Cox, 186–98. Ottawa: Carleton University Press, 1987.

Harris, Cole. *Making Native Space: Colonialism, Resistance, and Reserves in British Columbia.* Vancouver: University of British Columbia Press, 2002.

High, Steven. "Native Wage Labour and Independent Production during the 'Era of Irrelevance.'" *Labour/Le Travail* 37 (Spring 1996), 243–264.

Jamieson, Stuart. "Native Indians and the Trade Union Movement in British Columbia." *Human Organization* 1, no. 4 (1961–1962), 219–225.

Knight, Rolf. *Indians at Work: An Informal History of Native Labour in British Columbia, 1858–1930.* Vancouver: New Star Books, 1996.

Lutz, John. "After the Fur Trade: The Aboriginal Labouring Class of British Columbia, 1849–1890." *Journal of the Canadian Historical Association* 3 (1992), 69–93.

——. "Gender and Work in Lekwammen Families, 1843–1970." In *In the Days of Our Grandmothers: A Reader in Aboriginal Women's History*, edited by Mary-Ellen Kelm and Lorna Townsend, 216–250. Toronto: University of Toronto Press, 2006.

——. *Makúk: A New History of Aboriginal-White Relations.* Vancouver: University of British Columbia Press, 2008.

McCallum, Mary Jane. *Indigenous Women, Work, and History, 1940–1980.* Winnipeg: University of Manitoba Press, 2014.

Parnaby, Andrew. "'The best men that ever worked the lumber': Aboriginal Longshoremen on Burrard Inlet, BC, 1863–1939." *Canadian Historical Review* 87 (March 2006), 53–78.

Podruchny, Carolyn. "Unfair Masters and Rascally Servants? Labour Relations between Bourgeois and Voyageurs in the Montréal Fur Trade, 1770–1820." *Labour/Le Travail* 43 (Spring 1999), 43–70.

Raibmon, Paige. *Authentic Indians: Episodes of Encounter from the Late-Nineteenth-Century Northwest Coast.* Vancouver: University of British Columbia Press, 2005.

——. "The Practice of Everyday Colonialism: Indigenous Women at Work in the Hop Fields and Tourist Industry of Puget Sound." *Labor: Studies in Working-Class History of the Americas* 3 (Fall 2006), 23–56.

Tennant, Paul. *Aboriginal Peoples and Politics: The Land Question in British Columbia, 1849–1989.* Vancouver: University of British Columbia Press, 1990.

Van Kirk, Sylvia. *Many Tender Ties: Women in Fur Trade Society in Western Canada, 1670–1870*. Winnipeg: Watson Dwyer, 1980.

"The Battle of Ballantyne Pier: An Injury to One Is an Injury to All!"

Bernstein, Irvin. *The Turbulent Years: A History of the American Worker, 1933–1940*. Boston: Houghton-Mifflin Co., 1970.

Brown, Lorne. *When Freedom Was Lost: The Unemployed, the Agitator, and the State*. Montreal: Black Rose Books, 1987.

Dooley, Michael Kevin. "'Our Mickey': The Story of Private James O'Rourke, VC.MM (CEF), 1879–1957." *Labour/Le Travail* 47 (2001), 171–184.

Kimeldorf, Howard. *Reds or Rackets? The Making of Radical and Conservative Unions on the Waterfront*. Berkeley: University of California Press, 1992.

Larrowe, Charles P. *Harry Bridges: The Rise and Fall of Radical Labor in the U.S.* Rev. ed. Chicago: Chicago Review Press, 1977.

Leier, Mark. *Where the Fraser River Flows: The Industrial Workers of the World in British Columbia*. Vancouver: New Star Books, 1990.

McCandless, R.C. "Vancouver's 'Red Menace' of 1935: The Waterfront Situation." *BC Studies* 22 (1974), 56–70.

Nelson, Bruce. *Workers on the Waterfront: Seamen, Longshoremen and Unionism in the 1930s*. Urbana: University of Illinois Press, 1988.

Parnaby, Andrew. "On the Hook: Welfare Capitalism on the Vancouver Waterfront, 1919–1939." PhD diss., Memorial University, 2001.

Russwurm, Lani. "Constituting Authority: Policing Workers and the Consolidation of Police Power in Vancouver, 1918–1939." MA thesis, Simon Fraser University, 2007.

Selvin, David F. *A Terrible Anger: The 1934 Waterfront and General Strikes in San Francisco*. Detroit: Wayne State University Press, 1996.

Stanton, John. *Never Say Die! The Life and Times of a Pioneer Labour Lawyer*. Vancouver: Steel Rail Publishing, 1987.

Williams, David Ricardo. *Mayor Gerry: The Remarkable Gerald Grattan McGeer*. Vancouver: Douglas & McIntyre, 1986.

"Bill Williamson: Hobo, Wobbly, Communist, On-to-Ottawa Trekker, Spanish Civil War Veteran, Photographer"

Archival Collections

Imperial War Museum, London. Bill Williamson interview by British Video History Trust, Catalogue no. 14725, 1990; and Bill Williamson interview by Toby Haggirth, Catalogue no. 12385, 1990, reels 3, 4, and 6–9.

Library and Archives of Canada. Mackenzie-Papineau Battalion collection, MG 30, E 173. Walter E. Dent Papers, volume 5, file 24, letter from Bill Williamson to Lee Burke, August 21, 1980; and letter from Bill Williamson to Wally Dent, March 2, 1981.

Books

Agencia EFE, ed. *Imágenes inéditas de La Guerra Civil Española (1936–1939): Las mejores fotografías de la Agencia EFE*. Madrid: Agencia EFE, 2002.

Anikst, Mikhail, ed. *Soviet Commercial Design of the Twenties*. New York: Abbeville Press, 1987.

Beeching, William C. *Canadian Volunteers: Spain, 1936–1939*. Regina: Canadian Plains Research Center, University of Regina, 1989.

Carr, Raymond, ed. *Images of the Spanish Civil War*. New York: W.W. Norton & Company, 1989.

Dickerman, Leah, ed. *Building the Collective: Soviet Graphic Design, 1917–1937*. 2nd ed. Princeton: Princeton Architectural Press, 1996.

Hello Canada! Canada's Mackenzie Papineau Battalion, 1837–1937, 15th Brigade I.B. Toronto: Friends of the Mackenzie Papineau Battalion, 1937.

Howard, Victor with Mac Reynolds. *The Mackenzie-Papineau Battalion: The Canadian Contingent in the Spanish Civil War*. Ottawa: Carleton University Press, 1986.

Howard, Victor. *"We Were the Salt of the Earth!" A Narrative of the On-to-Ottawa Trek and the Regina Riot*. Regina: Canadian Plains Research Center, University of Regina, 1985.

Imperial War Museum. *The Spanish Civil War Collection: Sound Archive Oral History Recordings*. London: Imperial War Museum, 1996.

King, David. *Russian Revolutionary Posters: From Civil War to Socialist Realism, From Bolshevism to the End of Stalinism*. London: Tate Publishing, 2012.

Petrou, Michael. *Renegades: Canadians in the Spanish Civil War*. Vancouver: UBC Press, 2008.

Salvador, Tomas. *La guerra de España en sus fotografías*. Barcelona: Ediciones Marte, 1966.

Soviet Film Posters in the Silent Era. Tokyo: National Museum of Modern Art, 2009.

Turnball, Patrick and Jeffrey Burn. *The Spanish Civil War, 1936–39*. Oxford: Osprey, 1977.

Villarroya, Joan et al. *Guerra I Propaganda: Fotograies del Comissariat de Propaganda de la Generalitat de Catalunya (1936–1939)*. Barcelona: Viena Ediciones, 2006.

Waiser, Bill. *All Hell Can't Stop Us: The On-to-Ottawa Trek and Regina Riot*. Calgary: Fifth House, 2003.

Zuehlke, Mark. *The Gallant Cause: Canadians in the Spanish Civil War, 1936–1939*. Mississauga: John Wiley & Sons, 2008.

Films

Battleship Potemkin. Directed by Sergei M. Eisenstein. 1925.

Los Canadienses: Canadians in the Spanish Civil War, 1936–1939. Directed by Albert Kish. 1975.

The Spanish Earth. Directed by Joris Ivens. 1937.

"Coal Mountain: The 1935 Corbin Miners' Strike"
"Corbin: Another Ludlow Massacre." *B.C. Lumber Worker*, April 27, 1935. Available at the Centre for Socialist Education, 706 Clarke Drive, Vancouver, BC.

Griffin, Betty, and Susan Lockhart. *Their Own History: Women's Contribution to the Labour Movement of British Columbia*. New Westminster, BC: United Fishermen & Allied Workers Union/CAW Seniors Club, 2002.

Griffin, Sean. *Fighting Heritage: Highlights of the 1930s Struggle for Jobs and Militant Unionism in British Columbia*. Vancouver: Tribune, 1986.

Norton, Wayne R., and Naomi Miller. *The Forgotten Side of the Border*. Kamloops, BC: Plateau, 1998.

Stonier-Newman, Lynne. *Policing a Pioneer Province: The B.C. Provincial Police, 1858–1950*. Madeira Park, BC: Harbour, 1991.

"Madeleine Parent: A Life of Struggle and Solidarity"
Breault, Normand. "Madeleine Parent: Toujours dans l'action!" *Relations* 639 (April 1998), 73–78.

Connelly, Pat, with Marilyn Keddy. "Interview with Madeleine Parent." *Studies in Political Economy* 30 (Autumn 1989), 13–36.

Gillett, Margaret. *We Walked Very Warily: A History of Women at McGill.* Montréal: Eden Press, 1981.

Graveline, Pierre. "Développer nos solidarités: Rencontre avec Madeleine Parent." *Mouvements* (Fall 1984), 4–8.

Lacelle, Nicole. *Entretiens avec Madeleine Parent et* Léa Roback. Montréal: Les éditions du remue-ménage, 1988.

Lévesque, Andrée, ed. *Madeleine Parent: Activist.* Toronto: Sumach Press, 2005.

Palmer, Bryan D. et al. "Madeleine Parent (1918–2012)." *Labour/Le Travail* 70 (Fall 2012), 187–202.

Parent, Madeleine. "Remembering Police Surveillance in Quebec, 1940s–70s." In *Whose National Security? Canadian State Surveillance and the Creation of Enemies*, edited by Gary Kinsmen, Dieter K. Buse, and Mercedes Steedman, 235–245. Toronto: Between the Lines, 2000.

——. "Women in Unions: Past, Present and Future." In *Strong Women, Strong Unions: Speeches by Union Women*, edited by Joan Newman Kuyek. Toronto: Canada Employment and Immigration Union/Participatory Research Group, 1985.

Starr, Christina. "Usurping the Reign of the Favourites: Interview with Madeleine Parent." *Women's Education des femmes* 6, no. 3 (Summer 1988), 7–12.

"An 'Entirely Different' Kind of Labour Union: The Service, Office, and Retail Workers' Union of Canada"

Adamson, Nancy, Linda Briskin, and Margaret McPhail. *Feminist Organizing for Change: The Contemporary Women's Movement in Canada.* Toronto: Oxford University Press, 1988.

Ainsworth, Jackie et al. "Getting Organized...in the Feminist Unions." In *Still Ain't Satisfied! Canadian Feminism Today*, edited by Maureen Fitzgerald et al., 132–140. Toronto: The Women's Press, 1982.

The Bank Book Collective. *An Account to Settle: The Story of the United Bank Workers (SORWUC).* Vancouver: Press Gang Publishers, 1979.

Briskin, Linda and Patricia McDermott, eds. *Women Challenging Unions: Feminism, Democracy, and Militancy.* Toronto: University of Toronto Press, 1993.

Forrest, Anne. "Securing the Male Breadwinner: A Feminist Interpretation of PC 1003." In *Labour Gains, Labour Pains: Fifty Years of PC 1003*, edited by Cy Gonick, Paul Phillips, and Jesse Vorst, 139–162. Winnipeg: Fernwood Publishing, 1995.

Luxton, Meg. "Feminism as a Class Act: Working-Class Feminism and the Women's Movement in Canada." *Labour/Le Travail* 48 (Fall 2001), 63–88.

Maroney, Heather Jon. "Feminism at Work." *New Left Review* 1 (September–October 1983), 51–71.

Milligan, Ian. "Coming off the Mountain: Forging an Outward-Looking New Left at Simon Fraser University." *BC Studies: The British Columbian Quarterly* 171 (Autumn 2011), 69–91.

Nicol, Janet M. "'Unions Aren't Native': The Muckamuck Restaurant Labour Dispute, Vancouver, BC (1978–1983)." *Labour/Le Travail* 40 (Fall 1997), 235–251.

Palmer, Bryan D. *Canada's 1960s: The Ironies of Identity in a Rebellious Era.* Toronto: University of Toronto Press, 2009.

Potrebenko, Helen. *Two Years on the Muckamuck Line.* Vancouver: Service, Office, and Retail Workers' Union of Canada, 1981.

Rands, Jean. "Toward an Organization of Working Women." In *Women Unite! An Anthology of the Canadian Women's Movement*, edited by Bonnie Campbell et al., 141–148. Toronto: Canadian Women's Educational Press, 1972.

Sangster, Joan. *Transforming Labour: Women and Work in Post-war Canada*. Toronto: University of Toronto Press, 2010.

Smith, Julia. "An 'Entirely Different' Kind of Union: The Service, Office, and Retail Workers' Union of Canada (SORWUC), 1972–1986." *Labour/Le Travail* 73 (Spring 2014), 23–65.

Wasserlein, Francis Jane. "'An Arrow Aimed at the Heart': The Vancouver Women's Caucus and the Abortion Campaign, 1969–1971." MA thesis, Simon Fraser University, 1990.

White, Julie. *Sisters & Solidarity: Women and Unions in Canada*. Toronto: Thompson Educational Publishing, Inc., 1993.

"The Days of Action: The Character of Class Struggle in 1990s Ontario"

Camfield, David. "Assessing Resistance in Harris's Ontario, 1995–1999." In *Restructuring and Resistance: Canadian Public Policy in an Age of Global Capitalism*, edited by Mike Burke, Colin Mooers, and John Shields. Halifax: Fernwood Publishing, 2000.

Harvey, David. *A Brief History of Neoliberalism*. New York: Oxford University Press, 2005.

Panitch, Leo and Donald Swartz. *From Consent to Coercion: The Assault on Trade Union Freedoms*. Toronto: Garamond Press, 2003.

Pietropaolo, Vincenzo. *Celebration of Resistance: Ontario's Days of Action*. Toronto: Between the Lines, 1999.

Rapaport, David. *No Justice, No Peace: The 1996 OPSEU Strike Against the Harris Government in Ontario*. Montréal and Kingston: McGill-Queen's University Press, 1999.

"Kwentong Bayan: Labour of Love"

Arat-Koç, Sedef, and Fely O. Villasin. *Caregivers Break the Silence: A Participatory Action Research on the Abuse and Violence, Including the Impact of Family Separation, Experienced by Women in the Live-in Caregiver Program*. Toronto: INTERCEDE, 2001.

Axworthy, Lloyd. *Domestic Workers on Employment Authorizations: A Report of the Task Force on Immigration Practices and Procedures*. Ottawa: Government of Canada, Office of the Minister, Employment and Immigration, 1981.

Bakan, Abigail B, and Daiva K. Stasiulis. *Not One of the Family: Foreign Domestic Workers in Canada*. Toronto: University of Toronto Press, 1997.

Charlton, James I. Nothing about Us without Us: Disability Oppression and Empowerment. Berkeley: University of California Press, 1998.

Dunphy, Catherine. "Fely Villasin, 65: Activist Battled Marcos." *Toronto Star*, February 15, 2007, and March 8, 2007.

Hussan, Syed. "Why Is Stephen Harper Sending Domestic Workers Back to 1973?" *Huffington Post*, January 31, 2015, and February 2, 2015. Web.

Keung, Nicholas. "Juana Tejada, 39: Nanny Inspired Reforms for Caregivers." *Toronto Star*, March 11, 2009, and August 22, 2013.

Mascol, Philip. "Sherona Hall, 59: Fighter for Justice." *Toronto Star*, January 9, 2007, and March 8, 2007.

Ramirez, Judith. "Domestic Workers Organize!" *Canadian Woman Studies* 4, no. 2 (1982), 89–91.

Silvera, Makeda. *Silenced: Makeda Silvera Talks with Working Class West Indian Women about Their Lives and Struggles as Domestic Workers in Canada*. Toronto: Sister Vision Press, 1989.

Contributors

Jo SiMalaya Alcampo is an interdisciplinary artist who explores cultural/body memory and the healing of intergenerational soul wounds through community storytelling, installation-based art, and electroacoustic soundscapes. Jo has developed community arts projects with queer youth, consumer/survivors of the mental health system, and migrant domestic workers.

Althea Balmes is a multidisciplinary visual storyteller interested in playful collaborative creative expressions through illustration and video and is an artist-educator rooted in community work. She uses her strong connection to her Filipino culture and her place as a woman of colour in the diaspora to inform her art practice and her work.

Christine Balmes is a musician and community worker. She has worked as a Tagalog language instructor and is currently working as a settlement worker helping newcomer families and youth settle and thrive in Canada. Her research on Filipino Canadian arts and artists was published in the book *Filipinos in Canada: Disturbing Invisibility* by the University of Toronto Press in 2012.

Kwentong Bayan is a collective of two Filipina Canadian artists, Althea Balmes and Jo SiMalaya Alcampo. They are developing a longer stand-alone comic book, *Kwentong Bayan: Labour of Love*, in collaboration with Filipina migrant workers who work under Canada's Caregiver/Live-in Caregiver Program. *Kwentong Bayan* can be literally translated as "community stories" (www.lcpcomicbook.com).

Sam Bradd is a graphic facilitator and illustrator and a member of the Graphic History Collective. He listens and draws to help groups increase engagement, solve problems, and lead. He's collaborated with health researchers, sustainability visionaries, Indigenous leaders, labour unions, and groups who share his passion for innovative visuals. He's unionized with Unifor's Canadian Freelance Union and lives on unceded Coast Salish Territories.

Paul Buhle, a labour historian of 1960s vintage, published *Radical America Komiks* in 1969 and, after an explicable lapse of 35 years, has produced, since 2005, a number of non-fiction comics including *Wobbles!, Che*, and *Bohemians*.

Nicole Marie Burton is an artist, comics creator, and the founder of Ad Astra Comix. After 10 years of political activism, Nicole rekindled her love for comic books, focusing on the study, promotion, and creation of comics that address social justice issues, from marginalized history to gender and sexuality. She lives in Toronto with her imaginary cat.

David Camfield teaches Labour Studies and Sociology at the University of Manitoba and is the author of *Canadian Labour in Crisis: Reinventing the Workers' Movement*. During the Days of Action he was a Canadian Union of Public Employees activist.

Sean Carleton is a member of the Graphic History Collective and a co-author of *May Day: A Graphic History of Protest* and several of the comics in this collection. He has written about comics and critical pedagogy for both academic and popular audiences, and his academic research examines the history of colonialism, capitalism, and education in Canada.

Conely de Leon is a doctoral candidate in Gender, Feminist and Women's Studies at York University, 2013 Research Fellow at the Center for Women's Studies at the University of the Philippines Diliman, and proud member of GABRIELA-Ontario. Her doctoral research is about transnational Filipin@ care networks in Canada, the Philippines, and Hong Kong. She is also examining arts-based activism among caregivers as part of the SSHRC-funded Poverty and Precarious Employment in Southern Ontario (PEPSO) project.

Robin Folvik is a member of the Graphic History Collective and a co-author of *May Day: A Graphic History of Protest* and several of the comics in this collection. She has a strong background in history and women's studies, with a focus on feminist histories and British Columbia's working people, labour struggles, and social movements. Robin has a passion for translating academic knowledge to reach a broader public, and she has worked on films, curriculum development, walking tours, and public history installations through her position as Research Director at the BC Labour Heritage Centre.

Ethan Heitner is a cartoonist and member of the editorial collective of World War 3 Illustrated, the radical comics magazine. More of his work can be seen on his blog, https://freedomfunnies. wordpress.com.

Gregory S. Kealey is Emeritus Professor of History at the University of New Brunswick. His historical work has focused on Canadian working-class history and state repression of labour and the left. Major works include *Toronto Workers Respond to Industrial Capitalism* (1980); *Dreaming of What Might Be: The Knights of Labor in Ontario*, with Bryan Palmer (1982); *Workers and Canadian History* (1995); and *Secret Service: Political Policing in Canada from the Fenians to Fortress America*, with Reg Whitaker and Andy Parnaby (2012). He was the founding editor of *Labour/Le Travail* and is the editor of the University of Toronto Press Canadian Social History Series and the Athabasca University Press series Working Canadians (with Alvin Finkel).

Orion Keresztesi is an artist and activist inspired by the history of working people's struggles— how they have shaped the world we live in and how they can help us to do the same today. He is a proud member of Canadian Union of Public Employees Local 1281 and currently serving as the Communications Officer on the local's executive.

Mark Leier is a historian at Simon Fraser University and author of *Bakunin: The Creative Passion* (2006) and three books on labour and left history. The second edition of *Rebel Life: The Life and Times of Robert Gosden, Revolutionary, Mystic, Labour Spy* was published by New Star Books in 2013.

David Lester is guitarist in the rock duo Mecca Normal, with bandmate Jean Smith. David and Jean give a presentation/lecture called How Art & Music Can Change the World. David is the author of *The Gruesome Acts of Capitalism* (2006) and artist/writer of the graphic novel *The Listener* (2011). His poster "Malachi" was part of the 2014 Whitney Biennial in New York City at the Whitney Museum of American Art. He is art director of BC BookWorld. Visit http://davidlesterartmusicdesign.wordpress.com.

Andrée Lévesque is a feminist historian who has published widely in labour history and in women's history. In 2005, she published the proceedings of a colloquium on Madeleine Parent, under the title *Madeleine Parent: Activist* (Sumac Press).

Zenee May Maceda is a community organizer and labour activist based in Toronto. She has recently obtained her master's degree at the University of Toronto and is currently a National Representative for the United Food and Commercial Workers Union.

Dale McCartney is a researcher and instructor in the Morgan Centre for Labour Studies at Simon Fraser University. He was previously the editor of *Seven Oaks Magazine* and has been on picket lines with both Teamster's Local 213 and more recently the Teaching Support Staff Union (TSSU) at SFU, of which he is still a proud member. He is currently working on a PhD at the University of British Columbia, examining neoliberal restructuring of education in BC.

Doug Nesbitt is an organizer for Service Employees International Union Local 2 and an editor at *RankandFile.ca*. He is writing a history of the Ontario Days of Action for his PhD in History at Queen's University.

Bryan D. Palmer, a Canada Research Chair at Trent University, is the author of 13 books and five edited collections. His published works have been translated into Korean, Chinese, Italian, Portuguese, Spanish, and Greek. *Revolutionary Teamsters: The Minneapolis Truckers' Strikes of 1934* (2013) is his latest book. In the fall of 2015, the Historical Materialism book series will publish a two-volume collection of his essays, *Marxism and Historical Practice*. A forthcoming study, co-authored by anti-poverty activist Gaetan Heroux, will appear in 2016, titled *"Bread I Want, Bread I Will Have": Economic Crises, Resistance, and the Long History of Toronto's Poor and Out-of-Work, 1830–2015*.

Andrew Parnaby is an Associate Professor of History at Cape Breton University.

Joan Sangster teaches in Gender and Women's Studies and the Frost Centre for Canadian Studies and Indigenous Studies at Trent University. Her scholarship has addressed themes concerning working women, the labour movement, the Canadian left, the criminalization of women and girls, Indigenous women and the law, and feminist historiography. Her most recent book on women and labour is *Transforming Labour: Women and Work in Postwar Canada* (University of Toronto Press, 2010).

Kara Sievewright is a writer, artist, and designer who creates comics, zines, websites, prints, and more. She lives on Haida Gwaii, which have been claimed by Canada for the past 150 years but have been the home of the Haida for over 12,000 years, where she is working on a graphic novel. You can see more of her work at http://makerofnets.ca and on Tumblr and Twitter.

Julia Smith is a member of the Graphic History Collective and co-author of several of the comics in this collection. Her research interests include labour and working-class history, gender and women's studies, and political economy. She has published articles on women, work, and union organizing, particularly in the service, office, and retail sectors.

Ron Verzuh is a writer, labour historian, videographer, and trade unionist who is currently completing his PhD in History at Simon Fraser University. Before retiring in 2008, he was national director of communications for the Canadian Union of Public Employees. In the 1960s, he worked as a labourer at the Trail smelter and was a member of the International Union of Mine, Mill and Smelter Workers when it merged with the United Steel Workers in 1967. He is the author of three books, one on the history of the pioneer labour press in Canada, several booklets, and many articles. His recent film documentary, *Joe Hill's Secret Canadian Hideout*, won the award for best historical documentary at the Oregon Independent Film Festival and was an official selection at the Workers' Unite Film Festival in New York City. His latest documentary is called *Remembering Salt*, the story of how a blacklisted movie brought the Cold War to small-town Canada.

Tania Willard (Secwepemc Nation) works within the shifting ideas of contemporary and traditional as it relates to cultural arts and production, often working with bodies of knowledge and skills that are conceptually linked to her interest in intersections between Indigenous and other cultures. Willard has worked as an artist in residence with Gallery Gachet in Vancouver's Downtown East Side, the Banff Centre's visual arts residency, *fiction*, and *Trading Post,* and was a curator in residence with grunt gallery. Collections of Willard's work include the Department of Foreign Affairs and International Trade, Kamloops Art Gallery, and Thompson Rivers University. Willard's recent curatorial work includes *Beat Nation: Art, Hip Hop and Aboriginal Culture*, presented at Vancouver Art Gallery in 2011 and touring until 2014. Willard is currently the Aboriginal Curator in Residence at the Kamloops Art Gallery.

The Graphic History Collective is made up of activists, artists, writers, and researchers passionate about comics, history, and social change. We produce alternative histories—people's histories—in an accessible format to help people understand the historical roots of contemporary social issues. Our comics show that you don't need a cape and a pair of tights to change the world. Members of the Graphic History Collective are organized with the Canadian Freelance Union, a Community Chapter of Unifor. www.graphichistorycollective.com.